FIFTH EDITION

MANAGING

CULTURAL

DIFFERENCES

THE MCD SERIES
MANAGING CULTURAL DIFFERENCES

Competing Globally: Managing Multicultural Management and Negotiations
Farid Elashmawi

Developing the Global Organization: Strategies for Human Resource Professionals
Robert T. Moran, Philip R. Harris, and William G. Stripp

Dynamics of Successful International Business Negotiations
William G. Stripp and Robert T. Moran

Intercultural Services: A Worldwide Buyer's Guide and Sourcebook
Gary Wederspahn

International Business Case Studies for the Multicultural Marketplace
Robert T. Moran, David O. Braaten, and John E. Walsh

International Directory of Multicultural Resources
Robert T. Moran and David O. Braaten

Managing Cultural Differences, Fifth Edition
Philip R. Harris and Robert T. Moran

Mentoring and Diversity
Belle Rose-Ragins, David Clutterbuck, and Lisa Matthewman

Multicultural Management 2000: Essential Cultural Insights for Global Business Success
Farid Elashmawi and Philip R. Harris

Succeeding in Business in Central and Eastern Europe: A Guide to Cultures, Markets, and Practices
Woodrow H. Sears and Audrone Tamulionyte-Lentz

Transcultural Leadership: Empowering the Diverse Workforce
George F. Simons, Carmen Vazquez, and Philip R. Harris

FORTHCOMING TITLES:

Eurodiversity: Cultural Considerations and Business Success in Western Europe
George Simons

NAFTA—Best Practices
Robert T. Moran and Jeff Abbott

FIFTH EDITION

MANAGING

LEADERSHIP STRATEGIES FOR

CULTURAL

A NEW WORLD OF BUSINESS

DIFFERENCES

PHILIP R. HARRIS • ROBERT T. MORAN

JUDITH E. SOCCORSY
Editorial Coordinator

G|P **Gulf Professional Publishing**
P| an imprint of Butterworth-Heinemann

FIFTH EDITION

MANAGING

CULTURAL

DIFFERENCES

Originally published by Gulf Publishing Company, Houston, TX.

10 9 8 7 6 5 4 3 2

For information, please contact:
Manager of Special Sales
Butterworth–Heinemann
225 Wildwood Avenue
Woburn, MA 01801–2041
Tel: 781-904-2500
Fax: 781-904-2620
For information on all Butterworth–Heinemann publications available, contact our World Wide Web home page at:
http://www.bh.com

Library of Congress Cataloging-in-Publication Data

Harris, Philip R. (Philip Robert), 1926–
  Managing cultural differences / Philip R. Harris and
Robert T. Moran.— 5th ed.
    p. cm. — (Managing cultural differences series)
  Includes bibliographical references and index.
  ISBN 0-87719-345-2 (alk. paper)
    1. International business enterprises—Management. 2. Acculturation. 3. Cross-cultural studies. I. Moran, Robert T., 1938– II. Title. III. Series.

HD62.4 .H37 2000
658.1'8—dc21   00-032488
                                                                    CIP

Printed in the United States of America.

Printed on acid-free paper (∞).

Book design by Roxann L. Combs.

To our wives,

the late Dorothy L. Harris

and Virgilia M. Moran,

whose career paths crossed ours

on foreign soil and international assignments,

and who taught us so much in marriage

about managing cultural differences!

CONTENTS

UNIT 2

CULTURAL IMPACTS ON GLOBAL BUSINESS

FOREWORD

Don't be fooled by Moran and Harris's statement, "The realities about which we write are not only complex, but constantly changing, and our material represents a starting point . . ." This is an understatement. In their fifth edition of *Managing Cultural Differences,* they have provided a terrific springboard for understanding the complexities, challenges, and rewards of running global operations. What I appreciate most about their work is its blend of concepts combined with everyday practicalities and pragmatism. Whether the reader is a student hoping to enter the world of international business, or a practioner trying to keep pace with unprecedented historical changes, this book has something to offer.

Managing Cultural Differences documents critical sensitivities the business person must exhibit in various parts of the world. While some would argue the essence of business need only be concerned with "the bottom line," this book intelligently points out that many paths lead concurrently to that bottom line. When Bob Moran visited our organization, he used a quote from Blaise Pascal that summarizes a mind-set the business person of today must possess: "There are truths on this side of the Pyrénées which are falsehoods on the other." The world of business demands a repertoire of style, a respect for diversity, an understanding of cultures. It means taking a keen interest in how a person might possess a widely divergent perspective on a matter that seems abundantly clear to you. While this may cause discomfort to a newcomer on the international scene, Moran and Harris are quick to point out cultural differences can be a *resource,* not a impediment. Our organization is learning to see the world from a customer's point of view. And a customer in Germany may have a different persepctive than a customer in Tokyo or Mexico. Who's right? They all are.

I have personally lived many of the statements made in this book. The comment in Chapter 2, ". . . the very vitality and creativity of an organization or nation depends upon the content and character of its communications . . .," hit the target dead center. Someone told me it was important to communicate messages ten times more than I felt comfortable doing. And that was just for North American audiences! Imagine the challenge when doing business internationally. Communication on a world-wide basis is a continuous and active process. It is a message without beginnings or endings. It means listening to people from all parts of the world in terms of how they can help us meet business objectives. It means projecting a vision of where the organization is headed in a manner that connects with these same people. It means forming a corporate culture capable of coping with competition and change anywhere in the world. *Managing Cultural Differences* has captured these ideas in a chapter that should be read by anyone who hopes to understand the "hard" work of running the "soft" side of a business.

Of course, it does my heart good to read the acknowledgment that ". . . no industry has come farther and faster than the U.S. auto industry" in terms of recovering our corporate well-being. While Moran and Harris rightly say we have learned some techniques from the Japanese, I would add a benefit of doing business around the world is that we have learned from everyone. An international business today must be more than producer of goods and services. It must be a teacher and student simultaneously—a craftsman and an apprentice dedicated to continually improving the arts and sciences of managing without borders. The global enterprise we call Delphi Automotive Systems is inclusive, not exclusive; it consists of customers, employees, stockholders, stakeholders, partners, suppliers, and communities around the world. Further evidence why *Managing Cultural Differences* is such a contribution to its field. Moran and Harris recognize that the organization of the future is beyond technologies and machines—it is people. People with cultural differences. The clever and successful organization will recognize that these differences, properly managed, are among its core competencies. *Managing Cultural Differences* is not only relevant and current, it is prophetic. And it's a good read!

J. T. Battenberg III
Chairman of the Board, CEO, President
Delphi Automotive Systems
Worldwide Headquarters
Troy, Michigan

SERIES PREFACE

Culture is a fascinating concept. It has many applications whether between nations, organizations, or peoples. Communicating effectively across cultures, negotiating on a global scale and conducting international business are always challenging. To thrive and in many cases to survive in the 21st century, individuals and institutions must incorporate cultural sensitivity and skills into their relations, strategies, and structure. The new millennium has no tolerance for ethnic cleansing, anti-Semitism, or any other form of religious or racial discrimination.

As originally conceived, *Managing Cultural Differences* was intended to increase human effectiveness with people who differ in cultural backgrounds. With the new century, our "flagship" sails into her fifth edition. We are particularly gratified that business organizations have not only found the book useful but in academia more than 120 universities worldwide have adopted our work as a textbook. But this unique publication has also spawned many "offspring." The prototype in 1982 was *Managing Cultural Synergy;* in 1991 the **Managing Cultural Differences Series** was launched and has subsequently grown into many titles written by a variety of authors.

As series editors, we are pleased with the outstanding products of Butterworth-Heinemann's Book Division and its competent editorial staff. We trust that our readers will continue to find our literary efforts helpful as you seek to address global transcultural challenges in our rapidly changing, highly interdependent human communities.

Philip R. Harris, Ph.D.
Robert T. Moran, Ph.D.
Series Editors

PREFACE

The beginning of a new millennium is a fitting time to launch the fifth edition of *Managing Cultural Differences*. When first published more than two decades ago, it was ahead of the market, which is only now beginning to appreciate the importance of culture related to human behavior and performance. Yet, its message is still relevant as the human family struggles with two contrary forces—globalization and diversity in an Information Age versus increasing racism and ethnic hatreds.

Culture is not just a tool for coping, but a means for creating awareness and for learning. It underpins all human activities, and explains much of our behavior. Our favorite analogy is to compare it to a beautiful jewel—hold it to the light, turn it, and reveal its multiple dimensions. With each new writing of this text, we plumb its depths for meaning, and discover more applications—from national, to organizational, to team, to work culture. Now we perceive its insights for the global marketplace.

In the twenty-one years since the first edition of *Managing Cultural Differences*, we have had ample confirmation of our thesis that cross-cultural competency is essential not only for meaningful human relationships, but also for success as professionals, managers, or technicians. Numerous trends, such as globalization and work force diversity, have emerged to underscore the importance of effective intercultural relations to improve job performance and productivity. We are grateful to the more than 100,000 readers and 120 university professors whose text adoptions have proven the validity of that message. It is their needs and feedback that motivate us to this major revision.

At the opening of the 21st century, the fifth edition of *Managing Cultural Differences* (MCD) takes on profound contemporary changes—

economic, social, political, and technological—that foster the creation of a unique, post-industrial culture worldwide. *MCD* reflects the transition to a new work culture with its emphasis on communication technologies and knowledge workers. It seeks to respond to the challenges of the global market.

Those familiar with previous editions of *MCD* will find many differences in this version. First, the layout and content make this volume more "user friendly." We hope you will like the appearance in terms of typeface, graphics, and other format improvements provided by the talented people at Gulf Publishing Company. Both content and references have been extensively updated. The substance of these pages that initially attracted readers is still here but streamlined. There are fewer chapters—15 in all, some from prior editions have been combined, and a new chapter added on "Women in Global Business." Just as organizations are being "re-invented and re-engineered," so too this publication. Yet, in our content we still seek a balance of theory and practice, as well as between research findings and models.

As in the past, we open with two units that examine the cultural influences and impacts on global management and performance. However, the focus in the first five chapters (Unit I) is upon *leadership* in globalization, communication, negotiation, change, and cultural synergy. In the next four chapters (Unit II) improving one's management through cross-cultural effectiveness especially in the midst of relocation and transition is considered, as well as how to take advantage of emerging global market opportunities and diversity in the global work culture. In Unit III we end with the specifics of doing business or serving people in cultures different from our own. The United Nations recognizes 226 nations in the world, and we obviously could not treat all their unique cultures in this text. Instead, we choose a representative sample to provide culture specifics in terms of six major regions—North America, Latin America, Asia, Europe, the Middle East, and Africa.

Although this work has always been written for both practitioners and students, we recognize that many of our readers are in various departments of universities and colleges. Thus, we have enhanced the accompanying *Instructor's Guide,* so as to facilitate the learning process. Therefore, professors and human resource development (HRD) professionals will find that the latter not only contains information on teaching each chapter, but also material on cross-cultural HRD and training, instruments that can be reproduced for use with groups, and a comprehensive bibliography.

The most valuable auxiliary to this parent book is the *Managing Cultural Differences Series,* that is, the supplemental volumes with other co-authors that augment our themes. For example, the message of Chapter 1 is more fully developed in *Developing the Global Organization;* that of Chapter 3 is expanded upon in *Dynamics of Successful International Business Negotiations;* that of Chapters 10, 12, and 14 elaborated upon in *Multicultural Management 2000.*

We welcome your continued evaluation as to how *Managing Cultural Differences,* both as a book and a series, can better serve your needs.

Philip R. Harris, Ph.D.
Harris International, Ltd.
LaJolla, CA

Robert T. Moran, Ph.D.
American Graduate School of International Management
Glendale, AZ

ACKNOWLEDGMENTS

Our fifth edition would not have been possible without the aid of our very capable editorial coordinator, Judith E. Soccorsy.

Writing *Managing Cultural Differences* was not only a synergistic effort by the authors, but required assistance of many colleagues. We have tried to acknowledge them in the text. However, we are especially appreciative of the work of Tim Calk of Gulf Publishing Company.

We thank J. T. Battenberg III, chairman, CEO, and president of Delphi Automotive Systems for the foreword. Keith Wander, executive director, Organization and Employee Development of Delphi Automotive Group, for his assistance.

We are grateful to the following individuals for permitting us to use portions of their research: Nancy Baldwin, Maria Brightbill, Terry Finnegan, Ralph Krueger, and Corrine Pfund.

In addition we recognize, thank, and acknowledge Sarah Moran, Elizabeth Moran de Longeaux, Sebastien de Longeaux, Molly Ann Haney, as well as the following graduate students for their assistance in reviewing culture specific materials: Laurel Cool, Mary Mitchell, Mary Pietanza, Jeni Chávez, Cecile C. Ramírez de Arellano, Jie Zhang Yuanlim, Kim Sung-do, B. W. Lee, Yoon Park, Rebekhab Henry, Regina Sy-Facunda, Raj Kohli, William Everett, Fernando Garcia-Pretel, Eduardo Magailanes, Sato Masatoshi, Barbara Goodman, Karin Romano, Ardnt Luebbers, Larissa Koursova, ByungKi An, John Bechtold, Biswajit Mukherjie, Eric-Jan Van der Byl, and Kristen Kelly.

UNIT 1

CULTURAL IMPACTS ON GLOBAL MANAGEMENT

Today, almost 20% of world output—about $6 trillion of the $28 trillion world gross domestic product (GDP)—is produced and consumed in global markets. . . .

Within 30 years we estimate at least 80% of world output will be in global markets. By then, worldwide GDP will be $91 trillion, so the globally accessible arena could be $73 trillion—a twelve-fold increase in 30 years. Thirty years may seem a long time, but it is not if you consider that far more economic integration will occur, if our prediction comes true, than was achieved in the previous 13,000 years of economic history.

L. Bryan, J. Fraser, J. Oppenheim, and
W. Rall, Race for the World,
Boston, MA: Harvard Business School Press, 1999

GLOBAL LEADERS
AND CULTURE

As we begin the new millennium, the process of globalization is quickening. In an interconnected global world, the tradition of independent and stable organizations and cultures is no more. Our world is marked by accelerating change and greater diversity. The increasing diversity in virtually every culture and organization requires global knowledge, global attitudes and global skills. It is even difficult now to envision what successful organizations and their members will look like in a decade or two.

Between 1995 and 2000, the following is a sampling of events that have impacted the lives of a large percentage of the world's population.

❑ Eleven European Countries Adopt the Euro as Their Common Currency
❑ Oklahoma City's Alfred P. Murrah Building Is Bombed
❑ Pope John Paul II Visits Cuba
❑ Hurricane Mitch Devastates Central America
❑ Seran Gas Kills Japanese Commuters
❑ El Niño Affects World Weather
❑ Hong Kong Is Returned to China
❑ Good Friday Peace Accords Signed in Northern Ireland
❑ Major Famine in North Korea

If change is the constant, can much be said of the future? As the next century begins, however, we do have some inkling of the necessary qualitites and competencies of tomorrow's leaders.

In 1994, the *Economist Intelligence Unit*[1] asked 10,000 senior executives in North America, Europe, and Asia what competencies and qualities will managers and executives need in the future and what successful organizations will look like. An analysis of responses found:

- Management's handling of diversity will be the most significant factor affecting corporate success in North America and Europe.
- Senior executives need to possess the attribute of leadership that combines a blend of discipline and flexibility.
- In an era of constant change, corporate culture is a way to bring about organizational change.

Will the 21st century change these conclusions? It is our thesis that all management or professional development requires global intercultural education and skill. More than ten years ago, the American Association of Collegiate Schools of Business *required* all business schools to have an international component to their courses.

Today we must learn to move beyond the mere coping with cultural differences to creating more synergy and embracing the wellspring of diversity. Today's managers must provide the leadership. According to Goman who quotes Boyett and Conn,[2] "In the 1980s, most American workers were managed. Few were led. Americans didn't work for leaders. They worked (or more precisely 'put in their hours') for managers. As a result, American businesses were overmanaged and underled. Such will not be the case in the future. Workplace 2000 will require leadership, not management. Stable organizations can be managed. Chaotic (global) organizations must be led." Further, Pattison[3] states that "global skills and perspectives cannot be viewed as a specialty or segment of business today, they must be an integral part of an enterprise, totally integrated throughout all operations."

As a result of increasing diversity in all institutions, rapid change and other factors, the role of the leader has changed. Today, loyalty and connections are not sufficient to guarantee one's position. Leadership performance is necessary. To survive, become and maintain a best-in-class organization, as well as to develop and retain talent from many different cultures at all levels, strong leadership is essential.

Smart leaders are convinced of the necessity to manage cultural differences and to develop the skills necessary to participate effectively in a global environment. Skillful global managers and leaders understand the significance of the following statements:

- Japanese culture promotes a sense of group identity. Japanese ambiguity is an unconscious cultural process that often leads foreigners to draw false conclusions based on Japanese appearances.
- During the first business meeting in Saudi Arabia, Mexico, Japan and in many other countries, one does not conduct much business, but uses the time to become acquainted and build trust.

As a result of increasing diversity in all institutions, rapid change and other factors, the role of the leader has changed.

- In matters of recruitment and selection, Asian managers interview and often select family and trusted friends to fill positions, while Western managers use more impersonal measures of recruitment.
- In an era of mergers, acquisitions, and consolidations, many of these ventures fail within five years not because they were ill conceived, but rather the cultures of the organizations were not successfully integrated.
- When doing business in Indonesia, shaking hands with either gender is acceptable, but using the left hand for taking food or giving a gift is unacceptable.
- Los Angeles has a diverse multicultural and multilingual population. Spanish and Korean are the second and third largest foreign-language groups.
- The Business Council for International Understanding estimates that international personnel who go abroad without cross-cultural preparation have a failure rate much higher than those who had the benefit of such training.

Since this book's first edition in 1979 the awareness of business and government leaders has risen relative to the importance of the cultural influences on our behavior. Whether one is concerned about the supervisors of minority employees, the acquisition of a U.S. firm by a foreign owner, joint ventures or strategic alliances, increasing tourism, world trade, or global economic cooperation, **culture** will impact the relationships and the operations. Schein[4] states it profoundly:

> Consider any complex, potentially volatile issue—Arab relations, the problems between Serbs, Croats and Bosnians, corporate decision making, getting control of the U.S. deficit or health care costs, labor/management relations, and so on. At the root of the issue we are likely to find communication failures and cultural misunderstandings that prevent the parties from framing the problem in a common way, and thus make it impossible to deal with the problem constructively.

CULTURE AND ITS CHARACTERISTICS

Culture is a distinctly human capacity for adapting to circumstances and transmitting this coping skill and knowledge to subsequent generations. Culture gives people a sense of who they are, of belonging, of how they should behave, and of what they should be doing. Culture impacts behavior, morale, and productivity at work as well, and includes values and patterns that influence company attitudes and actions.

Culture is often considered the driving force behind human behavior everywhere. The concept has become the context to explain politics, economics, progress, and failures. In that regard, Huntington[5] has written:

> It is my hypothesis that the fundamental source of human conflict in this new world will not be primarily ideological or primarily economic.

The great divisions among humankind and the dominating source of conflict will be culture.

Culture and cultural identities . . . are shaping the patterns of cohesion, disintegration and conflict in the post-cold war world . . . global politics is being reconfigured along cultural lines . . . peoples and countries with similar cultures are coming together. Peoples and countries with different cultures are coming apart.

The following ten categories can be a means for understanding either a macroculture or a microculture, and can be useful for studying any group of people, whether they live in the rural South of the United States or the bustling city of Hong Kong.

Sense of Self and Space. The comfort one has with self can be expressed differently by culture. Self-identity and appreciation can be manifested by humble bearing in one place, and macho behavior in another. Independence and creativity are countered in other cultures by group cooperation and conformity. Americans have a sense of space that requires more distance between individuals, while Latins and Vietnamese will stand closer together. Some cultures are very structured and formal, while others are more flexible and informal. Some cultures are very closed and determine one's place very precisely, while others are more open and changing. Each culture validates self in a unique way.

Communication and Language. The communication system, verbal and nonverbal, distinguishes one group from another. Apart from the multitude of "foreign" languages, some nations have fifteen or more major spoken languages (within one language group there are dialects, accents, slang, jargon, and other such variations). Furthermore, the meanings given to gestures, for example, often differ by culture. So, while body language may be universal, its manifestation differs by locality. Subcultures, such as the military, have terminology and signals that cut across national boundaries (such as a salute, or the rank system).

Dress and Appearance. This includes the outward garments and adornments, or lack thereof, as well as body decorations that tend to be distinctive by culture. We are aware of the Japanese kimono, the African headdress, the Englishman's bowler and umbrella, the Polynesian sarong, and the Native American headband. Some tribes smear their faces for battle, while some women use cosmetics to manifest beauty. Many subcultures wear distinctive clothing; the formal look of business, the jeans of the youth throughout the world, and uniforms that segregate everyone from students to police. In the military microculture, customs and regulations determine the dress of the day, length of hair, and equipment to be worn.

Food and Feeding Habits. The manner in which food is selected, prepared, presented, and eaten often differs by culture. One man's pet is another person's delicacy—dog, anyone? Americans love beef, yet it is forbidden to Hindus, while the forbidden food in Moslem and Jewish culture is normally pork, which is eaten extensively by the Chinese and others. Many restaurants cater to diverse diets and offer "national"

Independence and creativity are countered in other cultures by group cooperation and conformity.

dishes to meet varying cultural tastes. Feeding habits also differ, and the range goes from hands and chop sticks to full sets of cutlery. Even when cultures use a utensil such as a fork, one can distinguish a European from an American by which hand holds the implement. Subcultures, too, can be analyzed from this perspective, such as the executive's dining room, the soldier's mess, the worker's hero or submarine sandwich, the ladies' tea room, and the vegetarian's restaurant.

Time and Time Consciousness. Sense of time differs by culture; some are exact and others are relative. Generally, Germans are precise about the clock, while many Latins are more casual. In some cultures, promptness is determined by age or status, thus, in some countries, subordinates are expected on time at staff meetings, but the boss is the last to arrive. Some subcultures, like the military, have their own time system of twenty-four hours—1:00 p.m. civilian time becomes 1300 hours in military time. In such cultures, promptness is rewarded, and in battles, the watches are synchronized. Yet, there are people in some other cultures who do not bother with hours or minutes, but manage their days by sunrise and sunset.

Time, in the sense of seasons of the year, varies by culture. Some areas of the world think in terms of winter, spring, summer, and fall; but for others the more meaningful designations may be rainy or dry seasons. In the United States, for example, the East and Midwest may be very conscious of the four seasons, while those in the West or Southwest tend to ignore such designations—Californians are more concerned with rainy months and mud slides, or dry months and forest fires.

Many industries operate on a round-the-clock schedule. This is of concern to chronobiologists who specialize in research on the body's internal clock by analysis of body temperature, chemical composition of blood serum and urine, sleepiness and peak periods of feeling good. Drastic changes in time, such as can be brought on by shift work, can undermine both performance and personal life, leading to serious accidents on the job.

Relationships. Cultures fix human and organizational relationships by age, gender, status, and degree of kindred, as well as by wealth, power, and wisdom. The family unit is the most common expression of this characteristic, and the arrangement may go from small to large—in a Hindu household, the joint family includes under one roof, mother, father, children, parents, uncles, aunts, and cousins. In fact, one's physical location in such houses may also be determined with males on one side of the house, females on the other. There are some places in which the accepted marriage relationship is monogamy, while in other cultures it may be polygamy or polyandry (one wife, several husbands).

In some cultures, the authoritarian figure in the family is the head male, and this fixed relationship is then extended from home to community, and explains why some societies prefer to have a dictator head up the national family. Relationships between and among people vary by

Cultures fix human and organizational relationships by age, gender, status, and degree of kindred, as well as by wealth, power, and wisdom.

category—in some cultures, the elderly are honored, whereas in others they are ignored; in some cultures, women must wear veils and appear deferential, while in others the female is considered the equal, if not the superior of the male.

The military subculture has a classic determination of relationships by rank or protocol, such as the relationships between officers and enlisted personnel. Even off duty, when on base, the recreational facilities are segregated for officers, noncommissioned, and enlisted personnel. The formalization of relationships is evident in some religious subcultures with titles such as "reverend," "guru," "pastor," "rabbi," or "bishop."

Values and Norms. The need systems of cultures vary, as do the priorities they attach to certain behavior in the group. Those operating on a survival level value the gathering of food, adequate covering and shelter; while those with high security needs value material things, money, job titles, as well as law and order. America is a country in the midst of a values revolution as the children of the Depression give way to the children of affluence who are concerned with the quality of life, self-fulfillment, and meaning in experiences. In some Pacific Island cultures, the greater one's status becomes, the more one is expected to give away or share.

In any event, from its value system, a culture sets norms of behavior for that society. These acceptable standards for membership may range from the work ethic or pleasure to absolute obedience or permissiveness for children; from rigid submission of the wife to her husband to women's total liberation. Because conventions are learned, some cultures demand honesty with members of one's own group, but accept a more relaxed standard with strangers. Some of these conventions are expressed in gift-giving; rituals for birth, death, and marriage; guidelines for privacy, showing respect or deference, expressing good manners, etc. The globalization process and telecommunications are leading to the development of shared values that cross borders and express planetary concerns, such as protection of the environment.[6]

Beliefs and Attitudes. Possibly the most difficult classification is ascertaining the major belief themes of a people, and how this and other factors influence their attitudes toward themselves, others, and what happens in their world. People in all cultures seem to have a concern for the supernatural that is evident in their religions and religious practices. Primitive cultures, for example, have a belief in spiritual beings labeled by us as "animism." In the history of human development there has been an evolution in our spiritual sense until today many individuals use terms like "cosmic consciousness" to indicate their belief in the transcendental powers. Between these two extremes in the spiritual continuum, religious traditions in various cultures consciously or unconsciously influence our attitudes toward life, death, and the hereafter. Western culture seems to be largely influenced by the Judeo-Christian-Islamic traditions, while Eastern or Asian cultures have been dominated by Buddhism, Confucianism, Taoism, and Hinduism. Religion, to a degree,

People in all cultures seem to have a concern for the supernatural that is evident in their religions and religious practices.

expresses the philosophy of a people about important facets of life—it is influenced by culture and vice versa.

A people's religious belief system is somewhat dependent on their stage of human development: Tribesmen and primitives tend to be superstitious and the practice of voodoo is illustrative of this; some religions are deeply locked into the agricultural stage of development, while many so-called advanced technological people seem to be more irreligious, substituting a belief in science for faith.

Mental Process and Learning. Some cultures emphasize one aspect of brain development over another, so that one may observe striking differences in the way people think and learn. Anthropologist Edward Hall maintains that the mind is internalized culture, and the process involves how people organize and process information. Life in a particular locale defines the rewards and punishment for learning or not learning certain information or in a certain way, and this is confirmed and reinforced by the culture there. For example, Germans stress logic, while the Japanese and the Navajo reject the Western idea of logic. Logic for a Hopi Indian is based on preserving the integrity of their social system and all the relationships connected with it. Some cultures favor abstract thinking and conceptualization, while others prefer rote memory and learning. What seems to be universal is that each culture has a reasoning process, but then each manifests the process in its own distinctive way.

Work Habits and Practices. Another dimension for examining a group's culture is its attitude toward work, the dominant types of work, the division of work, and the work habits or practices, such as promotions or incentives. Work has been defined as exertion or effort directed to produce or accomplish something. There are a variety of terms related to the concept, such as labor, toil, undertaking, employment, as well as career, profession, occupation, and job. Some cultures espouse a work ethic in which all members are expected to engage in a desirable and worthwhile activity. In other societies this is broadly defined, so that cultural pursuits in music and arts or sports are included. For some cultures, the worthiness of the activity is narrowly measured in terms of income produced, or the worth of the individual is assessed in terms of job status. In the past, or where a religious view of work still prevails, work is viewed as an act of service to God and people, and is expressed in a moral commitment to the job or quality of effort. In Japan, the cultural loyalty to family is transferred to the organization that employs the person and the quality of one's performance—it is expressed in work group participation, communication, and consensus.

Work within a country can be analyzed as to the dominant vocational activity of the majority. Thus, in the context of stages of human development, a people can be characterized primarily as hunters, farmers, factory or knowledge/service workers. Most economically advanced societies are in transition from an industrial work culture to a metaindustrial or technological type of work. Prior to this century, work

Most economically advanced societies are in transition from an industrial work culture to a metaindustrial or technological type of work.

required considerable expenditure of physical energy; today more emotional and mental energy is necessary because the nature and tools of work have changed. The attitude change is away from work as subsistence, and the distinctions between work and play are eroding. New conceptions of work are evolving so that it is seen as more than earning a living, and the shift in work is away from material production to nonmaterial goods, like information processing and service. The emphasis is upon quality of work life.

The manner in which work is divided in a culture can also be evaluated. From the feudal ages through the industrial age, whether in the military, trading companies, or industrial corporation, the bureaucratic culture was expressed in a hierarchy. The pyramid organization that resulted was divided by level and functions, each with its own head. The trend is away from this form of defined, individualistic activities toward teams, work sharing, and other new norms of an emerging work culture.

Another way of observing a culture is to note the manner and method for offering praise for accomplishments, which can include testimonial dinners, pay increases, business commendations, and medals.

These ten general classifications are a simple model for assessing a particular culture. It does not include every aspect of culture, nor is it the only way to analyze culture. This approach enables one to examine a people systemically. The categories are a beginning for cultural understanding as one travels and visits different cultures. Likewise, the model can be used to study the microcultures within a majority national culture. All aspects of culture are interrelated, and to change one part is to change the whole. There is a danger in trying to compartmentalize a complex concept like culture, yet retaining a sense of its whole.

All aspects of culture are interrelated, and to change one part is to change the whole.

SYSTEMS APPROACH TO CULTURE

Because there are many different anthropological approaches to cultural analysis, some readers may prefer to use this coordinated systems approach as an alternative. A system, in this sense, refers to an ordered assemblage or combination of correlated parts that form a unitary whole.[7]

Kinship System—the family relationships and the way a people reproduce, train, and socialize their children. The typical American family is nuclear and a rather independent unit. In other countries, there may be an extended family that consists of several generations held together through the male line (patrilineal) or through the female line (matrilineal). Such families have a powerful influence on child rearing, and often on nation building. The global manager needs to understand the significance of the family's influence to supervise effectively. Family influences and loyalties can affect job performance or business negotiations.

Educational System—how young or new members of a society are provided with information, knowledge, skills, and values. Educational systems may be formal and informal within any culture. If one is opening up a factory in India, for instance, the training plan had better include the rote method of education, whereas in some societies the training would be for sophisticated technological positions.

Economic System—the manner in which the society produces and distributes its goods and services. The Japanese economic system is an extension of the family and is group-oriented. Today, while much of the world is divided into capitalistic or socialistic economic blocks, it is evident that regional economic cooperatives are merging to cross national and ideological boundaries. Macroeconomics is the study of such systems.

Political System—the dominant means of governance for maintaining order and exercising power or authority. Some cultures are still in a tribal stage where chiefs rule, others have a ruling royal family with an operating king, while still others prefer democracy or communism. Although world society seems to be evolving beyond the nation-state, the global manager is forced to understand and deal with governments as they presently are structured with all their diversity.

Religious System—the means for providing meaning and motivation beyond the material aspects of life, that is, the spiritual side of a culture or its approach to the supernatural. This transcending system may lift a people to great heights of accomplishment, as is witnessed in the pyramids of Egypt and the Renaissance of Europe, or it may lock them into a static past. It is possible to project the history and future of India, for instance, in terms of the impact of its belief in reincarnation, which is enshrined in its major religion. Diverse national cultures can be somewhat unified under a shared religious belief in Islam or Christianity, for example. In some countries, such as Iran, Islam is becoming the basis of governance, legal and political systems. In others, religion dominates the legal and political systems, such as Judaism in Israel, or Roman Catholicism in the Republic of Ireland. The influence of religion is still culturally strong as Roman Catholicism in France and Lutheranism in Sweden. Religion can also be a source of divisiveness and conflict in a society, i.e. Northern Ireland, Yugoslavia (especially Bosnia and Kosovo), and Africa (including Algeria and Rwanda). Unfortunately, history demonstrates that in the name of religion, zealots and extremists may engage in culturally repressive behavior, such as religious persecutions, ethnic cleansing, and even "holy" wars.

Association System—the network of social groupings that people form. These may range from fraternal and secret societies to professional/trade associations. Some cultures are very group oriented and create formal and informal associations for every conceivable type of activity. Other societies are individualistic and avoid such organizing.

Health System—the way a culture prevents and cures disease or illness, or cares for victims of disasters or accidents. The concepts of

Although world society seems to be evolving beyond the nation-state, the global manager is forced to understand and deal with governments as they presently are structured with all their diversity.

health and wholeness, well being and medical problems differ by culture. Some countries have witch doctors, spiritual remedies and herb medicines, others like India have few government-sponsored social services, while Britain has a system of socialized medicine. The U.S. is in the midst of a major transition in its health management, care and delivery systems. There is increasing emphasis on universal coverage, prevention and wellness health models and alternative holistic medical treatments.[8]

Recreational System—the ways in which a people socialize, or use their leisure time. What may be considered play in one culture may be viewed as work in another, and vice versa. In some cultures "sport" has considerable political implications, in others it is solely for enjoyment, while in still others, it is big business. Certain types of entertainment, such as a form of folk dancing, seem to cut across cultures. Global communications are forcefully impacting the media and entertainment industries. Music, sports, films, and special cultural or athletic events can be quickly broadcast worldwide. As a result, the youth subculture today has similar tastes that go beyond national differences. The Internet becomes a forum for electronic commerce and exchange, as well as recreation.

KEY CULTURAL TERMINOLOGY

The specialists who make a formal study of culture use terms that may be helpful to those trying to comprehend the significance of this phenomena in business or international life.[9]

Patterns and Themes

Some cultural anthropologists try to search for a single integrated pattern to describe a particular culture. Thus, the Pueblo Indians may be designated as "apollonian"—people who stick to the "middle of the road" and avoid excess or conflict in their valuing of existence. The pinpointing of a consistent pattern of thought and action in a culture is difficult, so other scholars prefer to seek a summative theme. This is a position, declared or implied, that simulates activity and controls behavior; it is usually tacitly approved or openly promoted in the society. One can note that in most Asian cultures there is a "fatalism" theme, while in the American business subculture the theme is profits or the "bottom line."

Explicit and Implicit

Some aspects of culture are overt, while others are covert. Anthropologists remind us that each different way of life makes assumptions about the ends or purposes of human existence, about what to expect from each other, and about what constitutes fulfillment or frustration. Some of this is explicit in folklore and may also be manifest in law, regulations, customs, or traditions. Other aspects are implicit in the culture, and one must infer such tacit premises by observing consistent trends in word and deed. The distinction between public and hidden culture

Some aspects of culture are overt, while others are covert.

points up that much of our daily activity is governed by patterns and themes of which we may be only dimly aware, or totally unaware of their origin or meaning. Such culturally governed behavior facilitates the routine of daily living, so that one may perform many actions in a society without thinking about them. This cultural conditioning provides the freedom to devote conscious thinking to new and creative pursuits. It is startling to realize that some of our behavior is not entirely free or consciously willed by us. At times this can be a national problem, such as when a society finally realizes that implicit in its culture is a form of racism, which requires both legislation and education to rectify.

Micro or Subcultures

Within a larger society, group, or nation sharing a common majority or macroculture, there may be subgroupings of people possessing characteristic traits that set them apart and distinguish them from the others. These subcultures may be described in group classification by age, class, gender, race, or some other entity that distinguishes this micro- from the macroculture. Youth, or more specifically teenagers, share certain cultural traits as do other ethnic groups. There are many microcultures, such as white- or blue-collar workers, police or the military, college students or drug culture.

Universals and Diversity

The paradox of culture is the commonalities that exist in the midst of its diffusion or even confusion. There are generalizations that may be made about all cultures that are referred to as *universals*: age-grading, body adornments, calendar, courtship, divisions of labor, education, ethics, food taboos, incest and inheritance rules, language, marriage, mourning, mythology, numerals, penal sanctions, property rights, supernatural beliefs, status differentiation, tool making and trade, visiting, and weaning, etc. Thus, certain activities occur across cultures, but their manifestation may be unique in a particular society. And that brings us to the opposite concept of cultural *diversity*. Some form of sports or humor or music may be common to all peoples, but the way in which it is accomplished is distinctive in various cultural groupings.

Rational/Irrational/Nonrational Behavior

Among the many definitions of culture, consider it as historically created designs for living that may be rational, irrational, and nonrational. *Rational* behavior in a culture is based on what that group considers as reasonable for achieving its goals. *Irrational* behavior deviates from the accepted norms of a society and may result from deep frustration of an individual in trying to satisfy needs; it would appear to be done without reason and possibly largely as an emotional response. *Nonrational* behavior is neither based on reason, nor is it against reasonable expectations—it is dictated by one's own culture or subculture. A great deal of behavior is of this type, and we are unaware of why we do it, why we

The paradox of culture is the commonalities that exist in the midst of its diffusion or even confusion.

believe what we do, or that we may be biased or prejudiced from the perspective of those outside our cultural group. How often and when to take a bath frequently is a cultural dictate, just as what food constitutes breakfast. What is rational in one culture may be irrational in another, and vice versa. Some societies send political dissidents to mental institutions for what is considered irrational behavior.

Tradition

This is a very important aspect of culture that may be expressed in unwritten customs, taboos, and sanctions. Tradition can program a people as to what is proper behavior and procedures relative to food, dress, and certain types of people, what to value, avoid, or deemphasize. As the song on the subject of "Tradition" from the musical, *Fiddler on the Roof,* extols:

> Because of our traditions, we keep our sanity. . . . Tradition tells us how to sleep, how to work, how to wear clothes. . . . How did it get started? I don't know—it's a tradition. . . . Because of our traditions, everyone knows who he is and what God expects of him![10]

Traditions provide a people with a "mindset" and have a powerful influence on their moral system for evaluating what is right or wrong, good or bad, desirable or not. Traditions express a particular culture, giving its members a sense of belonging and uniqueness. But whether one is talking of a tribal or national culture, a military or religious subculture, traditions should be reexamined regularly for their relevance and validity. Mass global communications stimulate acquisition of new values and behavior patterns that may more rapidly undermine ancient, local or religious traditions, especially among women and young people worldwide.

CULTURAL UNDERSTANDING AND SENSITIVITY

The global leader, sensitive to cultural differences, appreciates a people's distinctiveness and seeks to make allowances for such factors when communicating with representatives of that cultural group. He/she avoids trying to impose his/her own cultural attitudes and approaches. Thus, by respecting the cultural differences of others, we will not be labeled as "ethnocentric," defined by *The Random House Dictionary* as

> Belief in the inherent superiority of one's own group and culture; it may be accompanied by feelings of contempt for those others who do not belong; it tends to look down upon those considered as foreign; it views and measures alien cultures and groups in terms of one's own culture.

Through cross-cultural experiences, we become more broadminded and tolerant of cultural "peculiarities." When this is coupled with some

Traditions provide a people with a "mindset" and have a powerful influence on their moral system for evaluating what is right or wrong, good or bad, desirable or not.

formal study of the concept of culture, we not only gain new insights for improving our human relations, but we become aware of the impact of our native culture. Cultural understanding may minimize the impact of culture shock and maximize intercultural experiences, as well as increase professional development and organizational effectiveness. Cultural sensitivity should teach us that culture and behavior are relative and that we should be more tentative, and less absolute, in human interactions.

The first step in managing cultural differences effectively is increasing one's general cultural awareness. We must understand the concept of culture and its characteristics before we can fully benefit from the study of cultural specifics and a foreign language.

Further, we should appreciate the impact of our specific cultural background on our own mindset and behavior, as well as those of colleagues and customers with whom we interact in the workplace.[11] This takes on special significance within a more diverse business environment, often the result of increasing migration from less-developed to more-developed economies. Transcultural leadership may be manifested by helping locals communicate with immigrants and visitors. That means building upon the newcomer's cultural heritage, rather than imposing our own. A case in point: many in Central and Eastern Europe look to the West for education and training in modern management. Because management itself is a highly cultural activity, our development programs must be within the cultural context of people coming out of centralized planning and totalitarianism into an unknown—the market economy and democracy.

CROSS-CULTURAL LEARNING

To increase effectiveness across cultures, *training* must be the focus of the job, while *education* thought of with reference to the individual, and *development* reserved for organizational concerns. Whether one is concerned with intercultural training, education, or development, all employees should learn about the influence of culture and be effective cross-cultural communicators if they are to work with minorities within their own society or with foreigners encountered at home or abroad. For example, there has been a significant increase in foreign investments in the United States—millions of Americans now work within the borders of their own country for foreign employers. All along the U.S.-Mexico border, twin plants have emerged that provide for a flow of goods and services between the two countries.

A new reality of the global marketplace is the information highway and its impact on jobs and cross-cultural communications. Many skilled workers in advanced economies are watching their positions migrate overseas where college-educated nationals are doing high-technology tasks for less pay. Consider this:

Because management itself is a highly cultural activity, our development programs must be within the cultural context of people coming out of centralized planning and totalitarianism into an unknown—the market economy and democracy.

Texas Instruments is designing some of its more sophisticated computer chips in India. Motorola Inc. recently set up computer programming and equipment design centers in China, Hong Kong, Singapore, Taiwan, and Australia, and it is looking for a site in South America.[12]

Beside computer language, most international exchanges occur with individuals using English as a second language. While a few corporate representatives will travel abroad, the main communication will occur by means of satellites on the Internet through modems connected to laptop or personal computers. Offshore operations done electronically in developing countries are stimulated by growing software applications that turn skilled tasks into routine work. Cross-cultural sensitivity is essential when participating in teleconferences or video conferences. Electronic media also requires appropriate etiquette and protocols to create cultural synergy.

GLOBAL TRANSFORMATIONS

In only 10% of 191 nations are the people ethnically or racially homogenous.

To stay competitive globally more and more corporations are increasing their investments and activities in foreign countries. U.S. engineers can work on a project during the day, then send it electronically to Asia or elsewhere for additional work while they sleep. Such trends represent an enormous challenge for cross-cultural competence.

An example of going global is in the personalized service firms such as law and accounting. These professions are increasingly engaging in cross-border activities, hiring local practitioners who comprehend their own unique culture, language, and legal or accounting systems. One reason is the need for international expertise and capital. Companies of professionals are forming alliances with their foreign counterparts such as the Alliance of European Lawyers. Furthermore, the divide between professions is being eliminated with accounting firms acquiring law firms as Arthur Andersen did in Britain and Spain. The process then requires an integration of *national, organizational,* and *professional cultures* if the acquisition is to be successful. Under these circumstances, culture becomes a critical factor ensuring business success, particularly with the 21st century trend toward economies of scale favoring large, multidisciplinary and multinational professional service organizations.[13]

In only 10% of 191 nations are the people ethnically or racially homogeneous. Never before in history have so many inhabitants traveled beyond their homelands, either as tourists or expatriate workers abroad, or to flee their countries as refugees or émigrés. In the host countries, the social fabric is being reconfigured and strained by massive waves of immigrants, whether legal or illegal.[14]

It is estimated that Chinese now constitute 3% of New York City's population, and a quarter of a million of them are concentrated in Manhattan Island's Chinatown, which overflows into older ethnic neighborhoods. This represents the largest Chinese expatriate group outside Southeast Asia.[15]

Too many corporate and government leaders, business students, and citizens still operate with dated mindsets of the world, the people in various societies, the nature of work, the worker, and the management process itself. The Industrial Age has given way to the Information Age, and we can only speculate on its replacement in the next one hundred years. Capra and Steindl Rast[16] state:

> Now, in the old paradigm it was also recognized that things are interrelated. But conceptually you first had the things with their properties, and then there were mechanisms and forces that interconnected them. In the new paradigm we say the things themselves do not have intrinsic properties. All the properties flow from their relationships. This is what I mean by understanding the properties of the parts from the dynamics of the whole, because these relationships are dynamic relationships. So the only way to understand the part is to understand its relationship to the whole. This insight occurred in physics in the 1920s and this is also a key insight of ecology. Ecologists think exactly in this way. They say an organism is defined by its relationship to the rest.

"Global managers must reframe the boundaries of their world . . . of space, time, scope, structure, geography and function. . . ."

Thus, today's leaders are challenged to create new models of management systems. For that to happen, managers and other professionals must become more innovative and recognize the contribution of each individual or unit to the effective workings of the whole.

As Peter Drucker has consistently observed, the art and science of management are in their own revolution, and many of the assumptions on which management practice was based are now becoming obsolete. Thinking managers alter not only their images of their role, but their managerial style and activities.

Foreign competition and the need to trade more effectively overseas has forced most corporations to become more culturally sensitive and globally minded. Some companies are investing in university programs to educate global managers. Managing people from different cultures is receiving the attention of business students, as well as those in education or human resource development. Global management is a component in most executive education/training programs worldwide.

According to Rhinesmith,[17]

> Global managers must reframe the boundaries of their world . . . of space, time, scope, structure, geography and function; of functional, professional, and technical skills from a past age; of thinking and classification relative to rational to intuitive, national versus foreign, we versus they; of cultural assumptions, values and beliefs about your relations with others, and your understanding of yourself.

How do companies foster and create effective global managers? What is a global manager? Many companies with worldwide operations are pondering these questions, plus many others. They find that the human resource component of the answer is, at times, more limiting then the capital investment in globalization. Bartlett and Ghoshal[18] state:

> Clearly, there is no single model for the global manager. Neither the old-line international specialist nor the more recent global generalist can cope with the complexities of cross-border strategies. Indeed, the dynamism of today's marketplace calls for managers with diverse skills. Responsibility for worldwide operations belongs to senior business, country, and functional executives who focus on the intense interchanges and subtle negotiations required. In contrast, those in middle management and front-line jobs need well-defined responsibilities, a clear understanding of their organization's transnational mission, and a sense of accountability.

Percy Barnevik, former president and CEO of Asea Brown Boveri (ABB), responded when asked if there is such a thing as a global manager,

> Global managers are made, not born. This is not a natural process. We are herd animals. We like people who are like us. But there are many things you can do. Obviously, you rotate people around the world. There is no substitute for line experience in three or four countries to create a global perspective. You also encourage people to work in mixed nationality teams. You force them to create personal alliances across borders, which means that sometimes you interfere in hiring decisions.
>
> You also have to acknowledge cultural differences without becoming paralyzed by them. We've done some surveys, as have lots of other companies, and we find interesting differences in perception. For example, a Swede may think a Swiss is not completely frank and open, that he doesn't know exactly where he stands. That is a cultural phenomenon. Swiss culture shuns disagreement. A Swiss might say, "Let's come back to that point later, let me review it with my colleagues." A Swede would prefer to confront the issue directly. How do we undo hundreds of years of upbringing and education? We don't, and we shouldn't try to. But we do need to broaden understanding.[19]

KEY CONCEPTS FOR GLOBAL LEADERSHIP

The following ten concepts contain the underlying message of this book. An awareness of and an application of these concepts to one's organization has direct relevance to the effectiveness of global managers, international lawyers, economic and community development specialists, engineers and technicians, public health officials, and ultimately everyone working in today's multicultural environment. An understanding and appplication of these concepts is critical to one's successful global performance.

Global Leadership—being capable of operating effectively in a global environment while respecting cultural diversity. This is an individual who can manage accelerating change and differences. The global leader is open and flexible in approaching others, can cope with situations and people disparate from his or her background, and is willing to reexamine and alter personal attitudes and perceptions.

Cross-Cultural Communication—recognizing what is involved in one's image of self and one's role, personal needs, values, standards, expectations, all of which are culturally conditioned. Such a person understands the impact of cultural factors on communication, and is willing to revise and expand such images as part of the process of growth. Furthermore, he or she is aware of verbal and nonverbal differences in communication with persons from another culture. Not only does such a person seek to learn another language, but he or she is cognizant that even when people speak the same language, cultural differences can alter communication symbols and meanings and result in misunderstandings.

Cultural Sensitivity—integrating the characteristics of culture in general, with experiences in specific organizational, minority, or foreign cultures. Such a person understands the cultural influences on behavior. This individual translates such cultural awareness into effective relationships with those who are different.

Acculturation—effectively adjusting and adapting to a specific culture, whether that be a subculture within one's own country or abroad. Such a person is alert to the impact of culture shock in successfully managing transitions. Therefore, when operating in an unfamiliar culture or dealing with employees from diverse cultural backgrounds, this person develops the necessary skills and avoids being ethnocentric.

Cultural Influences on Management—understanding that management philosophies are deeply rooted in culture, and that management practices developed in one culture may not easily transfer to another. However, this insight can be used to appreciate the universal character of management, and to identify with the subculture of modern managers. In the global marketplace, all management is multicultural.

Effective Intercultural Performance—applying cultural theory and insight to specific cross-cultural situations that affect people's performance on the job. Such a person makes provisions for the foreign deployment process, overseas adjustment and culture shock and the reentry of expatriates.

Changing International Business—coping with the interdependence of business activity throughout the world, as well as the subculture of the managerial group. There is an emerging universal acceptance of some business technology, computers and management information systems, for example. Yet, the global manager appreciates the effect of cultural differences on standard business practice and principles, such as organizational loyalty.

Cultural Synergy—building upon the very differences in the world's people for mutual growth and accomplishment by cooperation. Cultural synergy through collaboration emphasizes similarities and common concerns and integrates differences to enrich human activities and systems.

Acculturation—effectively adjusting and adapting to a specific culture, whether that be a subculture within one's own country or abroad.

By combining the best in varied cultures and seeking the widest input, multiple effects and complex solutions can result. Synergy is separate parts functioning together to create a greater whole and to achieve a common goal. For such aggregate action to occur, cross-cultural skills are required.

Work Culture—applying the general characteristics of culture to the specifics of how people work at a point in time and place. In the macro sense, work can be analyzed in terms of human stages of development—the work cultures of hunter, farmer, factory worker, and knowledge worker. In the micro sense, work cultures can be studied in terms of specific industries, organizations, or professional groups.

Global Culture—understanding that while various characteristics of human culture have always been universal, a unique global culture with some common characteristics may be emerging. The influences of mass media and telecommunications including the fax, email, the Internet, CNN/TV are breaking down barriers among groups of peoples and their diverse cultures. Global managers are alert to serving this commonality in human needs and markets with strategies that are transnational.

GLOBAL ORGANIZATIONS

The corporate culture of global organizations effects how an organization copes with competition and change, whether in terms of technology, economics, or people. Terpstra and David[20] recommend that people in global businesses be triply socialized—to their culture, their business culture, and their corporate culture. When we operate in the global marketplace it is imperative that we be informed about these three cultures of our customers, competitors, venture partners, suppliers, or government officials. Trompenaars[21] states:

> As markets globalize, the need for standarization in organizational design, systems, and procedures increases. Yet, managers are also under pressure to adapt their organization to the local characteristics of the market, the legislation, the fiscal regime, the socio-political system and the cultural system. This balance between consistency and adaptation is essential for corporate success.

As we evolve from a post-industrial culture to an information culture, McCarthy[22] envisions knowledge as culture. She states that knowledge is a powerful force, creating and affecting culture's attitudes and forms. Knowledge—its creation, storage, and use—becomes basic economic activity contributing to social transformation. Knowledge workers in various professions and technologies cut across the traditional boundaries of both nationality and disciplines.

By the end of the millennium, the number of global organizations is phenomenal. However, in 1994 there were 37,000 transnational corpo-

Global Culture— understanding that while various characteristics of human culture have always been universal, a unique global culture with some common characteristics may be emerging.

rations with 207,000 affiliates that controlled one-third of all private sector assets, and had worldwide sales of U.S. $5.5 trillion.[23] With great vision in 1974, Barnett and Muller forecast this post-industrial trend, and separately Wriston spoke of its influence. Barnett and Mulle:[24]

> The global corporation is the first institution in human history dedicated to centralized planning on a world scale. Because its primary activity is to organize and to integrate economic activity around the world in such a way as to maximize global profit, it is an organic structure in which each part is expected to serve the whole. . . . The rise of such planetary enterprises is producing an organizational revolution as profound for modern man as the Industrial Revolution and the rise of the nation-state itself.

Wriston:[25]

> The world corporation has become a new weight in an old balance and must play a constructive role in moving the world toward the freer exchange of both ideas and the means of production so that the people of the world may one day enjoy the fruits of a truly global society.

In discussing the evolution of the various corporations, the four types of corporations—ethnocentric, polycentric, regiocentric, and geocentric—are cited.[26]

Ethnocentric Corporations. These corporations are home-country oriented. Ethnocentric managers believe that home-country nationals are more intelligent, reliable, and trustworthy than foreign nationals. All key management positions are centered at the domestic headquarters. Home-country nationals are recruited and trained for all international positions.

The ethnocentric approach is fostered by many internal and external influences. The CEO may be limited by the biases of the owners and stockholders. Labor unions may impose intense pressure in favor of domestic employment. Home government policy may force emphasis on the domestic market.

The ethnocentric philosophy is exhibited in many international companies. The standard international company finds great difficulty communicating in different languages and in accepting cultural differences. International strategic alternatives are limited to entry modes such as exporting, licensing, and turnkey operations because "it works at home so it must work overseas."

Polycentric Corporations These are host-country oriented corporations. Profit potential is seen in a foreign country, but the foreign market is too hard to understand. The polycentric firm establishes multinational operations on condition that host-country managers "do it their way." The polycentric message is: "Local people know what is best for them. Let's give them the responsibility and leave them alone as long as they make us a profit."

The polycentric firm is a loosely connected group with quasi-independent subsidiaries as profit centers. Headquarters is staffed by home-country nationals, while local nationals occupy the key positions in their

Ethnocentric Corporations. These corporations are home-country oriented. All key management positions are centered at the domestic headquarters.

respective local subsidiaries. Host-country nationals have high or absolute sovereignty over the subsidiary's operations. There is no direction from headquarters and the only controls are financially oriented. No foreign national can seriously aspire to a senior position at headquarters.

The polycentric approach often results from great external pressures such as laws in different countries requiring local management participation. Engineering standards may have to be determined locally. The host-country government may be a major customer and therefore influence the ways of doing business.

The polycentric philosophy is often exhibited in multinational corporations. MNCs face a heterogeneous environment where product needs and preferences are diverse. In addition, governmental restrictions may be severe. Strategically, the MNC competes on a market-by-market basis because it believes that "local people know what is best for them."

Regiocentric Corporations. These corporations capitalize on the synergistic benefits of sharing common functions across regions. A regiocentric corporation believes that only regional insiders can effectively coordinate functions within the region. For example, a regiocentric organization might select a Japanese subsidiary to manage its Asian operations and a French subsidiary to manage its European operations. The regiocentric message is: "Regional insiders know what neighboring countries want."

The regiocentric firm is highly interdependent on a regional basis. Regional headquarters organize collaborative efforts among local subsidiaries. The regional headquarters is responsible for the regional plan, local research and development, product innovation, cash management, local executive selection and training, capital expenditure plans, brand policy, and public relations. The world headquarters takes care of world strategy, country analysis, basic research & development, foreign exchange, transfer pricing, intercompany loans, long-term financing, selection of top management, technology transfer, and establishing corporate culture.

Geocentric Corporations. Being world-oriented, a geocentric corporation's ultimate goal is creating an integrated system with a worldwide approach. The geocentric system is highly interdependent. Subsidiaries are no longer satellites and independent city-states. The entire organization is focused on worldwide and local objectives. Every part of the organization makes a unique contribution using its unique competencies. The geocentric message is: "All for one and one for all. We will work together to solve problems anywhere in the world."

Geocentrism requires collaboration between headquarters and subsidiaries to establish universal standards with permissible local variations. Diverse regions are integrated through a global systems approach to decision-making. Good ideas come from and flow to any country. Resources are allocated on a global basis. Geographical lines are erased and functional and product lines are globalized.

Within legal and political limits, the best people are sought to solve problems. Competence is what counts, not national origin. The reward

Regiocentric Corporations. These corporations capitalize on the synergistic benefits of sharing common functions across regions.

system motivates managers to surrender national biases and work for worldwide objectives.

The geocentric firm overcomes political barriers by turning its subsidiaries into good citizens of the host nations. It is hoped that the subsidiary will become a leading exporter from the host to the international community. Furthermore, the geocentric organization will provide base countries with an increasing supply of hard currency, new skills, and a knowledge of advanced technology.

SUMMARY

Having a sense of culture and its related skills are unique human attributes. Culture is fundamentally a group problem-solving tool for coping in a particular environment. It enables people to create a distinctive world around themselves, to control their own destinies, and to grow. Sharing the legacy of diverse cultures advances institutions' and individuals' social, economic, technological, and human development. Culture can be analyzed in a macro context, such as in terms of national groups, or in a micro sense, such as within a system or organization. Increasingly, we examine culture in a global sense from the perspective of work, leadership, or markets.

Because management philosophies and practices are culturally conditioned, it stands to reason that there is much to be gained by including cultural studies in all management or professional development. This is particularly relevant during the global transformation underway. Culturally skilled leaders are essential for the effective management of global corporations, as well as for the furtherance of mutually beneficial world trade and exchange. In these undertakings, the promotion of cultural synergy by those who are global professionals will help us to capitalize upon the differences in people, while ensuring their collaborative action.

In summary, here are parallel reasons why all managers and professionals should advance their culture learning, or why global organizations should include it in their human resource development strategies.

❑ Culture gives people a sense of identity, whether in nations or corporations, especially in terms of the human behavior and values to be encouraged, and through it organizational loyalty and performance can be improved.
❑ Cultural knowledge provides insight into people. The appropriate business protocol can be employed that is in tune with local character, codes, ideology, and standards.
❑ Cultural awareness and skill can be helpful in positively influencing organizational culture. Furthermore, subsidiaries, divisions, departments, or specializations have subcultures that can foster or undermine organizational goals and communications.

Culture is fundamentally a group problem-solving tool for coping in a particular environment.

- Cultural concepts and characteristics are useful for the analysis of work culture in global work environments.
- Cultural insights and tools are helpful in the study of comparative management techniques, so that we become less culture bound in our approach to leadership and management practice.
- Cultural competencies are essential for those in international business and trade.
- Cultural astuteness enables one to comprehend the diversity of market needs and to improve strategies with minority and ethnic groups at home, or foreign markets abroad.
- Cultural understanding is relevant to domestic relocation experiences. This is valid for individual managers or technicians who are facing a geographic transfer, as well as for their families and subordinates.
- Cultural understanding and skill development should be built into international deployment systems. Acculturation to overseas environments can improve the experience and productivity, and facilitate re-entry into the home and organizational culture.
- Cultural capabilities can enhance one's participation in international organizations and meetings. This is true whether one merely attends a conference abroad, is a delegate to a regional or foreign association, is a member in a world trade or professional enterprise, or is a meeting planner for transnational events.
- Cultural proficiency can facilitate one's coping with the changes of any transitional experience.
- Cultural diversity is not only evident on this planet, but also in the migration of our species aloft where multicultural crews of astronauts and cosmonauts are creating a new space culture.

Cultural proficiency can facilitate one's coping with the changes of any transitional experience.

Learning to manage cultural differences is a means for all persons to become more global in their outlook and behavior, as well as more effective personally and professionally. When cultural differences are perceived and used as a resource, then all benefit.[27]

REFERENCES

1. Mackiewicz, A. and Daniels, N. Caroline. "The Successful Corporation of the Year 2000," *Economist Intelligence Unit 1994*, Research Report, New York.
2. Goman, C. *Managing in a Global Organization*, Menlo Park, CA: Crisp Publications, 1994.
3. Pattison, J. E. *Acquiring the Future*, Homewood, IL: Dow Jones-Irwin, 1990.
4. Schein, E. H. "On Dialogue, Culture and Organizational Learning," *Organizational Dynamics*, Fall 1993, Vol. 22, Is. 2, pp. 40–51.
5. Huntington, S. *The Clash of Civilizations and the Remaking of World Order*, New York: Simon & Shuster, 1996.

6. Kidder, R. M. *Shared Values for a Troubled World,* 1994; Bryson, J. M. and Crosby, B. C. *Leadership for the Common Good,* 1992. San Francisco, CA: Jossey-Bass Publishers.

7. Miller, J. G. *Living Systems,* Niwot, CO: University Press of Colorado, 1994. See also *Systems Research and Behavioral Science,* Wiley Interscience, Buffins Lane, Chichester, West Sussex, UK, P019 1UD.

8. Clever, L. W. (ed.) "Cross-Cultural Medicine—A Decade Later," *The Western Journal of Medicine* (P.O. Box 7602, San Francisco, CA 94120, USA), Vol. 157:3, Sept. 1992.

9. Wallman, S. *Contemporary Futures: Perspectives for Social Anthropology.* London, UK: Routledge, 1992. . . . Foulkes, R. A. (ed.) *Astroanthropology: Issues and Perspectives on the Next Stage of Human Evolution.* Gainesville, FL: University of Florida Copy Center, 1993 (or contact editor at P.O. Box 14906, Gainesville, FL 32604).

10. Stein, J. "Tradition," *Fiddler on the Roof.* Harnick, S., lyrics, Bock, J., music, 1964.

11. Thiederman, S. *Bridging Cultural Barriers to Success: How to Manage the Multicultural Workforce,* 1990. *Profiting in America's Multicultural Workplace,* 1991. Lexington, MA: Lexington Books.

12. Bradsher, K. "Skilled Workers Watch Their Jobs Migrate Overseas," *New York Times,* Aug. 28, 1995, p.1, C6.

13. *The Economist,* August 29, 1998, p.59.

14. Harris, P. R. *The Cultural Diversity Handbook,* Simons, Abramms, Hopkins, and Johnson (eds). Princeton, NJ: Pacesetter Books, 1996.

15. *National Geographic,* August 1998, p.62.

16. Capra, F. and Steindl Rast, D. *Belonging to the Universe,* San Francisco, CA: Harper, 1991.

17. Rhinesmith, S. H. *A Manager's Guide to Globalization,* Second Edition, Chicago, IL: Irwin/ASTD, 1996, pp. x.

18. Bartlett, C. A. and Ghoshal, S. "What Is a Global Manager?" *Harvard Business Review,* September/October 1992, p. 131.

19. Taylor, W. "The Logic of Global Business: An Interview with ABB's Percy Barnevik," *Harvard Business Review,* March/April, 1991, p. 95.

20. Terpstra, V. and David, K. *The Cultural Environment of International Business,* Cincinnati, OH: South-Western Publishing, 1985.

21. Trompenaars, F. *Riding the Waves of Culture,* London: Economist Books, 1997, p. 3.

22. McCarthy, E. D. *Knowledge as Culture: The New Sociology of Knowledge,* London: Routledge, 1996.

23. *The Economist,* July 30, 1994, p. 57.

24. Barnett, R. J. and Muller, R.E. *Global Reach: The Power of the Multinational Corporation,* New York: Simon & Schuster, 1974.

25. Wriston, W. B., "The World Corporation—New Weight in an Old Balance," *Sloan Management Review,* Winter 1974.

26. Moran, R. T., Harris, P. R., and Stripp, W. G. *Developing the Global Organization: Strategies for Human Resource Professionals,* Houston, TX: Gulf Publishing Co., 1993.

27. Gesteland, R. R. *Cross-Cultural Business Behavior—Marketing, Negotiating, and Managing Across Cultures,* Copenhagen, DK: The Copenhagen Business School Press (Handelshojskolens Forlag), 1999.

GLOBAL LEADERS AND COMMUNICATIONS

If the global world in which we live had one thousand people, it would include:

❑ 584 Asians
❑ 124 Africans
❑ 150 Europeans and former Soviets
❑ 84 Latin Americans
❑ 52 North Americans
❑ 6 Australians and New Zealanders

About 50% of the people of the village speak the following languages:

❑ 165 Mandarin
❑ 86 English
❑ 83 Hindu/Urdu
❑ 64 Spanish
❑ 58 Russian
❑ 37 Arabic

The other half speak Bengali, Portuguese, Indonesian, Japanese, German, French and 200 other languages. Communication, indeed, would be challenging in this global village.[1]

The following quotation expresses well the diversity of values and truths in our global village and why global leaders must be skillful communicators—

"There are truths on this side of the Pyrénées that are falsehoods on the other."
Blaise Pascal,
Pensées

25

"There are truths on this side of the Pyrénées that are falsehoods on the other."

Blaise Pascal, Pensées

Perhaps the importance of international business communication can best be highlighted by contrasting some economic developments in the global marketplace:

❑ The pace of economic change has accelerated. It took the United Kingdom 58 years to double its output per worker, the United States 47 years, Japan 34 years, South Korea 11 years and China less than 10 years.[2]

❑ In the past, food preferences were considered very culturally oriented. Coca-Cola, McDonalds, and Pizza Hut have proven that tastes can be changed.[3]

❑ In some segments of the electronics industry, the shelf life of new products is 16 months. If products are not developed and introduced within this time frame, they risk not being highly competitive.[4]

❑ According to Jupiter Communications' predictions, by 2002, 56% of U.S. homes will have an Internet connection, compared to 32% currently.[5]

❑ Because of new communication technologies, people are increasingly communicating across cultures and borders.

With our globally interdependent economy, it is imperative to understand our world trade partners. But persons working internationally and participating in these intercultural experiences have learned that there are many challenges when working or living in a foreign environment. Communication across cultural boundaries is difficult. Differences in customs, behavior, and values result in problems that can be managed only through effective cross-cultural communication and interaction.

When people have misunderstandings or commit "errors" when working with persons from different cultures, they are often unaware of any problem. Cross-cultural *faux pas* result when we fail to recognize that persons of other cultural backgrounds have different goals, customs, thought patterns, and values from our own. This is particularly true in a more diverse workforce with increasing numbers of expatriate workers not familiar with the home culture, its language, and communication systems.

The personnel files of multinational corporations and government agencies are replete with documentation of intercultural communication misunderstandings. Some are not serious, while others result in organizational and personal tragedies and affect company presidents and ambassadors, as well as tourists. Usually, interpersonal work or social relations with the host nationals have gone sour, not because of person-

With our globally interdependent economy, it is imperative to understand our world trade partners.

ality factors, but because of ineffective communication and a misreading of verbal and nonverbal communication signals.

CULTURAL DIFFERENCES AS COMMUNICATION RESOURCES

In the past, many assumed that cultural differences were barriers and impeded communication and interaction. Today effective global leaders believe that cultural differences, if well managed, are resources, and not handicaps. In one's homeland, both students and workers can be taught how to communicate more effectively with colleagues and customers, as well as how to create cultural synergy with those from different racial, ethnic, or national backgrounds. Training, briefing, and adequate preparation for an overseas assignment will make the experience positive and enlightening. However, an effective communicator working with American nationals in the United States is not necessarily an effective communicator working with Japanese or Saudi Arabians in the United States, Japan, or Saudi Arabia.

Comprehending Communication

Studies of what managers do each day indicate that 75% of their time is spent writing, talking, and listening—that is communicating. In fact, all business ultimately comes down to transactions or interactions between individuals. The success of the transaction depends almost entirely on how well managers understand each other.

In our combined forty years of experience in international consulting in the United States and overseas, we have heard business people make one consistent request of presenters, consultants, seminar leaders and speakers. They ask that the material be relevant and useful in their worlds, as opposed to only academic and theoretical.

To better understand the global leader's role as a communicator, it is vital that we comprehend what is involved in the complex process of communication. As shown in the next section, it is a dynamic exchange of energy, ideas, information—knowledge—between and among peoples. It is verbal and nonverbal and occurs at different levels—informal or formal, intellectual or emotional.

Most communication is manifest through symbols that globally differ in their meaning according to time, place, culture or person. Human interaction is characterized by a continuous updating of the meaning of these symbols. In the past twenty-five years, we have expanded our capacities for symbolic communication beyond what was accomplished in the previous twenty-five hundred years. The human species is extend-

All business ultimately comes down to transactions or interactions between individuals. The success of the transaction depends almost entirely on how well managers understand each other.

ing its communication capabilities beyond print to that of electronic technology; in the process our whole thought pattern is being transformed.

Despite the technological wonders of today's communications, international relations require us to deal with one another on a person-to-person basis. For this to be effective interaction, we have to overcome language and stereotype barriers. This may require the mental elimination of terms like "foreigner" or "alien" and more appropriately viewing the individual as having a background that is different.

Axioms of Communication

Every person is a versatile communicator. Language sets us apart from other creatures and seemingly is characteristic of the more developed brain. But humans have a wide range of communication skills that go beyond words to include gestures, signs, shapes, colors, sounds, smells, pictures, and many other communication symbols. The diversity of human culture in this regard may be demonstrated by the "artist" who may communicate both thought and feeling in paintings, sculpture, music, and dance. Through such media, artists project themselves into people, things, and surroundings. They project their way of thinking, their temperament and personality, joys and sorrows into the world around them.

Every individual communicates a unique perspective of the world and reality. Every culture reflects the group view of the world.

Every person operates within his or her own private world or perceptual field. This is what is referred to as life space, and it applies to individuals as well as to organizations and nations. Every individual communicates a unique perspective of the world and reality. Every culture reflects the group view of the world. From time to time, one must check whether one's view of the world, or that of an organization synchronizes with the collective reality. This is particularly essential when "objective reality" is subject to the phenomenon of accelerating change. Cultural groups may have distorted views of world reality, as did China during the period of the Maoist Cultural Revolution.

Every person projects himself or herself into human communication. We communicate our image of self including our system of needs, values, and standards; our expectations, ideals, and perceptions of peoples, things, and situations. We project this collective image through body, bearing, appearance, tone of voice, and choice of words.

Every person is a medium or instrument of communication, not just a sender and receiver of messages. If a person is comfortable with himself or herself and congruent, people usually respond positively. If one is uncomfortable and incongruent, people will respond negatively. The more aware the individual is of the forces at work within himself or herself that affect behavior, the more able that person is to control his or her own life space.

Every generation perceives life differently. For example, the previous concepts of behavioral communication can be applied to a generation of people. The people of each generation project a unique image of "their" world at a certain point in time. This image reflects a generation's system of needs, values, standards, and ideals. The children of the "depression age" experienced life differently from today's children of affluence. The problem of communication between the generations and even cultures becomes more understandable. The supervisor of a young worker, for example, usually projects his or her generation's view of the world (past-oriented) and finds it difficult to facilitate communication by coming into the reality of the younger employee (future oriented).

Communication is at the heart of all organizational operations and international relations. It is the most important tool we have for getting things done. It is the basis for understanding, cooperation, and action. In fact, the very vitality and creativity of an organization or a nation depends upon the content and character of its communications. Yet, communication is both hero and villain—it transfers information, meets people's needs, and gets things done, but far too often it also distorts messages, causes frustration, and renders people and organizations ineffective.

The Communication Process

Communication is a process of circular interaction that involves a sender, receiver, and message. In human interaction, the sender or receiver may be a person or a group of people. The message conveys meaning through the medium or symbol used to send it (the how), as well as in its content (the what). Because humans are such intelligent, symbol-making creatures, the message may be relayed verbally, or nonverbally—words (oral or written), pictures, graphs, statistics, signs, gestures. Humans are versatile communicators; we can communicate with nature, animals, and other humans. Humankind's capacity to communicate ranges from smoke signals and the sound of drums to television and the Internet. As a dynamic being, humans constantly invent new and improved ways of communicating. Regardless of the communication symbol, a sender and receiver are normally involved.

Both sender and receiver occupy a unique field of experience, different for each person. Essentially, it is a private world of perception through which all experience is filtered, organized, and translated; it is what psychologists call the individual's life space. This consists of the person's *psychological environment* as it exists for him or her. Each person experiences life in a unique way and psychologically structures his/her own distinctive perceptual field. Among the factors that comprise one's field of experience are one's family, educational, cultural, religious, and social background. The individual's perceptual field affects the way he or she receives and dispenses all new information. It influences both the content and the media used in communicating.

An individual's self-image, needs, values, expectations, goals, standards, cultural norms, and perception have an effect on the way input is received and interpreted. Essentially, persons *selectively perceive* all new

Humans are versatile communicators; we can communicate with nature, animals, and other humans.

data, determining that which is relevant to, and consistent with, their own perceptual needs. Literally, two people can thus receive the same message and derive from it two entirely different meanings. They actually perceive the same object or information differently. Communication, then, is a complex process of linking up or sharing perceptual fields between sender and receiver. The effective communicator builds a bridge to the world of the receiver. When the sender is from one cultural group and the receiver from another, the human interaction is intercultural communication.

Once the sender conveys the message, the receiver analyzes the message in terms of his or her particular field of experience and pattern of ideas. Usually, decoding the message, interpreting it for meaning and encoding or sending back a response. Thus, communication is a circular process of interaction.

The communicator, whether as an individual from a cultural group or as a member of an organization, exhibits or transmits many kinds of behavior. First, the intended message is communicated on verbal and nonverbal level. We also communicate unintended behavior, or subconscious behavior, on verbal and nonverbal levels. In other words, communication at any level involves a whole complex of projections. There is a "silent language" being used also in the process of human interaction, including tone of voice, inflection of words, gestures and facial expressions. Some of these factors that affect the real meaning and content of messages are referred to as "body language," that is, the positioning of various parts of the sender's physique conveys meaning. The person is both a medium and a message of communication and the way in which one communicates is vastly influenced by our cultural conditioning.

GLOBAL COMMUNICATION

Klopf[6] defines communication as "the process by which persons share information meanings and feelings through the exchange of verbal and nonverbal messages." For the individual working and communicating in a multicultural environment, one must "remember that the message that ultimately counts is the one that the other person gets or creates in their mind, not the one we send."[7]

The following are practical guidelines for developing skills to become a more effective intercultural communicator. These statements briefly outline several important characteristics of intercultural communication. Some are obvious, others not, but all, if internalized and understood will result in more effective communication.

❏ **No matter how hard one tries, one cannot avoid communicating.** All behavior in human interaction has a message and communicates something. Body language communicates as well as our activity or inactivity, the color of our skin, the color of our clothes or the gift we give. All behavior is communication because all behavior contains a message, whether intended or not.

❑ **Communication does not necessarily mean understanding.** Even when two individuals agree that they are communicating or talking to each other, it does not mean that they have understood each other. Understanding occurs when the two individuals have the same interpretation of the symbols being used in the communication process whether the symbols be words or gestures.

❑ **Communication is irreversible.** One cannot take back one's communication (although sometimes one wishes that he or she could). However, one can explain, clarify, or restate one's message. Once one has communicated, it is part of his or her experience and it influences present and future meanings. Disagreeing with a Saudi Arabian in the presence of others is an "impoliteness" in the Arab world and may be difficult to remedy.

❑ **Communication occurs in a context.** One cannot ignore the context of communication that occurs at a certain time, in some place, using certain media. Such factors have message value and give meaning to the communicators. For example, a business conversation with a French manager in France during an evening meal may be inappropriate.

❑ **Communication is a dynamic process.** Communication is not static and passive, but rather it is a continuous and active process without beginning or end. A communicator is not simply a sender or a receiver of messages but can be both at the same time.

Each of us has been socialized in a unique environment. Important aspects of the environment are shared and these constitute a particular culture. Culture poses communication problems because there are so many variables unknown to the communicators. As the cultural variables and differences increase, the number of communication misunderstandings also increase.

Every person is part of many different identity groups simultaneously, thus learning and becoming part of all their cultures. Each of us is culturally unique because each adopts or adapts differently the attitudes, values, and beliefs of the groups to which he or she belongs. Thus, all communication becomes intercultural because of variations in group identities of those communicating. Our challenge is to examine the differences that make us unique and discover ways to be more effective in overcoming the barriers these differences create.[8] That is why,

> When we travel to another culture or interact with people from another culture in our culture, we cannot base our predictions of their behavior on our cultural rules and norms. This inevitably leads to misunderstanding. If we want to communicate effectively, we must use our knowledge of the other culture to make predictions. If we have little or no knowledge of the other person's culture, we have no basis for making predictions.[9]

Each of us is culturally unique because each adopts or adapts differently the attitudes, values, and beliefs of the groups to which he or she belongs.

CULTURAL FACTORS IN COMMUNICATION

Intercultural communication is a process whereby individuals from different cultural backgrounds attempt to share meanings. Lustig and Koester[10] provide definitions of communications. For example, *intercultural* communication is "the presence of at least two individuals who are culturally different from each other on such important attributes as their value orientations, preferred communication codes, role expectations, and perceived rules of social relationship," exemplified by a Japanese and an English negotiator discussing a joint venture. *Intracultural* communication occurs between culturally similar individuals. The study of child-rearing practices in different cultures would be referred to as *cross-cultural* or communication that pertains to the "study of a particular idea or concept within many cultures." *Interracial* communication refers to the "differences in communication between members of racial and ethnic groups," such as African Americans and Asian Americans.

In the classical anthropological sense, culture refers to the cumulative deposit of knowledge, beliefs, values, religion, customs, and mores acquired by a group of people and passed on from generation to generation. Imagine yourself participating in the following cross-cultural situations that affect communication and understanding between two culturally different individuals.

Intercultural communication is a process whereby individuals from different cultural backgrounds attempt to share meanings.

❑ You are involved in a technical training program in China and one of your responsibilities is to rate persons under your supervision. You have socialized on several occasions, spending time with one of the Chinese you are supervising. The Chinese is an extremely friendly and hardworking individual, but has difficulty exercising the leadership expected of him. On the rating form you so indicated, and this was discussed with him by his supervisor. Subsequently, he came to you and asked how you could have criticized his leadership skills. You indicated that you had an obligation to report deficiencies and areas of improvement. What cultural differences might cause misperceptions of performance appraisal and evaluation?

❑ You are in Saudi Arabia attempting to finalize a contract with a group of Saudi businessmen. You are aware these people are excellent negotiators, however, you find it difficult to maintain eye contact with your hosts during conversations. Further, their increasing physical proximity to you is becoming more uncomfortable. You also have noticed that a strong handgrip while shaking hands is not returned. When invited to a banquet, because you are left-handed, you use your left hand while eating. Your negotiations are not successfully concluded. What may have been the reason for this? What cultural aspects are evidenced in this interaction, which if known, could improve your communication with your Arab clients?

❑ You are the manager of a group of Puerto Rican workers in a New York factory, but you only speak English. You resent the use of Spanish among your subordinates. Why do your subordinates feel more comfortable in their native language? How could your company facilitate their instruction in the English language? Or should it?

In the past, many business people were not overly concerned with the ways that culture influenced individual or organizational behavior. But serious and costly errors have made those working in a multicultural environment aware that insensitivity and lack of cultural knowledge can do much to injure permanently or temporarily the relationship with their coworkers and colleagues. These questions may prove helpful and expedient.

1. What must I know about the social and business customs of country X?
2. What skills do I need to be effective as a negotiator in country Y?
3. What prejudices and stereotypes do I have about the people in country Z?
4. How will these influence my interaction?

COMMUNICATION KEYS— CONTEXT AND LISTENING

Anthropologist Edward Hall makes a vital distinction between high- and low-context cultures, and how this matter of *context* impacts communications. A high-context culture uses high-context communications, i.e., information is either in the physical context or internalized in the person with little being communicated in the explicit words or message. Japan, Saudi Arabia, Spain and China are cultures engaged in high-context communications. On the other hand, a low-context culture employs low context communications, i.e., most information is contained in explicit codes, such as words. Canada and United States as well as most European countries, engage in low-context communications.

When individuals are communicating, they are attempting to find out how much the listener knows about whatever is being discussed. In a low-context communication the listener knows very little and must be told practically everything. In high-context cultures the listener is already "contexted" and doesn't need to have much background information. Communication between high- and low-context people is often fraught with impatience and irritation because low-context communicators may give more information than is necessary, while high-context communicators may not provide enough information or background.

When communicating with individuals of our native culture, we can more readily assess the communication cues so that we know when our conversation, our ideas and words are being understood and internal-

A high-context culture uses high-context communications, i.e., information is either in the physical context or internalized in the person with little being communicated in the explicit words or message.

ized. However, when communicating across cultures, communication misunderstandings can occur. Usually they are not serious and can be rectified. However, Exhibit 2-1 illustrates a communication misunderstanding that had grave results. Excerpted is the transcript of the conversation between the captain, copilot and controller of the Avianca flight that crashed on Long Island in 1991.

EXHIBIT 2-1

Captain to Copilot:
"Tell them we are in emergency."

Copilot to Controller:
"We are running out of fuel. . ."

Controller:
"Climb and maintain 3,000"

Co-pilot to Controller:
"Uh, we're running out of fuel."

Controller:
"I'm going to bring you about 15 miles northeast and then turn you back. . . .
Is that fine with you and your fuel?"

Copilot:
"I guess so."

The jet ran out of fuel and crashed.

However, when communicating across cultures, communication misunderstandings can occur. Usually they are not serious and can be rectified.

The communication misunderstanding involves the high- and low-context of communication styles. It can be seen from the dialogue between the pilot, copilot, and controller that there was a crucial error of misunderstanding between the copilot who was Colombian (native language Spanish—high-context) and the American controller, who was a low-context communicator. "Emergency" is low-context. "We are running out of fuel" is more high context (literally, all airplanes, once they take off, are running out of fuel). The controller's last question, "Is that fine with you and your fuel?" is more high-context.

The controller could have asked, "Are you declaring a fuel emergency?" If the controller had asked this question, perhaps the copilot would have responded "yes" because he had just heard the pilot say, "Tell them we are in emergency."

Unless global leaders are aware of the subtle differences, communication misunderstandings between low- and high-context communicators can result. Japanese communicate by not stating things directly, while Americans usually do just the opposite—"spell it all out." The former is looking for meaning and understanding in what is not said—in the nonverbal communication or body language, in the silences and pauses, in relationships and empathy. The latter places emphasis on sending and receiving accurate messages directly, usually by being articulate with words.

Exhibit 2-2 illustrates the high-low context of communication on performance appraisals between Japanese, Americans, and Saudi Arabians.

EXHIBIT 2-2
CULTURAL VARIATIONS: PERFORMANCE APPRAISALS

Dimensions General	U.S. Low Context	Saudi Arabia High Context	Japan High Context
Objective of P.A.	Fairness, Employee development	Placement	Direction of company/employee development
Who does appraisal	Supervisor	Manager—may be several layers up—appraiser has to know employee well	Mentor and supervisor; Appraiser has to know employee well
Authority of appraiser	Presumed in supervisory role or position	Reputation important (Prestige is determined by nationality, age, gender, family, tribe, title, education)	Respect accorded by employee to supervisor to appraiser
	Supervisor takes slight lead	Authority of appraiser important—don't say "I don't know"	Done equally
How often	Yearly or periodically	Yearly	Developmental appraisal monthly; Evaluation appraisal—after first 12 years
Assumptions	Objective appraiser is fair	Subjective appraiser more important than objective; Connections are important	Objective and subjective important; Japanese can be trained in anything
Manner of communication and feedback	Criticism direct; Criticisms may be in writing; Objective/authentic	Criticisms subtle; Older more likely to be direct; Criticisms not given in writing	Criticisms subtle; Criticisms given verbally; Observe formalities
Rebuttals	U.S. will rebut appraisal	Saudi Arabians will rebut	Japanese will rarely rebut
Praise Motivators	Given individually Money and position strong motivators Career development	Given individually Loyalty to supv. strong motivator	Given to entire group Internal excellence strong motivator

*Adapted from report of the Association of Cross-Cultural Trainers in Industy, now Pacific Area Communicators of International Affairs, 16331 Underhill Lane, Huntington Beach, CA 92647.

Unless global leaders are aware of the subtle differences, communication misunderstandings between low- and high- context communicators can result.

Another related consideration for global leaders is the importance of *listening*. Education seems to emphasize articulation over the acquisition of listening skills, which are essential to international negotiations. Lyman Steil pioneered scientific research on listening and discovered that it is the communication competency that is used most but taught least in the United States. He summarized his findings in Exhibit 2-3.

EXHIBIT 2-3
COMMUNICATION SKILLS

	Listening	Speaking	Reading	Writing
Learned	1st	2nd	3rd	4th
Used	Most	Next most	Next least	Least
(%-100)	(45%)	(30%)	(16%)	(9%)
Taught	Least	Next least	Next most	Most

We learn to listen and talk before we read and write. Should we have difficulties with reading, writing, and talking, we will receive special assistance while at school. Why is listening not accorded the same attention, the same importance as speaking, reading, and writing?

Listening is a complex activity. The average person speaks approximately 12,000 sentences every day at about 150 words per minute, while the listener's brain can absorb around 400 words per minute. What do we do with this spare capacity? Many of us do nothing. We become bored. A good listener is seldom bored. He or she uses this extra capacity to listen to the entire message and to more fully analyze the meanings behind the words.

Listening means different things to different people. It can mean different things to the same person in different situations. There are various types of listening behaviors:

1. *Hearing* is a physiological process by which sound waves are received by the ear and transmitted to the brain. This is not really listening in and of itself, though the two are often equated. Hearing is merely one step in the process.
2. *Information gathering* is absorbing stated facts. It does not pertain to the interpretation of the facts and is indifferent as to the source.
3. *Cynical listening* is based upon the assumption that all communication is designed to take advantage of the listener. It is also referred to as defensive listening.
4. *Offensive listening* is the attempt to trap or trip up an opponent with his own words. A lawyer, when questioning a witness, listens for contradictions, irrelevancies, and weakness.

5. *Polite listening* is listening just enough to meet the minimum social requirements. Many people are not listening—they are just waiting their turn to speak and are perhaps rehearsing their lines. They are not really talking to each other, but at each other.

6. *Active listening* involves a listener with very definite responsibilities. In active listening, the listener strives for complete and accurate understanding, for empathy, and assistance in working out problems.

Active listening is what our normal listening mode should be, but rarely is.

Listening is, above all, a sharing of oneself. It is impossible for one to become an active listener without becoming involved with the speaker. Listening demonstrates the respect and concern that words alone cannot fully express. It has the unique power of diminishing the magnitude of problems. By speaking to someone who listens, a person has the sense of already accomplishing something.

Listening fulfills another vital function as well. The listener provides feedback to the speaker concerning the latter's success in transmitting his or her message clearly. In doing this, the listener exerts great control over future messages that might or might not be sent. Feedback will influence the speaker's confidence, delivery, the content of the words, and the nonverbal facets of communication.

Simons, Vázquez, and Harris[11] state that working within our own culture we are very perceptive. We know what ideas are being accepted or rejected, and when others are following our conversation. However, when communicating across cultures there is the real possibility of reading people incorrectly and they us. Problems arise when one does not pay close enough attention or actively listen to what an individual is trying to communicate. Instead, when at work, focusing on getting the job done and meeting business deadlines and agendas, one can easily pretend to listen or listen halfheartedly. Today the workplace is filled with individuals from different cultures, as well as a mix of age, gender and work values. One must listen at three levels in cross-cultural exchanges.

1. *Pay attention to the person and the message.* One may subconsciously ignore another because the thought process or thinking patterns they use are more convoluted or subtle then one's own. Also, the behavior of the speaker may be so emotional or subdued that one may selectively listen or not listen at all. To further complicate the listening process, an individual may speak with an accent that can cause the listener to struggle to determine the words and put them in an understandable order.

2. *Emphasize and create rapport.* Empathy, especially with people who have visible differences in language and culture, can build trust and loyalty. The verbal and nonverbal cues of the speaker

In active listening, the listener strives for complete and accurate understanding, for empathy, and assistance in working out problems. Listening is, above all, a sharing of oneself . . . it demonstrates the respect and concern that words alone cannot fully express.

reveal his or her thinking patterns. Attempting to emulate cues, after reading them properly and matching their style increases the comfort and effectiveness of communication, especially a cross-cultural one.

3. *Share meaning.* Share your understanding of what you think the individual is saying. Paraphrasing is an "active listening" skill enabling one to check the accuracy of what you understand the message to be.

ATTRIBUTION

Triandis[12] cites the following interesting cross-cultural situation. In many cultures domestic help does most of the tasks around a home, including the cleaning of shoes. In the United States, such employees usually do not clean shoes as part of their responsibilities. If Mr. Kato, a Japanese businessman, were a house guest of Mr. Smith, an American businessman, and asked the "cleaning person" to shine his shoes there could be a problem. It is, or at least could be, an inappropriate request. However, the crucial question is, what *attributions* does the cleaning person make concerning Mr. Kato's request? There are probably two possibilities. One is that he or she could say Mr. Kato is ignorant of American customs and in this case the person would not be too disturbed. The cleaning person could respond in a variety of ways, including telling the Japanese guest of the American custom, ignoring the request, and speaking to his or her employer. However, if the cleaning person attributes Mr. Kato's request to a personal consideration (he is arrogant), then there will be a serious problem in their interpersonal relationship. If a person from one culture is offended by a person from another culture and one believes it is because of culture ignorance, this is usually forgiven. If one "attributes" the offense or "error" to arrogance, there will be serious problems.

Attribution theory is concerned with how people explain things that happen. We interpret behavior in terms of behaviors appropriate for a role. Mr. Kato expected that it would be acceptable to ask the cleaning person to shine his shoes. From the perspective of the cleaning person, this is not acceptable. When each one's expectations were not realized they attributed motives to the "offender" based on their cultural construct. It helps to answer such questions as:

1. Why did Mr. Kato ask the cleaning person to shine his shoes?
2. Why did I pass or fail an examination?
3. Why can't Molly read?

There are many ways of perceiving the world, and given the almost limitless possibilities, we must subconsciously and habitually "screen" and organize the stimuli.

Paraphrasing is an "active listening" skill enabling one to check the accuracy of what you understand the message to be.

Attribution theory helps to explain what happens and is applicable to cross-cultural management situations for the following reasons:

- ❏ *All behavior is rational and logical from the perspective of the behaver.* At a seminar involving Japanese and American business people, an American asked a Japanese what was most difficult for him in the United States. The Japanese replied that "the most difficult part of my life here is to understand Americans. They are so irrational and illogical." The Americans listened with amusement and surprise.
- ❏ *Persons from different cultures perceive and organize their environment in different ways, so that it becomes meaningful to them.* To be effective in working with people from different cultures requires that we make *isomorphic attributions* of the situation, i.e., we put ourselves "in the other person's shoes." Isomorphic attributions result in a positive evaluation of the other person because they help us to better understand his or her verbal and nonverbal behavior.

Triandis[12] provides another attribution in Exhibit 2-4. As background, Greeks perceive supervisory roles as more authoritarian than Americans who prefer participatory decision-making. Read the verbal conversation first, then the attributions being made by the American and the Greek.

EXHIBIT 2-4

Verbal Conversation	Attribution
American: How long will it take you to finish this report?	*American:* I asked him to participate. *Greek:* His behavior makes no sense. He is the boss. Why doesn't he tell me?
Greek: I do not know. How long should it take?	*American:* He refuses to take responsibility. *Greek:* I asked him for an order.
American: You are in the best position to analyze time requirements.	*American:* I press him to take responsibility for own actions. *Greek:* What nonsense! I better give him an answer.
Greek: 10 days.	*American:* He lacks the ability to estimate time; this estimate is totally inadequate.
American: Take 15. Is it agreed you will do it in 15 days?	*American:* I offer a contract. *Greek:* These are my orders: 15 days.

(Exhibit continued on next page)

There are many ways of perceiving the world, and given the almost limitless possibilities, we must subconsciously and habitually "screen" and organize the stimuli.

EXHIBIT 2-4 (CONTINUED)

Verbal Conversation	Attribution

In fact the report needed 30 days of regular work. So the Greek worked day and night, but at the end of the 15th day, he still needed one more day's work.

American: Where is the report?	*American:* I am making sure he fulfills his contract. *Greek:* He is asking for the report.
Greek: It will be ready tomorrow.	Both attribute that it is not ready.
American: But we had agreed it would be ready today.	*American:* I must teach him to fulfill a contract. *Greek:* The stupid, incompetent boss! Not only did he give me wrong orders, but he does not even appreciate that I did a 30-day job in 16 days.
The Greek submits his resignation.	The American is surprised. *Greek:* I can't work for such a man.

This example illustrates that each statement of a person in cross-cultural communication leads to an intimation that does not match the attribution of the other. These are extreme examples of non-isomorphic attributions, and accordingly work to the detriment of the relationship.

The intercultural skill of making isomorphic attributions is vital to appropriate protocol and effective technology transfer.[13]

Levels of Culture and Human Interaction

Using the analogy that culture is like an iceberg (part of it is seen but most is not), the *technical* level of culture is the part of the iceberg that is visible. The technical aspects of a culture can be taught and there is little emotion attached to this level. Few intercultural misunderstandings arise at this level, because the reason for the misunderstanding is usually quite easy to determine. Managers operate at the technical levels of culture when discussing the tolerance points of certain metals; however, when two managers are interacting over a period of time, it is difficult to remain exclusively at the technical level.

Continuing with the analogy of the cultural iceberg, the *formal* level of culture is partially above and partially below sea level. We learn aspects of our culture at the formal level usually by trial and error. We may be aware of the rules for a particular behavior, such as the rituals of marriage, but

The intercultural skill of making isomorphic attributions is vital to appropriate protocol and effective technology transfer.

we do not know why. The emotion at the formal level of culture is high and violations result in negative feelings about the violator even though the violation is often unintentional. The fact that the violated rule is local, i.e., an aspect of one culture and not another and therefore does not apply to everyone, is difficult to admit. A visiting business representative who uses a social occasion in France to discuss business with a French executive is violating a rule at the formal level of that culture.

The *informal* level of culture lies below "sea level" and actions and responses are automatic and almost unconscious. The rules of such behavior are usually not known although we realize that something is wrong. Informal rules are learned through a process called *modeling*. One example is the male and female role behavior in cultures. In France, for instance, when is it appropriate for the American manager to begin calling her colleague, "Denise" instead of "Mademoiselle Drancourt?" Emotion is usually intense at the informal level when a rule is broken and the relationship between the persons involved is affected. Violations are interpreted personally and calling a person by his or her first name too soon could be interpreted as overly friendly and offensive.

VARIABLES IN THE COMMUNICATION PROCESS

Samovar and Porter[14] identify several variables in the communication process whose values are determined to some extent by culture. Each variable influences our perceptions, which in turn influence the meanings we attribute to behavior. Seeking to work effectively in a multicultural environment one should recognize these and study the cultural specifics for the country or area to be visited.

Attitudes are psychological states that predispose us to behave in certain ways. An undesirable attitude for managers working in a multicultural environment is ethnocentrism or self-reference criterion. This is the tendency to judge others by using one's own personal or cultural standards. For example, instead of attempting to understand the Japanese within their own cultural context, an ethnocentric person tries to understand them as similar to or different from Americans. It is vital to refrain from constantly making comparisons between our way of life and that of others. Rather, one must understand other people in the context of their unique historical, political, economic, social, and cultural backgrounds. In that way it is possible to become more effective interactors with them.

Stereotypes are sets of attitudes that cause us to attribute qualities or characteristics to a person on the basis of the group to which that individual belongs. Stereotypes are outsiders' beliefs about groups. Stereotypes are certain generalizations reached by individuals that allow us to organize and understand our environment. For humans to survive, we need to be able to form instant judgments about a situation, object or

> *Attitudes are psychological states that predispose us to behave in certain ways. It is vital to refrain from constantly making comparisons between our way of life and that of others.*

person and to commit those judgments to memory. We draw on these stereotypes during similar situations so that we can quickly make judgments and act appropriately. Stereotypes aid us in predicting behavior by reducing our uncertainty. It was once said that "Stereotypes are in some ways a shorthand for us, but they have absolutely nothing to do with the person sitting across from you at the negotiating table."

Many studies of comparative management facilitate the development of stereotypes in that "management" is discussed largely in terms of the management system in the United States, and thus becomes the basis of comparison for management practices in other countries. An underlying assumption usually is that the American management system is the norm and other systems are compared to the United States.

Social organization of cultures is also a variable that influences one's perceptions. A *geographic society* comprises members of a nation, tribe, or religious sect; and a *role society* comprises members of a profession or the elite of a group. Managers are members of the same role society, i.e., the business environment, but they are often members of different geographic societies. At one level communication between managers from two different cultures should be relatively smooth. On another level, significant differences in values, approach, pace, priorities, and other factors may cause difficulties.

Thought patterns or forms of reasoning may differ from culture to culture. The Aristotelian mode of reasoning prevalent in the West is not shared by people in the East. What is reasonable, logical, and self-evident to an American may be unreasonable, illogical, and not self-evident to a Japanese.

Roles in a society and expectations of a culture concerning behavior affect communication. Some roles have very prescriptive rules. For example, the *meishi* or name card of the Japanese business person identifies his or her position in a company and determines the degree of respect that is appropriately due the individual.

Language skill in a host country is acknowledged as important by global leaders, but many believe that a competent interpreter can be helpful and at times necessary.

Space is also a factor in the communication process. Americans believe that a comfortable space around them is approximately two feet. The United States is a non-contact society. Latin Americans and Middle Easterners, for example, are contact societies and are comfortable with close physical proximity to others. Touching is common between males and handshakes are frequent.

Time sense also impacts human interaction. North American cultures perceive time in lineal-spatial terms in the sense that there is a past, a present and a future. In being oriented to the future, and in the process of preparing for it, one saves, wastes, makes up, or spends time. Zen treats time as a limitless pool in which certain things happen and then

North American cultures perceive time in lineal-spatial terms in the sense that there is a past, a present and a future. Zen treats time as a limitless pool in which certain things happen and then pass.

pass. A different time orientation can cause confusion when doing business in other cultures.

INTERNATIONAL BODY LANGUAGE

> Words representing perhaps 10% of the total (communication) emphasize the uni-directional aspects of communication—advocacy, law and adversial relationships—while behavior, the other 90% stresses feedback on how people are feeling, ways of avoiding confrontation and the inherent logic that is the birthright of all people. Words are the medium of business, politicians and our world leaders. All in the final analysis deal in power. . . . The nonverbal, behavioral part of communication is the provenance of the common man and the core culture that guides life.
>
> Edward T. Hall[15]

Do your actions really speak louder than your words? A classic study by Dr. Albert Mehrabian found the total impact of a message on a receiver is based on: 7% words used; 38% how the words are said—tone of voice, loudness, inflection and other paralinguistic qualities; 55% nonverbal: facial expressions, hand gestures, body position etc.

Nonverbal signals or gestures are used in all cultures, and understanding the differences can help us become better cross-cultural communicators. An example of similar body language cues having different cultural reactions was reported by Furnham,[16] who states that "research in the U.S. has shown that tips tend to be larger if the waiter touches the diner . . . and if the waiter gives a big and 'authentic' initial smile." However, in the U.K. that same body language exhibited by a waiter may result in no tip at all. Body language is frequently culturally distinct. International body language can fall under three categories, two of which can create problems.

1. A gesture can mean something different to others than it does to you. For example, the "A-OK" gesture, as used in the United States, means that things are fine, great, or that something has been understood perfectly. But Brazilians interpret it as an obscene gesture, and to the Japanese it means money.
2. A gesture can mean nothing to the person observing it. Scratching one's head or drawing in breath and saying "saa" are common Japanese responses to embarrassment. One can miss these cues because these gestures may have no particular meaning in one's native culture.
3. A gesture can mean basically the same in both cultures and the meaning is accurately communicated with few possible misunderstandings.

Nonverbal signals or gestures are used in all cultures, and understanding the differences can help us become better cross-cultural communicators.

Hand and Arm Gestures

Most persons use their hands when speaking to punctuate the flow of conversation, refer to objects or persons, mimic and illustrate words or ideas. Often, gestures are used in place of words. Generally, Japanese speakers use fewer words and fewer gestures than American speakers; French use more of both and Italians much more.

In the United States, patting a small child on the head usually conveys affection. But, in Malaysia and other Islamic countries, the head, considered the source of one's intellectual and spiritual powers, is sacred and should not be touched.

Australians signal "time to drink up" by folding three fingers of the hand against the palm, leaving the thumb and little finger sticking straight up and out. In China, the same gesture means six.

To get someone's attention or to summon a waiter or waitress is often a problem. This task requires different gestures in different countries. For example, in restaurants in North American countries, one would call a waiter or waitress quietly, "sir," "miss," "waiter," raise a finger to catch their attention, or tilt one's head to one side. Do not snap your fingers. On the Continent one would clink a glass or cup with spoon or your ring. In the Middle East clapping one's hands is effective. In Japan, extend your arm slightly upward, palm down, and flutter your fingers. In Spain and Latin America extend your hand, palm down, and rapidly open and close your fingers.

Eye Contact

In many Western cultures, a person who does not maintain "good eye contact" is regarded as being slightly suspicious. Those who avoid eye contact are unconsciously considered unfriendly, insecure, untrustworthy, inattentive, and impersonal. However, in contrast, Japanese children are taught in school to direct their gaze at the region of their teacher's Adam's apple or tie knot, and, as adults, Japanese lower their eyes when speaking to a superior, a gesture of respect.

In Latin American cultures and some African cultures, such as Nigeria, prolonged eye contact from an individual of lower status is considered disrespectful. In the U.S., it is considered rude to stare—regardless of who is looking at whom. In contrast, the polite English person is taught to pay strict attention to a speaker, to listen carefully, and to blink his or her eyes to let the speaker know he or she has been understood as well as heard. Americans signal interest and comprehension by bobbing their heads or grunting.

A widening of the eyes can also be interpreted differently. For instance, the case of an American and a Chinese discussing the terms of a proposed contract. Regardless of the language in which the transaction is carried out, the U.S. negotiator may interpret a Chinese person's widened eyes as an expression of astonishment instead of as a danger signal (its true meaning) of politely suppressed Asian anger.

GUIDELINES FOR ENGLISH AND FOREIGN LANGUAGES

Much of the world's international business is conducted in English. When the mother languages in international business are different, generally, the most commonly understood language is English. When Swedes negotiate with the Saudis in Saudi Arabia the language most likely used is English. Following are twenty propositions for "internalizing" the use of English.[17]

1. Practice using the most common 3,000 words in English, that is, those words typically learned in the first two years of language study. Be particularly careful to avoid uncommon or esoteric words; for example, use "witty" rather than "jocose," or "effective" rather than "efficacious."

2. Restrict your use of English words to their most common meaning. Many words have multiple meanings, and non-native speakers are most likely to know the first or second most common meanings. For example use "force" to mean "power" or "impetus" rather than "basic point." Other examples include using "to address" to mean "to send" (rather than "to consider") or using "impact" to mean "the force of a collision" (rather than "effect").

3. Whenever possible, select an action-specific verb (e.g., "ride the bus") rather than a general action verb (e.g., "take the bus"). Verbs to avoid include "do," "make," "get," "have," "be," and "go." For example, the verb "get" can have at least five meanings (buy, borrow, steal, rent, retrieve) in, "I'll get a car and meet you in an hour."

4. In general, select a word with few alternate meanings (e.g., "accurate"—1 meaning) rather than a word with many alternate meanings (e.g., "right"—27 meanings).

5. In choosing among alternate words, select a word with similar alternate meanings rather than a word with dissimilar alternate meanings. For example, "reprove" means to rebuke or to censure—both similar enough that a non-native speaker can guess the meaning accurately. In contrast, "correct" can mean either to make conform to a standard, to scold, or to cure, leaving room for ambiguity in interpretation by a non-native speaker.

6. Become aware of words whose primary meaning is restricted in some cultures. For example, outside of the Untied States, "check" most commonly means a financial instrument and is frequently spelled "cheque."

Restrict your use of English words to their most common meaning. Non-native speakers are most likely to know the first or second most common meanings.

7. Become aware of alternate spellings that exist of commonly used words and the regions in which those spellings are used: for example, colour/color, organisation/organization, centre/center.
8. Resist creating new words by changing a word's part of speech from its most common usage; for example, avoid saying "a warehouse operation" or "attachable assets."
9. Avoid all but the few most common two-word verbs such as "to turn on/off (the lights)" or "to pick up" meaning "to grasp and lift."
10. Maximum punctuation should be used, e.g., commas that help clarify the meaning, but could technically be omitted, should be retained.
11. Redundancy and unnecessary quantification should be avoided as they are confusing to the non-native speaker who is trying to determine the meaning of the sentence. For example, factories cannot operate at greater than capacity—"peak capacity" is redundant.
12. Conform to basic grammar rules more strictly than is common in everyday conversation. Make sure that sentences express a complete thought, that pronouns and antecedents are used correctly, and that subordination is accurately expressed. For example, the sentence, "No security regulations shall be distributed to personnel that are out of date," needs to be rewritten as, "Do not distribute out-of-date security regulations to personnel."
13. Clarify the meaning of modal auxiliaries; for example, be sure that the reader will understand whether "should" means moral obligation, expectation, social obligation, or advice.
14. Avoid "word pictures," constructions that depend for their meaning on invoking a particular mental image (e.g., "run that by me," "wade through these figures," "slice of the free world pie"). A particular form of mental imagery likely to cause misunderstandings if taken literally is the use of absurd assumptions; for example, "suppose you were me" or "suppose there were no sales."
15. Avoid terms borrowed from sports (e.g., "struck out," "field that question," "touchdown," "can't get to first base," "ballpark figure"), the military (e.g., "run it up the flag pole," "run a tight ship), or literature (e.g., "catch-22").
16. When writing to someone you do not know well, use their last name and keep the tone formal while expressing personal interest or concern. Initial sentences can express appreciation (e.g., "We are extremely grateful to your branch . . .") or personal connection (e.g., "Mr. Ramos has suggested . . ."). Closing phrases can express personal best wishes (e.g., "With warmest regards, I remain sincerely yours . . .").
17. Whenever the cultural background of the reader is known, try to adapt the tone of the written material to the manner in which such information (i.e., apology, suggestion, refusal, thanks, request, directive) is usually conveyed in that culture. For example, apologies may

Avoid terms borrowed from sports, the military, or literature.

need to be sweeping and unconditional (e.g., "My deepest apologies for any problems . . ."); refusals may need to be indirect (e.g., "Your proposal contains some interesting points that we need to study further . . .").

18. If possible, one should determine and reflect the cultural values of the reader on such dimensions as espousing controlling versus qualitative changes. When in doubt, a variety of value orientations should be included: "I want to thank you [individual] and your department [collective]. . . ."

19. When the cultural background of the reader is known, try to capture the spoken flavor of the language in writing. For example, communications to Spanish-speakers would be more descriptive and expressive and lengthy than those to German-speakers.

20. Whenever possible, either adopt the cultural reasoning style of your reader or present information in more than one format. For example, the following sentence contains both a general position statement and inductive reasoning: "Trust among business partners is essential; and our data show that our most successful joint ventures are those in which we invested initial time building a personal trusting relationship."

Besides these points, we recommend the following:

❑ Oral presentations should be made plainly, clearly, and slowly, using visual aids whenever possible.
❑ Paraphrase in intercultural conversations, encouraging your counterpart to do the same with your input.
❑ International business communications by telephone on important issues should be confirmed by fax or written reports.
❑ International meetings are facilitated with a written summary, preferably in the language of the receiver or client.
❑ Written brochures, proposals, and reports should be translated into the native language of the receiver or client.

Foreign Language Competency

To survive and communicate, the average European speaks several languages. The typical Japanese studies English as well as other languages. This is not true of most U.S. citizens who even when they study a foreign language, often lack fluency.

Although English is becoming a global language, bear in mind that many speak it as a second language. Also, American English is different from, though rooted in, British English, which is further modified as it is used in the British Commonwealth nations. Thus in countries where "English" is the official language, human resource leaders should consider training programs for those workers whose native language is not

Although English is becoming a global language, bear in mind that many speak it as a second language.

English. These can be group sessions or self-learning modules that some-time can be presented by organizations under the title, "Improving Communications at Work." This instruction should also include improving pronunciation of employees born in other countries.

To further reduce misunderstanding in business and international relations, one can use interpreters. But translations are given in a cultural context, and linguistic specialists themselves require cross-cultural training. International education and business can be facilitated by competent simultaneous interpretation. New equipment for simultaneous interpreting, graphic presentations, and reporting have done much to foster international communication. The global use of the computer creates a universal language of another type. Also, through the wizardry of electronic technology, forthcoming inventions will translate for us.

The following selections of announcements in English illustrate the problems in intercultural communication.[18]

SOMETHING GOT LOST IN THE TRANSLATION

- Sign on door in Hong Kong curio shop—Teeth extracted by latest Methodists.
- Sign in elevator in Germany—Do not enter lift backwards and only when lit up.
- Sign in Paris dress shop—Elegant dresses designed for street walking.
- Sign in an Acapulco, Mexico hotel—We are pleased to announce that the manager has personally passed all the water served here.

Poorly translated materials can cause problems for corporations. For example, when Coca-Cola introduced its product into the Asian market, the Chinese characters sounded correct, but actually read, "Bite the wax tadpole." Pepsi-Cola had a comparable communication disaster when it moved into the Thai market using the American slogan, "Come alive, you're in the Pepsi generation." Only later did Pepsi discover that the real Thai translation said, "Pepsi brings your ancestors back from the dead."

TECHNOLOGY AND INTERCULTURAL COMMUNICATION

The following underscores the challenges and prospects in current communication technologies, particularly relative to the intercultural factors. Cross-cultural skills and sensitivity are just as much in demand when people meet electronically as when they meet in person.

Communicating Via Electronic Mail

Citizens of the global village increasingly use email for business and personal reasons, with Internet subscriptions predicted to increase significantly every year. When emailing across cultures avoid ambiguous messages, be specific, provide background or context for the communication so there can be no misinterpretation. Summarize information in different words to clarify, remembering that body language and voice intonation are not present to "complete" the message.

Computers and Language

New communications technologies constantly expand our capacity for exchanges with one another regardless of distance. They enable us to transmit our *brains* and the information stored there rather than moving our *bodies* from place to place. The wonders of modern telecommunications are wide ranging—from telegraph, typewriter, telephone, television to radio, personal computers, electronic mail and facsimile machines. Movies have moved from theaters to cassettes or diskettes that can be player on one's television or computer monitor; CD-ROM disks offer a wide range of learning and entertainment for playing on a personal computer. A combination of communication satellites and computers plus fiber optics on the ground enhance our global interactions. Instead of using a computer keyboard, we can now talk to our computers in our own language. The emerging generation of communicating devices are called "thin client appliances"—fixed screen Web phones, smart mobile telephones, energy efficient and supposedly easy to use. Processing power for computing doubles every 18 months, while the speed and simplicity for transmission of messages increases as well. The cost of this communication also goes down thanks to the advances in cheap chips and high-bandwidth connections.

To plumb the depths of information on the global computer network, most messages and stored data are in English. Great numbers of the world's population do not speak English and often are handicapped in their use of the Internet. English, the language of science and business, is also the language of the computer world. To meet the demand for more multicultural media, a consortium of computer companies has developed Unicode, a universal digital code that allows computers to represent the letters and characters of virtually all of the world's languages. As a result of new multilingual software, people are adding data bases and home pages or websites in their own languages, enabling greater numbers of individuals to communicate on the world wide web. Automatic translation capabilities now help one to transmit messages in one language and have them be received in another.[19]

Cross-cultural skills and sensitivity are just as much in demand when people meet electronically as when they meet in person.

Video Conferencing

Video conferencing is forecast to grow 60% a year through the 21st century. In 1998, equipment sales were already a $5 billion industry. Frost & Sullivan Market Intelligence predict for the near future that North America will buy 50% of the video conferencing systems; Europe, 26%; Pacific Rim countries 20% while the rest of the world accounts for the remaining 4%.

Exxon Chemical employees use video conferencing more than 1,600 times a year saving more than $4 million in travel costs. For example, a 90-minute transpacific video conference in Hong Kong will cost $500 compared to three executive's expenses for travel and lodging at approximately $12,000. Annually, the corporation has more than 3,000 electronic meetings at 45 video centers worldwide. Team problem solving and short reviews are important benefits of this technology. Combined with interactive computers, a person in Europe can change numbers on a spreadsheet sketched on a board in the United States.[20]

Video-bridging is making it possible to connect multiple locations without degrading audio and video quality. The next century will demonstrate the capability of 300 linkups in the same video conference. Inexpensive equipment will permit knowledge workers to turn their offices and homes into video studios, conducting video conferences from desktop computers with colleagues around the world.

SUMMARY

To facilitate our interactions with persons who do not share our values, assumptions, or learned ways of behaving requires new competencies and sensitivities, so that the very cultural differences become resources.

The most basic skill that global leaders must cultivate is cross-cultural communications. To facilitate our interactions with persons who do not share our values, assumptions, or learned ways of behaving requires new competencies and sensitivities, so that the very cultural differences become resources. The complexities of the communication process have been reviewed here from the perspectives of cross-cultural behaviors and factors; listening, attribution and foreign language skills levels and variables when interacting; body language and gestures.

Also, this chapter has emphasized the possibilities and the pitfalls in intercultural communication, whether in personal or electronic encounters. The new media has increased the prospects for positive or negative interchanges across cultures, both macro and micro. Culturally sensitive senders and receivers are still vital in the communication process. Global leaders should give a high priority to intercultural communication proficiency, for as Hall and Hall[21] observe:

> Each cultural world operates according to its own internal dynamic, its own principles, and its own laws—written and unwritten. . . . Any culture is primarily a system for creating, sending, storing, and processing infor-

mation. Communication underlies everything. . . . Culture can be likened to an enormous, subtle, extraordinarily complex computer. It programs the actions and responses of every person, and these programs can be mastered by anyone wishing to make the system work.

And, as the late Janice Hepworth[22] observed:

Each culture is a unique arrangement of "components" characterizing different lifestyles which distinguish one culture from another. "Components" is a broad term used here to refer to attitudes, values, beliefs, and institutions that each culture creates and defines to serve its own particular needs. The problems for intercultural communication arise out of unique definitions and arrangements made by each culture. . . . While this may seem obvious to you, the "rightness" of your way of doing things can stand in the way of intercultural communication.

REFERENCES

1. Meadows, D. H. "If the World Were a Village of 1,000 People," *Futures by Design: The Practice of Ecological Planning*, Aberley, D. (ed.), New Society Publishers: Philadelphia, PA: 1994.
2. Schnitzer, M. C. *Comparative Economic Systems*, Cincinnati, OH: South-Western College Publishing, 1997.
3. Bartlett, C. A. and Ghoshal, S. *Managing Across Borders*. Boston, MA: Harvard Business School Press, 1989.
4. Napuk, K. *The Strategy Led Business*. London: McGraw-Hill Book Company Europe, 1993.
5. Burrows, P. "Beyond the PC," *Business Week*, March 8, 1999 p. 86.
6. Klopf, D. W. *Intercultural Encounters*. Englewood, CO: Morton Publishing Co, 1991.
7. Simons, G. F. and Vázquez, C. and Harris, P. R. *Transcultural Leadership*. Houston, TX: Gulf Publishing Co., 1993.
8. Singer, M. R. *Perception & Identity in Intercultural Communication*. Yarmouth, ME: Intercultural Press, 1998.
9. Gudykunst, W. B. *Bridging Differences: Effective Intergroup Communications*. Thousand Oaks, CA, Sage Publications, 1994. See also Bennett, M. J. (ed.) *Basic Concepts of Intercultural Communication*. Yarmouth, ME: Intercultural Press, 1998.
10. Lustig, M. W. and Koester, J. *Intercultural Competence*, New York: Addison Wesley, 1998.
11. Simons, G. F. and Vázquez, C., and Harris, P. R. *Transcultural Leadership*. Houston, TX: Gulf Publishing Co., 1993. See also Elashmawi, F. and Harris, P. R. *Multicultural Management 2000*. Houston, TX: Gulf Publishing Co., 1998.
12. Triandis, H. C. (ed.) *Variations in Black and White Perceptions of the Social Environment*. Urbana, IL: University of Illinois Press, 1976.
13. Nelson, C. A. *Protocol for Profit—A Manager's Guide to Competing Worldwide*, London, UK: International Thomson Business Press, 1998.

14. Samovar, L. A. and Porter, R. E. *Intercultural Communication: A Reader*. Belmont, CA: Wadsworth Publishing Co., 1988.
15. Hall, E. T. *Dance of Life*. Garden City, NY: Anchor Press/Doubleday, 1983.
16. Furnham, A. "Actions Speak Louder Than Words," *Financial Times*, April 4, 1999.
17. Riddle, D. I. and Lanham, Z. D. *The Journal of Language for International Business*, "Internationalizing Written Business English: 20 Propositions for Native English Speakers," 1985.
18. Landers, Ann, *Los Angeles Times*, "At Times Everything Gets Lost in the Translation" January 28, 1996.
19. A. W. Pollack, *New York Times*, August 7, 1995, C1/6.
20. Meyers, G. *Exxon Magazine*, Summer 1998, pp. 10–11.
21. Hall, E. T. and Hall, M. R. *Hidden Differences—Doing Business with the Japanese*, Garden City: NY: Anchor/Doubleday, 1987.
22. Hepworth, J. *International Communication* (1990) and *Things to Know About Americans* (1991), Denver, CO: University Centers, Inc. See also Lustig, M. W. and Koester, J. *Intercultural Competence*, NY: Harper Collins, 1999.

GLOBAL LEADERSHIP IN NEGOTIATIONS AND ALLIANCES

Global business leaders travel the world seeking business relationships. Some are buyers, others are sellers, some are both. Just as infants learn to walk by trial and error, so too these executive global travelers develop a pattern and style that works.

It is also an era of mergers, acquisitions, and consolidations. This business activity by which one company melds or is integrated into another does not occur very frequently, it usually is a one-time event. Therefore, most leaders of organizations cannot draw on their previous experience base in making decisions about the acquisition or merger or the integration of the companies involved. Many claim the success rate of mergers and acquisitions, after five years, is less than 50% for successful integration, although little hard data are available.

Today's leaders seek business ventures in the global arena crisscrossing the world to negotiate, bargain or form strategic alliances. Appreciating the complexities of labor negotiations in the home culture or negotiating a contract in a foreign country, has made these leaders understand the competency and skill needed to effectively work out these situations.

As we enter the 21st century, the biggest change in the negotiating situation is the media available within the world marketplace. Today's global leaders increasingly do their negotiating *electronically*, by telephone, fax, email and video conferencing. One of the most powerful communication tools for this purpose is the Internet. It offers quick and easy negotiation opportunities with manufacturers, suppliers, customers, and even government regulators, but requires more openness, transparency, and trust in business communications and negotiations. The Internet and computers are altering the whole situation in international negotiations.

Many claim the success rate of mergers and acquisitions, after five years, is less than 50% for successful integration, although little hard data are available.

This chapter is about international business negotiations and strategic collaborations—negotiations and collaborations that result in mutual benefit. The goal is to be conceptual, practical, and useful. The first section of the chapter focuses on negotiations.

NEGOTIATING ACROSS CULTURES

Negotiation is a process in which two or more entities come together to discuss common and conflicting interests to reach an agreement of mutual benefit. In international business negotiations, the differences in the negotiation process from culture to culture include language, cultural conditioning, negotiating styles, approaches to problem solving, implicit assumptions, gestures and facial expressions, and the role of ceremony and formality.

For international negotiations to produce long-term synergy, and not just short-term solutions, individuals involved in the negotiation must be aware of the multicultural facets in the process. The negotiator must understand the cultural space of his or her counterparts. It is our belief that negotiating is a skill and it can be improved. It is the purpose of this section to suggest some of the cultural variables and considerations.

Glen Fisher[1] addresses five considerations for analyzing cross-cultural negotiations: (1) the players and the situation; (2) styles of decision-making; (3) national character; (4) cross-cultural noise; and (5) interpreters and translators. Each consideration presents questions that should be answered before entering international negotiations.

The Players and the Situation

Fisher asserts that there is a cultural dimension in the way negotiators view the negotiation process. This raises several issues. Form, hospitality, and protocol are important to the success of international negotiations. Difficulties sometimes arise because there is a difference in what negotiators expect of a negotiation's social setting. The negotiator should discover what the foreign negotiator expects and then provide a tension-free environment that encourages cooperation and problem-solving.

There also may be a national style in choosing negotiators and in selecting negotiating teams. Negotiators can anticipate a counterpart's behavior by researching biographical data and analyzing the negotiator's organizational or institutional role. In the case of negotiating teams, it is useful to discover how corporate culture affects internal dynamics.

Styles of Decision Making

Fisher contends that there are patterns in the way officials and executives structure their negotiation communication systems and reach institutional decisions. The organizational culture of a foreign corporation may provide formal rules and regulations guiding its decision-making process. A negotiator can find ways to influence a foreign corporation's decisions by analyzing its corporate culture and structuring arguments to fit within established guidelines.

Furthermore, there are general cultural patterns by which individual negotiators develop personal styles of decision-making behavior. By discovering how foreign counterparts look at facts and analyze data, successful negotiators can provide information that will increase the probability of a successful outcome.

National Character

Studies of national character call attention both to the patterns of personality that negotiators tend to exhibit and to the collective concerns that give a nation a distinctive outlook in international relationships. Foreign negotiators concerned with international image may be preoccupied with discussions of their national heritage, identity, and language. Cultural attitudes, such as ethnocentrism or xenophobia, may influence the tone of their argument.

Fisher maintains that foreign negotiators display many different styles of logic and reasoning. International negotiators frequently find that discussions are impeded because the two sides seem to be pursuing different paths of logic. Negotiation breakdown may result from the way issues are conceptualized, the way evidence and new information are used, or the way one point seems to lead to the next.

During the discussions, the foreign counterpart may pay more attention to some arguments than to others. Greater weight may be given to legal precedence, expert opinion, technical data, amity, or reciprocal advantage. A good international negotiator will discover what is persuasive to the foreign counterpart, and use that method of persuasion.

Foreign negotiators may place different values on agreements and hold different assumptions as to the way contracts should be honored. The negotiator must find out what steps the counterpart intends to take in implementing the agreement. A signature on a piece of paper or a handshake may signify friendship rather than the closing of a contract.

The danger of misinterpretation of messages necessitates analysis of various contextual factors.

Cross-Cultural Noise

Noise consists of background distractions that have nothing to do with the substance of the foreign negotiator's message. Factors such as gestures, personal proximity, and office surroundings may unintentionally interfere with communication. The danger of misinterpretation of messages necessitates analysis of various contextual factors.

Interpreters and Translators

Fisher points to limitations in translating certain ideas, concepts, meanings, and nuances. Subjective meaning may not come across through words alone. Gestures, tone of voice, cadence, and double entendres are all meant to transmit a message. Yet these are not included in a translation.

Sometimes a negotiator will try to communicate a concept or idea that does not exist in the counterpart's culture. For example, the American and English concept of "fair play" seems to have no exact equivalent in any other language. How then can an English national expect "fair play" from a foreign counterpart?

Interpreters and translators may have difficulty in transmitting the logic of key arguments. This is especially true in discussions of abstract concepts such as planning and international strategy. The parties may think that they have come to an agreement when in fact they have entirely different intentions and understandings.

Fisher's five-part framework provided scholars and consultants with a launching pad for both theory-building and practical applications.

AMERICANS AND NEGOTIATING

When people communicate with one another, they make certain assumptions about the process of perceiving, judging, thinking, and reasoning patterns of each other.

When people communicate with one another, they make certain assumptions about the process of perceiving, judging, thinking, and reasoning patterns of each other. They make these assumptions without realizing they are making them. Correct assumptions facilitate communication, but incorrect assumptions lead to misunderstandings and miscommunication often results.

The most common assumption is *projective cognitive similarity,* that is, one assumes that the other perceives, judges, thinks, and reasons the same way he or she does. Persons from the same culture but with a different education, age, background, and experience often experience difficulty in communicating. American managers communicating with managers from other cultures experience greater difficulties in communication than with managers from their own culture. However, in some regards American managers share more interests with other members of the world managerial subculture than with their own workers or union leaders. The effects of our cultural conditioning are so pervasive that people whose experience has been limited to the rules of one culture can have difficulty understanding communication based on another set of rules.

To create cultural synergistic solutions to management problems and international negotiating, U.S. managers must identify and understand what is American about America, what common cultural traits are shared by Americans, and what values and assumptions are their foundation. Mark Twain stated, "The only distinguishing characteristic of the American character that I've been able to discover is a fondness for ice water." There is much more, as Chapter 10 will show.

Awareness of cultural influences is essential for transferring concepts, technology, or ideas. Depending on the cultures, there may be an overlap of values in a specific area, and therefore, the problems related to transferring ideas will be minimal. However, in some instances the gap will be significant and cause serious problems. According to Graham[2], there are four problems in international business negotiations: (1) language, (2) nonverbal behavior, (3) values, and (4) thinking and decision-making.

The problems increase in importance and complexity because of their subtle nature. For instance, it is easy to ascertain the language differences between the French and the Brazilians. The solution is either state-of-the-art translating headsets or interpreting/translating teams to accommodate each side. The problem is obvious and relatively easy to address.

Cultural differences concerning nonverbal behavior often are not as obvious or are we as aware of these behaviors. In face-to-face negotiations, we give off and receive nonverbal behavioral cues. Some argue that these cues are the critical messages of a negotiation. The nonverbal signals from our counterparts can be so subtle that we may feel a sense of discomfort but may not know exactly why. For example, when a Japanese negotiator fails to make eye contact, it may produce a sense of unease but we may not know the cause. Often nonverbal intercultural friction effects business negotiations but goes undefined and more often uncorrected.

Laver and Trudgill in Lottgen and Campoy[3] also point out that during conversations one almost must act as a detective, considering the words and speech but also attempting to establish, from an array of clues, the state of mind and the profile and perspective of his or her identity.

The difference in values is even more obscure and harder to understand. For example, Americans value objectivity, competitiveness, equity, and punctuality, and often presume that other cultures hold the same values in high esteem. As regards punctuality Graham states, "Everyone else in the world knows no negotiation tactic is more useful with Americans. Nobody places more value on time. Nobody has less patience when things slow down."

Generally, during a complex negotiation Westerners divide the large tasks up into smaller task. One can move through the smaller tasks, fin-

Cultural differences concerning nonverbal behavior often are not as obvious or are we as aware of these behaviors.

ishing one and then move onto the next, sensing accomplishment along the way. Issues are resolved at each step in the process and the final agreement is the sum of the sequence. However, in Eastern thinking often all issues are discussed with no apparent order, and concessions, when made, are done so at the conclusion of negotiations. The Western approach is sequential and the Eastern holistic—the two are worlds apart. Therefore, American negotiators have difficulty measuring progress during negotiations with the Japanese, and the differences in the thinking and decision-making processes can result in blunders. For the Japanese the long-term goal is a mutually beneficial ongoing business relationship. "The economic issues are the *context*, not the *content* of the talks*.*" Conversely, to Americans, negotiations are a problem solving activity with the best solution for both parties being the goal.

Graham and Herberger[4] suggest a combination of characteristics that American negotiators typically use. They are part of the cultural baggage such nationals bring to the negotiating table and, according to Graham and Herberger, typify the "American John Wayne" style of negotiating.

- ❑ "I can go it alone." Many U.S. executives seem to believe they can handle any negotiating situation by themselves, and they are outnumbered in most negotiating situations.
- ❑ "Just call me John." Americans value informality and equality in human relations. They try to make people feel comfortable by playing down status distinctions.
- ❑ "Pardon my French." Americans aren't very talented at speaking foreign languages.
- ❑ "Check with the home office." American negotiators get upset when halfway through a negotiation the other side says, "I'll have to check with the home office." The implication is that the decision makers are not present.
- ❑ "Get to the point." Americans don't like to beat around the bush and want to get to the heart of the matter quickly.
- ❑ "Lay your cards on the table." Americans expect honest information at the bargaining table.
- ❑ "Don't just sit there, speak up." Americans don't deal well with silence during negotiations.
- ❑ "Don't take no for an answer." Persistence is highly valued by Americans and is part of the deeply ingrained competitive spirit that manifests itself in every aspect of American life.
- ❑ "One thing at a time." Americans usually attack a complex negotiation task sequentially, that is, they separate the issues and settle them one at a time.
- ❑ "A deal is a deal." When Americans make an agreement and give their word, they expect to honor the agreement no matter what the circumstances.

❏ "I am what I am." Few Americans take pride in changing their minds, even in difficult circumstances.

These comments on American negotiators may appear to be harsh. They are not intended to isolate Americans alone as lacking in global negotiating skills. In today's marketplace other nationalities can learn just as Americans can how to negotiate more effectively and skillfully.

Frank Acuff[5] is not complimentary in his report card on American negotiators' skills (see box).

THE U.S. NEGOTIATOR'S GLOBAL REPORT CARD

Competency	Grade
❏ Preparation	B-
❏ Synergistic approach (win-win)	D
❏ Cultural I.Q.	D
❏ Adapting the negotiating process to the host country environment	D
❏ Patience	D
❏ Listening	D
❏ Linguistic abilities	F
❏ Using language that is simple and accessible	C
❏ High aspirations	B+
❏ Personal integrity	A-
❏ Building solid relationships	D

Adapted from Frank Acuff

As the global experience broadens all of us, hopefully, we are getting better at understanding the national character of our negotiating counterparts, confronting cultural stereotypes, and putting the negotiating process into a cultural context.

FRAMEWORK FOR INTERNATIONAL BUSINESS NEGOTIATIONS

A successful negotiation is a "win-win situation" in which both parties gain. Many factors affect its outcome.

There are varied negotiation postures, bases from which to negotiate. One framework by Weiss and Stripp[6] maintains there are 12 variables in

We are getting better at understanding the national character of our negotiating counterparts, confronting cultural stereotypes, and putting the negotiating process into a cultural context.

every international negotiation that impact the negotiation and therefore can significantly influence the outcome either positively or negatively.

- ❏ *Basic Conception of Negotiation Process.* There are two opposing approaches to the concept of negotiation: strategic and synergistic. In the strategic model, resources are perceived as limited. The sides are competitive and bargaining is perceived as who will get the larger portion of the pie. In the synergistic model, resources are unlimited. Each party wants to cooperate so that all can have what they want. Counterparts look for alternative ways to obtain the desired results.

- ❏ *Negotiator Selection Criteria.* These criteria include negotiating experience, seniority, political affiliation, gender, ethnic ties, kinship, technical knowledge and personal attributes (e.g., affability, loyalty, and trustworthiness). Each culture has preferences and biases regarding selection.

- ❏ *Significance of Type of Issue.* Defining the issues in negotiation is critical. Generally substantive issues focus on control and use of resources (space, power, property). Relationship-based issues center around the ongoing nature of mutual or reciprocal interests. The negotiation should not hinder relationship and future negotiations.

- ❏ *Concern with Protocol.* Protocol is the accepted practices of social behavior and interaction. Rules of protocol can be formal or informal. Americans are generally less formal than Germans.

- ❏ *Complexity of Language.* Complexity refers to the degree of reliance on nonverbal cues to convey and interpret intentions and information in dialogue. These cues include distance (space), eye contact, gestures and silence. There is high- and low-context communication. Cultures that are high context in communication (China) are fast and efficient communicators and information is in the physical context or pre-programmed in the person. Low-context communication, in contrast, is information conveyed by the words without shared meaning implied. The United States is a low-context culture.

- ❏ *Nature of Persuasive Arguments.* One way or another, negotiation involves attempts to influence the other party. Counterparts can use an emotional or logical approach.

- ❏ *Role of Individuals' Aspirations.* The emphasis negotiators place on their individual goals and need for recognition may also vary. In some cases, the position of a negotiator may reflect personal goals to a greater extent than corporate goals. In contrast, a negotiator may want to prove he or she is a hard bargainer and compromise the goals of the corporation.

- ❏ *Bases of Trust.* Every negotiator at some point must face the critical issues of trust. One must eventually trust one's counterparts otherwise resolution would be impossible. Trust can be based on the written laws of a particular country or it can be based on friendship and mutual respect and esteem.

Complexity of Language refers to the degree of reliance on nonverbal cues to convey and interpret intentions and information in dialogue.

❑ *Risk-Taking Propensity.* Negotiators can be perceived as either "cautious" (low risk takers), or "adventurous" (high risk takers). If a negotiator selects a solution that has lower rewards but higher probability of success he or she is not a risk taker. If the negotiator chooses higher rewards but a lower probability of success than he or she is "adventurous" and a risk taker.

❑ *Value of Time.* Each culture has a different way of perceiving and acting upon time. Monochronic cultures emphasize making agendas, being on time for appointments and generally seeing time as a quantity to be scheduled. Polychronic cultures stress the involvement of people rather than preset schedules. The future cannot be firm so planning takes on little consequence.

❑ *Decision-Making System.* Broadly understood, decision-making systems can be "authoritative" or "consensual." In authoritative decision-making, an individual makes the decision without consulting with his or her superiors. However, senior executives may overturn the decision. In consensus decision-making, negotiators do not have the authority to make decisions unless they consult their superiors.

❑ *Form of Satisfactory Agreement.* Generally, there are two broad forms of agreement. One is the written contract that covers possible contingencies. The other is the broad oral agreement that binds the negotiating parties through the quality of their relationship.

With these 12 variables in mind, the international negotiator is now able to develop a profile of his negotiating counterparts.

Chapters in Unit Three will cover culture-specific information to assist the negotiator in developing profiles for various countries.

Using Interpreters During Negotiations

The importance of an interpreter in business negotiations cannot be overstressed. It is the interpreter who can assist with the accurate communication of ideas between the two teams. A linguistic interpreter can also be a cultural interpreter and let the negotiators know of actual or potential cultural misunderstandings. It is advisable to remember the following points concerning the use of interpreters:

❑ Brief the interpreter in advance about the subject. Select an interpreter knowledgeable about the product or subject).
❑ Speak clearly and slowly.
❑ Avoid little-known words.
❑ Explain the major idea two or three different ways, as the point may be lost if discussed only once.
❑ Avoid talking more than a minute or two without giving the interpreter a chance to speak.

The importance of an interpreter in business negotiations cannot be overstressed.

- While talking, allow the interpreter time to make notes about what is being said.
- Do not lose confidence if the interpreter uses a dictionary.
- Permit the interpreter to spend as much time as needed in clarifying points whose meanings are obscure.
- Interrupting the interpreter as he or she translates may cause misunderstandings.
- Avoid long sentences, double negatives, or the use of negative wordings of a sentence when a positive form could be used.
- Avoid superfluous words. Your point may be lost if wrapped up in generalities.
- Try to be expressive and use gestures to support your verbal messages.
- During meetings, write out the main points discussed. In this way both parties can double check their understanding.
- After meetings, confirm in writing what has been agreed.
- It is unwise to expect an interpreter to work for more than two hours without a rest.
- Consider using two interpreters if interpreting is to last an entire day or into the evening, so that when one tires the other can take over.
- Don't be concerned if a speaker talks for five minutes and the interpreter covers it in half a minute.
- Be understanding if the interpreter makes a mistake.
- Ask the interpreter for advice if there are problems.

Skills of Successful Negotiators

Negotiations bring together two parties each with an expected outcome as to what they want.

Negotiations bring together two parties each with an expected outcome as to what they want. On examination the two parties evaluate their leverage, authority and tactics. To close a negotiation, which was the best possible deal for both sides, means that most probably neither side feels cheated or duped, and that a spirit of fairness pervaded the negotiation. When international negotiations occur, the cultural differences and implications can spin the negotiation in unanticipated directions. Weiss[7] establishes five steps for analyzing and developing a culturally responsive strategy for international negotiations.

- *Study Your Own Culture's Negotiation Script.* When we are in our home culture we behave almost automatically. Studying observations about our home culture by outsiders as well as our own self examinations will enable a negotiator to construct an accurate national profile. What does your side bring to the party?
- *Learn the Negotiation Script of Your Counterpart.* A first time negotiator should build from the ground up a profile of his or her counterparts. An experienced negotiator should review and research his or her counterparts, adding new information. Beware of cultural biases. What does this party bring to the negotiations?

❑ *Consider the Relationship and Circumstance.* Whether you are the buyer or the seller in a negotiation will affect the relationship, and an adjustment of strategy will have to occur. Any previous negotiating relationship with a counterpart, as well as their home culture and its familiarity with yours will also affect the outcome. What is the context of the relationship?

❑ *Predict the Counterpart's Approach.* If your counterpart's approach is similar to yours, or you perhaps can influence the selection of the approach, these deliberations will preview the possible interactions during the negotiation preparation. Generally, approaches will be complementary or conflicting.

❑ *Choose Your Strategy.* After completing the first four steps, the selection of the strategy must be feasible given the cross cultural dimensions of the negotiations, the counterpart's approach, be appropriate to the relationship, and, hopefully, a win-win for both parties.

The following is a summary of a research project that analyzed actual negotiations.[8] The researchers' methods allowed them to distinguish between skilled negotiators and average negotiators by using behavior analysis techniques as they observed the negotiations and recorded the discussion. They identified "successful" negotiators as those who:

❑ Were rated as effective by both sides.
❑ Had a "track-record" of significant success.
❑ Had a low incidence of "implementation" failures.

A total of 48 negotiators were studied who met all of these three success criteria. They included union representatives (17), management representatives (12), contract negotiators (10), and others (9).

The 48 successful negotiators were studied over a total of 102 separate negotiating sessions. In the following description, the successful negotiators are called the "skilled" group. In comparison, the negotiators who either failed to meet the criteria or about whom no criterion data were available, were called the "average" group.

During the Planning Process

Negotiation training emphasizes the importance of planning.

❑ *Planning Time.* No significant difference was found between the total planning time that skilled and average negotiators claimed they spent prior to actual negotiation.

❑ *Exploration of Options.* The skilled negotiator considers a wider range of outcomes or options for action, than the average negotiator.

❑ *Common Ground.* The research showed that the skilled negotiators gave over three times as much attention to common ground areas as did average negotiators.

❑ *Long-Term or Short-Term?* With the average negotiator, approximately one comment in 25 met the criteria of a long-term consideration, namely a comment that involved any factor extending beyond the immediate implementation of the issue under negotiation.

❑ *Setting Limits.* The researchers asked negotiators about their objectives and recorded whether their replies referred to single-point objectives (e.g., "We aim to settle at 83") or to defined range (e.g., "We hope to get 85 but we would settle for a minimum of 77"). Skilled negotiators were significantly more likely to set upper and lower limits—to plan in terms of range. Average negotiators, in contrast, were more likely to plan their objectives around a fixed point.

❑ *Sequence and Issue Planning.* The term "planning" frequently refers to a process of sequencing—putting a number of events, points, or potential occurrences into a time sequence. Critical path analysis and other forms of network planning are examples.

Typical sequence plan used by average negotiators:
A then B then C then D
Issues are linked.

Typical issue plan used by skilled negotiators:

A

B

D

C

Issues are independent and not linked by sequence.

The clear advantage of issue planning over sequence planning is flexibility.

Face-To-Face Behavior

Skilled negotiators show marked differences in their face-to-face behavior, compared with average negotiators. They use certain types of behavior significantly more frequently while other types they tend to avoid.

❑ *Irritators.* Certain words and phrases that are commonly used during negotiation have negligible value in persuading the other party, but do cause irritation. Probably the most frequent example of these is the term "generous offer" used by a negotiator to describe his or her proposal.

❑ *Counter-Proposals.* During negotiation, one party frequently puts forward a proposal and the other party immediately responds with a

Skilled negotiators show marked differences in their face-to-face behavior, compared with average negotiators.

counter-proposal. Researchers found that skilled negotiators made immediate counter-proposals much less frequently than average negotiators.

❑ *Argument Dilution.* This way of thinking predisposes us to believe that there is some special merit in quantity. Having five reasons for doing something is considered more persuasive than having only one reason. One may feel that the more he or she can put on his or her scale, the more likely it is to tip the balance of an argument in his or her favor. The researchers found that the opposite was true. The skilled negotiator used fewer reasons to back up each of his or her arguments.

❑ *Reviewing the Negotiation.* The researchers asked negotiators how likely they were to spend time reviewing the negotiation afterwards. More than two-thirds of the skilled negotiators claimed that they always set aside some time after a negotiation to review it and consider what they had learned. Just under half of average negotiators, in contrast, made the same claim.

This research clearly indicates some of the behaviors of skilled negotiators. These behaviors, and others, negotiators need to practice to increase their skills.

STRATEGIC COLLABORATIONS

"Companies are just beginning to learn what nations have always known: In a complex, uncertain world filled with dangerous opponents, it is best not to go it alone."[9] Mergers and acquisitions result. Some thrive, some survive, and some die. Some are perceived as an act of desperation, and others are more strategic. The following points are relevant:

❑ Internal growth possibilities are diminished for many organizations and mergers or acquisitions as a way to survive or grow.
❑ Acquisitions or mergers are viewed as a fast way to grow.
❑ Increasing products, markets and technology lowers risk.
❑ Organizational culture clash is a major problem in integrating different companies.
❑ Making the deal is easy, making it work is difficult.

Ashkenas et al.[10] outline the lessons learned by GE Capital. They state the following lessons:

❑ Acquisition integration begins with the due diligence studies of all aspects of the organization.
❑ Integrating management is a full-time business function like marketing.

Organizational culture clash is a major problem in integrating different companies.

❑ Decisions on structure, roles, and other important aspects of integration should be announced soon after the merger or acquisition is reported.
❑ Integration involves not only technologies and product, but cultures.

These lessons are relevant when the organizations being integrated are from the same national culture. When they are from different national cultures, the challenges are more significant, and the skills required to make them succeed are broader, deeper, and more sophisticated.

Global leaders are required to meet, socialize, and negotiate with foreign business persons and government officials. The manager must be able to communicate and work with persons who have grown up and who have been socialized in a different cultural environment. Customs, values, life-styles, beliefs, management practices, and other aspects of their personal and professional life are therefore different. To be effective, the global leader must be aware of the many beliefs and values that underlie his or her country's business practices, management techniques, and strategies. Awareness of such values and assumptions is critical for managers who wish to transfer technology to another culture or who wish to collaborate with those who have different values and assumptions.

Exhibit 3-1 identifies several U.S. values with possible alternatives. Examples of how the cultural system might influence management are also indicated in the third column.

To be effective, the global leader must be aware of the many beliefs and values that underlie his or her country's business practices, management techniques, and strategies.

EXHIBIT 3-1
U.S. VALUES AND POSSIBLE ALTERNATIVES

Aspects* of U.S. Culture	Alternative Aspect	Examples of Management Function Affected
The individual can influence the future (where there is a will there is a way).	Life follows a preordained course and human action is determined by the will of God.	Planning and scheduling
The individual can change and improve the environment.	People are intended to adjust to the physical environment rather than to alter it.	Organizational environment, morale, and productivity
An individual should be realistic in his aspirations.	Ideals are to be pursued regardless of what is "reasonable."	Goal setting career development
We must work hard to accomplish our objectives (Puritan ethic).	Hard work is not the only prerequisite for success. Wisdom, luck and time are also required.	Motivation and reward system
Commitments should be honored (people will do what they say they will do).	A commitment may be superseded by a conflicting request or an agreement may only signify intention and have little or no relationship to the capacity of performance.	Negotiating and bargaining

EXHIBIT 3-1 (CONTINUED)
U.S. VALUES AND POSSIBLE ALTERNATIVES

Aspects of U.S. Culture	Alternative Aspect	Examples of Management Function Affected
One should effectively use one's time (time is money which can be saved or wasted).	Schedules are important but only in relation to other priorities.	Long and short range planning
A primary obligation of an employee is to the organization.	The individual employee has a primary obligation to family and friends.	Loyalty, commitment, and motivation
The employer or employee can terminate their relationship.	Employment is for a lifetime.	Motivation and commitment to the company
A person can only work for one company at a time (one cannot serve two masters).	Personal contributions to individuals who represent an enterprise are acceptable.	Ethical issues, conflict of interest
The best qualified persons should be given the positions available.	Family considerations, friendship, and other consideration should determine employment practices.	Employment, promotions, recruiting, selection, and reward
A person can be removed if he or she does not perform well.	The removal of a person from a position involves a great loss of prestige and will rarely be done.	Promotion
All levels of management are open to qualified individuals (a clerk can rise to become company president).	Education or family ties are the primary vehicles for mobility.	Employment practices and promotion
Intuitive aspects of decision-making should be reduced and efforts should be devoted to gathering relevant information.	Decisions are expressions of wisdom by the person in authority and any questioning would imply a lack of confidence in his or her judgment.	Decision-making process
Data should be accurate.	Accurate data are not as highly valued.	Record-keeping
Company information should be available to anyone who needs it within the organization.	Withholding information to gain or maintain power is acceptable.	Organization, communication, managerial style
Each person is expected to have an opinion and to express it freely even if his or her views do not agree with his or her colleagues'.	Deference is to be given to persons in power or authority and to offer judgment that is not in support of the ideas of one's superiors is unthinkable.	Communications, organizational relations
A decision-maker is expected to consult persons who can contribute useful information to the area being considered.	Decisions may be made by those in authority and others need not be consulted.	Decision-making, leadership

(Exhibit continued on next page)

EXHIBIT 3-1 (CONTINUED)

U.S. VALUES AND POSSIBLE ALTERNATIVES

Aspects* of U.S. Culture	Alternative Aspect	Examples of Management Function Affected
Employees will work hard to improve their position in the company.	Personal ambition is frowned upon.	Selection and promotion.
Competition stimulates high performance.	Competition leads to unbalances and leads to disharmony.	Career development and marketing
A person is expected to do whatever is necessary to get the job done (one must be willing to get one's hands dirty).	Various kinds of work are accorded low or high status and some work may be below one's "dignity" or place in the organization.	Assignment of tasks, performance, and organizational effectiveness
Change is considered an improvement and a dynamic reality.	Tradition is revered and the power of the ruling group is founded on the continuation of a stable structure.	Planning, morale and organizational development
What works is important.	Symbols and the process are more important than the end point.	Communication, planning, quality control
Persons and systems are evaluated.	Persons are evaluated but in such a way that individuals not highly evaluated will not be embarrassed or caused to "lose face."	Rewards and promotion, performance evaluation and accountability

Aspect here refers to a belief, value, attitude or assumption which is a part of culture in that it is shared by a large number of persons in any culture.

The connectivity of the Internet enables us to create information partnerships with personnel, customers, suppliers, contractors, and consultants.

The exercise not only compares cultural values affecting management practices in culture X with those in culture Y, but also provides a basis whereby a manager might "synergistically" relate to managers trained in another cultural system and management practices developed in other cultures.

The observations in this section assume added significance when computer networking and the Internet are used to form strategic alliances and partnerships. The *connectivity* of the Internet enables us to create *information partnerships* with personnel, customers, suppliers, contractors, and consultants. The key in such electronic endeavors is to treat them as *collaborators* rather than competitors.

Learning About *Other Management Cultures*

To create opportunities for collaboration, global leaders must learn not only the customs, courtesies, and business protocols of their counterparts from other countries, they must also understand the national character, management philosophies, and mindsets of the people. Dr. Geert Hofstede, a European research consultant who has helped identify important dimensions of national character, identifies following four dimensions of national culture:[11]

1. *Power distance*—indicates "the extent to which a society accepts that power in institutions and organizations is distributed unequally."
2. *Uncertainty avoidance*—indicates "the extent to which a society feels threatened by uncertain or ambiguous situations."
3. *Individualism*—refers to a "loosely knit social framework in a society in which people are supposed to take care of themselves and of their immediate families only." *Collectivism*, the opposite of individualism, occurs when there is a "tight social framework in which people distinguish between in-groups and out-groups; they expect their in-group (relatives, clan, organizations) to look after them, and in exchange for that owe absolute loyalty to it."
4. *Masculinity*—with its opposite pole, femininity, expresses "the extent to which the dominant values in society are assertiveness, money, and material things, not caring for others, quality of life and people."

The most significant dimension related to leadership in Hofstede's study of 40 countries was the power dimension. On the basis of mean ratings of employees on a number of key questions he assigned an index value to each country.

Exhibit 3-2 shows the positions of the 40 countries on the power distance and uncertainty avoidance scales, and Exhibit 3-3 shows the countries' positions on the power distance and individualism scales.

The United States ranked fifteenth on power distance, ninth on uncertainty avoidance (both of these are below the average), fortieth on individualism (the most individualist country in the sample), and twenty-eighth on masculinity (above average).

In Hofstede's study the United States ranked fifteenth out of 40 on the power distance dimension. If this had been higher, then the theories of leadership taught in the United States might have been expected to be more "Machiavellian." We might also ask how U.S. leaders are selected. Most are selected on the basis of competence, and it is the position of the person that provides the authority in the United States, which is, theoretically at least, an egalitarian society. In France, there is a higher power distance index score, and little concern with participative management, but a great concern with who has the power.

Even today, French industry and the managers who run it are a mixture of the old and the new. France is still an industry of family empires with many paternalistic traditions. There is also a remnant of a feudalis-

To create opportunities for collaboration, global leaders must also understand the national character, management philosophies, and mindsets of the people.

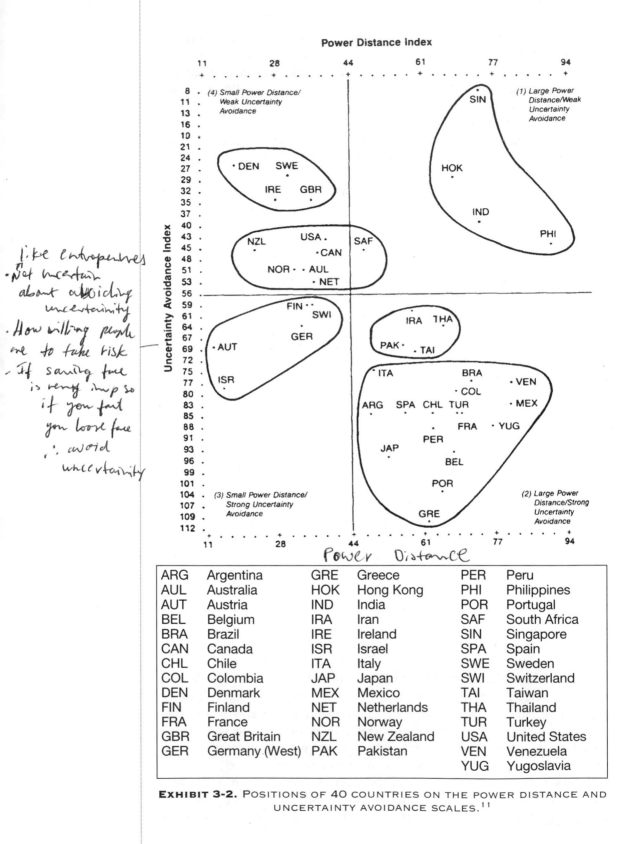

Power Distance Index

Handwritten notes (left margin):
- like extroverts
- Not uncertain about avoiding uncertainty
- How willing people are to take risk
- If saving face is very imp so if you fail you loose face ∴ avoid uncertainty

Chart labels:

(4) Small Power Distance/Weak Uncertainty Avoidance

(1) Large Power Distance/Weak Uncertainty Avoidance

(3) Small Power Distance/Strong Uncertainty Avoidance

(2) Large Power Distance/Strong Uncertainty Avoidance

Uncertainty Avoidance Index

Power Distance (handwritten)

ARG	Argentina	GRE	Greece	PER	Peru
AUL	Australia	HOK	Hong Kong	PHI	Philippines
AUT	Austria	IND	India	POR	Portugal
BEL	Belgium	IRA	Iran	SAF	South Africa
BRA	Brazil	IRE	Ireland	SIN	Singapore
CAN	Canada	ISR	Israel	SPA	Spain
CHL	Chile	ITA	Italy	SWE	Sweden
COL	Colombia	JAP	Japan	SWI	Switzerland
DEN	Denmark	MEX	Mexico	TAI	Taiwan
FIN	Finland	NET	Netherlands	THA	Thailand
FRA	France	NOR	Norway	TUR	Turkey
GBR	Great Britain	NZL	New Zealand	USA	United States
GER	Germany (West)	PAK	Pakistan	VEN	Venezuela
				YUG	Yugoslavia

EXHIBIT 3-2. POSITIONS OF 40 COUNTRIES ON THE POWER DISTANCE AND UNCERTAINTY AVOIDANCE SCALES.[11]

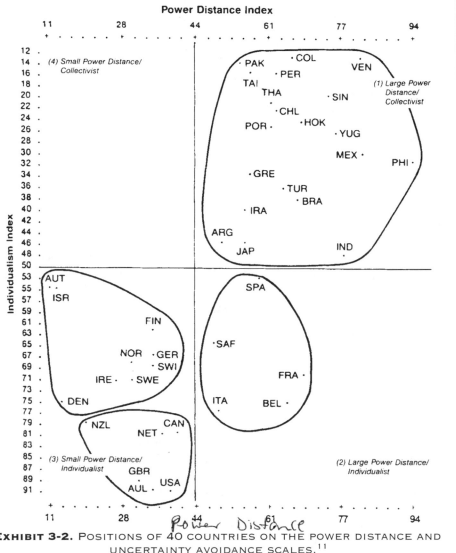

EXHIBIT 3-2. POSITIONS OF 40 COUNTRIES ON THE POWER DISTANCE AND UNCERTAINTY AVOIDANCE SCALES.[11]

eg: used is IBM in diff countries

Interaction of organizational structure is influenced by national culture

tic heritage that is deeply rooted within the French spirit, which could account for the very conservative and autocratic nature of their business methodology.

Hofstede has shown that in countries with lower power distance scores than the United States, such as Sweden and Germany, there is considerable acceptance of leadership styles and management models that are even more participative than presently exist. Industrial democracy and codetermination is a style that does not find much sympathy in the United States.

Hofstede has demonstrated that in Germany there is high uncertainty avoidance and, therefore, industrial democracy is brought about first by legislation. In Sweden, where uncertainty avoidance is low, industrial democracy was started with local experiments.

Hofstede[11] continues,

> The crucial fact about leadership in any culture is that it is a comple-
> ment to subordinateship. The Power Distance Index scores . . . are in fact
> based on the values of people as *subordinates*, not on the values of superi-
> ors. Whatever a naive literature on leadership may try to make us believe,
> a leader cannot choose his style at will; what is feasible depends to a large
> extent on the cultural conditioning of his/her subordinates. I therefore
> show . . . a description of the type of subordinateship that, other things
> being equal, a leader can expect to meet in societies at three different levels
> of Power Distance, and to which his/her leadership has to respond. The
> middle level represents what most likely is found in the U.S. environment.

The underlying assumptions regarding leadership in the United States are clearly seen in the practice of management by objectives.

Where does this leave us as global managers? Perhaps we pick and
choose, and adopt what is appropriate in the home culture. The matter is
brought into focus as we examine a specific management system. The
underlying assumptions regarding leadership in the United States are
clearly seen in the practice of management by objectives. This assumes
that a subordinate is independent enough to negotiate meaningfully with
a superior (not too high of a power distance), that both the superior and
the subordinate are willing to take risks (a low uncertainty avoidance)
and that performance is important to both (high masculinity).
Hofstede continues to demonstrate the importance of cross-cultural
research as management by objectives is applied to Germany.

> Let us now take the case of Germany. This is also a below-average
> Power Distance country, so the dialogue element in MBO should present
> no problem. However, Germany scores considerably higher on Uncertain-
> ty Avoidance; consequently, the tendency towards accepting risk and
> ambiguity will not be present to the same extent. The idea of replacing
> the arbitrary authority of the boss by the impersonal authority of mutual-
> ly agreed-upon objectives, however, fits the low Power Distance, high
> Uncertainty Avoidance cultural cluster very well. The objectives become
> the subordinates' "superego."

The consequences of Hofstede's conclusions are significant. Leadership, decision-making, teamwork, organization, motivation, and in fact
everything managers do is learned. Management functions are learned
and they are based on assumptions about one's place in the world. Managers from other business systems are not "underdeveloped" American
managers.

Learning From Other Management Cultures

The crow imitating the cormorant drowns in the water.
                                                    Japanese proverb

It is our conviction that all persons and organizations can learn from
others and adapt aspects of those systems to fit their own. Here is an

example of what we might learn from another culture based on one of the author's experiences in Japan:

Between 1965 and 1968, I was the playing coach of the Seibu Railroad Ice Hockey Team, the best team in Japan. The owner of the team and the president of the company, Yoshiaki Tsutsumi (identified by *Fortune* magazine as one of the world's 10 wealthiest people), decided to devote some of his time to developing ice hockey in Japan in preparation for the 1972 Winter Olympics, which had just been awarded to the city of Sapporo in northern Japan . . .

In October 1968, shortly before leaving with a group of 25 Japanese hockey players for a one-month, 17-game series against Canadian amateur and semi-professional hockey teams throughout Canada, I was asked to attend a meeting with Mr. Tsutsumi. I was told the purpose of the meeting was to decide on the wardrobe for the players during their tour of Canada, which was to take place in January (Canada's coldest month).

There were six persons at the meeting, including the owner/president, his secretary, three other staff persons, and myself. After exchanging pleasantries, we began the serious business of selecting what would go into each player's luggage bag.

Department managers from the Seibu Department Store were waiting in an adjoining room with samples of the various possibilities. The meeting lasted over four hours. First, we decided on the outerwear—coats, hats, gloves, and overshoes. Then the formal and informal suits and sweaters, and finally the underwear. Yes, we even decided on the kind and number of undershorts that each player would be allocated. The person making these decisions was the president himself, Mr. Tsutsumi. Of course, many hundreds of hours were spent planning other aspects of the tour.

Of the 17 games played in Canada, the Japanese team won 11, and from both Canadian and Japanese perspectives, the tour was a total success. On several occasions, during the pregame discussion and between-period pep talks, the fact that the company president was concerned about them to the extent of assisting with the selection of their wardrobe was mentioned. He also telephoned before and after each game and spoke to several of the players a number of times. In my opinion, this was an example of Japanese management in its purest form.

What is the moral of this story? Is it that the owners of amateur and professional hockey teams (and perhaps baseball, football, and other teams as well) should select the underwear for their players? No, it isn't. But having worked and conducted communication and team-building workshops for a professional hockey team in the National Hockey League, I certainly believe that a little more care on the part of the owners in communicating and working with the players might have done wonders for their morale and have had a positive impact on their ability to win hockey games.

Can the crow learn to imitate the cormorant? Can any management system borrow from another? In some cases, yes, and in others, no. Work environments in various countries are culturally different, but often cultural synergy can occur.

GLOBAL STUDY OF MANAGEMENT

Most studies in the management literature are comparative in nature. A book compares, for example, managerial processes and interdepartmental relations in the United States and Germany, or an article compares the career paths of Japanese and American managers. These kinds of cross-cultural studies are useful. However, because our world is becoming more pluralistic and interdependent, it is vital, though difficult, to study interactions between managers from more than one country.

Much of the management literature and textbooks (there are more MBA programs in the United States than most, if not all countries combined), and much of the organizational and management behavior research is conducted in the U.S. However, researchers in the United States should not assume that the U.S. management techniques are necessarily the best for American managers or for managers of other countries. American management techniques are based on American values and assumptions (for example, that we can influence and control the future to a high degree). Managers from other countries do not necessarily have such values and assumptions—at least they do not place as much emphasis or importance on them.

Improved individual and organizational performance is the purpose of most organizational change. This is generally accepted by managers. But attempts in the U.S. to improve individual and organizational performance by studying and adopting other nations' management systems have been insufficient and inconsistent. Many managers feel that there's no need to do this. After all, they ask, "Hasn't the United States developed the most highly sophisticated system of management in the world? Don't the managers of the best foreign companies come to U.S. business schools for MBA degrees and executive management courses?" Yes, it may be true that many foreign managers come to the U.S. for training, but Americans can still learn from and borrow aspects of foreign management systems.

Today many foreign countries, especially Europe and Canada, have their own world-class programs in management education. Some of their MBA degree programs have unique features and adaptions worthy of emulation, particularly in cross-cultural management and organizational behavior.

Japanese and American Management

Studying managers solely through comparisons is not enough. One must also consider what happens when differences come together, namely *interactions*. Aspects of North American or European managerial systems are not necessarily appropriate for managers of other geographic areas and may not even be the best for their own managers. Further-

Because our world is becoming more pluralistic and interdependent, it is vital, though difficult, to study interactions between managers from more than one country.

more, management is a dynamic process and is constantly changing. However, we can learn from the "way it was" by contrasting it with practices current at the end of the century. For example, the following research was conducted more than 25 years ago but shows how American and Japanese management styles have influenced one another and caused changes. Recent economic problems in Japan have forced many companies in that country to abandon some traditional customs like "lifetime employment."

The Type Z Hybrid

Ouchi and Jaeger[12] identify characteristics of typical American organizations (Type A):

1. Short-term employment
2. Individual decision-making
3. Individual responsibility
4. Rapid evaluation and promotion
5. Explicit, formalized control
6. Specialized career path
7. Segmented concern

and characteristics of typical Japanese (Type J) organizations:

1. Lifetime employment
2. Consensual decision-making
3. Collective responsibility
4. Slow evaluation and promotion
5. Implicit, formal control
6. Nonspecialized career path
7. Holistic concern

They then compare these organizations and relate them to their socio-cultural roots. They conclude by presenting a hybrid organizational form (Type Z), which they suggest may be useful in the United States.

Each of the two types of organizational structures (American and Japanese) represent a natural outflow and adaptation to the environments to which they belong. However, several U.S. companies are now using aspects of Japanese management with great success.

Ouchi and Jaeger suggest the following characteristics for Type Z organization (modified American):

1. Long-term employment
2. Consensual decision-making
3. Individual responsibility
4. Slow evaluation and promotion
5. Implicit, informal control with explicit formalized measures

Management is a dynamic process and is constantly changing.

6. Moderately specialized career path
7. Holistic concern for individuals

One of the most dramatic cases for East-West synergy lies in the interdependent relationship between Japan and the United States. This relationship has been tested many times but overall it has been mutually beneficial.

Despite current economic setbacks, Japanese previous success in production, distribution, and marketing has been the ability of Japanese to learn from Western nations and then apply this to their own business situations. Nowhere is this more evident than in the field of management where Japanese executives borrowed ideas from the United States, then refined these for increased productivity. Later some of these renewed techniques and practices would be re-exported to North America. That such a synergistic strategy works is attested by the hundreds of Japanese-owned or controlled firms now operating in the U.S. By adapting their own and our methods to the U.S. workplace, Japanese companies have been able to overcome differences in culture and work attitudes. Japanese managers abroad have pursued their concepts of job flexibility, training employees for more than one job; have emphasized quality over quantity; have interacted daily on the plant floor with personnel and have drawn upon worker knowledge and resources to improve productivity.

Hamel and Prahalad[13] suggest a pitfall in taking aspects of another culture, namely Japan, and integrating them into one's business philosophy. They cite a survey in which 80% of U.S. managers polled believed that "quality would be a fundamental source of competitive advantage."

However, less than 50% of Japanese managers surveyed anticipated that quality would be a source of competitive advantage at the turn of the millennium, although 82% believed quality was an advantage now. Japanese managers believed "the ability to create fundamentally new products and businesses will be the primary source of competitive advantage."

Many American companies have made significant changes in manufacturing techniques, including Kanban manufacturing, quality control circles, and just-in-time (JIT) purchasing which are part of mainstream American/Japanese industrial production. Boosting the morale, knowledge, responsibility, and therefore productivity of a corporation's workforce by using these techniques can only be accomplished if employees realize that they have a growing role in the firm's processes, problems, and profits.

JIT Production

JIT production is a major evolution in the manufacturing process. Its essence is the constant, efficient production of small units of parts. The major JIT productivity enhancements include less buffer stock, less

Many American companies have made significant changes in manufacturing techniques.

scrap, less rework labor, lower inventory interest, less in-process storage space, less inventory handling equipment, and less inventory accounting.

To fully implement JIT production a firm's purchasing department must adopt JIT purchasing methods. Instead of supporting a handful of suppliers of a particular item "just-in-case" they are needed, manufacturers can determine which supplier is the most efficient and develop just-in-time purchasing ties with only this firm.

The JIT system is centered on the notion that goods should be *pulled* through the factory by demands from the next work station, the next department, and in reality, from the marketplace (as opposed to the practice of management *pushing* a quantity of goods through the factory to the market). The key elements of the system were perfected by Toyota, where it is called Kanban manufacturing, after the cards used to signify parts orders from farther down the line. This system is now used by Toyota in their plant in Georgetown, Kentucky.

Quality Control Circles

Another major element of Japanese management that has found acceptance in America is quality control circles (QCC), originated in the U.S., perfected in Japan, and reapplied here.

Many American firms have already taken recovering steps toward corporate well-being through usage of Japanese and other foreign management techniques. And no industry has come farther faster than the U.S. auto industry. Chrysler has dodged the bankruptcy bullet and saved millions of dollars of interest charges by repaying government-backed loans seven years early. But how can this be? American automakers were up against the ropes in the mid-1980s. Overall vehicle production had been nearly cut in half from the peak year. And still today, Michigan congressional representatives pander to their beleaguered constituencies by claiming that Japanese refusal to arbitrarily extend their voluntary restriction to free market access in the U.S. auto market is a second Pearl Harbor. Such comments fly in the face of the current booming market, the unprecedented industry profit forecasts, and the fantastic job American automakers have done in applying Japanese techniques to their operations.

SYNERGISTIC SKILLS FOR GLOBAL MANAGEMENT

Let us now consider the question of being an effective manager in an overseas assignment. In the cross-cultural management literature, there is a lack of precise statements or criteria concerning the factors that are related to cross-cultural adaptation and effectiveness.

Many American firms have already taken recovering steps toward corporate well-being through usage of Japanese and other foreign management techniques. And no industry has come farther faster than the U.S. auto industry.

Cross-cultural communication behaviors or skills can be learned, so a manager can function effectively with host nationals. We are making important distinctions between cognitive competency or awareness and behavioral competency at this time. Behavioral competency is the ability to demonstrate or use the skills. Cognitive competency is the intellectual awareness or knowledge base.

The following skills have been identified by Ruben's research[14] as being associated with effectiveness in a multicultural environment in transferring knowledge. We shall refer to these skills as abilities. Most of these are common sense but often not demonstrated by multinational managers or supervisors of minority employees in one's own culture:

❑ *Respect.* The ability to express respect for others is an important part of effective relations in every country. All people like to believe and feel that others respect them, their ideas and their accomplishments. However, it is difficult to know how to communicate respect to persons from another culture. The following are questions that should be considered in the case of an overseas manager working in another culture with persons from that culture. What is the importance of age in communicating respect? What is the significance of manner of speaking? Do you speak only when spoken to? What gestures express respect? What kind of eye contact expresses respect? What constitutes "personal questions" as an invasion of privacy and a lack of respect? These are only a few of the many questions that could be generated relating to the important question, "How do I demonstrate that I respect the people I am working with?

❑ *Tolerating Ambiguity.* This refers to the ability to react to new, different, and at times, unpredictable situations with little visible discomfort or irritation. Excessive discomfort often leads to frustration and hostility, which are not conducive to effective interpersonal relationships with persons from other cultures. Learning to manage the feelings associated with ambiguity is a skill associated with adaptation to a new environment and effectively working with managers who have a different set of values.

❑ *Relating to People.* Many Western managers, concerned with getting the job done, are overly concerned with the task side of their jobs. In transferring skills and knowledge to persons in another culture, there is a requirement of getting the job done, but also the ability to get it done in such a way that people feel a part of the completed project and have benefited from being involved. Too much concern for getting the job done and neglect of "people maintenance" can lead to failure in transferring skills.

❑ *Being Nonjudgmental.* Most people like to feel that what they say and do is not being judged by others without having the opportunity of fully explaining themselves. The ability to withhold judgment and remain objective until one has enough information requires an understanding of the other's point of view and is an important skill.

❑ *Personalizing One's Observations.* As has been indicated previously, different people explain the world around them in different terms. A manager should realize that his or her knowledge and perceptions are valid only for self and not for the rest of the world. Thus, one would be able to personalize observations, be more tentative in conclusions and demonstrate a communication competence that what is "right" or "true" in one culture is not "right" or "true" in another. As one author said, "this is my way, what is your way? There is no 'the way' way"—it is all relative.

❑ *Empathy.* This is the ability to "put yourself in another's shoes." In this context, most people are attracted to and work well with managers who seem to be able to understand things from their point of view.

❑ *Persistence.* The multinational manager may not be successful at getting things done immediately, but with patience and perseverance, the task can be accomplished. There are many self-learning aids to acquire more synergistic skills for global management.

CHALLENGES IN INTERNATIONAL MANAGEMENT

We invite our readers to analyze the following material[15] and complete the exercise with colleagues from other cultures in light of the chapter messages:

Trivial Pursuit™ is a board game that has sold millions of copies throughout the world. The game requires players to answer questions in a number of categories such as geography, entertainment, history, art and literature, science, and nature and sports. The category of the question is determined by a roll of the dice.

I would like to invite you, the reader, to play this game. You have rolled the dice and drawn the category "International Management." This is your question: "Which countries produce the most competent internationalists in business?"

If the question were in Trivial Pursuit™, it would be in the genius edition—a very difficult question. Two words in the question contribute to the difficulty—competent and internationalists. A standard dictionary provides this definition of competent: "well qualified, capable, fit." "Internationalist" is a little more murky. The dictionary definition is "a person who believes in internationalism." But what is internationalism? Again, with help from the dictionary: "The principle or policy of international cooperation for the common good."

Before giving my answer, I'd like to discuss the origin of the question and the process of arriving at the "correct" answer. The question was suggested by a friend of a friend. This means I really don't know whose question it is. But the suggester of the question thought the answer was Japan. My friend disagreed for the following reasons.

"This is my way, what is your way? There is no 'the way' way"—it is all relative.

Japan indeed has a successful track record of best-selling products, including cars, electronic equipment and steel, among others. This is largely accomplished through Japanese businessmen who work for the nine giant Japanese trading companies—the *sogo shosha*. But the Japanese cheat in trade, he said. They have been found guilty of commercial piracy, bribery and falsifying documents. They also distort the international value of the yen, my friend said, so that some Japanese goods sell for less in other countries than in Tokyo. Moreover, they have exploited the open-door policy of some countries while vigorously pursuing a closed-door policy for themselves.

A Vote for the United States

Another businessman who was listening to this conversation said he thought the United States produced the most competent internationalists in business. The United States is the biggest economic entity in the history of the world, with dominant positions worldwide in computers, space, medicine, biology, and so on. Its competent internationalists in business make this possible.

This was overheard by a French manager, who said that Americans are naïve internationally. American businessmen, according to him, are the most ethnocentric of all businessmen (the dictionary definition is "one who judges others by using one's own personal or cultural standards").

Besides, he said, American businessmen have their priorities mixed up. They are too materialistic, too work-oriented, too time-motivated, and equate anything "new" with best. Americans also have the highest attrition rate (dictionary definition—"return early from an international assignment") of any country, said the French manager.

The question is indeed a tough one. At a recent meeting of American managers attending a seminary on international joint ventures, I posed the same question. It evoked considerable discussion but no agreement. One person suggested they vote and most hands were raised when Sweden was proposed. But Sweden, said one person who voted for another country, couldn't be the winning answer. Sweden is too small and the Swedish economy has declined sharply since the late 1970s because Swedish internationalists aren't aggressive enough. At this point, another participant suggested the right answer was the Soviet Union. Most people laughed at this suggestion. I assume that meant disagreement.

Britain has had foreign operations for centuries. Maybe the British manager is the most competent internationalist. But when business travelers from several countries discussed this possibility while caught in Geneva International Airport recently during a snowstorm, no one thought Britain was the winning answer because Britain has lost so much in the international marketplace. Several businessmen from Britain were among those who participated in the discussion.

Since no agreement could be reached on the correct answer to my first question, I decided to rephrase it: What contribution to a multinational organization is made by managers of various nationalities?

Different Contributions

Hari Bedi, and Indian expatriate working for a large multinational company in Hong Kong, believes that Asian internationals use the 5 Cs of *continuity* (a sense of history and tradition), *commitment* (to the growth of the organization), *connections* (where social skills and social standing count), *compassion* (balancing scientific and political issues), and *cultural sensitivity* (a respect for other ways).

These qualities are among the contributions made by Asian managers to a multinational organization, he says. Western managers, according to Bedi, use the 5 Es: *expertise* (experience in managerial and technical theory), *ethos* (practical experience), *eagerness* (the enthusiasm of the entrepreneur), *esprit de corps* (a common identity), and *endorsement* (seeks unusual opportunities).

The answer is that the managers of every country contribute something to a multinational organization. The usefulness of that contribution depends on the situation. Competent internationalists (we're back to my first and discarded question) are able to recognize the contribution made by managers of various nationalities. They are also able to develop solutions to problems faced by multinational organizations by using these contributions and cultural diversity as a resource, rather than a barrier to be overcome.

The Beginning or the End of Cooperation

With international trade and foreign investments increasing at unprecedented rates, a deep understanding of the forces at work and skills to manage these forces will be keys to successful international management. Thus, organizational strategy of the future will account for differences in strength and direction. Human resources will be used to contribute the maximum to the organizational objectives, emphasizing the individual's special skills or values. The criteria applied in decision-making will increasingly consider differences of the cultural values, while at the same time will also make maximum use of them. Thus, the global manager's task is recognizing these differences and combining them in an optimal way. This must be accomplished within the contexts of the indigenous national and organizational cultures if synergy is to be achieved.

Thus, organizational strategy of the future will account for differences in strength and direction.

SUMMARY

Trends in the global marketplace have made organizations from various countries more interdependent. Leaders who seek to be effective in international negotiations and the forming of strategic alliances or partnerships cultivate the mindset and skills presented in this chapter. The creation of cultural synergy is the key to success, whether in a global enterprise or within the micro-culture of a single entity. The new work culture avoids rugged individualism and destructive competition, while fostering cooperation and collaboration that is win-win for all involved—managers, workers, customers, and even competitors at times. Unit III offers culture specifics for increasing one's effectiveness abroad.

REFERENCES

1. Fisher, G. *International Negotiation: A Cross-Cultural Perspective,* Chicago: Intercultural Press, 1980.
2. Graham, J. "Vis-a-Vis: International Business Negotiations," *International Business Negotiations,* Ghauri, P. and Usunier, J. C. (eds.), Oxford, UK: Pergamon, 1996
3. Scheu-Lottgen, U. D. and Hernandez-Campoy, J. M. "An Analysis of Sociocultural Miscommunication: English, Spanish and German," *International Journal of Intercultural Relations,* Vol. 22, No. 4, November 1998.
4. Graham, J. and Herberger, R. "Negotiating Abroad—Don't Shoot From the Hip," *Harvard Business Review,* July-August, 1983.
5. Acuff, F. L. *How to Negotiate with Anyone, Anywhere Around the World.* New York: AMACOM, 1993.
6. Weiss, S. and Stripp W. *Negotiation with Foreign Business Persons: An Introduction for Americans with Propositions on Six Cultures,* New York University/Faculty of Business Administration, February 1985.
7. Weiss S. E. "Negotiating with 'Romans'—Part 2," *Sloan Management Review,* Massachusetts Institute of Technology, Spring 1994.
8. *Behavior of Successful Negotiators,* Huthwaite Research Group Report, 1976, 1982.
9. Ohmae, K. "The Global Logic Strategic Alliances," *Harvard Business Review,* March-April, 1989.
10. Ashkenas, R. N., DeMonaco, L. J., and Francis, S. C. "Making the Deal Real: How GE Capital Integrates Acquisitions," *Harvard Business Review,* January-February, 1998.
11. Hofstede, G. *Cultures' Consequences: International Differences in Work-Related Values,* Beverly Hills, CA: Sage Publications, 1984. See also Hofstede, G. *Cultures and Organizations,* London: McGraw-Hill, 1991.
12. Ouchi, W. G. and Jaeger, A. M. "Made in America Under Japanese Management," *Harvard Business Review,* Vol. 52, No. 5, pp. 61–69, 1974. See also Chen, M. *Asian Management Systems,* London: Routledge, 1995; and Funakawa, A. *Transcultural Management,* San Francisco: Jossey-Bass, 1997.
13. Hamel, G. and Prahalad, C. K. *Competing for the Future,* Boston: Harvard Business School Press, 1994.
14. Ruben, B. *Handbook of Intercultural Skills,* Vol. 1, New York: Pergamon Press, 1983. See also Kenton, S. B. and Valentine, D. *Crosstalk: Communicating in a Multicultural Workplace,* Upper Saddle River, NJ: Prentice Hall, 1997.
15. "Cross-cultural Management," *International Management,* March 1985.

LEADERSHIP IN CULTURAL CHANGE

Some have referred to organizational culture as "the way we do things around here." Organizational or corporate culture can facilitate or inhibit change.

The concepts of culture, communication and change are all inter-connected, each influencing the other whether within a nation or region, a system or corporation. For example, changes in communication technologies are impacting both national and work cultures. This chapter focuses on the role of the global manager and the conscious exercise of leadership in managing change. We will focus especially on the application of leadership to changing organizational culture. Some have referred to organizational culture as "the way we do things around here." Organizational or corporate culture can facilitate or inhibit change. As we move into the 21st century, accelerating social and technological change require leaders who do not merely "manage change," but use it to competitive advantage. This organizational change may mean servicing better and faster the needs of the customer, consumer, or public. Like individuals, institutions whose cultures are flexible and adaptive usually outperform their counterparts. Individuals can be trained to move toward a culture of continuous change, but the organization's "way of doing things" must also continuously reaffirm this norm of human behavior.[1]

CHANGE

When a computer system or area networking is introduced into a corporation, there is a change in role relationships. When a management information system is introduced into an office, the data available for decision-making affect relationships. When a local company moves beyond its borders into the international marketplace, there is not only a transformation of company strategy, policies, and procedures, but structures change as well. When minorities become part of the workforce in greater numbers, there is an altering of relationships with the majority personnel. When women are promoted to increasingly higher levels in business, the working relationships between women and men are influenced. All such actions provoke change in organizational culture. So too, when managers, sales persons or technicians, as well as their families, are deployed overseas for a lengthy assignment, there is a profound transposition in their relationships to their "world" and the "foreigners" in it.

The paradox of change is that it is inevitable and constant. Today's managers operate in a global environment that has changed more rapidly and extensively than any other period in human history. To survive and develop, leaders not only need new skills for coping with change, but must learn to build an environment that is open to dynamic change within their systems, as well as within the life-styles of their colleagues and themselves.

This chapter views planned change in terms of three interactive cultures: (1) *cyberculture*—the urban, technological, superindustrial society that is emerging; (2) *national culture*—the people and place in which one seeks to live and conduct business; (3) *organizational culture*—the base from which the global manager or professional operates. Increasingly, these cultures are different from the culture in which we were born and socialized. Human behavior can be modified and we are changed by the impact of these three cultures upon us, especially in leadership roles. But we need not passively react, for we have the means to temper or tamper with these interacting cultures. Specifically, modern management theory maintains that managers have a responsibility to be proactive agents of change. That is, we can initiate actions to correct obsolescence.

Not all change is desirable. Critical choices have to be made about the overall wisdom of an alteration. Because accelerating change is a reality of our world, change must be managed if it is not to cause disastrous dislocation in the life of people and their organizations or societies. Perhaps the place to begin is for the reader to assess his or her attitudes toward change, as well as to consider why planned change is more desirable. It is a challenge to reeducate ourselves and to reevaluate our psychological constructs—the way we read meaning into the events and experiences of our lives.

Human Factors in Change

Individuals have a set of highly organized constructs around which we organize our "private" worlds. We construct a mental system for putting order, as we perceive it, into our worlds. This intellectual synthe-

To survive and develop, leaders not only need new skills for coping with change, but must learn to build an environment that is open to dynamic change within their systems

sis of sense perceptions relates to our images of self, family, role, organization, nation, and universe. These constructs then become anchors or reference points for our mental functioning and well being. Our unique construct systems exert a pushing/pulling effect upon all other ideas and experiences we encounter. They assign meaning quickly and almost automatically to the multiple sensations and perceptions that bombard us daily.

Not only do individuals have such unique sets of constructs through which they filter experience, but groups, organizations, and even nations develop such mental frameworks through which they interpret information coming from their environment. The intense interactions of various segments of their group form construct sets that enable them to achieve collective goals. In this way a group, organizational or national "style" or type of behavior emerges. Through communication in such groupings, people share themselves and their individual perceptions converge into a type of "consensus" of what makes sense to them in a particular environment and circumstance. Culture, then, transmits these common, shared sets of perceptions and relationships. But since human interaction is dynamic, pressures for change in such constructs build up in both individuals and institutions. For example, when a manager from Grand Rapids, Michigan, is transferred for three years to Riyadh, Saudi Arabia, that person is challenged to change many of his or her constructs about life and people. The same may be said for the corporate culture that individual's company attempts to transplant from Midwest America to the Middle East. These forces for change can be avoided, resisted, or incorporated into the person's perceptual field. If the latter happens, then change becomes a catalyst for a restructuring of constructs and an opportunity for growth. In other words, the employee and the company can adapt and develop.

By practicing skill in planned change, we cannot only facilitate people's preparation and acceptance of change, but we also reduce stress and energy waste. Maximum two-way communication about the proposed change can create the necessary readiness for its eventual implementation and the negative impact of sudden changes can be defused. While proposing innovations, leaders can endeavor to reduce the uncomfortable threat of those involved. Thus, negative reactions like apathy or sabotage, protest or revolt can be minimized.

It is important for today's global managers to appreciate that much of human history, most of the globe's inhabitants were raised in hierarchical societies where personal choice and progress were limited, and one's place was immutable. For generations people survived by remaining within their prescribed roles, adapting to the pattern of thought, belief, and action of their local cultural group. Except for less developed countries, all this is changing—humankind is in the midst of a mind-boggling

By practicing skill in planned change, we cannot only facilitate people's preparation and acceptance of change, but we also reduce stress and energy waste.

transformation that offers seemingly unlimited choices and opportunities. We change our environment and are changed by it. We create technology, and we are physically and psychologically changed by it. In the process traditional customs, values, attitudes, and beliefs are disrupted. Yet, as our culture and social institutions change, we learn to change ever more effectively and our capacity for such learning is seemingly inexhaustible. Global leaders are in the forefront of this phenomenon and should be on the cutting edge of innovation, while mindful of the human dimensions involved.[2]

In today's *culture of change,* people are challenged to alter the way in which they perceive or think about their work and how it is to be performed. The shifting context of the nature of work and the environment in which employees function has been described as the *new work culture.*[3] The driving forces behind these social and technological changes are globalization of consumerism; transformation of traditional corporate hierarchy into a multinational or global network; fragmentation of work and creation of global jobs; ascendency of knowledge as a primary global product. One outcome of this phenomenon is the reshaping of our views of the various roles we have in society whether in the community, family or workplace.

Role Changes

Differences in gender roles are largely created and kept in place by social, not biological forces, and therefore, are subject to change.

For two decades, Cynthia Fuchs Epstein[4] has researched the changing roles of men and women, discovering that gender differences are mostly in our minds. Epstein found that the differences in gender roles are largely created and kept in place by social, not biological forces, and therefore, are subject to change. As the research of Ann M. Morrison[5] confirmed, it is not necessary for individuals to be typecast and culture bound in their career aspirations. In many societies changes in this regard are rapid as workers move beyond traditional role concepts and fight for equality.

Similar representations may be made of *organizations,* because human systems—collections of people—also suffer identity crises. Caught between a disappearing bureaucracy and an emerging "ad-hocracy," the institution may experience down-turns in sales, poor morale, membership reductions, bankruptcy threats, obsolete product lines and services, and increasing frustration with unresponsive management. Organizations, then, are challenged to go through planned renewal and to reproject their public images.[6]

So too with *nations.* When the social fabric unravels or wavers, there are national identities in crisis. Examples include the loss of "face" by the U.S. in Vietnam and the seizure of U.S. diplomats in Iran; Great Britain, which lost its empire and nearly went bankrupt as a nation; Japan whose very economic and technological progress threatens its traditional culture; East Germany, where the Communist state collapsed and the country was incorporated into The Federal Republic of Germany. As with the underlying hostilities in the Balkans where human suffering has not diminished, people of various countries have sought to rediscover their collective selves in the post-national period, and geographers continuously have to redraw the changes in maps of national borders.

In some societies, the struggle for national identity is epitomized in a name change, as from Congo to Zaire or Rhodesia to Zimbabwe. Elsewhere, as in the former U.S.S.R., especially the Baltic Republics of Lithuania, Latvia, and Estonia, individuals seek greater ethnic identity and autonomy from centralized control. Whereas, in the People's Republic of China, often turmoil centers around democratization and the totalitarian control by the Communist Party.

After the collapse of communism in Yugoslavia, the national federation broke up into conflicting republics, such as Croatia, Bosnia, and Serbia, who not only warred against one another in the 1990s, but the latter sought dominance by *ethnic cleansing* or genocide against groups like Moslems in Bosnia or Albanians in Kosovo. Such violence based on ancient rivalries not only transgresses the U.N. Declaration on Human Rights, but acts to reverse changes toward a more modern, multicultural society.

Peter Drucker[7] provides a disturbing perspective of the changes ongoing in society. He examines our altered perceptions of government's role, and thinks politicians are falling behind the new realities. For example, he presaged the "decolonization" of the Soviet empire, and anticipated the breakup of that huge country into European and Asian parts. So-called Western leaders failed to consider the revolutionary consequences of these changes. National economies, he says, are shaped increasingly by global events.

Drucker addresses the changing role of owners, workers, managers, and the corporation itself. He describes a world of knowledge workers in companies reorganized to be leaner and more specialized and in growing nonprofit and volunteer sectors. He stresses the need for new approaches to politics, economics, and management, and increased innovation in how we define problems and organize ourselves for work now and in the future.

While reengineering advocates call for a business revolution, Christopher[8] suggests that business itself has an identity problem in this metaindustrial period in which we live:

> If we have no concept of what we are as a business enterprise, our journey into the future will be haphazard. . . . If our actions, adjustments, and reactions derive from a philosophy in tune with the world around us, we will find some kind of identity . . . that is consciously articulated and made central to every action taken everywhere in the organization. . . .

Christopher proposes that this search for a more relevant business identity seek answers to these questions. What business are we in? What

People of various countries have sought to rediscover their collective selves in the post-national period, and geographers continuously have to redraw the changes in maps of national borders.

are we as an organization? What should we become? We would add two more questions: Who are our customers? Where are our markets? Many corporations are afraid to enter the global marketplace, cope with diverse customs or import/export regulations.

Environmental Forces Influencing Change

Why must most business organizations, non-governmental organizations (NGOs), and many other institutions become global to survive? Moran and Riesenberger[9] identify and describe twelve environmental forces impacting organizations and influencing change. The **proactive** environmental forces are:

1. *Global sourcing*—organizations are seeking non-domestic sources of raw materials because of cost and quality.
2. *New and evolving markets* are providing new opportunities for growth.
3. *Economies of scale*—today's marketplace requires new approaches resulting in competitive advantages in price and quality.
4. *Movement towards homogeneous demand*—globalization is resulting in similar products being required worldwide.
5. *Lowered transportation costs*—the global transportation costs of many products have fallen significantly since the 1960s.
6. *Government tariffs and taxes*—the protectionist tendencies of many governments is declining as evidenced by the North America Free Trade Agreement (NAFTA) and the European Union (EU).
7. *Telecommunications*—falling prices as a result of privatization and new technologies are impacting globalization.
8. *Homogeneous technical standards*—the International Organization for Standardization (ISO) has been successful in developing global standards known as ISO 9000.

The **reactive** forces are:

9. *Competition for non-domestic organizations*—new competitive threats are experienced by organizations regularly.
10. *Risk for volatile exchange rates*—the constant fluctuation of exchange rates in many countries impacts profits.
11. *Customers are becoming more global consumers*—globalization is impacting customers in ways that "local content" in subsidiary produced goods is increasing.
12. *Global technological change*—technological improvements coming from many areas of the world are requiring organizations to adjust their strategies to survive.

TRANSFORMING
GLOBAL BUSINESS CULTURE

Leading-edge thinkers maintain that the computer and the Internet are the most transforming inventions in human history with the capacity to change everything—the way we work, the way we learn and play, and perhaps the way we sleep and cohabit.[10] Andrew Grove, founder and chairman of Intel, predicts in five years all companies will be Internet companies. Grove[11] talks about "Internet time" when referring to change, citing his own experience as a chip maker when the Pentium processor was in full-scale production. As CNN reported the story worldwide, a minor design error resulted in "a rounding error in division once every nine billion times." After this global report, the new Pentium users immediately requested replacement chips. Intel's response was to quickly set up a "war room" so as to instantly answer a flood of inquiries on the subject. Gradually, they replaced chips with this minor defection by the hundreds of thousands. This incident not only shows the planetary power of satellite communications, but the kind of global leadership necessary to *manage such change!*

Symonds[12] observes that, "The Internet is turning business upside down and inside out. It is fundamentally changing the way companies operate, whether in high tech or metal bashing. This goes far beyond buying and selling over the Internet, and deep into the processes and culture of an enterprise." Some of the sociotechnical changes Symonds underscores are:

❑ Connecting through the Internet with buyers and sellers, as well as trading partners.
❑ Using the Internet to lower costs dramatically across integrated supply and demand chains.
❑ Developing e-business (electronic) at hyper-growth rates by inter-company trade over the Internet.
❑ Using websites to enrich the multimedia experience by integrating customer/suppliers, databases, monitoring sites visited, supporting online transactions, integrating personal/telephone call center operations, and supporting multiple payment operations.
❑ Establishing organizational *Intranets* to improve departmental and personnel exchanges, manage travel and expenses, employee benefits, and share the latest information.

This whole process is also transforming organizational cultures and business strategies. It fosters synergistic relations by the practice of connecting and collaborating. It encourages the formation of *information*

Intel's response was to quickly set up a "war room" so as to instantly answer a flood of inquiries on the subject.

partnerships between suppliers and customers, as well as between systems. It facilitates customized services, outsourcing for both personnel and manufacturing, inventory control, as well as innovating with new products and services. The emerging e-speak technology connects us with electronic experts from mediators and brokers to physicians and consultants. Through networking, these software inventions permit business to become part of a worldwide, dynamic eco-system.

This communication revolution is connecting in new ways industry, government, and academia; researchers in both the private and public sectors as well as scattered family members over the globe. In fact, research at the Salk Institute in La Jolla, California, has an automated computer program that currently recognizes 62 facial cues of any human being filmed on video. Such computer image analysis has myriad applications from health care to law enforcement. Universities are also daily creating new communication technologies and applications. For example, the University of California-San Diego has a Link Family Computer System to connect electronically various segments of its community for information exchanges. Components include StudentLink, FinancialLink, EmployeeLink, TravelLink, and DataLink, as well as EZPay for paperless financial payments. This is a Web-based system providing easy access to information about a wide-range of institutional operations and resources. It is another dimension for using modern media to streamline business practice, decrease costs, increase productivity, while enhancing customer satisfaction and employee accountability and morale. This, then, is another indicator why global leaders must learn to be high performing managers of accelerating change.

Innovators may respect the established system, while working to bend or beat it to make it more responsive to satisfying human need.

DEVELOPING CHANGE STRATEGIES

Global managers should be sources of innovation, yet skillful in "managing" change. Agents of change may apply their efforts, in this context, to altering personal, organizational, and cultural goals. With a global leader operating in diverse cultures and circumstances, for example, the very differences require appropriate adaptation of organizational objectives, processes and procedures. Their revision might include a goal of learning to be knowledgeable and comfortable as possible wherever they are located, even if it means creative circumvention of local constraints. Innovators may respect the established system, while working to bend or beat it to make it more responsive to satisfying human need.

The *New York Times* once ran this interesting advertisement:

WANTED—CHANGE AGENTS—Results-oriented individuals able to accurately and quickly resolve complex tangible and intangible problems. Energy and ambition necessary for success.

Within an organization or culture, what then would be the focus of such a change agent when employed? Probably, the initial concern would be to examine the change possibilities in six categories:

1. Structure (the system of authority, communication, roles, and work flow).
2. Technology (problem solving mechanisms, tools, and computers).
3. Tasks (activities accomplished, such as manufacturing, research, service).
4. Processes (techniques, simulations, methods, scenario building procedures, such as management information systems).
5. Environment (internal or external atmosphere).
6. People (personnel or human resources involved).

Having decided upon which category or combinations to focus one's energy for change, the leader might follow these steps:

1. Identify specific changes that appear desirable to improve effectiveness.
2. Create a readiness in the system for such change.
3. Facilitate the internalization of the innovation.
4. Reinforce the new equilibrium established through the change.

The skilled change maker is aware that any change introduced in one element of the previous chain affects the other factors.[13] The parts of complex systems are interdependent, so the innovator attempts to forecast the ripple effect. Change agents must take a multidimensional approach, considering legal, economic, and technological aspects of the change without ignoring its social, political, and personal implications. They also operate on certain assumptions:

❑ People are capable of planning and controlling their own destinies within their own life space.
❑ Behavioral change, knowledge and technology should be incorporated into the planning process.
❑ Human beings are already in the midst of profound cultural change—it's evolution!

The implication of the latter statement is that the people involved in the change process may be suspicious of simplistic solutions as a result of the information/media blitz to which they have been exposed. They may already be suffering from information overload, experiencing a sense of powerlessness and loss of individuality; and they expect innovative and involving communication about the change. Essentially, the change maker may employ three change models to bring about a shift in the status quo:

Human beings are already in the midst of profound cultural change—it's evolution!

1. Power—political or legal, physical or psychological—coercion to bring about change may be legitimate or illegitimate, depending on the purpose, the ingredients, and the method of application (legislative power may be used to promote equal employment opportunity or to prevent a disease epidemic, while the authority of role or competence may be called upon to overcome resistance to change).
2. Rationale—the appeal to reason and the common good, but this approach must face the fact that people are not always altruistic and self-interest may block acceptance of the proposed change, no matter how noble or worthwhile for the majority.
3. Reeducative—conditioning, training, and education become the means to not only create readiness for the change, but to provide the information and skills to implement it.

Each model has its strength and weaknesses, so a combination of the models is most effective.

The "how" of planned change offers a variety of approaches. It can be as simple as "imagineering" at a staff meeting regarding the likely changes to become realities in a decade based on present trend indicators. Or it may be using the more elaborate Delphi technique, in which a questionnaire is developed with about a dozen likely situations that may occur in the future within a company or a culture. Members or experts may then be asked to rate on a percentage basis the probability of the event happening. Results are then tabulated and median percentages for each item determined. A report of results is circulated among participants, and they are asked to again rate the alternative possibilities after studying peer responses.

Today the words "reengineering" or "re-inventing" the organization are used to describe planned system-wide change. Hammer[14] states that reengineering is not about downsizing, reorganizing, or restructuring. It is about thinking outside of the box, rethinking your work and company. It is a fundamental rethinking and radical redesigning of all the processes of business to obtain improvements in critical measures of performance (cost, quality, capital, service and speed). It is throwing away what is and replacing it. For instance, if IBM, Merck, Boeing, etc. did not exist today, how would they be created/structured?

Responding to change in today's organizations is difficult. At times, organizations that do not change or transform themselves effectively open the door to being merged with or acquired by another company. According to Beatty and Ulrich[15] four principles can serve as the framework if change and renewal are to be understood and implemented in mature organizations. However, we believe their guidelines are applicable to all organizations not only mature ones involved in change and renewal.

At times, organizations that do not change or transform themselves effectively open the door to being merged with or acquired by another company.

Organizations renew by focusing on the customer's perspective and demands. To sustain a competitive advantage, organizations must be devoted to customers' needs in unique ways. When a mindset is embedded in employees that affects their work habits, changing focus is exceedingly difficult. When employees can focus on the customers' perspective and let go of the political boundaries and internal company policies, renewal can happen. Hewlett Packard, an innovator in this area, in order to advance renewal, asked their teams to pretend they were the buyers of a particular product. As customers they were to shop their four major competitors and evaluate why they chose one supplier over another, what the image of the supplier/competitor was and the reasons for their choice. After going through this analysis, from a customer's perspective, teams were better able to understand the perceived mindsets of their competitors, which gave them insight into their customer's needs. The teams were also able to determine how this mindset differed from Hewlett Packard. Instilling customer perspective can refocus attention outside to produce change inside an organization.

Organizations renew by increasing their capacity for change. Like humankind, organizations have internal clocks that determine how swiftly change will move from definition to action. Today, organizations want to reduce their cycle time on how and when decisions are made and activities completed so they can move quicker from idea conception to production and increase their capacity for change and flexibility. "Alignment, symbiosis and reflexiveness" can be helpful in this process. Alignment refers to the common goals of the company. When organizations have a sense of alignment they can move toward shared goals in a shorter time frame because less time is spent building commitment and more time can be spent on work. Symbiosis is the speed with which organizations can remove barriers inside and outside the company to effect change. The Ford Taurus is a good example. To reduce boundaries and speed up internal clocks, Ford chose a cross-functional team removing boundaries between departments to design and deliver the car. Consequently, the Taurus moved from conception to production in 50% less time than established internal clocks. Reflexiveness is the time to reflect and learn from past activities, ensuring a sense of continuity.

Organizations renew by adjusting both the hardware and software within their company. Beatty and Ulrich[15] refer to the hardware as issues of strategy, structure and systems. "These domains of activity are malleable and measurable and can be heralded with high visibility—for example, timely announcement about new strategies, structures or systems." Unless the hardware is connected to the appropriate software, however, computers are useless. The same is true of the less visible domains of the organization, the software, which includes employee

Organizations have internal clocks that determine how swiftly change will move from definition to action.

behavior and mindset. Change begins by altering hardware, but often not enough resources are spent making sure that employee behavior, mindset, and work activities match the change.

Organizations need empowered employees to act as leaders at all levels. "Employees are trusted and empowered to act on issues that affect their work performance. Leaders have the obligation of articulating and stating a vision and of ensuring that the vision will be implemented." Leaders must be credible. They must be good communicators, articulating changes so that they are readily understood, acceptable, and inspirational as well to all employees. All leaders at all levels must be able to express the new vision/strategy/mindset, encouraging the extra effort needed to make the vision a reality.

Leaders may find the following tips for fostering change especially helpful in intercultural situations.[16]

❏ Include in the planning process everyone concerned about the change.
❏ Avoid discrepancies between words and actions relative to the change.
❏ Set realistic time frames for bringing about the change.
❏ Integrate the activities involved in the change with available budget and resources.
❏ Avoid overdependence on external or internal specialists.
❏ Avoid data gaps between the change efforts at the top, middle and lower levels of the system.
❏ Avoid forcing innovations into old structures incapable of handling them.
❏ Avoid simplistic, cookbook solutions to the problems connected with change.
❏ Realize that effective relations are a condition for change, not an end.
❏ Apply change intervention strategies appropriately.
❏ Identify personnel capable of diagnosing the need for change.
❏ Capitalize on the pressures both from within and without the system for the change.
❏ Search the system at all levels for the leadership to effect the change.
❏ Promote collaborative efforts between line and staff in planning and implementing the change.
❏ Take strategic risks to inaugurate necessary change.
❏ Maintain a realistic, long-term perspective relative to the change.
❏ Initiate systems to reward people who cooperate in carrying out the change and in establishing more effective behaviors.
❏ Collect data to support the change and evaluate it.
❏ Set measurable objectives and targets relative to the change that are both tangible and immediate.

Introducing change in multicultural organizations is more difficult than in domestic organizations. Exhibit 4-1 suggests a way change

Avoid forcing innovations into old structures incapable of handling them.

agents can anticipate resistance to change and measure the degree of risk. It can be used in the following way. Suppose there are five nationalities (national culture 1 = France, national culture 2 = U.S., etc.) working together in an organization. A decision was made that detailed performance appraisals were to be implemented every six months for all employees, and the decision was of high importance to the success of the organization. If the compatibility of this change in the organization was plotted on Exhibit 4-1, the likelihood of success could be determined. In reality, often a change is compatible with one group but not another. The change agent then needs to consider the cultural underpinnings resisting the change, and make appropriate interventions.

Technological, economic, market and social forces, such as mass immigrations, drive changes in the workplace. Pritchett & Associates, a Dallas-based consultancy in organizational change, specializes in down-

Technological, economic, market and social forces, such as mass immigrations, drive changes in the workplace.

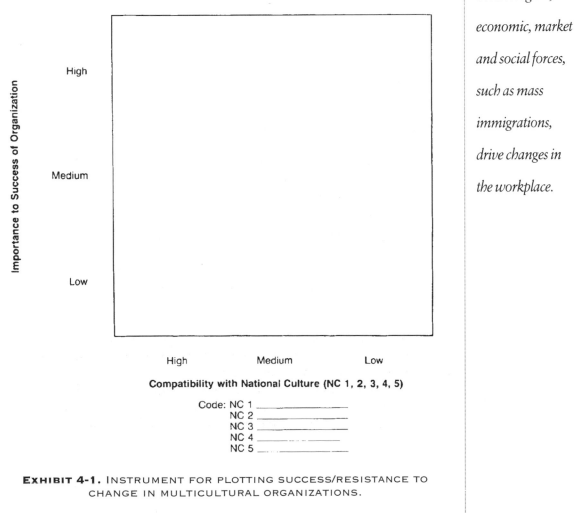

EXHIBIT 4-1. INSTRUMENT FOR PLOTTING SUCCESS/RESISTANCE TO CHANGE IN MULTICULTURAL ORGANIZATIONS.

sizing, turn-arounds, and mergers during the "Age of Instability." In an employee handbook on the subject, Pritchett and Pound,[17] write that myths about change influence worker mindsets, and must be dispelled. Reality is that:

❑ Change is dynamic and here to stay.
❑ Controlling emotions helps workers to control the fluid situation.
❑ Progress often masquerades as trouble.
❑ Company changes necessitate that workers also change.
❑ Problems are a natural side effect of implementing change.
❑ Management usually tries to be straightforward as the situation permits, while making the tough decisions about the alterations.
❑ Workers can be part of the problem or the solution.
❑ Both management and worker must work as a team to make the change plan succeed.

In the shift to emerging global economy and work culture, Pritchett advises that *new work habits* are essential. In another handbook, he provides thirteen ground rules for worker success in our changing world:

❑ Become a quick-change artist, that is, flexible and adaptable.
❑ Commit fully to your job—it makes work satisfying and ensures success.
❑ Speed up—accelerate with the organization.
❑ Accept ambiguity and uncertainty—change is the only certainty.
❑ Behave like you are in business for yourself—assume personal responsibility.
❑ Stay in school—life-long learning is essential.
❑ Hold yourself accountable for outcomes—set goals and targets.
❑ Add value—contribute more than you cost.
❑ See yourself as a service center—customers are a source of job security.
❑ Manage your own morale—be responsible for attitude control.
❑ Continuously strive for performance improvement.
❑ Be a fixer, not a finger-pointer—assume ownership of problems.
❑ Alter your expectations—rely on yourself to develop work skills for success in the information age!

A fourteenth might be—*openness to differences in people and situations*.
To conclude this section, remember change is more acceptable when it is understood; is related to one's security; results from previously established principles; follows other successful changes; prior changes have been assimilated; new people, departments or programs are involved; personnel share in the planning and benefits; and people are trained for it.

Problems are a natural side effect of implementing change.

LEADERSHIP AND CHANGE

Global leaders cope more effectively with change by means of strategic planning and management. For global corporations, discontinuous change can be costly in terms of loss of profits and in reversing losses. Ansoff[18] advocates a form of strategic response to change that is both decisive and planned. He concludes that behavioral resistance to change is a natural reaction because our culture and power are threatened. Therefore, effective leaders anticipate resistance, diagnose it, and then "manage" it, or incorporate it into the system.

Just as our cultural conditioning affects our attitudes toward the phenomenon of change, so too it influences our concepts of leadership. For our purposes here, the *Random House Dictionary* definition may provide a base for understanding—a leader is one who guides, directs, conducts, while leadership is the position or function or ability to influence or lead others.

For the past 40 years behavioral science research has focused upon the *function* of leadership.[19] The consensus is that leadership style should be situational; that is, appropriate to the time, place, culture, and people involved. Thus, the leader should operate within a continuum as described in Exhibit 4-2. However, in an advanced, technological society, the middle-to-right-side range of the continuum is preferable, especially when dealing with knowledge workers. The words in the center of the continuum highlight the dominant style in each leadership posture from telling to complete delegation. The diagonal line symbolizes the delicate balance between leader authority and group freedom. This balance shifts according to whether the authority is shared or centered in the ruling person or class. For example, an authoritarian leader dictates policy and tells the group members, whereas, in a group that has much freedom and authority is wholly shared, the leader abdicates total control in favor of total delegation.

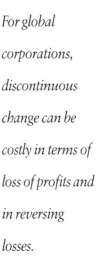

For global corporations, discontinuous change can be costly in terms of loss of profits and in reversing losses.

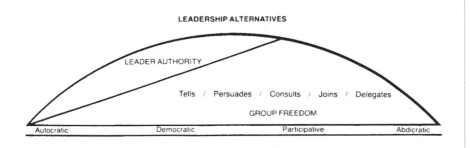

EXHIBIT 4-2. LEADERSHIP IS SITUATIONAL AND OPERATES WITHIN A CONTINUUM OF ALTERNATIVE STYLES.

The trend is now away from leadership centered in a single person, to members of a group contributing toward the leadership function by sharing talent and resources. The research of social scientists confirms that participation and involvement of members in the decision-making process can result in more effective and productive behavior. In terms of participative management this principle is expressed as follows: Those who will be substantially affected by decisions should be involved in those decisions. But it takes a skillful and competent leader to implement such an ideal.[20] According to Gambrell and Stevens,[21] to maximize the chances of a positive outcome the following skills need to be used to effectively facilitate organizational change.

- ❑ Unbiased open-mindedness
- ❑ Good strategic planning abilities
- ❑ Commitment to leadership; a history of commitment
- ❑ Team building skills
- ❑ Good communication skills

Synergistic organizational or institutional forms encourage self-actualization. But throughout this process these new human systems must educate and train their members in new interpersonal and organizational skills, so that adherents can communicate and cooperate across cultures, and act together for mutual benefit. It also implies helping participants to conserve and develop human and natural resources for the common good. Finally, it means that leaders must acquire and practice a partnership or collaborative form of power; namely, that of group initiative and cooperative action.

In the literature of education and training today, there is increasing emphasis on use of left/right brain learning activities. It appears that certain capacities are associated with either side of the cortex. Similarly, every person has qualities that are associated with both the female and male psyche. Holistic learning of males would include cultivation of those aspects commonly associated with the feminine character, and vice versa for the female. Furthermore, it has also been observed that one of the major problems with global leadership, whether political or corporate, is its male domination. Many decision makers tend to be chauvinistic and skewed toward the male perception of "reality" and the male approach to problem-solving. If we are to have synergistic leadership, male and female thinking and powers must be integrated. Perhaps the world's persistent, unsolved problems—mass unemployment, hunger, violence, aggression, underutilization of human resources, among others exist partly because our attempts to manage them have been so lopsided. That is, over one half of the human race, women, are too frequently excluded from the decision-making process and power. Synergy is thwarted as long as beliefs, attitudes, and traditions in which distinctions are made of people's intrinsic worth on the basis of gender prevail.

The trend is now away from leadership centered in a single person, to members of a group contributing toward the leadership function by sharing talent and resources.

Leaders who promote planned change in the work culture practice synergistic leadership that:

- Emphasizes quality of life, rather than just quantity of goods/services.
- Promotes concepts of interdependence and cooperation, rather than just competition.
- Encourages work and technology in harmony with nature, rather than conquering it and avoiding environmental/ecological considerations.
- Is conscious of corporate social responsibility and goals, rather than just technical efficiency and production.
- Creates an organizational culture that encourages self-achievement and fulfillment through participation, rather than dogmatism and dependency.
- Restates relevant traditional values such as personal integrity, work ethic, respect for other's property, individual responsibility, and social order.
- Encourages the capacity for intuition, creativity, flexibility, openness, group sensitivity, and goal-oriented planning.

To exercise any leadership in complex systems in transition today is a challenge. It is an illusion that the single leader or decision maker can make the difference, and this explains why so many people internationally are disillusioned with contemporary political "leaders." Now, only the combined brainpower of multiple executives or teams is most appropriate, so that many become involved with their unique resources and mobilized toward complex solutions. Contemporary changes in markets and workers call for a new type of leadership development.

Innovative leaders assist people and their social institutions to build upon, yet to transcend, their cultural past. Anthropologist Edward Hall recalled that formerly one stayed relatively close to home so behaviors around us were fairly predictable. But today we constantly interact personally or through media with strangers, often at great distances from our home. Such extensions have widened our range of human contact and caused our "world" to shrink. Multicultural leaders not only have insights and skills for coping with such changed circumstances, but readily share them with their colleagues and systems. To be comfortable with changing cultural diversity and dissonance, we must literally move beyond the perceptions, imprints, and instructions of our own culture.

Cultures worldwide are in the midst of profound change, and nowhere is this more evident than in the matter of *work culture*.[22] But the speed and progress of that change varies considerably by where one is located. For example, the people in Brazil's Amazon who were thought locked into the hunting stage of human development and tribal culture are being catapulted into industrial culture. There are farmers everywhere, products of the agricultural stage of development, who because of new technologies are being swept up into a post-industrial

To exercise any leadership in complex systems in transition today is a challenge.

culture. There are manufacturers, formed by the Industrial Age, who in decades are being forced into the metaindustrial work culture. Similarly, tribes in Africa or Latin America must cope with rapid modernization, while former Communists countries must quickly abandon centralized planning to learn the intricacies of free market economies and entrepreneurship. So while the pace of change varies, its focus and challenge differ by region and global community.

LEADERSHIP IN CHANGING ORGANIZATIONAL CULTURE

Organizations grow in many ways. If global managers are to be effective leaders, then we need not only understand the influence of culture upon organizations, but use that culture to improve performance, productivity, and service. Organizations create culture; to be renewed and restructured, they alter it. Organizational culture represents understandings and practices regarding the nature of people and the entity—whether it is a corporation, association, or government agency—about reality and truth, vocational activity, or work. Such organizational culture is manifested in values, attitudes, beliefs, myths, rituals, performance, artifacts, and myriad other ways.

Coping with Organizations' Cultural Differences

What have these people in common?

❑ Hari just received his MBA from an American university and is employed in his own country of Pakistan for a Middle Eastern airline.
❑ Frank has been an American expatriate for six years and has been reassigned to corporate headquarters in Boise, Idaho.
❑ Mohammed, an Egyptian who was educated in Britain, is posted temporarily for additional training at a factory of his transnational employer in Fort Wayne, Indiana.
❑ Lee is leaving his native Korea to supervise a construction crew of his fellow nationals in Saudi Arabia where his company has a subcontract with the U.S. petroleum manufacturer.
❑ Alicia, a Hispanic high school graduate, has just been recruited to work in a government law enforcement agency that has been dominated until now by Anglo males.

Each of these individuals may face with the problem of integration into an unfamiliar organizational culture. Perhaps, it would be better to think of it as the challenge of acculturation. Their approach to the different institutional contexts can facilitate their success or failure in the corporation or agency. Writing on "The Organization as a Microcul-

Organizations create culture; to be renewed and restructured, they alter it.

ture," Leonard Nadler reminds persons that their "cultural baggage" can impose limitations on creativity.

There are many dimensions to this concept of the organization as a microculture, which are influenced by the larger macroculture in which it operates. Everything the reader has learned previously in this text about culture in general can be applied to organizational culture.

The organization's culture affects employee, supplier, and customer behavior, as well as community relationships. Furthermore, the issues of this chapter have implications regionally, nationally, and internationally. The corporate culture of Coca-Cola influences and is influenced by the regional culture wherein are located its headquarters and principal activities, Atlanta, Georgia. That same corporate culture interfaces with American culture in its domestic marketing, as well as when it produces and sells its soft drinks abroad, whether in China or Mexico.

The organization's culture has a powerful impact on the worker's or member's morale and productivity. It even influences the organization's image of itself which, in turn, is communicated to its public. Those associated with the organization can either accept or reject its culture. If it is the former, then the member may conform or modify that culture. If it is the latter, then its personnel become frustrated or leave that organization.

Organizations are actually *microcultures* that operate within the larger context of a national macroculture. Thus, an organizational culture may be the Mexican government, an American multinational or foundation, a British university or trust, the Roman Catholic Church, the Russian airline, Swedish Employers Federation, or the Association of Venezuelan Executives. Other transcultural organizations are synergistic in their structural make-up, such as UNESCO, International Red Cross, The European Union, Management Centre Europe, or OPEC.

Exhibit 4-3 illustrates many of the aspects of organizational culture.

There are aspects of an organization's culture that are formal, explicit, and overt, just as there are dimensions that are informal, implicit, and covert. Fundamentally, the organization, viewed as an energy exchange system, inputs into the social system information and resources. Physical and psychic energy pours into the organization, along with capital, to be transformed into output. In attempting to achieve its goals and mission, the organizational culture is further influenced by leadership practices, norms and standards, rules and regulations, attitudes and principles, ethics and values, policies and practices, structures and technologies, products (artifacts) and services, roles and relationships. To facilitate these activities, cultural mandates or traditions are established concerning dress codes, work hours, work space and facilities, tools and equipment, communication procedures and special language, rewards and recognitions, as well as various personnel provisions. The resulting cultural behavior and activities are manifested in the outputs, such as products, services, personnel, or public information.

There are aspects of an organization's culture that are formal, explicit, and overt, just as there are dimensions that are informal, implicit, and covert.

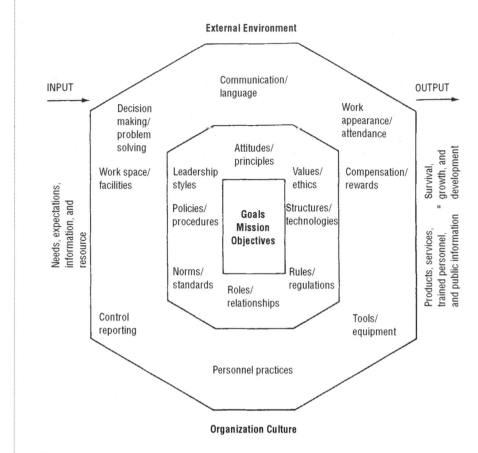

External Environment

INPUT →

OUTPUT →

Communication/language

Decision making/problem solving

Work appearance/attendance

Attitudes/principles

Work space/facilities

Leadership styles

Values/ethics

Compensation/rewards

Policies/procedures

Goals Mission Objectives

Structures/technologies

Norms/standards

Roles/relationships

Rules/regulations

Control reporting

Tools/equipment

Personnel practices

Needs, expectations, information, and resource

Survival, growth, and development / Products, services, trained personnel, and public information

Organization Culture

EXHIBIT 4-3. CONCEPTUAL ILLUSTRATION OF THE VARIOUS ASPECTS OF ORGANIZATIONAL CULTURE.

The largest transnational corporations adapt themselves to the culture and circumstances in which they operate, while trying to retain that which gives them their distinctiveness and accomplishments.

An organization as large as General Motors, for example, has many subcultures in the form of divisions for manufacturing, marketing, and other functions or models of cars. It may have many domestic and foreign subsidiaries that also have unique subcultures. The largest transnational corporations adapt themselves to the culture and circumstances in which they operate, while trying to retain that which gives them their distinctiveness and accomplishments. The GM culture is quite different from that of competitors within one's own country, such as Ford Motor Company, but it is especially different from a comparable company abroad. The formal aspects of GM's culture are like the tip of an iceberg—its overt activities are written objectives, technological processes, raw materials, and manpower skills; the informal or covert elements involve attitudes and feelings, values and group norms that dominate the organization and affect both productivity and quality control. When General Motors, for example, opened a subsidiary plant in Juarez, Mexico, it developed a Mexican-American management team to create a plant culture appropriate to that community. It provided the Mexican and American managers and their spouses with language and cultural training to enhance the success of the intercultural operation.

Today most successful corporate cultures are in the process of transition from an industrial to metaindustrial work environment.[23] Many global organizations are reengineering themselves as well as their subcultures. Contemporary organizations, like General Motors, must cope with more than the cultural differences in companies or divisions that occur because of acquisitions, mergers, or foreign expansion. They also struggle to transform an industrial into a technological work culture centered around information processing and microelectronics.

Sherwood[24] makes a compelling case for high-performance, high-commitment work cultures, citing many progressive companies, such as General Electric, Proctor and Gamble, Digital Equipment, and Ford, which are innovating in the redesign of work and organizational structure. Sherwood maintains that personnel exhibit energy because work is challenging and significant; in such firms, continuous "learning" is emphasized and rewarded for quality performance. He recommends as a tool for this purpose design teams to redesign sociotechnical systems.

Sherwood believes that management will succeed in gaining a competitive advantage only when leaders change their views about people and the design of work, linking human and technical resources in a collaborative work system.

Whether in a corporation, association, or government agency, culture is multifaceted and can be diagnosed in various ways, such as in terms of the subsystems that compose it. One model proposed in this chapter uses ten major classifications for organizational analysis:

Culture is multifaceted and can be diagnosed in various ways, such as in terms of the subsystems that compose it.

1. Identity or image and mission—its rationale
2. Space and scope—its demarcations
3. Attitudes, beliefs, and myths—its philosophy
4. Values and norms—its priorities and standards
5. Communication and languages—its media and message
6. Processes and learnings—its operational mode
7. Personnel and leadership—its recognitions and rewards for behavior models
8. Rites, rituals, and feeding habits—its customs and traditions
9. Relationships—its roles and their interface
10. Look, style, and reputation—its appearance and public aura.

TRANSNATIONAL DIFFERENCES AND ORGANIZATIONAL CULTURES

Because the microculture is a reflection of the macroculture, it stands to reason that the location of an organization will be affected by the culture of the community that surrounds it. There is an interaction continuously between the majority and minority cultures, each influencing the other. Thus, when a manager goes abroad, outside his or her native culture, the organizational culture that person represents should adapt to local circumstances. Furthermore, the organizational cultures in the host country with whom the expatriate interfaces are quite unique manifestations of the indigenous culture. Should this person who is a foreigner in a strange land go to work for one of the local companies or government agencies as a consultant or even an employee, the individual should expect that things will be done quite differently from "back home" and that people in the native organization will behave very differently from colleagues in one's own country.

The state of technological, economic, and social development of a nation will also affect the organizational culture. First World nations, for instance, may have more organizations using the emerging adhocracy model, while developing countries might still use the industrial or traditional organizational modes. Typical managerial activities such as planning and innovating, organizing and controlling, recruiting and selecting, evaluating and rewarding/punishing, leading and relating, communicating, problem-solving and decision-making, negotiating and managing conflict, supervision, and training are all conducted within the context of the dominant local culture. Thus, that unique people's perception of their world and of human beings, their motivational orientation, their ways of associating, their value and activity emphasis, will be reflected in the social institutions they establish. A corporation or government agency mirrors the images and imprints of the indigenous population to various degrees.

Perhaps some examples of such cross-cultural differences in organizations and their workers will best illustrate this point. In the old traditional Latin organization that is rapidly disappearing, the supervisor-subordinate relationships are such that an employee would never *directly* approach a foreman or manager to discuss a problem—in the old authoritarian mode, one does not question the boss. In Japan the corporation's first duty is to its employees, and it is not considered demeaning for the worker to identify with the organization that employs him or her. In Japanese industry, the adversary labor-management relationship is considered unhealthy and an elitist attitude from the industrial revolution. For the most part, corporate, not government enterprises provide for employee welfare. In fact, corporate elitism is frowned upon, and group harmony is accented.

Consider that a language is a means of communicating within a particular culture. There are approximately 3,000 different languages, and each represents a different perceptual world. Many nations may share an official language, such as English, but have a variety of versions of it, such as British or American. In India, the official language is Hindi, but English is a "link" language among fifteen major languages and numerous dialects; organizations in that country may be expected to speak the official language, but only 30% of the population do so, and personnel in many companies will probably speak the local language and all that it implies.

There are approximately 3,000 different languages, and each represents a different perceptual world.

Thus, in the matter of organizational communications, a social institution may reflect the nation's language homogeneity or heterogeneity.

Consider the cross-cultural implications of *time* and *time consciousness*. In some countries, company representatives may start a meeting within an hour of the time agreed upon, and the sequence of one's arrival at that staff conference may depend upon one's status in the organization, or one's age. The length of the work day differs among cultures—in some starting and stopping is exact, and may be spelled out in a union contract, whereas in others it goes by the sunrise and sunset, or the heat of the day, or the seasons.

The rhythm of life for a people is determined by their stage of human development; therefore for populations in the pre-industrial nations, time is shaped by the natural cycles of agriculture; whereas in industrialized nations, the artificial time of the clock and the assembly line regulate workers. In the superindustrial society, time becomes a scarce resource, while in underdeveloped nations time is abundant. Sociologist Daniel Bell reminds American "clock-watchers" that the computer with its nanoseconds is considered a time saver in organizational cultures of high technology. For some populations, the rhythm of life is linear, but for others it is cyclical.

The culture of a work system must be adapted to the macroculture in which it operates. Organizational leaders everywhere can learn from each other, regardless of where in the world the entity functions.

The transnational corporation that moves beyond the culture of a single country and operates comfortably in the multicultures of many nations obviously will develop a unique microculture of its own. Its organization model and environment will reflect the synergy of the diverse macrocultures in which it functions, as well as the varying managerial approaches to business, government, and people. Thus, far-flung business activities require a new organizational culture that is able to accommodate itself to cross-cultural realities. Japanese business leaders, for example, are gradually changing their attitudes towards mergers and acquisitions. Although their culture and language disinclined them toward such actions, farsighted executives now realize its necessity as part of the global marketplace. The restructured Japanese organizations may produce both synergy and strength.

The multinational entity becomes a conglomerate of organizational cultures. For example, through acquisitions and mergers, the corporation may develop a variety of overseas subsidiaries. The central base operation then impacts considerably upon the organizational culture of its affiliate, but that company abroad inputs and influences the headquarters' culture.

The multinational enterprise adapts to the larger culture in which it functions, depending on its experiences with the external environment. Terpstra[25] identifies five factors to be considered in international business:

Far-flung business activities require a new organizational culture that is able to accommodate itself to cross-cultural realities.

- *Cultural Variability*—the degree to which conditions within a macroculture are at a low or high, stable, or unstable rate. The more turbulent the macroculture, for instance, the more unpredictable are business operations. The internal structure and processes in that situation requiring rapid adjustment to change, would demand open channels of communication, decentralized decision-making, and predominance of local expertise.
- *Cultural Complexity*—that is the issue of high- and low-context cultures. It requires a response from corporate leaders that considers the covert and overt approaches of the macroculture.
- *Cultural Hostility*—the degree to which conditions locally are threatening to organizational goals, norms, values, et al. Depending upon how the transnational corporation is perceived, the indigenous environment may range from munificent to malevolent in terms of acceptability, cooperation, political climate, material and human resources, capital and good will. In response, the organizational culture may range from integration and collaboration to tightening up and finally being forced to leave.

Professor Terpstra maintains that the previous three dimensions occur within cultures, but that the next two can be observed among macrocultures.

- *Cultural Heterogeneity*—the degree to which cultures are dissimilar or similar. It is easier for a transnational corporation to deal with a culture that is relatively homogeneous, or like the base culture (e.g., English-based multinationals would have an edge possibly in British Commonwealth nations). But when a culture is diverse and disparate, then it is difficult for the central headquarters to coordinate the behavior of subsidiaries and their employees. Management may have to be more differentiated, semiautonomous, and decentralized units may have to be established. Expatriates from the base culture may be more prone to culture shock on assignment in the host culture.
- *Cultural Interdependence*—the degree of sensitivity of the culture to respond to conditions and developments in other cultures. This dimension may range from economic dependence on other nations for raw materials, supplies, and equipment, to adaptation and adoption of new technology and processes from other interacting cultures, to being subject to scrutiny in the host culture for attitudes and actions that occurred on the part of the corporation in another culture.

Thus, all such factors impact upon the multinational's organizational culture, influencing decisions, planning, information systems, and conflict resolution. Terpstra cites a variety of strategies that a transnational corporation can use to cope with the vagaries of international operations—environmental impact assessments, comparative and/or cluster

The more turbulent the macroculture, for instance, the more unpredictable are business operations.

analysis, cultural scanning and intelligence systems, computer simulations, social cost/benefit analysis, systems dynamics and modeling, social indicators/quality-of-life monitoring, risk analysis and scenario writing, trend extrapolation and technological forecasting, and establishment of external affairs units. For a multinational to be effective, synergy should occur between the host, base, and international business environments. It requires adaptations within the transnational organization's culture to factors of language and communication, law and politics, values and beliefs, education and training, technology and material resources, and local social organization.

Probably, the source of greatest cross-cultural difference in organizations throughout the world is in the concept of management. For the global manager, there is much to be gained from mutual exchanges on this issue of organizational culture.

PEOPLE AND FUTURE ORGANIZATIONAL CULTURES

There must be a fit between people and their organizational culture if synergy is to occur. Effective global leaders will direct more effort toward promoting that match.

One strategy is to carefully search and select personnel who will be comfortable in a particular system, then acculturate them to a strong culture. Strong culture firms further ensure commitment with transcendental values. Organizational cultures reaffirm continually the company folklore on watershed events in their pasts and "how we do things around here." Behavior models among management display the same traits and become mentors to young proteges. To better manage organizational energies, the strong culture offers a consistent set of implicit understandings that help in dealing with ambiguities of business politics and relationships.

Another strategy is to adapt the organization to its people, especially in terms of a particular place or time. It is not only plant and equipment that can rust and deteriorate. Within human systems, values and norms, policies and practices, leadership and technologies can also lag or become obsolete. That may call for planned renewal when the people and their productivity are being undermined by outdated or archaic approaches or processes. In the behavioral sciences, technologies have been created for such organization development (OD). Consultants, either internal or external, are used to solve people and structural problems, while facilitating planned change by management of the organization's culture. More recently, a new type of consultant is emerging who is concerned about promoting organizational transformation (OT). The emphasis is upon the practices of transformational leadership or new management; upon

The source of greatest cross-cultural difference in organizations throughout the world is in the concept of management.

organizational vision and futuring regarding what the organization should become in the light of changing times and peoples.

Corporate culture is dynamic, and leaders should not underestimate the adaptive changes necessary for survival.

The new organizational culture should enable people to—

❑ Spend their lives on something worthwhile that will outlast them.
❑ Live a life of consequence without stress and undue cultural restraints.
❑ Preserve for tomorrow what we can use up today.
❑ Value the work as much as we did the work ethic.
❑ Accept differences and appreciate similarities.
❑ Seize opportunities for personal and professional development, while overcoming the disadvantages to developing one's potential.

Relative to the people in tomorrow's organization, it is obvious that these will be largely knowledge/technical and service workers of multicultural backgrounds. Because managerial skills will be scarce and in demand, one can envision the development of a cadre of executives and administrators capable of being transferred across the traditional boundaries of nations, industries, and public/private sectors. Dr. Chris Argyris[26] believes that the organizational culture of the future will include personnel policies that—

❑ Encourage employees to be authentic with one another and management.
❑ Fully appreciate the value of human resources, as well as other factors that contribute to organization success.
❑ Foster individual responsibility for career development.
❑ Take a holistic approach to promoting organizational health.

Significantly, management consultants are beginning to appreciate that an organization's informal culture has as much influence on corporate effectiveness as the formal structure of jobs, authority, technical and financial procedures. Thus, the target now for planned change must be the organizational climate, along with the work attitudes and habits of employees. Organizations of the future will be excellent to the extent that they maximize their human energy assets, and minimize their human energy losses. They must be able to capitalize on ad hoc, unstructured relationships among people, to cope effectively with uncertainty and accelerating change, and to cooperate in multicultural environments.

Many scholars believe that we are now entering into the period of the "Third Industrial Revolution." Mechanization and computerization were the focus of the first and second industrial revolutions. But the current revolution, sometimes called metaindustrial, centers around the needs and aspirations of employees in the design and implementation of production and other work systems. Thus, the shift in these three work

An organization's informal culture has as much influence on corporate effectiveness as the formal structure of jobs, authority, technical and financial procedures.

revolutions has been from products to things to people and information processing.

Cornish[27] lists possible ways our lives may change by the year 2025. According to Cornish the evolving "cyber society" will affect technology and the world of humankind more profoundly than the Industrial Revolution. He cautions that the power of new technology be used wisely remembering that current value systems were formed over thousands of years when agriculture, the pastoral life and industry were the mainstays of our world. During the cyber era, the new resources offered by technology can bridge the gap between people everywhere to sort out and confront issues as we struggle to manage the future.

Cornish predicts:

❑ Some sort of infotech will be implanted in our bodies making it unnecessary to carry credit cards, identification, passport etc.
❑ As a global culture arises from technology, languages and cultures may disappear.
❑ With the gigantic increase in information at libraries and databases, a critical question will arise, What do our children really need to learn?
❑ Nations will become more economically specialized, squeezing out other international competitors.
❑ If a computer program can win at speed chess, a financial software package may be able to make fast paced decisions about stock and bond investments and commodity exchanges.
❑ Technology will allow citizens more input into government, perhaps voting at home during elections or on current issues.
❑ Electronic gambling may be a major social problem in the future as it moves into people's homes and billion-dollar jackpots are commonplace.
❑ People's attention may become the world's most precious resource.

To humanize the workplace Michael Maccoby[28] proposes the application of four principles:

1. *Security*—employees must be free from fear and anxiety concerning health and safety, income, and future employment.
2. *Equity*—employees should be compensated commensurate with their contributions to the value of the service or product.
3. *Individuation*—employees should have maximum autonomy in determining the rhythm of their work and in planning how it should be done.
4. *Democracy*—employees should, whenever possible, manage themselves, be involved in decision-making that affects their work, and accept greater responsibility in the work of the organization.

Efforts to improve the organizational culture based on such premises can be found throughout the world, especially in North America and

The evolving "cyber society" will affect technology and the world of humankind more profoundly than the Industrial Revolution.

western Europe. Managers, consultants, and researchers are cooperating in sharing their findings relative to quality of work life and participation experiments.

Convergence of endeavors to "humanize the organizational environment or work culture" is happening on a universal scale and calls for more synergy on the part of corporate and government leaders.

Organizational Change in Transitional Economies

The decade of the '90s produced remarkable alterations in nations and organizations under totalitarian, communist rule, as well as in developing countries, where economies generally have moved toward greater freedom and emphasis on human rights. The transition from centralized planning of socialist economies to a free-market economy and political democracy is evident from Eastern Europe, Africa, and the People's Republic of China.

As the macroculture shifts, so does the microculture of institutions. Thus, organizational cultures within these societies are experiencing profound transformations. Free enterprise within the private sector is being encouraged, while the public sector companies are being sold to investors or cooperatives.

Culture is a dynamic concept that changes, as does the way we communicate it.

One of the most dramatic examples is in Germany within its two Western and Eastern regions. With political unification comes economic integration progress, but progress is slow and unemployment is high. Consider the executive challenges involved in integrating such disparate organizational cultures, one conditioned by capitalist and the other by communist systems! Imagine the differences in workers—one group attuned to participation, innovation, and profit motivation, and the other to totalitarianism, bureaucracy, and autocratic management.

SUMMARY

Global leaders need to understand and analyze the impact of culture on organizations. Furthermore, they should lead in influencing cultural change within their institutions. When groups of people formulate an organization, its culture reflects that of the larger community, and impacts behavior both within and without the enterprise. The human and material energy exchanged through the organization is affected by culture, which may foster or undermine productivity and profits. Organizational culture may motivate or obstruct high performance.

Culture is a dynamic concept that changes, as does the way we communicate it. Those with the mindset and skills of a global manager exercise proactive leadership in altering both the macro and micro levels of culture. To cope effectively with accelerating change, global managers continuously revise their images of self, role, and organization, so that attitudes and behavior are modified accordingly.

Although our outlooks on change and leadership are culturally conditioned, global managers realize that the new work culture worldwide requires us not only to be open to change, but to build it into our social systems. Thus, we must stay relevant in meeting human needs by creating new markets, processes, products, and services.

Effective leadership styles are dependent to a degree on the people and culture at a given point in time. Generally, the metaindustrial work culture calls for more participative, team-oriented management that responds rapidly and synergistically to the changing environment. In the emerging work culture, leadership opportunities are shared with competent knowledge workers, regardless of gender, race, religion, or nationality. The underlying assumption of this chapter is that global managers should be change makers, and this begins with one's self!

REFERENCES

1. Benveniste, G. *The Twenty-first Century Organization,* San Francisco, CA: Jossey-Bass, 1994.
2. Bennis, W. *An Invented Life: Reflections on Leadership and Change,* Reading, MA: Addison-Wesley, 1993.
3. O'Hara-Devereaux, M. and Johansen, R. *Globalwork-Bridging Distance, Culture & Time,* San Francisco, CA: Jossey-Bass, 1994. Also see, Harris, P. R. *New Work Culture: HRD Transformational Management Strategies,* Amherst, MA: Human Resource Development Press, 1998.
4. Epstein, C. F. *Deceptive Distinctions: Sex, Gender, and Social Order,* New Haven, CT: Yale University Press, 1989. Morrison, A. M. *The New Leaders-Guidelines on Leadership Diversity in America,* San Francisco, CA: Jossey-Bass, 1992.
5. Morrison, A. M. *The New Leaders—Guidelines on Leadership Diversity in America,* San Francisco, CA: Jossey-Bass, 1992.
6. Kaufman, H. *The Limits of Organizational Change,* Rutgers, NJ: Transaction Publishers, 1994.
7. Drucker, P. F. *The New Realities,* New York, NY: Harper & Row, 1989. See also, *The Future of Industrial Man.* Rutgers, NJ: Transaction, Publishers, 1994.
8. Christopher, W. C. *Management for the 1980s,* Englewood Cliffs, NJ: Prentice Hall, 1980. Also see Hammer, M. and Champy, J. *Reengineering the Corporation: A Manifesto for Business Revolution,* New York, NY: Harper/Collins, 1993.
9. Moran R. T. and Riesenberger, J. R. *The Global Challenge: Building the New Worldwide Enterprise,* London: McGraw-Hill, 1994.
10. Woodcok, M. and Francis, D. *25 Training Activities for Creating and Managing Change,* Amherst, MA: HRD Press, 1994 (accompanying training video is entitled *Managing Change Creatively).*
11. Grove, A. S. *Only the Paranoid Survive,* New York: Currency: Doubleday, 1996.
12. *The Economist,* "When Companies Connect—How the Internet Will Change Business," June 26–July 2, 1999, Special Survey Insert, pp. 1–40.

13. Woodcok, M. and Francis, D. *25 Training Activities for Creating and Managing Change,* Amherst, MA: HRD Press, 1994 (accompanying training video is entitled *Managing Change Creatively).*

14. Hammer, M. "Reengineering and the Process-Oriented Corporation," EFI International 1995 Executive Forum, Honeywell, Orlando, FL. See also, Limerick, D. and Cunnington, B. *Managing the New Organization—A Blueprint for Networks and Strategic Alliances;* Bergquist, W. *The Postmodern Organization-Mastering the Art of Irreversible Change,* San Francisco, CA: Jossey-Bass, 1993.

15. Beatty, R. W. and Ulrich, D. "Re-Energizing the Mature Organization," *Organizational Dynamics,* Summer 1991, Vol. 20.

16. Harris, D. School of Business and Management, United States International University, San Diego, CA.

17. Pritchett, P. and Pound, R. *The Employee Handbook for Organizational Change,* Pritchett, P. *The Employee Handbook of New Work Habits for a Radically Changing World,* 1994. Copies are available from Pritchett & Associates, Inc. (P.O. Box 802889, Dallas, TX 75380, USA; tel: 1-800-992-5922).

18. Ansoff, H. I. *Implanting Strategic Management,* Englewood Cliffs, NJ: Prentice Hall, 1994; Nutt, P. C. and Backer, R. W. *Strategic Management of Public and Third Sector Organizations—A Handbook for Leaders,* San Francisco, CA: Jossey-Bass, 1992.

19. Freeman, F. H., Knott, K. B., and Schwartz, F. H. (eds.) *Leadership Education Sourcebook,* 5th ed. Greensboro, NC: Center for Creative Leadership, 1994; Sayles, L. *The Working Leader: The Triumph of High Performance over Conventional Management Practice.* New York, NY: The Free Press, 1993.

20. Buker, E. A., Leiserson, M. A., and Rinehard, J. A., (eds.), *Taking Part: Ingredients for Leadership, Participation, and Empowerment,* Lantham, MD: University Press of America, Inc., 1994.

21. Gambrell, S. and Stevens, C. "Moving Through the Three Phases of Organizational Change," *International Management,* July/August, 1992, pp. 4–6.

22. Harris, P. R. *The New Work Culture—HRD Transformational Management Strategies,* Amherst, MA: Human Resource Development Press, 1998.

23. Bellingham, R., Cohen, B., Edwards, M. R., and Allen, J. (eds.), *The Corporate Culture Sourcebook,* Amherst, MA: Human Resource Development Press, 1994.

24. Sherwood, J. "Creating Work Culture with Competitive Advantages," *Organizational Dynamics,* Winter 1988, pp. 5–26.

25. Terpstra, V. and David, K. *The Cultural Environment of International Business,* Cincinnati, OH: Southwest Publishing Co., 1985. Also see Hofstede, G. *Cultures and Organizations,* New York, NY: McGraw-Hill, 1991.

26. Argyris, C. *Knowledge for Action—A Guide to Overcoming Barriers to Organizational Change,* San Francisco, CA: Jossey-Bass, 1993.

27. Cornish, E. "The Cyber Future," *The Futurist,* 1996, World Future Society, Bethesda, MD.

28. Maccoby, M. *The Leader—The New Face of American Management,* New York, NY: Simon & Schuster, 1981. Also see, Ginzberg, E. (ed.) *Executive Talent-Developing and Keeping the Best People,* Rutgers, NJ: Transaction Publishers, 1994.

LEADERSHIP IN CULTURAL SYNERGY

The complexity and shrinking of today's world literally forces people to capitalize on their differences.

Synergy, which comes from the Greek word meaning "working together,"

1. Represents a dynamic process.
2. Involves adapting and learning.
3. Involves the joint action of many in which the total effect is greater than the sum of effects when acting independently.
4. Creates an integrated solution.
5. Does not signify compromise, yet in true synergy nothing is given up or lost.

Synergy is cooperative or combined action. It can occur when diverse or disparate groups of people work together. The objective is to increase effectiveness by sharing perceptions, insights, and knowledge. The complexity and shrinking of today's world literally forces people to *capitalize* on their differences.

The very differences in the world's people can lead to mutual growth and accomplishment that is more than the single contribution of each party. As people, we can go beyond awareness of our own cultural heritage to produce something greater by cooperation and collaboration.

Cultural synergy builds upon similarities and fuses differences resulting in more effective human activities and systems. The very diversity of people can be used to enhance problem solving by combined action. Using information and technology to promote cooperation among disparate elements in a human system creates something better than existed by separate endeavors.

Since our beginnings as a species, we have shared information and experience, either formally or informally. Culture itself is an attempt, consciously or unconsciously, by a people to transmit to future generations their acquired wisdom and insight relative to their knowledge, beliefs, customs, traditions, morals, law, art, communication, and habits. Peers in a particular career, trade, or profession have long banded together to exchange ideas and pursue a common interest. Opportunities for the practice of synergy will take on more urgency within the global electronic business community as computers and the Internet permit unprecedented possibilities for collaboration worldwide, regionally and locally.

Some cultures are more synergistic and inclined toward cooperation, while other cultures are inclined toward competition and conflict. The late anthropologist, Ruth Benedict, studied this phenomenon. Her research was amplified by ground breaking humanistic psychologist, Abraham Maslow. A summary of their characterizations of "high-synergy" and "low-synergy" societies is presented in Exhibit 5-1.

In terms of the model described in Exhibit 5-1, analyze various cultures throughout the world as to their synergistic relations or their lack of same. Japan and Sweden are seemingly two national cultures that are high synergistically, while the Balkan countries, as well as Iraq, would seem less so. The most dramatic example of creating synergy among national cultures is occurring within the European Community and Parliament. Sometimes the diverse membership can agree on policies and procedures, such as in establishing a common European Space Agency; on other occasions, as in attempting a common euro currency some members opted out of the plan. For humanity to succeed in space development, for instance, space culture will have to be highly synergistic. Space is a place for synergy because the high risk, the huge cost, and the complexity of living and working on the high frontier demand it.[1]

SYNERGY IN ORGANIZATIONAL CULTURE

It is critical to understand the importance of synergy when working or managing teams and organizations. Global leaders can promote cultural synergy, thereby influencing social change in human behavior and improving system effectiveness.

According to Adler,[2] there are five strategies when working in teams or managing in the global marketplace. Often, Adler states, a balance is created by using all these options when the appropriate business situation calls for it.

1. *Cultural dominance.* When one organization is in a more powerful position than the other, the more powerful organization will dominate, usually continuing to do things as they are done in the

Some cultures are more synergistic and inclined toward cooperation, while other cultures are inclined toward competition and conflict.

EXHIBIT 5-1

High-Synergy Society	Low-Synergy Society
❑ Emphasis is upon cooperation for mutual advantage.	❑ Uncooperative, very competitive culture; enhances rugged individualistic and "dog-eat-dog" attitudes.
❑ Conspicuous for a nonaggressive social order.	❑ Aggressive and antagonistic behavior toward one another, leading to either psychological or physical violence toward the other.
❑ Social institutions promote individual and group development.	❑ Social arrangements self-centered; collaboration is not reinforced as desired behavior.
❑ Society idealizes win/win.	❑ Society adheres to win/lose approach;
❑ Leadership fosters sharing wealth and advantage for the common good. Cooperatives are encouraged, and poverty is fought.	❑ Leadership encourages private or individual gain and advantage, especially by the power elite; poverty is tolerated, even ignored.
❑ Society seeks to use community resources and talents for the commonwealth and encourages development of human potential of all citizenry.	❑ Society permits exploitation of poor and minorities, and tolerates the siphoning of its wealth by privileged few; develops power elites and leaves undeveloped the powerless.
❑ Open system of secure people who tend to be benevolent, helpful, friendly and generous; its heroes are altruistic and philanthropic.	❑ Closed system with insecure people who tend toward suspiciousness, ruthlessness and clannishness; idealizes the "strong man" concerned with greed and acquisition.
❑ Belief system, religion or philosophy is comforting and life is consoling; emphasis is on the god of love; power is to be used for benefit of whole community; individuals/groups are helped to work out hurt and humiliations.	❑ Belief system is frightening, punishing, terrifying; members are psychologically beaten or humiliated by the strong; power is for personal profit; emphasis is on the god of vengeance; hatreds go deep and "blood feuds" abound; violence is the means for compensating for hurt and humiliation.
❑ Generally, the citizenry is psychologically healthy, and mutual reciprocity is evident in relationships; open to change; low rate of crime and mental illness.	❑ Generally, the citizenry tends to be defensive, jealous; mass paranoia and hostility; fears change, and advocates status quo; high rate of crime and mental illness.

home culture. "On an individual level, managers often choose the cultural dominance approach when they strongly believe their way is the only right way and especially when they perceive the situation to involve a fundamental ethical issue"

2. *Cultural accommodation.* This option is the opposite of cultural dominance. Mangers implementing this option tend to imitate the host culture, attempting to blend in. Fear often surfaces at headquarters that a manager can represent the interests of the organization properly. Examples of cultural accommodation occur when managers learn or become fluent in the native language or construct contracts using the local currency of the host culture instead of the home culture.

3. *Cultural compromise.* This approach is a combination of the first two, with both sides conceding something to work together more successfully. Most often the most powerful partner gives up less, however both sides must make concessions.

4. *Cultural avoidance.* Often Asian managers use this approach. They work and manage as if no conflict of cultures exists. This approach emphasizes saving face and is most often used when the unresolved issue is less important than the final outcome of a situation or negotiation.

5. *Cultural synergy.* This option develops new solutions that respect all cultures involved and often increases the choices for working effectively in a cross-cultural business environment. What language to conduct business in offers an example of these options When working, international business people often do not share the same language and must then decide which language to use. If, for example, a French firm insists that negotiations with the Germans be conducted in French it is an example of cultural dominance. If the Germans agree at once, it is cultural accommodation. If both sides decide that interpreters are better, their choice reflects cultural compromise. However, if the Germans and French agree to negotiate in English it is a cultural synergy approach, whereby no side will have a language advantage.

As there are high- and low-synergy societies, there are high- and low-synergy organizations. A high-synergy corporation is one in which employees cooperate for mutual advantage because the customs and traditions of the corporation or organization support such behavior. In this noncompetitive atmosphere the individual works toward his or her betterment as well as that of the group. Employees work to ensure that mutual benefits are derived from their common undertakings.

A low-synergy business is one that finds it difficult to adapt too quickly to change. Employees are not empowered and often systems and policies are more important than the customer or the people. Managers impose "their way" or organizational culture upon others, often to their mutual detriment. A better approach is being aware of a person's cultural strengths and biases in terms of their national and organizational characters, objectively evaluating what is of value and building on such foundations with sensitivity to cultural differences and opportunities for mutual growth and development.

In culturally synergistic organizations, the best of each culture is melded together without infringing on the other. This diversity and respect enables leaders to solve problems synergistically. Adler[2] advocates three steps in synergistic problem solving that high-synergy corporations would manifest.

1. *Describe the situation.* Often not as easy as it sounds when working across cultures. Actually, this is one of the most difficult and critical steps. This process involves describing the situation/problem well from the perspective of one's own culture. Then describing, from the perspective of each of the culture involved, their perception of the situation. Each individual's divergent business and cultural values will challenge us to describe and see the situation from their perspective.
2. *Culturally interpret the situation.* Global leaders in high-synergy organizations must ask, What historic and cultural assumptions exist in this cross-cultural situation? All behavior is understandable from the perspective of the person who is behaving; our cultural biases often lead us to misinterpret the logic of other culture's behavioral patterns. Role reversal is an effective tool in identifying the similarities and differences between our own cultural assumptions and actions and those of other cultures.
3. *Increasing cultural creativity.* Many alternatives are investigated and searched out in high-synergy organizations. Individuals from all cultures involved offer solutions. The resolution should be compatible with all but not imitate anyone culture's solution, transcending the behavior and patterns of each culture.

After the problem solving, implementing a culturally synergistic solution should be planned carefully. Employees need to have an awareness of their own culture as well as cross-cultural awareness of others' values, assumptions, and behaviors. Without this cultural understanding, implementation may not make sense nor be viable.

SYNERGY IN GLOBAL ORGANIZATIONS

Synergy is a dimension of organizational culture that takes on increasing importance as international business and government activities become more global in scope, more complex in practice, and more sophisticated in technology. Chapter 1 cited it as one of the characteris-

In culturally synergistic organizations, the best of each culture is melded together without infringing on the other.

tics of the global leader—the need to create cultural synergy so that the enterprise values cooperation, collaboration, and team management. Promoting synergy in and through the organization is one of the characteristics of the new work culture.

To facilitate understanding of this key concept, imagine the following scenarios for which we will later provide examples of how synergistic relations can be fostered in acquisitions, relocation, structural change, personnel change, role change, consortium formation, and global consultation.

❏ The chief executive officer of a large global corporation visits the facilities of a newly acquired subsidiary to determine which of the parent company's policies, procedures, and personnel should be utilized in the merged firm, and which approaches or strategies should be retained.

❏ A New England plant is being relocated to Alabama. Its employees have been given the opportunity to move to the South and join an enlarged workforce of local Southerners. The plant manager at the Alabama plant is a technocrat from England who immigrated to the United States five years ago.

❏ A major retailer is in the midst of profound organizational change. A traditional enterprise with branches throughout the country, it is proud of its seventy-five years of customer service and the long employment records of its faithful employees. Declining sales, fierce competition, and inflation led to the election of a new chairman of the board who has hired some new competent and effective managers, and together they have begun to shake up the corporation.

❏ A European conglomerate has purchased controlling rights of an American steel manufacturer. Key management positions have been filled with French, Italian, and German managers, and most of the competent American management has been retained. Plans are underway to improve operations and turn the company into a profitable venture.

❏ As employees become more sophisticated at computers and information processing, competent and well trained information technologists must be able to assist all.

❏ European partners are successfully involved in producing innovative aircraft at Airbus Industrie. It began with three major companies from three different countries, and eventually a fourth company/country entered into the agreement.

❏ A Canadian consulting firm agreed to assist a Mexican corporation in the use of advanced technology. It is part of a larger deal between the governments of both countries in which Mexican energy is to be supplied in return for Canadian expertise and equipment.

The common element in each of these scenarios is the opportunity to exercise leadership in cultural synergy. Differences in organizational cultures in these situations can either undermine the intended actions, or the differences can be used to enhance goal achievement.

Managers can either impose "their way" or organizational culture upon others, often to their mutual detriment, or they can be aware of a person's cultural strengths and biases, in terms of their national and organizational characters. But a better approach is to objectively evaluate what is of "value" in each of the existing enterprises, and build upon such foundations, being sensitive to cultural differences and opportunities for mutual growth and development.

There are seven specific situations when synergy in organizational culture is most desirable. They are exemplified by the previous incidents, and they include:

Acquisition. Whenever a corporation acquires or merges with another entity domestically or internationally, synergy skill is required. For organizational effectiveness, there must be a synthesis of two distinct microcultures, not just an imposition by the more powerful company. This is particularly true in the case of a newly acquired subsidiary. The executives from the parent company can do much to facilitate the integration process if they will take time to analyze the subsidiary's culture. Furthermore, this merger of two organizational worlds and climates can be aided when management from the acquired firm melds its distinct culture with the other, perhaps creating new policy, procedures, and processes, as well as corporate goals, attitudes, and strategies.

Relocation. When a company moves an existing facility and employees to another site, at home or abroad, synergistic efforts must be undertaken. Relocation services offered by the corporation must go beyond moving and new community information, as employees require orientation to the realities and opportunities of the new cultural environment.

Structural/Environmental Change. When there is a major change within the organizational structure, employees should be prepared for the new shift in policy, procedure, product or service. Planned change strategies can be used to ready personnel for reorganization and renewal without abrupt disruption of the work climate. The quickening of the work pace on understaffed operations can lead to greater resentment, exhaustion, and "burn out." Involving employees in cooperative efforts to regulate and monitor change or growth requires organizational synergy.

Personnel Change. Whenever the composition of a workforce shifts, planned endeavors are needed to integrate the new employees. In addition to hiring large numbers of women and minorities, there are many diverse cultures represented in today's workforce. The global insights and the knowledge of international markets that is gained validates the talents of heterogeneous personnel.

Managers can either impose "their way" or organizational culture upon others, often to their mutual detriment, or they can be aware of a person's cultural strengths and biases, in terms of their national and organizational characters.

Role Change. The introduction of new technology into an organization usually means that personnel roles and relationships change. In the traditional industrial-age corporation, work disciplines, units, and departments were fairly stable and separate. But in complex, post-industrial organizations the divisions between line and staff are fluid. New interpersonal skills are required that enable personnel to form quick, intense organizational relations of a cooperative, mission-oriented nature. This is evident in today's project/product teams and matrix management.

Consortium. Organizations often move outside their own orbit to seek partners who will join together for their mutual benefit. Synergy is required for a combination of institutions to pool their talent and capital for a successful operation. Project management, for instance, provides opportunities for diverse departments and activities within a single organization to come together to achieve desired objectives. This approach has brought together different companies from the same or several industries, from the same or many nations. The very complexities of the global economy demand such collaboration.

Global Consulting. Whenever a group of "experts" enters the organizational culture of a client synergistic skills are necessary. Knowingly or not, the representatives from a consulting group merge their organizational culture into the client's environment. When such assistance is rendered on an international scale, the intervention may also include two or more national cultures. Consultants should attempt to integrate themselves into the organizational culture of their customers, and not impose the mindset or systems of the consultants.

These seven dimensions can be used as a model for better understanding synergy in organizational culture.

In the transitional work environment marked by acquisitions, mergers and downsizing, many employees report dehumanizing practices by myopic managers only concerned with immediate "bottom-line" considerations. At the same time, there are wise leaders who appreciate the long term implications of a synergistic work culture and strive to create an "internal strategic unity within a chaotic external environment."[3]

TRANSFORMING THE WORK CULTURE

High-synergy organizations are part of the new work culture. Global leaders must create cultural synergy through the enterprise values of cooperation, collaboration, and team management. Promoting synergy in and through the organization is one of the characteristics of the new work culture.

Global leaders must create cultural synergy through the enterprise values of cooperation, collaboration, and team management.

It is impossible to fully describe this new work culture, but Exhibit 5-2 outlines this metaindustrial work scene in terms of eight classifications.

For the past forty years a wide range of behavioral scientists, in cooperation with executives and other organizational leaders, have been engaged in transforming the work environment from that of the industrial age toward the directions indicated in Exhibit 5-2.

Our research has identified ten general characteristics of the emerging work culture.[4] Workers at all levels in the future will generally manifest or seek more—

- ❏ Enhanced quality of work life
- ❏ Autonomy and control over their work space
- ❏ Organizational communication and information orientation
- ❏ Participation and involvement in the enterprise
- ❏ Creative organizational norms or standards
- ❏ High performance and improved productivity
- ❏ Emphasis on new technology
- ❏ Emphasis on research and development
- ❏ Emphasis on entrepreneurialism/intrapreneurialism
- ❏ Informal and synergistic relationships

SYNERGISTIC TEAMS AND MANAGEMENT

Traditional organizational models and managerial styles are gradually being replaced and reworked as they become inadequate and unproductive in the new work culture. A major transition is underway in social systems from "disappearing bureaucracies" to "emerging ad hocracies." Global leaders facilitate the transcendence from past to futuristic operations by promoting team management approaches. Whether the strategy is called a project, task force, product or business systems team, or ad hoc planning committee, work is organized around a "temporary" group that involves permanent (functional) and impermanent lines of authority. Teams are altering and designing bridges from the way we have been doing work to the way we will be working in the decades ahead. Today's microelectronic and semiconductor companies often result from the synergy of entrepreneurial teams.[5]

The dictionary defines a "team" as a number of persons associated in some joint action, while "teamwork" is described as cooperative or coordinated effort on the part of persons working together. Dyer notes that "teams are collections of people who must rely upon group collaboration if each member is to experience the optimum of success and goal achievement."[6]

Changing technology and markets have stimulated the team approach to management and multicultural and multifunctional teams are becom-

Traditional organizational models and managerial styles are gradually being replaced and reworked as they become inadequate and unproductive in the new work culture.

EXHIBIT 5-2
THE METAINDUSTRIAL WORK CULTURE*

Components of Organizational Culture	Organizational Manifestations	Metaindustrial Organizational Illustrations
Rationale and Identity	Reasons for existing Self-image Beliefs, attitudes Philosophy Space, boundaries Strategies, structures	Profitable, quality service transnational system Energy exchange system Promotion of innovation, synergy, excellence Corporate social responsibility Business computer or conceptual modeling; futuristic, long-term planning; goal- and results-oriented.
Purposes and Standards	Mission, goals Objectives Corporate assumptions Norms Priorities, schedules Performance criteria Personnel rules Code of ethics	Multinational operations; Pacific Rim focus MBO system to link levels of operations Use of new technologies to facilitate mission. Criteria of competence; creativity; tough-minded analysis High achievement; performance emphasis Rules customized, developed by implementers High standards, integrity; culturally sensitive behavior; commission, yes; bribery, no
Look and Style	Corporate leadership style Policies, procedures Time sense Appearance, dress Food, fitness habits Corporate environment	Participative; consensus oriented Management of responsibility, accountability 24-hour operations; long-term, futuristic Informal, casual appropriate Healthful diet; wellness programs Dynamic, flexible, stimulating environment
Processes and Activities	Operational practices, projects Products, services Manufacturing, technology R&D Systems and program emphasis	Matrix, team management Knowledge, information processing Microelectronic technologies Technical, human factor research Interdisciplinary, software creation

EXHIBIT 5-2 (CONTINUED)
THE METAINDUSTRIAL WORK CULTURE*

Components of Organizational Culture	Organizational Manifestations	Metaindustrial Organizational Illustrations
Communications and Information Systems	Formal, informal systems External, internal systems Management info systems (MIS) Community, government relations Specialized languages, vocabularies, codes signals	Functional, open, authentic circular Mass media, closed circuit TV; feedback Centralized EDP, decentralized minicomputer Synergistic partnerships Computerized languages security systems; nonverbal awareness; multilevel communications and interactions
Human Resource and Personnel Pattern	Recruitment and selection Role and task assignments Career, professional development Education, training Skills acquisition, learning Performance regulation, control Human energy conservation, utilization	EEO, pluralistic; competency criteria Broad, flexible; self-designed Investment in human assets Teleconferencing; teleprocessing CAI, self-learning, AV systems Results-and-achievement-oriented; monitoring by individual and team Emphasis on actualizing human potential
Interpersonal Relations	Organizational networks Personnel and contractor relations Client, customer relations Human-machine relations Intra-, inter-group subsidiary relations Intercultural relations	Global electronic connections Integrated, helpful Consultative, facilitative Robotics interface Cooperative, collaborative Sensitive, skillful, interdependent
Recognition and Rewards	Quality of work life and morale Personnel needs and motivations Employee status and respect Intrinsic, extrinsic rewards Compensation plans Incentives, ownership	Increase employee control over work space Ego, self-fulfillment emphasis to energize Democratization, participation opportunities More autonomy, professionalization Tailor to individual needs and choices Profit sharing, stock options, formation of multinational operatives

*Extracted with permission from Harris, P.R. The New Work Culture and HRD Transformational Management Strategies. Amherst, MA: Human Resource Development Press, 1998.

ing commonplace. Furthermore, the complexity of society, and the human systems devised to meet continuing and new needs, requires a pooling of resources and talents. Inflation, resource scarcity, reduced personnel levels, budget cuts, and similar constraints have underscored the demands for better coordination and synergy in the use of "brainpower."

In effect, the team management model causes a new organizational culture to be formulated. The term used currently is *self-managed teams,* which contribute to employee empowerment and problem-solving. Such work units evolve their own unique *team culture.*[7] As noted previously, high technology corporations are indicative of this change, with project teams consisting of a variety of skilled specialists from management information systems, accounting, and new technologies. Obsolete business separations give way to synergistic, functional arrangements among those employed in manufacturing, marketing, and administration; line and staff activities overlap and often merge.

Synergy through team efforts can occur within a single enterprise, or among different organizations that formerly competed or rarely mixed. The trend is evident among companies, agencies, and associations, as well as between the private and public sectors. The computer has been the most powerful tool in making team management feasible, and it has fostered a revolution in organizational culture.

Globalism and *regionalism* have also promoted team management strategies. Government entities find that problems of planning, economics, ecology, conservation, and even population control are too big for local solutions. Only by the integration of overlapping jurisdictions and efforts can the public sector meet the challenges of today's business environment. Thus, there is a remarkable growth in the establishment of interagency task forces in planning, training, or criminal justice activities. For effective macro problem-solving in complex societies, regional commissions are sometimes formed in which local governmental power is delegated to a more comprehensive organization, bringing together a technical support staff with representatives of each local government. An interdisciplinary team at the Cleveland Clinic, for example, used high tech surgery and a health care team to kill brain tumors. Known as CAMIS (computer-assisted minimally invasive surgery), the technique and equipment represents a marriage between aerospace and medical technologies. It is the result of a team effort among two companies, four hospitals, four universities, the U.S. Air Force and NASA, facilitated by the Ohio Aerospace Institute. To bring together diverse organizations in a common undertaking is called *levering of resources.* Such synergy transcends organizational boundaries by creating new entities that develop *integrated cultures* of their own.[8]

Increasingly, team management is employed when the organization's activities are less repetitive and predictable. Such an approach increases the need for liaison, management by exception, and sharing of authority and information. All this is contrary to traditional organizational cul-

Synergy through team efforts can occur within a single enterprise, or among different organizations that formerly competed or rarely mixed.

tures. Management in transition today challenges organizations to improve information processing, enhance integration of realistic schedules, and share decision-making, subject to continuing revision and change.

Furthermore, there is a fundamental shift in the way power is exercised. Interfunctional product teams, for example, involve a delicate balance of power among peer specialists. Because joint decisions are to be made, each member must be sensitive to the others if the contributions of all are to lead to the team's success. The product manager's task is to facilitate collaboration across functional lines. For many this will necessitate an attitude change. In America, there is much discussion about "reengineering," which demands cooperation rather than confrontation in the triple relationship between business, labor, and government. Even where a functional approach to business is still in force, labor and management can develop team relations. Today it is common to have quality-control circles composed of workers and supervisors who meet regularly to discuss how to improve product quality and service.

The following observations on what is considered desirable in a team culture might be questioned in whole or part by readers from other national backgrounds. For purposes of discussion, here are seventeen guidelines to facilitate team success:

1. Tolerance of ambiguity, uncertainty and seeming lack of structure.
2. Taking interest in each member's achievement, as well as the group's.
3. Ability to give and accept feedback in a non-defensive manner.
4. Openness to change, innovation, group consensus, team decision-making and creative problem-solving.
5. Creation of a team atmosphere that is informal, relaxed, comfortable, and nonjudgmental.
6. Capacity to establish intense, short-term member relations, and to disconnect for the next project.
7. Keeping group communication on target and schedule, while permitting disagreement and valuing effective listening.
8. Urging a spirit of constructive criticism, and authentic, nonevaluative feedback.
9. Encouraging members to express feelings and to be concerned about group morale/maintenance.
10. Clarifying roles, relationships, assignments, and responsibilities.
11. Sharing leadership functions within group, and using total member resources.
12. Pausing periodically from task pursuits to reexamine and reevaluate team progress and communications.
13. Fostering trust, confidence, and commitment within the group.
14. Being sensitive to the team's linking function with other work units.

Interfunctional product teams involve a delicate balance of power among peer specialists.

15. Fostering a norm that members will be supportive and respectful of one another, and realistic in their expectations of each other.
16. Promoting an approach that is goal-directed, seeks group participation, divides the labor fairly, and synchronizes effort.
17. Setting high performance standards for the group.

Each team experience is different, and organizations should encourage such uniqueness. Yet at the same time, coordination and integration of team effort with other units and the whole enterprise is essential if the sum is to be greater than its parts. When team cultures contain the elements previously outlined, and are reflective of the whole organizational environment, then they become closely knit and productive. The more team participation is provided and employees are included in team decision-making the healthier and more relevant is that human system.

The teams may be part of the formal organization structure as in the case of matrix management. However, some traditional hierarchies are slow and difficult to change. Then collateral organizations of informal teams may be formulated as a secondary mode of problem-solving. This unofficial, parallel organizational arrangement is a change strategy to use with problems that are intractable in the formal system.

Team management is suitable for knowledge problems that require high-quality, creative solutions with rapid processing and high output. When complex problems are less structured, quantifiable, definable, and past experience is unreliable, team management is necessary.

Improving Team Performance

Just like the organization in general, we might have an image of the team as an "energy exchange system." When the group functions, human psychic and physical energy is used effectively. Team interaction is an energy exchange. As the group seeks to achieve its goals, members energize or motivate themselves and one another by their example. Team planning and changes become projections on energy use and its alteration. Every aspect of the group process can be analyzed in terms of this human energy paradigm. The key issue, then, is how the team manages its energies most productively, and avoids underutilizing or even wasting the group energies. There are ways that members can analyze their functions and performance in projects, task forces, or product teams.

Team behavior can be examined from the viewpoint of task functions, which initiate, give or seek information, clarify or elaborate on member ideas, and summarize or synthesize. It can also be seen from the angle of group maintenance or morale building, such as encouraging, expressing group feeling, harmonizing, and compromising.

Such data-gathering can be useful periodically to improve the group's effectiveness. Not only can the information help the person to change his or her team behavior, but when such data are combined into a visual

As the group seeks to achieve its goals, members energize or motivate themselves and one another by their example.

profile, they offer a diagnosis of team health from time to time. It is recommended that teams pause on occasion for self-examination of their progress. Sometimes a third-person facilitator, such as an internal or external consultant, can be most helpful in this regard. When the group's analysis of its maturity is summarized, the team can then view the total assessment and discuss its implications for effective energy use.

Team participation is an intensive learning experience. When members voluntarily involve themselves and fully participate, personal and professional growth is fostered. The team is like a laboratory of the larger organizational world in which it operates. Although a temporary experience, it is an opportunity for individual and team development. Each participant shares self and insights from the basis of unique life and organizational experiences. Synergy occurs when the members listen to each other and enter into the private worlds of the others. Total team perception and wisdom then become more than the sum of the parts.

Team Culture Characteristics

If the organization's culture emphasizes employee participation through team management, the group microcultures are likely to reflect that system's macroculture. Thus, collaborative management should be evident not only within an individual team, but in intergroup relations. There is an implicit assumption that the team culture exerts a significant influence on individual member's behavior. As a team member, one functions beyond the individual level, becoming representative of the group "persona." Those who serve in two or more interlocking groups are expected to act as linking pins in the accomplishment of organizational mission through these separate but interdependent entities.

Everything that anthropologists would examine in the culture of people in a national or organizational group can be analyzed in the miniature environment of the team. That can range from the group's beliefs and attitudes, to procedures and practices, to priorities and technologies. The team atmosphere, task orientation or processes, communication patterns, role clarification or negotiation, conflict resolution, decision making, action planning, intragroup and intergroup relations—all can be scrutinized for better diagnosis of the group's dynamics. When a global manager or consultant engages in such analysis, the team can be helped to become more effective in the use of its energies.

Whether it is a family group (a permanent work unit) or a special group (temporarily constituted for a particular purpose), each individual contributes uniquely to the team from his or her own experience and talents. The team's resources can be strengthened when intercultural differences are used for synergy, rather than allowed to become a cause for divisiveness. The differences of perception that arise from varied academic or training backgrounds, work expertise and experiences, ethnic and national origins can enrich the group's basis for creative problem-

As a team member, one functions beyond the individual level, becoming representative of the group "persona."

solving and achievement. The team's culture can be the means for capitalizing on such, so that all members accomplish something together. A strong team culture enhances group communications and permits confrontation, so as to stimulate group growth and cohesion. Then, as a team identity is strengthened, group morale, camaraderie, and "esprit de corps" are also improved.

Transcultural Teams

Social scientists are conducting research on what people can do in small groups to facilitate a meaningful experience and productive outcome. One exciting example of this occurred at the East-West Center in Honolulu, Hawaii. At its Culture Learning Institute, Dr. Kathleen K. Wilson spearheaded an investigation with 15 other distinguished colleagues on the factors influencing the management of International Cooperative Research and Development (ICRD) projects. Their findings have vital implications now for any professional seeking to improve human performance and collaboration. Although the researchers are examining project team effectiveness, their insights can be extrapolated to other forms of inter- and intragroup behavior, whether it is a matrix organization, product team, task force, or any work unit.

Reporting the researchers' progress to the Australian Commonwealth's Scientific and Industrial Research Organizations, Dr. Wilson reviewed the varied contexts in which international cooperative groups must operate. These external factors affect the environment within the project itself, and include such diverse elements as political, organizational, and cultural aspects, the size and scope of the endeavor, the disciplinary background of team members, and their individual characteristics, research, and development policies and problems. A summary of factors that foster or hinder professional synergy follows (Exhibit 5-3). Certainly, the exhaustive listing of situations that influence a project's effectiveness points up the need for strategies to manage the many cultural differences existing between and among professionals attempting to work together.

The East-West research on international cooperation projects offers some criteria that can be used in recruiting, selecting, and assessing professionals. *Team member characteristics* that foster group synergy are presented. Such benchmarks can be helpful in interviewing potential team members, choosing collaborators, and setting goals for self-improvement in organizational relations.

Finally, the ICRD researchers at the East-West Culture Learning Institute offer some indications for synergy assessment in professional cooperative efforts. They have established four criteria for evaluating project effectiveness and management competence:

A strong team culture enhances group communications and permits confrontation, so as to stimulate group growth and cohesion.

Exhibit 5-3
Human Factors That Foster or Hinder Professional Synergy Within a Project

- How project business is planned.
- Consideration of other problem-solving viewpoints.
- How the work should be organized.
- Approach to R & D tasks.
- Definition of R & D problems.
- Ambiguity resolution and problem formulation.
- Methods and procedures.
- Decision-making relative to recurring problems.
- Allocation of resources to team members.
- Accountability procedures relative to resource use.
- Timing and sequencing approaches.
- Determining objectives for an R & D effort.
- Affiliation and liaison with external groups and degree of formality in their work relations.
- Quantity and type of project human resources.
- Qualifications, recruitment, and selection of new members.
- New member orientation and training on the project.
- Management of responsibilities.
- Underutilization of workers relative to skill competencies.
- Motivating behavior and reward expectations.
- Coordination of long/short-term members.
- Agreement on degree of innovation required.
- Experience with cooperation especially relative to international R & D tasks.
- Official language(s) to use on project.
- Method of reporting everyone's involvement in the project.
- Coping with internal demands and visitors.
- Meeting face-to-face and having to resort to other forms of more impersonal communication.
- Involvement in making viewpoint known.
- Power differences because of institution resources each brought to the project.
- Prestige, risk-taking, tolerance of uncertainty, and perceptions.
- Project leadership and/or organizational policies changing unexpectedly.
- Quality of work presented in evaluation methods.
- What constituted success in project work, and what to do when members fail to meet group expectations.
- Clarification of roles on the relationships.

1. Individual team member satisfaction.
2. Group satisfaction and morale.
3. Work progress relative to intended goal statements.
4. Social and cultural impact of the endeavor on people.

The East-West Center's ICRD researchers have also identified interpersonal skills that influence a professional group's situation and accomplishments. Exhibits 5-4 and 5-5 present summaries of these self-management competencies.

These insights offer a compendium of the shared leadership skills that professionals should expect to contribute in the course of group collaboration. For those organizations that provide project management training or team building for their members, these are the types of competencies to be sought in the emerging "ad hocracies."

EXHIBIT 5-4
SELF-MANAGEMENT COMPETENCIES
PERMIT THE PROJECT MEMBER TO:

- ❏ Recognize other member participation in ways they find rewarding.
- ❏ Avoid unnecessary conflicts among other team members, as well as resolving unavoidable ones to mutual satisfaction.
- ❏ Integrate different team members skills to achieve project goals.
- ❏ Negotiate acceptable working arrangements with other team members and their organizations.
- ❏ Regard other's feelings and exercise tactfulness.
- ❏ Develop equitable benefits for other team members.
- ❏ Accept suggestions/feedback to improve his or her participation.
- ❏ Provide useful specific suggestions and appropriate feedback.
- ❏ Facilitate positive interaction among culturally different members, whether in terms of macro differences (nationally/politics), or micro differences (discipline or training).
- ❏ Accomplish required work while enjoying positive social relations with other team members.
- ❏ Build a support network for the benefit of the project team.
- ❏ Facilitate team exchanges and convert member ideas into specific tasks of accomplishment.
- ❏ Gain acceptance because of empathy expressed and sensitivity to end users.
- ❏ Encourage dissemination of project outcomes throughout its life.
- ❏ Recognize national/international differences in problem statements and procedures, so as to create appropriate project organizational responses.
- ❏ Anticipate and plan for probable difficulties in project implementation.
- ❏ Recognize discrete functions, coordinating discrete tasks with overall project goals.
- ❏ Coordinate transitions among different kinds of activities within the project.

EXHIBIT 5-5
THE EFFECTIVE TEAM MEMBER HAS THE CAPACITY FOR:

- ❑ Flexibility and openness to change and others' viewpoints.
- ❑ Exercising patience, perseverance, and professional security.
- ❑ Thinking in multidimensional terms and considering different sides of issues.
- ❑ Dealing with ambiguity, role shifts, and differences in personal and professional styles or social and political systems.
- ❑ Managing stress and tension well, while scheduling tasks systematically.
- ❑ Cross-cultural communication, and demonstrating sensitivity for language problems among colleagues.
- ❑ Anticipating consequences of one's own behavior.
- ❑ Dealing with unfamiliar situations and life-style changes.
- ❑ Dealing well with different organizational structures and policies.
- ❑ Gathering useful information related to future projects.

SYNERGY AMONG INDIVIDUAL PROFESSIONALS

To be a professional in our discussion, one can be an athlete, technician, or programmer, as well as an attorney, physician, or social scientist. Today professional relationships are often temporary and intense. Peers may come together on a project team, a research effort, or to write a handbook or report. It is a "bridge building process" among specialists who often come from a variety of microcultures within the fields of learning, or even within the organization. The link-up effort is even more complex when the participants are internationals from diverse macrocultures. To promote synergy in teams and networks four steps are evident:

1. Bring the new person "on board" quickly by various means of reaching out, briefing, and inclusion efforts.
2. Foster intense, ad hoc work relationships, as well as possible outside social relations.
3. Disengage rapidly when the task is completed and reassignment occurs, or another undertaking is begun.
4. Follow up on the aftermath of the professional activity and maintain limited communication with members of the prior consortium.

A project team is a "bridge building process" among specialists who often come from a variety of microcultures within the fields of learning, or even within the organization.

Local *world trade centers* are "passports to opportunity" for those engaged in international business. Usually operating in conjunction with the Chamber of Commerce in major cities, they offer global managers a chance for synergistic networking and career development. Often they sponsor a World Trade Day dealing with such subjects as business opportunities on the Internet, Russian and Mexican markets, tips for importing/exporting, gathering competitive intelligence and forming strategic alliances.

Networking as Synergy

Individuals have always formed linkages and exchanges with each other within a society or field of human endeavor. What is different in recent decades is the escalation of these phenomena on a global scale, across both cultures and disciplines of knowledge. Twentieth-century advances in communication and transportation have accelerated the process on a mass scale. They also contribute to professional obsolescence, and the need for continuous professional development to be relevant within a vocational activity.

One's peers within a career field provide a reference group against which individual performance can be measured, recognized, and motivated. Today, such professional colleagues may be found around the world, not just within one's own country or even within one's own field of learning. As more people study abroad, attend professional conferences overseas, or engage in career activities internationally, transnational linkages are formed. The potential for a new synergy among professionals through such developments is astounding.

In these new patterns of collaboration, it is important that self-reliance is fostered in the participants and that interdependence is perceived as the basis of the network. Networks, in effect, can represent reference groups for professionals. They form a new microculture of people working for more diverse and challenging practices, standards and perspectives that will be appropriate for life in the twenty-first century.

Networking can be a new work culture strategy for performance improvement, because it creates a system of interrelated people or groups, offices or work stations, linked together personally or electronically or both, for information exchange and mutual support. Networking is a modern mechanism for coping with complexity and change in the transition to the information society. Furthermore, it is in harmony with many national cultures.

For networking to achieve positive contribution for its participants and society, these characteristics should be cultivated among members:

1. Free-forming and adaptive relationship in which the person is the most important feature, the boundaries are unstructured, the power and responsibility are distributed, the participants may play

Networking is a modern mechanism for coping with complexity and change in the transition to the information society.

many roles, the balance is maintained between personal integrity and collective purpose, and the sharing of concerns and values is encouraged.

2. Willingness of those linked together to exercise initiative, take risks, be assertive, be autonomous, be informal, and be authentic in communications.

3. Ability to cope with differences, ambiguity, uncertainty, and with lack of closure.

Innovative Cooperation with Colleagues

Now that the concepts and means for promoting synergy in professional development have been reviewed, it may help to examine some creative approaches to the subject. It takes vision, courage, and risk to innovate. In 1931, Professor Neil Gordon of Johns Hopkins University had a brainchild for transmitting scientific information in a different way. Gordon wanted small groups of scientists to meet for summer seminars in a secluded and relaxed setting for informal, free give-and-take of information and knowledge exchange. Today this innovative concept yields 100 Gordon conferences annually in seven New Hampshire schools and colleges for 12,000 professionals. Among the participants are Nobel laureates who enjoy the relaxed exchange of data where there is no pressure, no publicity, and no need to publish.

But what is innovation? And are there already some models of it that demonstrate synergy among professionals?

Innovation has been defined as creative idea generation, or the act of introducing something new into the established order; a change or different way of doing things from the traditional pattern. Innovation, for survival and development, should be built into the operating mechanisms or policies of corporate systems. All social institutions, especially government agencies and corporations, have a desperate need to encourage creative deviations from the traditional norms and practices. One might take the *Fortune* 500 corporations in 2000 and inquire how many will be in that category by the year 2050. Those without innovative performance certainly will not be.

Peter Drucker's comments about innovation and business can be applied to all human systems:[9]

> Innovation means, first, the systematic sloughing off of yesterday. It means, next, the systematic search for innovative opportunities in the vulnerabilities of a technology, a process, a market, in the lead time of new knowledge; in the needs and wants of a market. It means willingness to organize for entrepreneurship, to creating new businesses. . . . It means, finally, the willingness to set up innovative ventures separately, outside the existing managerial structure, to organize proper accounting concepts for the economics and control of innovation, and appropriate compensation policies for the innovators.

Innovation, for survival and development, should be built into the operating mechanisms or policies of corporate systems.

The new work culture values creativity and innovation, and manifests this in its support of entrepreneurial activities. Innovative management builds mechanisms for this into organizational systems, such as developing an incentive system to reward risk-taking or creating a people-oriented climate that provides employees with a sense of ownership. Individuals from multiple disciplines and associations can be brought together cooperatively to accomplish something more than any one as an individual can achieve.

SUMMARY

After explaining the concept of cultural synergy, the chapter provided a contrast of societies that could be characterized as having high or low synergy, as well as organizational culture that reflects high and low synergy. The contemporary conflicts in Northern Ireland, the Middle East, Yugoslavia and Afghanistan are examples of low synergy cultures that breed violence and terrorism. The 1998 Good Friday Agreement to foster peace in Ulster, for example was an effort to build synergistic relations between the peoples of the United Kingdom and the Republic of Ireland. It takes openness and good will to end long time bitterness and foster cooperation.

Within groups, the research reported on the behaviors and practices that contribute to synergy and success among teams, particularly in terms of international projects. The concluding section described people who are truly "professionals" in their attitude toward their career and work, whether in traditional professions or the new technologies, and how they can mutually benefit by the practice of synergy.

Global leaders actively create a better future through synergistic efforts with fellow professionals. The new work culture favors cooperation, not excessive competition. This trend is evident, as well as necessary, in corporations and industries, in government and academic institutions, in non-profit agencies and unions, in trade and professional associations of all types. In an information or knowledge society, collaboration in sharing ideas and insights is the key to survival, problem solving, and growth. But high synergy behavior must be cultivated in personnel, so we need to use research findings, such as those outlined in this chapter, to facilitate teamwork and ensure professional synergy. In addition to fostering such learning in our formal education and training systems, we also should take advantage of the increasing capabilities offered to us for both personal and electronic networking.

Needed are synergistic professionals who can operate in two cultures: the industrial culture, which is disappearing, and the metaindustrial or cyberculture, which is emerging. Contemporary global leaders must be effective bridge builders between both worlds, between the realities of the past and future.

Contemporary global leaders must be effective bridge builders between both worlds, between the realities of the past and future.

REFERENCES

1. Harris, P. R. *Living and Working in Space,* Chichester, UK: Wiley-Praxis, 1996.
2. Adler, N. *Organizational Behavior,* 3rd ed., Cincinnati, OH: South-Western College Publishing, 1997.
3. O'Toole, J. *Leading Change—Overcoming the Ideology of Comfort and the Tyranny of Customs,* San Francisco: Jossey-Bass, 1995.
4. Harris, P. R. *The New Work Culture—HRD Transformational Management Strategies,* Amherst, MA: Human Resource Development Press, 1998. Moran, R. T., Harris, P. R. and Stripp, W. *Developing the Global Organization,* Houston, TX: Gulf Publishing, 1993.
5. Moran, R. T., Harris, P. R., and Stripp, W. G. *Developing the Global Organization,* Houston, TX: Gulf Publishing, 1993. Recommend readers get on the mailing list and request free newsletter of the Center for the Study of Work Teams at the University of North Texas (Denton, TX 76203, USA).
6. Dyer, W. *Team Building,* Reading, MA:Addison-Wesley, 1987. See also Dinkmeyer, D. and Eckstein, D. *Leadership By Encouragement,* Dubuque, IA: Kendall/Hunt Publishing Co., 1993
7. Parker, G. and Knopp, R. P. *50 Activities for Self-Directed Teams,* Amherst, MA: HRD Press Inc., 1994. Wellins, R. S., Byham, W. C., and Wilson, J. M. *Empowered Teams,* San Diego, CA: Pfeiffer & Company, 1991. Glasser, R. (ed.) *Classic Readings in Self-Managing Teamwork,* King of Prussia, PA: HRD Quarterly Press (2002 Renaissance Blvd., Ste. 100, zip code 19406, USA), 1993. [Reader Note: all three publishers are source of team development materials, including videos and simulations.]
8. Binder, J. D. "Levering Resources Through Collaboration," *Aerospace America*, March, 1998, p. 20.
7. Drucker, P. F. *Innovation and Entrepreneurship,* New York, NY: Harper & Row, 1985. See also Hesselbein, R., Goldsmith, M., Beckhard, R., and Schubert, R. F. (eds.). *The Community and the Future,* San Francisco: Jossey-Bass, 1998

UNIT 2

CULTURAL IMPACTS ON GLOBAL BUSINESS

Merging two organizations, it is said, is like mating two elephants and hoping to produce a gazelle. In the 1990s, only 30% of the corporate mergers in the U.S. realized anticipated synergies, even two years after the transaction. Thus, while looking after the financials of the deal, it's also important to exercise cultural due diligence: examining the way each organization does things, to see if, when they net out culturally, they might diminish or even negate the apparent value of the deal. In essence, this challenges the way many deal makers use the word "synergy." To them, it means the ability to remove costs by eliminating duplication, but it really means setting up two groups so they can, together, produce and develop capabilities that they might never have developed on their own.

P. Senge, et al., The Dance of Change,
New York: Doubleday, 1999

MANAGING TRANSITIONS AND RELOCATIONS

Cultural

homogeneity

exists in very few

cultures today.

Individuals, family groups and networks of people have been relocating and making transitions from early times. Historians and cultural anthropologists suspect survival has been the major motivator.

In today's global world, the number of people living in another country for lengthy periods of time is increasing. Virtually everyone comes in contact with individuals who speak a different language or who were reared in another culture. Cultural homogeneity exists in very few cultures today. Recent books such as Storti's *Figuring Foreigners Out*[1] help all individuals, not just Peace Corps volunteers or globe-trotting executives, understand people from different cultures.

Children from families who have lived extensively abroad and been reared in different cultures have also been studied, and are referred to Third Culture Kids (TCK). Pollock and Van Reken[2] have examined TCK for three reasons. First, the number of TCK has increased dramatically as the global economy generates many corporate relocations, not only Americans transferring to Latin America or Europe, for example, but also Asians to Eastern Europe and Canadians to Africa. International travel time frames have diminished so that it rarely takes more than one day of travel to reach a destination, making it relatively easy to have children accompany their parents. International schools have also increased. Second, the voice of TCK has grown louder and support groups and organizations have developed to encourage them to share the relevance of their experience. Lastly, the TCK experience is fast becoming the norm throughout the world. Growing up in a different culture may soon be the rule rather than the exception. There are benefits and challenges to developing a sense of identity when living or being reared outside one's home country.

Embarking on a "hero's journey" is the way the late anthropologist Joseph Campbell[3] describes the challenge of living or working abroad.

> Furthermore, we have not even to risk the adventure alone, for the heroes of all time have gone before us. The labyrinth thoroughly known. We have only to follow the thread of the hero path, and where we have thought to find an abomination, we shall find a god. And where we have thought to slay another, we shall slay ourselves. Where we had thought to travel outward we will come to the center of our own existence. And where we had thought to be alone, we will be one with the world.

Early researchers in cross-cultural studies were concerned primarily with what happened when a person transitioned from home culture to a host culture. Today, interdependence between nations has facilitated the cross border flow of people, ideas, and information.

We now have a broader view of *transition trauma* associated with life's turning points, be they a relocation or other personal or professional challenges. The trauma of change related to career assignments may be experienced domestically, as well as internationally. Apart from lifestyle transitions that everyone faces, individuals must cope with rapid alterations in their work and/or culture.

COPING WITH TRANSITIONAL CHALLENGES

Increasingly we interact with people who are very different from us, or in situations that are unfamiliar. Even when we share a common nationality, we may have to deal with citizens who are indeed "foreign" to us in their thinking, attitudes, vocabulary, and background. Individuals may face challenges within their environment due to their upbringing or local cultural conditioning. The challenges present opportunities for growth or disruption. Such experiences can include married couples who divorce, families who move from one geographic area to another, and those who change careers in midlife or have major alterations in jobs or roles.

To get a sense of transitional experience that can cause cultural shock, consider the following scenarios.

Majority to Minority Culture

Your company transfers you and your family to a section of your country where you feel like an "immigrant." From the Northeast you come to this Sunbelt state that is so different and unique. Your boss suggests you enroll at the local university to take a course entitled "Living Texas" to introduce you to the myths and mannerisms of Texans. The

The trauma of change related to career assignments may be experienced domestically, as well as internationally.

course teaches newcomers how to adapt to this former republic, rather than be considered "people from the outside." Texas is a state of contrasts, from huge ranches and high technology to Bible-belt mentality and laws. The course covers everything from "Talking Texas" and Texas cooking to the Mexican side of the Texas revolution and Texas folk heroes. If you can adapt, you will probably fall in love with these friendly people, their jalapeño lollipops, and chili pepper dishes and even discover their diverse ethnic mixture and the "Austin sound" of music.

Transitions in the Global Marketplace

You are a North American marketing consultant for high technology companies worldwide. Because of your expertise, you are in much demand traveling beyond your home culture on short assignments. Your professional activities take you to a variety of host cultures. Typically, you are there for one to two weeks, consulting with local executives, many of whom are quite different in their approach to you as a woman. Most of your clients are men from cultures as diverse as Indonesia, Malaysia, and Mexico to India, Hungary, and Russia. Their knowledge of English is limited, usually as a second or third language. You often experience changes in time zones and resultant "jet lag," as well as problems with the native foods, social customs, and the loneliness of the female consultant on the road.

Technology Transfer

You are an engineer from a highly industrialized nation. Your overseas assignments are mainly to less developed countries. You realize that the indigenous population is not ready for sophisticated technologies. To help them in their transition to modern economies, and rather than sell them expensive equipment that they cannot afford or maintain, you prefer to design appropriate machines that pump water, cook food, and meet their real and practical needs. Your company partners with local institutions, scales projects back for maximum benefit, and provides ample training in what is usable, affordable and appropriate technology. You are patient in your instructions and use bright natives to transmit your expertise to local workers. Furthermore, you encourage your company to underwrite scholarships for intelligent local youth to receive a more advanced technical education. Your attitude is that we are all part of the same human family.

These incidents are real transitional experiences. Having indepth, intercultural encounters can be stimulating or psychologically disturbing, depending on your preparation and approach to them. The process of adjustment or acculturation to a new living environment takes time, usually some months, for we have to learn new skills for responding and adapting to the unfamiliar. When abroad, the extent of the trauma depends on whether one lives among the native population or in a mili-

Having indepth, intercultural encounters can be stimulating or psychologically disturbing, depending on your preparation and approach to them.

tary/diplomatic/corporate compound. The experience of coping with human differences globally can be renewing or devastating. When we are in a place where the traditions and customs are foreign and unexpected, we may lose our balance and become unsure of ourselves. The same thing can happen within our own society when change happens so rapidly that the old traditions, the cues we live by, are suddenly undermined and irrelevant and our sense of self becomes threatened.

Transitional experiences offer two alternatives—to cope or to "cop out." One can learn to comprehend, survive in, and grow through immersion in a different culture. The positive result can be increased self-development. Whenever we leave home for the unfamiliar, it involves basic changes in habits, relationships, and sources of satisfaction. Inherent in cultural change is the opportunity to leave behind, perhaps temporarily, one set of relationships and living patterns, and to enrich one's life by experimenting with new ones. Implicit in the personal conflict and discontinuity produced by such experiences is the possible transcendence from environment or family support to self support. Intercultural situations of psychological, social, or cultural stress also stimulate us to review and redefine our lives; to see our own country and people in a new perspective. Or, we may reject the changes or new culture and possibly lose a growth opportunity.[4]

CULTURE SHOCK

As a scholarly issue, culture shock has only been researched in the past twenty or so years. However, the impact of culture shock has been written about in works of fiction as early as 1862 including Tolstoy in his book *The Cossacks*. Jack London, in a 1900 story, described what it felt like to be a foreigner in a literary not scientific way.[5]

London[6] describes what a sojourner should expect:

> He must be prepared to forget many of the things he learned, and to acquire such customs as are inherent with existence in the new land; he must abandon the old ideals and the old gods, and oftentimes he must reverse the very code by which his conduct has hitherto been shaped.

London cautions that:

> The pressure of the altered environment is unbearable, and they chafe in body and spirit under the new restrictions which they do not understand. This chafing is bound to act and react, producing diverse evils and leading to various misfortunes.

Essentially, culture shock, alluded to by London, is our psychological reaction to an unfamiliar or alien environment,[7] which often occurs during a major transitional experience. Culture shock is neither good or

Transitional experiences offer two alternatives—to cope or to "cop out."

bad, necessary or unnecessary. It is a reality that many people face when in strange and unexpected situations. Oberg[8] referred to culture shock as a generalized trauma one experiences in a new and different culture because of having to learn and cope with a vast array of new cultural cues and expectations, while discovering that your old ones probably do not fit or work. More precisely he notes:

> Culture shock is precipitated by the anxiety that results from losing all our familiar signs and symbols of social intercourse. These signs or cues include the thousand and one ways in which we orient ourselves to the situations of daily life: how to give orders, how to make purchases, when and when not to respond. Now these cues which may be words, gestures, facial expressions, customs, or norms are acquired by all of us in the course of growing up and are as much a part of our culture, as the language we speak or the beliefs we accept. All of us depend for our peace of mind and efficiency on hundreds of these cues, most of which we are not consciously aware.

According to Klopf[5] there are six stages of culture shock.

1. The *preliminary stage* involves the preparation for the experience. During the process, anticipation and excitement build as one packs, makes reservations and plans.
2. The arrival at the destination marks the *spectator stage,* during which there are many strange sights and different people. All of this newness produces fascination with the culture. This honeymoon stage may last from a few days to six months.
3. The *participation stage* is over when the individual must do the hard work of living in the culture and the honeymoon has ended. The sights have been visited and now the coping with everyday life by yourself must occur.
4. When problems begin to arise that are difficult to handle, usually the *shock stage* sets in. Often irritability, lethargy, depression and loneliness are symptoms. One must find ways to confront the differences in culture and adjust.
5. If the individual reaches the *adjustment stage,* identification with the host culture has progressed satisfactorily. Relationships with locals develop along with a sense of belonging and acceptance.
6. For individuals living permanently in a culture the adjustment stage finishes the transition period. For those who are temporarily living in another culture the return to the home culture introduces the *reentry stage.* Culture shock in reverse may set in with individuals going through the first five stages again at home. The pace at which one advances through the stages may quicken and perhaps the trauma is lessened.

When in a different culture, which may disturb or frustrate, one's concerns may be real or imagined. Those in culture shock manifest obvious symptoms such as excessive concern over cleanliness, feeling that what is new and strange is "dirty." This may be seen with reference to water, food, dishes, and bedding, or evident in excessive fear of servants and shopkeepers relative to the disease they might bear. Other indications of the person in such trauma are feelings of helplessness and confusion, growing dependence on long-term residents of one's own nationality, constant irritations over delays and minor frustrations, as well as undue concern for being cheated, robbed, or injured. Some may exhibit symptoms of mild hypochondria, expressing over concern for minor pains and skin eruptions—it may even get to the point of real psychosomatic illnesses. Often, such individuals postpone learning the local language and customs, dwelling instead on their loneliness and longing for back home, to be with one's own and to talk to people who "make sense." However, persons who seek international assignments as a means of escaping "back-home problems" with career, marriage, drugs or alcoholism will probably only exacerbate personal problems that would be better resolved in one's native culture.

Osland[9] uses the concept of "learning to live with paradox" instead of emphasizing the shock that may come from experiences in an alien society. Such paradox occurs when we have to hold ideas in mind that are seemingly opposite. Osland calls this the "road of trials" when we are confronted with obstacles and tests to our way of "normally" perceiving and functioning. To deal with such paradoxes more effectively, she proposes we learn from expatriates who have gone before us.

To facilitate acculturation, organizations responsible for sending others abroad should be careful in their recruitment and selection of individuals for assignments abroad. Surveys have shown that those who adjust and work well in international assignments are usually well-integrated personalities with qualities such as, flexibility, personal stability, social maturity, and social inventiveness. Such candidates for overseas work are not given to unrealistic expectations, irrational concepts of self or others, nor do they have tendencies toward excessive depression, discouragement, criticism, or hostility. Global corporations, government agencies, and international foundations must reduce culture shock among employees to become more cost effective, to promote productivity abroad, and to improve client and customer relations with host nationals.

One should also be realistic about the difficulties that may be experienced when living abroad. Intestinal disorders and exotic diseases are real, and may not always be avoided by inoculations or new antibiotics. In some countries, water, power, transportation, and housing shortages are facts, and one's physical comfort may be seriously inconvenienced. Political instability, ethnic feuds, and social breakdown may make an

To facilitate acculturation, organizations responsible for sending others abroad should be careful in their recruitment and selection of individuals for assignments abroad.

assignment in these countries unacceptable. Real difficulties can also arise from not knowing the language or in coping with strange climates and customs. But we are born with the ability to learn, to adapt, to survive, to enjoy. After all, human beings do create culture, so the shocks caused by such differences are not unbearable or without value. The intercultural experience can be most satisfying, contributing much to personal and professional satisfaction. One can discover friends everywhere.

Role Shock

The phenomenon and process of culture shock has applications to other life crises. There is the matter of role shock. Each of us chooses or is assigned or is conditioned to a variety of roles in society and its organizations—son or daughter, parent or child, husband or wife, teacher or engineer, manager or union organizer, man or woman. In these positions, people have expectations of us and we have expectations of them. These role expectations may often differ in another culture. A woman, for instance, may do in one culture what is forbidden in another. In some societies, senior citizens are revered, and in others ignored. In some cultures, the youth regard teachers with awe, while others treat them as inferiors or "buddies."

Role perception is subject to change, at times accelerated change. The person who has a particular understanding of what a manager is and does, may be upset when he or she finally achieves that role and finds it to be changed, so that one's traditional views of the function are suddenly obsolete. It can be very disconcerting, and the shock may be severe or long lasting. Role shock can lead to an identity crisis if one's life is tightly linked to a job or role. A cross-cultural assignment can accentuate role shock. Many individuals sent abroad find themselves in totally different role requirements than back home.

Role shock may manifest itself as a result of organizational mergers or acquisition, or as a result a reduction in the workforce, which may cause a person to lose a position and rejoin the job market search. In the past decade, many middle positions were simply eliminated in corporations trying to cope with new economic conditions. Even when one retains his or her position within a newly acquired company, the organization and its culture may perceive "your role" in an entirely different way.

Reentry Shock

When expatriates return from foreign deployment, there is another form of reverse culture shock that is faced. Having objectively perceived his or her culture from abroad, one can have a more severe and sustained jolt through reentry shock. Some returning "expats" feel a subtle downgrading and loss of prestige and benefits. Others bemoan the loss of household help and social contacts, as well as other overseas "perks."

After all, human beings do create culture, so the shocks caused by such differences are not unbearable or without value.

Many feel uncomfortable for six months or more in their native land, frustrated with their company, and bored with their narrow-minded colleagues. Some seem out of touch with what has happened in their country or corporation in their absence, and no longer seem to fit. The phenomenon can be temporary and the person helped by a reorientation program. But for some, culture and reentry shocks can be the catalyst for major choices and transitions to a new locale, job or career, and new life-style. Some expatriates never make the necessary adjustment and live as strangers in their own homelands.

Fostering Acculturation

After culture shock subsides acculturation settles in. Anyone adapting to a new cultural situation such as college, a foreign country as a business person, traveler or student, an immigrant or refugee to a new country, all must learn about and adapt to the new cultural environment.

As early as the 1930s, acculturation was being researched. The definition of acculturation is as valid now as then.

> . . . when groups of individuals having different cultures come into continuous first-hand contact, with subsequent changes in the original cultural patterns of either or both groups.[10]

Most obviously, one must acculturate to the physical concerns like finding doctors, schools, banks or grocery stores. Acculturation produces cultural changes as well, when one leaves behind the familiar cultural patterns and institutions of the old and takes on and assimilates into the new. Value systems and attitudes also undergo change in this process. There maybe biological changes as one adjusts to possible different bacteria and viruses or unfamiliar plant life. The social changes of acculturation will involve finding and forming new relationships and friendships. All of these changes result in stress. Stress or tension is no respecter of time, place, or persons. In today's "pressure-cooker" world, some tension is normal, so one must learn to defuse stress, reduce tension to controllable levels, and to alleviate pressures, otherwise, insecurity, instability, and insomnia result.

Sociologists point out that stable, healthy family relationships abroad can make the difference between success and failure in the foreign assignment. Families who interact in mutually supportive ways can be their own resource for acculturation and adjustment in another environment. Ten tips follow to deflate the stress and tension of acculturation.

Be Culturally Prepared. Forewarned is forearmed. Individual or group study and training are necessary to understand cultural factors and cultural specifics. Public libraries and the Internet provide a variety of material. Also, the public health service will advise about required inoculations, dietary clues, and other sanitary data. Before departure, the

Sociologists point out that stable, healthy family relationships abroad can make the difference between success and failure in the foreign assignment.

person scheduled for overseas service can experiment with the food or restaurants representative of the second culture. Furthermore, one might establish contact in his or her homeland with foreign students or visitors from the area to which one is going.

Osland[9] suggests seeking out a *cultural mentor*—a wise friend or counselor who has lived in the host country or is there upon arrival. The expatriate mentor is capable of guidance, encouragement, and help in mastering the intricacies of a new culture.

Learn Local Communication Complexities. Study the language of the place to which one is assigned. At least, learn some of the basics that will help in exchanging greetings and shopping. In addition to courses and books on the country, cassettes can advance one's communication skills in the host culture. Published guides can be helpful in learning expected courtesies and customs.

Interact with the Host Nationals. Meeting with people from the country one is going to is helpful. They may provide introductions to relatives and friends and information regarding their native culture. If one lives within a company or military colony avoid the "compound mentality." Immerse oneself in the host culture. Join in, whenever feasible, the artistic and community functions, the carnivals and rites, the international fraternal or professional organizations. Offer to teach students or business people one's language in exchange for knowledge of their language; share skills from skiing to tennis and it will be the means for making new international friends.

Be Creative and Experimental. Innovations abroad may mean taking risks to get around barriers of bureaucracy and communication to lessen social distance. This principle extends from experimenting with the local food to keeping a diary as an escape to record one's adventures and frustrations. Tours, hobbies, and a variety of cultural pursuits can produce positive results. One needs to be open and existential to the many opportunities that will present themselves.

Be Culturally Sensitive. Be aware of the special customs and traditions which, if followed by a visitor, will make one more acceptable. Recognize that in some cultures, such as in Asia and the Middle East, saving face and not giving offense is considered important. Certainly, avoid stereotyping the natives, criticizing their local practices and procedures, while using the standard of one's own country for comparison purposes. Americans are pragmatic and generally like to organize so it may be a challenge for them to relax and adjust to a different rhythm of the place and people they are visiting.

Recognize Complexities in Host Cultures. Counteract the tendency to make quick, simplistic assessments of situations. Most complex societies comprise different ethnic or religious groups, stratified into social classes or castes, differentiated by regions or geographical factors, separated into rural and urban settlements. Each of these may have distinct subcultural characteristics over which is superimposed an official language,

Innovations abroad may mean taking risks to get around barriers of bureaucracy and communication to lessen social distance.

national institutions, and peculiar customs or history that tie a people together. Avoid pat generalizations and quick assumptions. Instead, be tentative when drawing conclusions, realizing one's point of contact is a limited sample within a multifaceted society.

Understand Oneself as a Culture Bearer. Each person bears his or her own culture, and distortions, when going abroad. Thus, one views everything in the host culture through the unique filter of one's own cultural background. For example, if one is raised in democratic traditions, a society that values the authority of the head male in the family and extends this reverence to national leaders maybe unsettling.

Be Patient, Understanding, and Accepting of Self and Hosts. In an unfamiliar environment, one must be more tolerant and flexible. An attitude of healthy curiosity, a willingness to bear inconveniences, patience when answers or solutions are not forthcoming or difficult to obtain, is valuable to maintain mental balance. Such patience may also extend to other compatriots who struggle with cultural adjustment.

Be Most Realistic in Expectations. Avoid overestimating oneself, one's hosts, or the cross-cultural experience. Disappointments can be lessened if one scales down expectations. This applies to everything from airline schedules to renting rooms. Global managers, especially, must be careful in new cultures not to set unreasonable work expectations for themselves or others until both are acclimated.

Accept the Challenge of Intercultural Experiences. Anticipate, savor, and confront the psychological challenge to adapt and change as a result of a new cross-cultural opportunity. Be prepared to alter one's habits, attitudes, values, tastes, relationships, or sources of satisfaction. Such flexibility can become a means for personal growth, and the transnational experience can be more fulfilling. Of course, a deep interest and commitment to one's work—professionalism—can be marvelous therapy in intercultural situations, counteracting isolation and strangeness when living outside one's culture.

One views everything in the host culture through the unique filter of one's own cultural background.

COMPONENTS OF A DEPLOYMENT SYSTEM

In 2000, there are about 6.1 billion human beings inhabiting earth. Today, we experience a vast movement of people from the place where they are born to another nation to live, study or work. Almost a million of them now come yearly to the United States. In this relocation process, some leave home in an orderly fashion to dwell in unfamiliar worlds, some come and go in an unplanned way. The issue, then, is how can these transcultural exchanges be facilitated for the benefit of both the expatriate and the indigenous population? When an organization is responsible for sending people abroad, it has an obligation to ensure that such persons are adequately selected, prepared and supported, as well as assisted when they return. The sponsors need to have a *system* for sending and receiving people.

Behavioral scientists have now begun to investigate the whole phenomenon of people living and working in isolated and confined environments.[11] The latter range from offshore oil rigs and polar research stations to undersea submarines and space stations.

Stage One—Employee Assessment

The first major component in a relocation or foreign deployment system involves evaluating individuals who are sent abroad and evaluating the organizational program responsible for the transfer and reentry process. From the perspective of the organizations' responsibilities, a complete foreign deployment system needs to:

❑ Ascertain the adaptability of key personnel for foreign service, including their ability to deal with the host nationals effectively.
❑ Summarize a psychological evaluation of the candidate's skills in human relations within an intercultural context, as well as the candidate's ability for coping with changes and differences; the candidate's susceptibility to severe culture shock.
❑ Identify specific physical and intellectual barriers to successful adjustment in the foreign environment, if possible, to correct any deficiencies.
❑ Highlight any specific technical or management factors that need strengthening before the cross-cultural assignment.
❑ Find out any family problems or situations that would undermine employee effectiveness abroad.
❑ Provide this assessment for top and middle management personnel, supervisors, technicians and hourly employees.
❑ Provide a special review of individual suitability for foreign deployment in remote sites with limited input and support services.
❑ Adapt the process to meet the needs of foreign nationals brought on assignment to domestic operations.
❑ Interview candidates for foreign deployment with questions by psychologists and international personnel specialists.
❑ Provide group meetings for candidates, including employees who have returned from the foreign site, or host country nationals, to study interactions and determine suitability of prospects.
❑ Use instruments for data gathering about the candidates' attitudes and competencies regarding change, intercultural knowledge and relations, and communication skills—these may involve commercial or home-made questionnaires, inventories, checklists, and culture shock tests.

The overseas assessment process might further investigate:

❑ The tasks or activities the candidate might engage in, and the candidates' ability to accomplish them.

The first major component in a relocation or foreign deployment system involves evaluating individuals who are sent abroad and evaluating the organizational program responsible for the transfer and reentry process.

- ❏ The people with whom the individual will interact and the individual's ability to deal with representatives of the indigenous population.
- ❏ The extent to which the official position requires social interactions with host and third country nationals, as well as expatriates, and the capacity of the candidate to deal with such variety of human relationships.
- ❏ Whether the work can be handled by an individual or requires team collaboration, especially with persons outside the company.
- ❏ The language skills required (English or a foreign language) and the capacity of the candidate to meet them.
- ❏ Whether the individual is provincial in outlook, or has that person demonstrated prior interests in things outside his or her native country. How global in attitude is the candidate, and what is the individual's experience outside the home culture?
- ❏ Whether the candidate possesses a realistic concept of life overseas— job requirements, incongruities, opportunities, and frustrations—and if the candidate has previously visited the job site, what reactions did the candidate have?
- ❏ Provide hypothetical situations, critical incidents, or case studies that approximate the new assignment.
- ❏ How the person envisions the absence of several years from the homeland while on foreign assignment. (Is the individual realistic on how it will affect and change his or her personal life and that of dependents, as well as impact on career development and life plans?)
- ❏ How the candidate would be rated on overall assignment suitability relative to knowledge of the demands to be made upon him or her by the foreign job and society.

The assessment process should provide the candidate with factual information about the host country and assignment. Having seen films, slides, or videotapes of the onsite situation, and having discussed the salary adjustment, housing provisions, tax problems, and other such realities, the candidate should be given the opportunity to choose. This may result in the candidate refusing the foreign assignment.

The assessment center techniques used in some large companies may be modified to assist with recruitment and selection of overseas personnel. Or the organization may have to use an external resource, such as an international executive/management/technical search firm. Some companies use a selection review board made up of their own employees or members, qualified volunteers, and people who have served in the target culture. Existing specialists in corporate health and personnel services can provide valuable data.

Some criteria for selecting candidates for overseas service are empathy, openness, persistence, sensitivity to intercultural factors, respect for others, role flexibility, tolerance for ambiguity, and two-way communication skill. Research indicates that possession of these characteristics is correlated to adaptation and effectiveness outside an individual's home culture.

Some criteria for selecting candidates for overseas service are empathy, openness, persistence, sensitivity to intercultural factors, respect for others, role flexibility.

Russell[12] reviewed the literature for the past decades on what factors are associated with successful international corporate assignments. His "Dimension of Overseas Success in Industry" is found in Exhibit 6-1. The factors remain valid.

EXHIBIT 6-1
DIMENSIONS OF OVERSEAS SUCCESS IN INDUSTRY[12]

(Asterisks indicate most desirable characteristics of foreign deployment candidates.)
1. Technical Competence/Resourcefulness
   *Technical skill/competence
   Resourcefulness
   Imagination/creativity
   Demonstrated ability to produce results with limited resources
   Comprehension of complex relationships
2. Adaptability/emotional stability
   *Adaptability/flexibility
   Youthfulness
   Maturity
   Patience
   Perseverance
   *Emotional stability
   Variety of outside interests
   Ability to handle responsibility
   Feeling of self-worth/dignity
   Capacity for growth
3. Acceptability of Assignment to Candidate and Family
   *Desire to serve overseas
   Willingness of spouse to live abroad/family status
   Belief in mission/job
   Stable marriage/family life
   *Adaptability of spouse/family
   *Previous experience abroad
   *Motivation
   Willingness to take chances
   Willingness to travel
   (Negative trait: overly strong ties with family in home country)
4. Planning, Organization, and Utilizing Resources
   *Organization ability
   Self-sufficient as manager
   Ability to build social institutions
   Management skills
   Administrative skills

EXHIBIT 6-1 (CONTINUED)
DIMENSIONS OF OVERSEAS SUCCESS IN INDUSTRY[12]

5. Interpersonal Relationships/Getting Along with Others
    *Diplomacy and tact
    Consideration for others
    Human Relations skills
    Commands respect
    *Ability to train others
    Desire to help others
    Ability to get things done through others
    Sense for politics of situations
6. Potential for Growth in the Company/Organization
    *Successful domestic record
    Organizational experience
    Industriousness
    *Educational qualifications
    *Mental alertness
    Intellectual
    Dependability
7. Host Language Ability
    *Language ability in native tongue
8. Cultural Empathy
    *Cultural empathy/sensitivity
    *Interest in host culture
    Respects host nationals
    Understands own culture
    Open-minded
    Area expertise
    *Ability to get along with hosts
    *Tolerant of others' views
    Sensitive to others' attitudes
    Understands host culture
    Not ethnocentric/prejudiced
    Objective
9. Physical Attributes
    *Good health
    Sex gender acceptability
    Physical appearance
10. Miscellaneous
    *Character
    Generalist skills
    Independence on job
    Social acceptability
    *Leadership
    Friendliness
    Initiative/energy

Some organizations try to circumvent the selection problem by hiring persons with previous successful overseas assignment experience. Obviously, to assure effectiveness, some type of evaluation process should be utilized even in choosing such persons.

The corporate assessment process might include a survey of employees overseas regarding their special needs and problems related to foreign assignment, and how well the corporate or organizational orientation program helped them to cope with the onsite reality; or the investigation might be limited to expatriates who have returned home.

If a corporation or agency is not using an external consulting group to conduct its relocation services, then internal organizational resources should be developed before the next stage in the deployment process can occur. For example, a corporate library or data bank on cultural specifics could be developed for each overseas' location. In a large global organization, both management and employees would have access to this information.

Stage Two—Employee Orientation

The second component in a foreign deployment system is some type of self-learning/training about the culture. The content can include learning modules on cross-cultural communications and change, understanding culture and its influence on behavior, culture shock and cross-cultural relations, improving organizational relations and intercultural effectiveness. In the general program for increasing cultural awareness, several alternatives are possible.

Another approach to replace or supplement formal group instruction is individualized learning packages for the employee and their family. This is a programmed learning and media instructional system on cultural differences in general, and for the specific country to be visited. Such a self-instructional program could be used at home with one's family. It might also serve as a preparation for classroom instruction.

Culture specific briefing programs can be developed for a particular geographical area or country. Thus, the Middle East could be a subject of area study with particular emphasis on Saudi Arabia and Iran. A learning program of twelve or more hours can be designed with self-instructional manual for individual study, or use the materials for group training.

Obviously, no foreign deployment orientation is complete without adequate language and technical training. However, the focus here is on cultural training and preparation.

We would like to summarize current thinking on this second stage of foreign deployment in the form of some recommendations for orienting employees.

Obviously, no foreign deployment orientation is complete without adequate language and technical training.

Phase One—General Culture/Area Orientation

1. Become culturally aware of the factors that make a culture unique, and the characteristics of the home culture that influence employee behavior abroad.
2. Seek local cross-cultural experience and engage in intercultural communication with microcultures within the homeland so as to sensitize oneself to cultural differences.
3. Foster more global attitudes in the family, and counteract ethnocentrism—cook national dishes of other countries, attend cultural weeks or exhibits of foreign or ethnic groups.

Phase Two—Language Orientation

1. Undertake 60–80 hours of formal training in the language of the host country.
2. Supplement classroom experience with 132–180 hours of self-instruction in the language, listen to audio cassettes or records in the foreign tongue, read newspapers, magazines, or books in the new language, speak to others who have this language skill, listen to music in the language.
3. Build a 500-word survival vocabulary.
4. Develop specialized vocabularies for the job or marketplace, etc.
5. Seek further education in the language upon arrival in the host country.
6. Practice the language at every opportunity, especially with family members.

Phase Three—Culture Specific Orientation: Training and Learning

1. Learn and gather data about the specific culture of the host country.
2. Understand and prepare for "culture shock."
3. Check out specific company policies about the assigned country, relative to allowances for transportation, housing, education, expense accounts, and provisions for salaries, taxes, and other fringe benefits including medical service and emergency leave.
4. Obtain necessary transfer documents (passports, visas, etc.), and learn customs, policies and regulations, as well as currency restrictions, for entry and exit.
5. Interview fellow employees who have returned from the host country. Get practical information about banking, shopping, currency, climate, mail, and law enforcement.
6. Read travel books and other information about the country and culture.

Phase Four—Job Orientation: Information Gathering

1. Obtain information about the overseas job environment and organization.
2. Be aware of the government's customs, restrictions and attitudes regarding the corporation or project.
3. Arrange for necessary technical training to assure high performance abroad.

Strategies of foreign deployment should encompass the staff engaged in recruiting, selecting, and training; the employee and dependents assigned abroad; and the host culture managers who are responsible for organizational personnel in the new environment. The focus should be on the opportunities afforded by the international assignment for personal growth, professional exchange and development, and effective representation of country and corporation.

Stage Three—Support Service: Onsite Support and Monitoring

Once employees have been recruited, selected, trained, and transported abroad, the personnel responsibility should be to: (a) facilitate their integration into a different work environment and host culture, (b) evaluate their needs and performance, and (c) encourage morale and career development. Toward the end of the person's tour of duty, the HRD department should assist in an orderly transition to the home culture and the domestic organization.

As a follow-up to the predeparture training, some type of orientation and briefing should occur regarding the local situation soon after the family arrives in the host country. Back home there might have been a lack of readiness to listen to details about the job and new community. Now that the expatriates are faced with the daily realities of life they may have many questions.

The onsite orientation should be pragmatic, and meet the needs of the expatriate family. It should demonstrate that the organization cares about its people. It should aid the employee and his or her family to (a) resolve immediate living problems; (b) meet the challenge of the host culture and the opportunities it offers for travel, personal growth, and intercultural exchange; (c) attempt to reduce the culture shock and to grow from that experience; (d) provide communication links to the local community and the home organization. Much of this can be accomplished in a systematic, informal, friendly, group setting.

Onsite support services cannot just be for the first year abroad, or take for granted that the adjustment is satisfactory if the family manifests no overt problems in the first two years of a five-year tour of duty

Strategies of foreign deployment should encompass the staff engaged in recruiting, selecting, and training; the employee and dependents assigned abroad; and the host culture managers.

overseas. There must be a continuing follow-up and undergirding of the foreign deployment program with reinforcement inputs, "hotline" alerts and counseling, and other innovative means to reduce family stress and strain.

Furthermore, more emphasis should be given to mental health services in both the selection and support of overseas personnel. Ideally, a total system of transcultural personnel services should offer counseling and community services to expatriate families.

Three formal steps that the organization's human resource development staff might take abroad are:

1. *An adjustment survey*—Approximately 3–6 months after arrival, request the employee to supply feedback on the foreign deployment situation. The survey should be completed with other family members. Greater cooperation and authenticity might be forthcoming if on-site management does not have access to the individual responses. A second administration of the inquiry form might be considered twelve or eighteen months after arrival, or just prior to completing the assignment.

2. *Data analysis and reporting*—The information is analyzed from two viewpoints: individual need, and foreign deployment policies and practices. The material would be analyzed for the identification of problems and the recommendation of solutions. Reporting enables back-home management to monitor its foreign deployment system, while on-site management can improve the quality of working life for the expatriated employees. As group data are compiled and stored in a computer, a profile is drawn on overseas employee needs and concerns relative to foreign deployment at a particular location. This collection of significant information is then used in future orientation and training programs for planning. Data stored from deployment groups over a period of years provide insight into the requirements of overseas personnel in a geographic area. The results from such inquiry studies, whether used on a short- or long-term basis, have preventive value relative to problems of cultural adjustment, and lead to considerable savings in financial and human terms.

3. *Organizational communications*—To counteract alienation, loneliness, and feelings of being "cut off," an organization must establish communication links with its representatives abroad. Newsletters, other company publications, and video or audio cassettes need to be sent to expatriates and their families. The communications can reinforce previous learning and ego building at the foreign location. The employee would continue to be plugged into domestic operations, and be confident that his or her overseas assignment is important.

Reporting enables back-home management to monitor its foreign deployment system, while on-site management can improve the quality of working life for the expatriated employees.

Ideally, at least six months before completion of the foreign assignment, the employee should be getting assistance relative to departure, transition, and reintegration into his or her native country and domestic work environment.

Stage Four—Reacculturation: Reentry Program

The last component in the foreign deployment system involves reintegrating the expatriate into the home society and domestic organization. For the person or family who has been abroad for sometime, the homeland and the organizational culture will have changed upon their return. The reentry process begins overseas with the psychological withdrawal that the expatriate faces with returning home. Upon return, reentry shock may occur for six months or more, as the person struggles to readjust to the life-style and tempo of the changed home and organizational cultures. Apart from the challenge of reestablishing home and family life is the issue of reassignment in the parent company or agency.

For many expatriates, it is a time of crises and trauma, the last stage of the culture shock process. The experience abroad for those who are sensitive and who got involved in the host culture was profound. It causes many people to reexamine their lives, values, attitudes; to assess how they became what they are. It prompts others to want to change their life-style. The reentry home becomes the opportunity to carry out these aspirations. Individuals may not be satisfied to return to old neighborhoods, old friends, or the same job or company affiliation. Many wish to apply the new self-insights, and to seek new ways of personal growth. The organization that sent them abroad in the first place should be empathetic to this reality, and be prepared to deal with it.

The foreign deployment system is incomplete unless it helps returning employees to fit into the home culture and organization. The deployment system may involve group counseling with personnel specialists, psychologists, and former expatriates.

However, expatriates coming back from an overseas assignment are a valuable resource. The corporation can learn much from their cross-cultural experience.

Tung[13] examines the issue of managing personnel abroad. To bolster the contention that human resource management (HRM) is the key to successful international operations, she surveyed current programs at training institutes (UK's Center for International Briefings at Farnham Castle, as well as Japan's Institute for International Assignment and Japanese American Conversation Institute). In addition, she analyzed the expatriate policies and practices within British, Italian, Swiss, and German multinationals and two transnational corporations (an MNC owned by people of different nationalities with two or more parent headquarters. Tung concludes that European and Japanese multination-

The foreign deployment system is incomplete unless it helps returning employees to fit into the home culture and organization.

als have lower failure rates with "expats" because they are more international or global in their orientation, and select and train people who are more adept at living and working in a foreign environment. Global organizations must provide a cross-cultural component in the human resource development of not only those they send abroad, but also with the company's local host nationals who must learn to work effectively with internationals.

At the end of the 20th century, one conclusion is evident—personnel deployment strategies should be both dynamic and flexible. One relocation program might be designed within the home culture, while another is focused upon the global manager in a host culture. The latter may have two variations (1) for professionals, technicians, and sales representatives who operate abroad on short-term multinational assignments, often with limited time spent in a variety of countries; (2) for long-term expatriates assigned to a specific region or country. In either situation a modular program is preferable with standard learning modules or procedures to fit differing employee needs. For example, if dependents are included in the transfer, then there should be a family approach to relocation and travel, to identity crises and culture shock, and to reentry challenges. Trauma and dislocation problems can be managed if people are forewarned, trained to interact in a mutually supportive way, and use resources to facilitate adjustment within an alien environment.

MANAGING BUSINESS PROTOCOL

World trade is considered by many to be the human race's best chance to maintain global peace and prosperity. Luis Aranda[14] maintains the potential for substantial international commerce is largely untapped. To improve trade and lower deficits in the global marketplace, Aranda advocates more than training in managing change, interpersonal skills, and cultural difference. To perform effectively outside one's native country, Aranda believes companies should be providing employees with:

❑ *Technical knowledge* for penetrating foreign markets (e.g., introducing new products in foreign markets, licensing patents and dealing with non-tariff barriers abroad, identifying potential export opportunities.)
❑ *Comparative management* for dealing with foreign business and government (e.g., comparison of regional management practices, cross-cultural negotiating skills, current international business issues and trends.

The scope of foreign investment in other countries' economies is another reason for concern about observing their business protocols if one seeks a return on it. An Arthur Andersen study revealed that foreigners invested $26.2 billion in the U.S.A. in 1993, the biggest investors

World trade is considered by many to be the human race's best chance to maintain global peace and prosperity.

being Britain, Japan, Germany, The Netherlands, and France, along with Canada. Cross-cultural sensitivity on the part of such investors not only ensures that the right ventures and projects are chosen, but further trade and business relationships which assures their success.

Today the developed and developing countries all invest in each other's ventures, transferring funds to underwrite projects or to purchase stocks. It is a global market and the stock markets in each region are interdependent, networking, and exchanging with one another.

Another cultural dimension requiring caution is the legal system in various countries. U.S. legal practices are rooted in English Common Law whose premise is "you are innocent until proven guilty." However, Mexico is still guided by the Napoleonic Code where if accused, "you are guilty until you prove your innocence."

Some countries have underdeveloped legal systems as in China and Russia, while others lack a legal system. Thus, world-class law firms with offices around the globe hire cadres of local lawyers or barristers to ensure that provisions of local laws and regulations are respected in the course of their professional practice. LaPere[15] wrote of her ordeal caused by a persistent street peddler in Pamukkale, Turkey. To get rid of the pesky salesman, she paid $20 for three dirty marble heads that turned out to be ancient Roman sculpture from nearby ruins. Detained by customs officials, she was accused of smuggling antiquities, and faced Turkish law based again on the Napoleonic Code. The harrowing experience ended by an unauthorized escape. U.S. constitutional guarantees and passports are meaningless when abroad. One had best know and observe the laws of the foreign country in which one visits or does business.

Life is filled with turning points and crises that can be turned into challenges for personal and professional growth.

SUMMARY

Life is filled with turning points and crises that can be turned into challenges for personal and professional growth. Such transitional experiences are characteristic of going abroad and the passage from the industrial to metaindustrial work culture. The trauma experienced in this adjustment process can take many forms, whether it is called culture or reentry shock, role or organization shock, or even future shock. Essentially, cross-cultural transitions threaten our sense of identity. Such transitions force us to rethink and reevaluate the way we read meaning into our private worlds. They are opportunities to learn, to grow, and to transform our life-style, management, or leadership.

Organizations can assist personnel to reduce such shocks to their systems by coaching, counseling, and training. The stress and anxiety that result need not lead to severe disorientation, depression, and unhealthy behavior. These can be countered by increasing awareness and information, providing enjoyable intercultural experiences, as well as facilitating integration into the unfamiliar situation.

When considered in the context of sending employees overseas on assignment, the return on organizational investment in cross-cultural preparation and continuing support services can be considerable. We recommend that sponsoring multinational corporations or agencies institute a foreign deployment system. This approach to transnational activities cannot only reduce premature return costs and much unhappiness among expatriates and overseas' customers, it can improve performance, productivity, and profitability in the world market.

Furthermore, observing and practicing both national and international protocol facilitates human performance and cooperation, especially in development projects. Such counsel becomes even more meaningful in the context of technology transfer, whether within a nation, or across borders.

REFERENCES

1. Storti, C. *Figuring Foreigners Out,* Yarmouth, ME: Intercultural Press, 1999.
2. Pollock, D. C. and Van Reken, R. E. *The Third Culture Kid Experience,* Yarmouth, ME: Intercultural Press, 1999.
3. Campbell, J. *Hero With a Thousand Faces,* Princeton, NJ: Princeton University Press, 1968. See also Osland, J. S. *The Adventure of Working Abroad—Hero Tales from the Global Frontier,* San Francisco, CA: Jossey-Bass, 1995.
4. Books on lifestyle transitions are available from Knowledge Systems, Inc. (7777 W. Morris St., Indianapolis, IN 46231, USA): *Life Changes—Growing through Personal Transitions* by S. A. Spencer and J. D. Adams; *Transitions—Make Sense of Life's Changes* by W. Bridges; *Over Fifty—Resource Book for the Better Half of Your Life* by T. & N. Biracress; *Transitions—a Women's Guide to Successful Retirement* by D. Cort-Van Arsdale.
5. Klopf, D. W. *Intercultural Encounters,* 3rd ed., Englewood, CO: Morton Publishing Company, 1995.
6. Lewis, T. and Jungman, R. (eds.). *On Being Foreign: Culture Shock in Short Fiction,* Yarmouth, ME: Intercultural Press, 1986.
7. Furnham, A. and Bochner, S. *Culture Shock—Psychological Reactions to an Unfamiliar Environment,* New York: Methuen & Co., 1986. See also King, N. and Huff, K. *Host Family Survival Kit,* 2nd ed., Yarmouth, ME: Intercultural Press, 1997.
8. Oberg, K. "Culture Shock and the Problem of Adjustment to New Cultural Environments," Washington, DC: Foreign Service Institute, 1958.
9. Osland, J. S. "The Hero's Adventure: The Overseas Experience of Expatriate Business People," unpublished doctoral dissertation, Case Western University, 1990. Available through University Microfilms International, 300 N. Zeeb Road, Ann Arbor, MI 48106.
10. Berry, J. W. "Psychology of Acculturation," *Applied Cross-Cultural Psychology,* R. W. Brislin (ed.), Newbury Park, CA: Sage Publications, 1990.

Observing and practicing both national and international protocol facilitates human performance and cooperation

11. Harrison, A. A., Clearwater, Y. A., and McKay, C. P. (eds.). *From Antarctica to Outer Space—Life in Isolation and Confinement,* New York, NY: Springer-Verlag, 1991. . . . Harris, P. R., *Living and Working in Space—Human Behavior, Culture, and Organization.* Chichester, UK: Wiley/Praxis Publishing, 1996 (PRAXIS, White House, Church Lane, Eastergate, Chichester, West Sussex PO20 6 UR, England; in the USA, distributor is John Wiley); Harris, P. R. "The Influence of Culture on Space Developments," in *Social Concerns of Space Resources* edited by M. F. & D/ F. McKay (vol. 4, pp. 189–219) and M. B. Duke (Washington, DC: U.S. Government Printing Office, 1992, NASA SP-509, 5 vol.).

12. Russell, P. W. Jr., unpublished paper presented at SIETAR Conference, Phoenix, AZ, 1978.

13. Tung, R. L. *The New Expatriates—Managing Human Resources Abroad,* Cambridge, MA: Ballinger/Harper & Row, 1988; see also, Dowling, P. J., Schuler, R. S., and Welch, D. E. *International Dimensions of Human Resource Management,* Belmont, CA: Wadsworth Publishers, 1994.

14. Aranda, L. *Training and Development Journal,* April 1986, pp. 71–73.

15. LaPere, G. *Never Pass This Way Again,* Bethesda, MD: Adler and Adler, 1987.

16. Elashmawi, F. *Business Across Cultures,* Houston, TX: Gulf Publishing Co., 2000.

17. Nelson, C. A. *Protocol for Profit,* London: International Thomson Business Press, 1998.

18. Morrison, T., Conway, W., and Douress, J. *Dunn & Bradstreet Guide to Doing Business Around the World,* Englewood Cliffs, NJ: Prentice Hall, 1997.

19. Sheehy, G. *New Passages, Mapping Your Life Across Time,* New York: Random House, 1995.

MANAGING DIVERSITY IN THE GLOBAL WORK CULTURE

T he globalization of economies and marketplaces and advances in communication technologies are transforming worldwide the workplace culture, as well as the work force. Workers are moving in greater numbers across borders and national cultures, increasing diversity within societies and institutions.

The concept of diversity has many applications but this chapter examines only a few.

WORK FORCE DIVERSITY IN NORTH AMERICA

In many countries throughout the world, changing demographics is a driving force toward greater diversity in the work force. Nowhere is this more evident than in North America because of changes in laws and social mores. Furthermore, democracy and affluence in the United States and Canada have made them targets of opportunity for economic, as well as political, refugees and émigrés.

The demographics of U.S. society have changed significantly over the past 50 years. By the year 2000, women will constitute about 50% of the workforce and 29% of the workforce will be nonwhite. Organizations face the challenge of using this diverse workforce in increasingly productive ways. Research has shown that productivity decreases when relationships among diverse groups is poor. There is little research on the impact and effectiveness of diversity training.[1]

To unleash the talent and potential of this changing work force, the public and private sectors are increasing diversity training within their organizations.

To unleash the talent and potential of this changing work force, the public and private sectors are increasing diversity training within their organizations. However, there is much controversy over the definitions of diversity and the training that may result. Betances[2] states:

> Differences among people are wonderful facts of life. Problems emerge because of the meaning we attach to such differences as skin color, gender, age, or sexual orientation. The diversity agenda must be concerned with making sure that people understand that differences are okay. We must not send a message that to become successful in our society, women have to act like men, African-Americans need to straighten their hair, or Hispanics have to forget Spanish. We have to use diversity as a process of discovery and acceptance, of celebration of differences rather than thinking of differences as problems.

However, as a foil to this, Thomas[3] states that:

> . . . people want to act like diversity is synonymous with differences. They talk about diversity fracturing the country, fracturing the organization. For me diversity refers to both differences and similarities. So diversity, as opposed to fracturing, becomes the context within which you can talk about the ties that bind and also the differences that make us unique. . . . We can be different and still united. . . . Now it remains to be seen if we come together and move forward in a united way around similarities and still be very different.

Within the cultures of our civilizations, there is a universal microculture of work and that is changing worldwide as well.

Advances in telecommunications and mass transportation, and the breaking down of national borders and cultures has lead to the emergence of a global, information-oriented culture. While this happens at the macro level, counterforces are at work in some cultures locally, exhibited by the "ethnic cleansing" of people who are *different*. Humanity's mainstream needs to appreciate that our common survival and the satisfaction of our universal needs and concerns are interdependently linked.

Within the cultures of our civilizations, there is a universal *microculture of work* and that is changing worldwide as well. In business today, people are the most important source of sustainable competitive advantage. Every person brings a unique combination of background, heritage, gender, religion, education and experiences to the workplace. Their diversity represents an enormous source of new ideas and vitality. The authors attempted to outline some of these changes and ideas in both Chapters 1 and 3, as well as in their volume, *Developing the Global Organization*,[4] which describes the rise of a new work culture, and the requirements for global leadership therein. The principal new work culture driving forces are both economic and technological. Alvin and Heidi Toffler aptly observe our age of painful instability:[5]

The world economy today is undergoing its deepest restructuring since the Industrial Revolution. A fundamentally new system for creating wealth is emerging. It is not based on "First Wave" agrarian toil in the fields . . . nor on muscle work in "Second Wave" factories. The revolution is based instead on "Third Wave" knowledge-work that substitutes ideas and information for the transitional economic inputs of land, labor, capital and energy.

Bear in mind that the changes occurring within the work environment reflect substantial transitions happening in society at large. Howard suggests three dimensions to analyze.[6]

1. Work—its nature is being transformed both in terms of content and context, thus altering job designs and work roles.
2. Workers—as a result, personnel selection, placement, activities and relationships are in transition.
3. Working—is now different in manner, performance, association and experience.

PEOPLE ON THE MOVE

Migration helped create humans, drove us to conquer a planet, shaped our societies and promises to reshape them again. . . . If they (people) had not moved and intermingled as much as they did, they probably would have evolved into a different species.[7]

The numbers of workers going beyond their homelands in search of jobs may cause severe strain on the locals, while being a boon for their economy. In the U.S., for instance, the Southern states are reporting a large influx of unskilled laborers. The work force in the South is 10% Latino, while the Asian population in the region jumped 42% over the past decade. In Fayetteville, AR, Latinos comprise 9.1% of the inhabitants, taking jobs no one else seems to want. Most Arkansans welcome the input of Latino music, food, and tax dollars, while others complain about increased crime and lower wages. Arkansas "can either welcome and invest in its new immigrants, or it can waste a golden opportunity for growth and renewal."[8]

In the host countries and especially in local counties, the social fabric is being reconfigured and strained by massive waves of immigrants, whether legal or illegal, who come to live and work, permanently or temporarily. The demographic changes are often from developing economies to industrialized nations. The migrations are not just to North America, but to Europe. The geographic emigration pattern often is from South (Latin America, Africa, and the Middle East) to North (e.g., U.S., or England, France and Germany). The mass migrations are

Mass migrations are usually in pursuit of a better way of life, but frequently cause costly, complex social and financial problems for the host culture.

usually in pursuit of a better way of life, but frequently cause costly, complex social and financial problems for the host culture struggling to absorb the new arrivals.[9]

Categories of people on the move include:[10]

❑ **Refugees:** People living outside their country of nationality, afraid to return for reasons of race, religion, social affiliation or political opinion. The U.N. Office of the High Commissioner for Refugees counts more than 150 million refugees worldwide, including 5 million in Africa.

❑ **Internally displaced persons:** People forced to flee their homes because of armed conflict but who have not yet crossed international boundaries. There are an estimated 14 million. Like refugees, they have generally lost all they own and are not protected by their national governments.

❑ **Migrant workers:** People, both skilled and unskilled, who work outside their home country, including the legally employed migrants without legal permission to work abroad, and undocumented immigrants. It is estimated that there are as many as 50 million migrant workers and their families worldwide, with as many as half of them illegal.

Exhibit 7-1[11] summarizes the dual impact of the ongoing push and pull of immigration.

Throughout the world, societies, and particularly workplaces, are becoming more heterogeneous or multicultural. Scholars from the Urban Institute[12] forecast that by 2030, whites will constitute only 60% of the U.S. population in contrast to 75% today, while in some states, such as California, nonwhites may begin to approach a majority. With a sudden and massive influx of new arrivals, a social byproduct is compounding of tensions among racial groups, including more violence and hate crimes against minorities, more immigrant bashing and restrictive legislation. In 1994, civil strife over ethnic, racial or religious differences occurred in 51 nations—reportedly caused by the impact of global migration and lack of population control, as well as by quest for power, insecurity and limited resources.

The global work culture is best characterized by two words— change and diversity.

These recent arrivals bring new energy, talent, and enthusiasm to the pursuit of freedom and other democratic benefits—they add both human and financial capital. The mix of citizenry is more like a mosaic; in America, the racial or ethnic backgrounds of individuals increasingly defy categorization. Some high schools in Los Angeles, for instance, are composed of students who are first-generation or immigrants including black Hispanics, Chinese-Cubans, Portuguese-speaking Koreans from Brazil et al.—the new citizens of the world, a rainbow coalition. Thus, the global work culture is best characterized by two words—*change and diversity.* It is well to remind ourselves that just as in nature diversity makes for adaptation. As Sowell[13] observes, "differences in productive

Exhibit 7-1[11]
Root Causes of Immigration

When people leave their homes generally there is a "push" factor from the sending country and a "pull" factor from the receiving country. Of course, individual, religious, political or economic reasons play a critical role.

Principal "push" factors include:	"Pull" Factors in receiving countries include:
❑ war and civil strife, including religious conflicts ❑ economic decline and rising poverty ❑ rising unemployment ❑ population pressures (more specifically, burgeoning numbers of unemployed youth) ❑ political instability ❑ large-scale natural disaster and ecological degradation ❑ human rights violations ❑ denial of education and health care for selected minorities, and other kinds of persecution ❑ government resettlement policies that threaten ethnic integrity ❑ resurgent nationalism	❑ substantial immigration markets and channels opened up in the West ❑ family reunion with workers already living in Europe ❑ safety ❑ freedom from fear of violence, persecution, hunger and poverty ❑ economic opportunity ❑ education ❑ maintaining ethnic identity ❑ access to advances in communication and technology

skills and cultural values are key to understanding the advancement or regression of groups, countries, and civilizations.

As the 21st century begins, global leaders who understand what is happening to societies and workplaces should also be aware of two other counter trends impacting world development.

❑ Resurgence of people's popular interest in their ethnic identities, religious roots, and ancient affiliations.

❑ Emergence of transnational ethnic groups of *global tribes* who have a major influence on international trade and the economy.

These latter, whether Asian, British, Russian, or whatever their origin, are frequently venture capitalists, financiers, arbitragers and entrepreneurs who benefit by the discipline of their traditions. These commercial tribes are bound together by common heritage, language, and culture.

A third trend to recognize is the desire of enlightened migrants everywhere for freedom, democracy, and protection of their human rights, including at work. The United Nations has best articulated their aspirations in its Declaration of Human Rights. Those who would be global leaders, private sectors, recognize that both society and the work environment must follow the declaration's guidance.

Immigration Patterns in Europe

The Conference Board[11] reports that before the early '70s immigration into Western Europe was fueled by political unrest and harsh economic times under Communist regimes. Cultural similarities made integration into the expanding Western European workforces and labor pools relatively easy. Then during the early '70s Communist regimes tightened their control and consolidated their rule and few were permitted to leave. At the same time, nationals from developing countries outside Europe fled politically repressive regimes. But unlike the treatment accorded Eastern Europeans, these nationals were not the recipient of the same sensitivity to their adjustment and migration.

In 1989, with the East German wall coming down, millions of people surged across the border. Not since the end of World War II had there been such population shifts, but gradually the mass migration stabilized.

By 1990, according to the Conference Board,[11] 9 million migrants remained in the European Union and the continental-wide tightening of immigration policies ensued. Family reunification, expert labor and political asylum have been the only legal avenues of entry available to Western Europe. An increasing number of economic migrants have attempted to seek a back-door entry to Europe by applying for political asylum, causing the applications in Western Europe for asylum to skyrocket over 500,000 requests. Progress in the political and economic union of the European Community in the 21st century will further advance diversity. Agreements now permit citizens of the EC countries to travel and work in member countries with a minimum of regulation.

NEW WORK PROCEDURES

A reality of the new work order is diversity in production. As advanced economies move from the mass production of the Industrial Age, those types of jobs that facilitate mass production migrate to developing countries. In the "high performance workplace" quality has replaced quantity, and variety takes precedence over volume. Here, efficiency and service are the watchwords, along with ideas like lean inventories, flexible operations (i.e., customization, timeliness within

As advanced economies move from the mass production of the Industrial Age, those types of jobs that facilitate mass production migrate to developing countries.

economies of scale with global reach), diversified quality achieved through information technology and autonomous teams of skilled craftsman. The current American work environment is eclectic, pragmatically borrowing from the above approaches perfected abroad.[15] Two contemporary models in use are: (1) *lean production*—which is characterized by centralized coordination, performance measurement, and "reengineering" to cut overhead and reduce manufacturing or service cycle time; and (2) *team management*—which relies on innovative workers involved in decision-making and operating with self-management teams and quality circles.[16]

While global competitiveness pushes companies to "re-invent" the workplace, often the changes are cosmetic and faddish. Yet application of the lean production model among the largest U.S. corporations has resulted in elimination of 5 million jobs, one quarter of the work force. Downsizing forces the remaining employees to take up the slack and work longer hours, however, business is facilitated considerably by new communication technologies.

In the new work environment, even the size of a firm no longer matters. Large corporations reorganize themselves into smaller, autonomous business units that have more flexibility. Rubbermaid did that, while the Swedish-Swiss engineering giant, Asea Brown Boveri, subdivided itself into 1,300 independent companies and 5,000 autonomous profit centers. On the other hand, smaller firms can obtain the advantages of larger corporations by forming strategic alliances to lengthen their reach. Nike, the American sports-shoe manufacturer, has a local, core work force, but through its fluid networks and contract workers it seems to be a sprawling multinational operating across geographical and corporate boundaries.

Work Force Trends

Wrenching changes in work structure and composition are underway worldwide. In North America, management seeks to transform traditional practices of recruitment and hiring, compensation and benefits, career development and training. Based upon the Hudson Institute's "Work Force 2000"[17] study, futurists have identified some pertinent trends affecting the new work culture. These are:

Diversity of Personnel

Apart from more women, minorities, and migrants, the American workforce is aging. By the end of 2003, it is estimated that there will be more workers over the age of 40 than under 40.[18] Furthermore, the workforce is more mobile and diverse in attitudes and lifestyles.

By the end of 2003, it is estimated that there will be more workers over the age of 40 than under 40.

Expansion of Worker Support Services

With more women in the workforce and growth in dual career families, increasingly, employers are making provisions to lessen stress on personnel and to improve the integration of work with home (e.g., family leave to cope with sick dependents and elder-care, day-care for employee children).

Flexible Work Arrangements

To get more work done at less cost, as well as to attract the necessary skills, firms are varying work schedules, allowing job sharing (even by spouses), and permitting temporary or contract work, as well as distance work at home or in a satellite work center (40 million Americans now work out of a home office).

Focused Human Resource Development

To meet the need for new and critical knowledge and technological skills, training and education of workers on the job is being boosted, while companies reach out to school systems for future personnel offering internships, incentives and cooperative work arrangements with educational institutions.

Competing in the Global Talent Pool

To cope with changes in the world economy, organizations are not only re-structuring and engaging in mergers/acquisitions, but they are "wooing" knowledge workers across borders because birthrates are down in industrialized nations, and up in developing countries (e.g., offering more incentives to the technologists, involving workers directly in marketing/sales/customer relations, providing them with assistance from artificial intelligence, automation, robotics).[19]

Creating Virtual Corporations and Communities

Global leaders who tread the Information Highway enter into cyberspace, using computer networks, telecommunications, and virtual reality technologies to create new electronic relationships, as well as new commercial ventures.[20]

DIVERSITY

The popular understanding of diversity usually refers to differences in people of color, ethnic origin, gender, sexual or religious preferences, age

The popular understanding of diversity usually refers to differences in people of color, ethnic origin, gender, sexual or religious preferences, age and disabilities.

and disabilities. In his book on empowering a diverse work force Simons[21] has provided a glossary that defines diversity as:

> . . . the current term used to describe a vast range of cultural differences that have become factors needing attention in living and working together. Often applied to organizational and training interventions that seek to deal with the interface of people who are different from one another.

Stated definitions of *organizational* diversity recognize a wide range of characteristics. According to American Express Financial Advisors[22] they include:

> . . . race, gender, age, physical ability, physical appearance, nationality, cultural heritage, personal background, functional experience, position in the organization, mental and physical challenges, family responsibilities, sexual orientation, military experience, educational background, style differences, economic status, thinking patterns, political backgrounds, city/state/region of residence, IQ level, smoking preference, weight, marital status, non-traditional job, religion, white collar, language, blue collar and height.

Of course, each human being is unique and our basic differences stem from our perceptions of one another, influenced by our cultural backgrounds. South African Samuel Paul, a victim of apartheid, reminds us, "Differences are not deficits to be changed and corrected, but gifts to be cherished and enjoyed."[23]

By valuing differences, companies are facing up to historic shifts in the makeup of the labor market. They realize it is a business and bottom-line issue, for it involves also communicating with and motivating diverse minorities and immigrants.

Responding to these shifts in the labor market has placed cultural diversity training as the third most important issue for business right behind health care and downsizing, ahead of team building and other management concerns (*Personnel Journal*, March 1994). What does this training focus upon?

Jamieson and O'Mara[24] outline three paths companies take to address workplace diversity. The most common is the "diversity awareness training," designed to make people aware of their own diversity, biases, and discriminations. Much of that training is experiential and designed to help individuals get more in touch with how they think and behave. Companies on the second path view diversity as an organizational and management opportunity, not just a matter of political correctness and human relations. This path usually involves senior management sessions focused primarily on exploring how policies, systems, and leadership help or hinder diversity management. The enthusiasm and drive that employers bring to this path determine the speed with which real change occurs. The third and least-traveled path catapults compa-

By valuing differences, companies are facing up to historic shifts in the makeup of the labor market.

nies beyond talking to systematically revising company policies, procedures and rules to make them flexible enough to encourage differences in needs and preferences.

In the workplace, the complex concept of diversity may also be examined in terms of either the individual worker or work teams. It provides the basis for the formation of identity, and persons may have multiple identities—racial, gender, ethnic, functional group identity.

Globalization also has prompted domestic business to seek diverse partners abroad, sometimes as part of the process of "de-verticalizing" an organization in which manufacturing is left to others.[25]

International competition is another powerful force behind the diverse work culture. C. K. Prahalad believes that a company's competitiveness comes from its ability to develop unique core competencies that spawn unanticipated products. Thus, the firm must (a) seek workers, regardless of gender, race, or ethnic origin, who possess these core competencies; (b) create a work community in which these high performers freely exchange information and knowledge about optimum work practices, and (c) share collective knowledge to keep ahead of competition.[26]

Besides economic factors diversity must be responsive to the 1991 Civil Rights Act and the Americans with Disabilities Act. This legislation places significant constraints on making race, gender, religion or ethnicity a factor in employment decisions. However, diversity initiatives recognize and value what is different, and in so doing may cause a dilemma between Equal Employment Opportunity guidelines, affirmative action and anti-discriminatory laws. These contradictions appear often in other aspects of our culture. For example, a doctor cannot refuse treatment to an individual because they are different. Yet, physicians do treat each patient individually focusing on their particular situation. Organizations need to be "clear in their understanding of diversity and precise in their expectations of employee behavior. . . ."[27]

Changing the attitudes and behaviors of any work force is challenging, but changing them in an unreceptive environment is an enormous task requiring a strong visionary blessed with persistence and stamina. It is unrealistic to expect employees to throw off the deeply imbedded perceptions and embrace diversity overnight——no matter how charismatic or persuasive the leader. Rethinking diversity and establishing a strategy will affect every aspect of organizational culture.

In the Industrial Age, for instance, much emphasis was placed on loyalty to the organization and many employees stayed with the same department or work unit throughout their career. But that implicit employment contract between individual and organization is becoming "unglued," as David M. Noer writes.[28] As the old system disappears, the new work culture calls for dynamic, flexible and responsible adults committed to personal and professional excellence. With the diverse work environment previously described, loyalty is now transferred from

Changing the attitudes and behaviors of any work force is challenging, but changing them in an unreceptive environment is an enormous task requiring a strong visionary blessed with persistence and stamina.

the organization to the work team, colleagues and even to one's career enhancement. Noer suggests that:

> Leadership is very different in a liberated work force unencumbered by fear, false expectations of promotions, or the distractions of politics and trying to impress the boss.

Capitalizing on People Diversity

As a concept, diversity has different meanings and applications, depending on where you are in the world. Simons[21] points out that "euromanagers" focus on developing global management skills, whereas the U.S. diversity praxis has moved beyond a legal basis of equity concerns and "leveling the playing field" for all workers. Instead, the current American emphasis is upon using human resources to improve creativity and productivity of both the enterprise and the nation. Thus, that will be the concern of this closing section.

Within our Information Society, it is important to recognize that increasing *globalism* enormously impacts the workforce worldwide.[29] For leading-edge organizations, globalism means the creation of a culture that embraces diversity to maximize the potential of personnel, especially through cohesive work teams.[30] For global managers, the challenge is to innovate in finding ways to improve human commitment and performance at work. Because so many people achieve their full potential through their work and career, the new work culture fosters values like empowerment and character development, gauging success not in terms of organizational status but in the quality of work life. For metaindustrial workers, Nair[31] suggests the quest for personal/professional excellence and meaningful business relationships take precedence over climbing the corporate ladder and the pursuit of external rewards.

If results are to be achieved, readjusting to the demands of today's work realities requires a revision of cultural assumptions about the external global environment, the organization, the manager and the group as suggested in Exhibit 7-2, which illustrates the main components influencing the new work culture.[32]

EMPOWERMENT

Empowerment refers to altering management style and transforming organizational set-ups from hierarchical to more participatory, sharing authority and responsibility with workers in a variety of ways.

Empowerment, as a concept, originated in North America. Generally, it refers to altering management style and transforming organizational set-ups from hierarchical to more participatory, sharing authority and responsibility with workers in a variety of ways. To empower means that leaders, be they heads of organizations, groups or families give individual members more freedom to act, more control over their own life. Inclusion rather exclusion, particularly with regard to women and

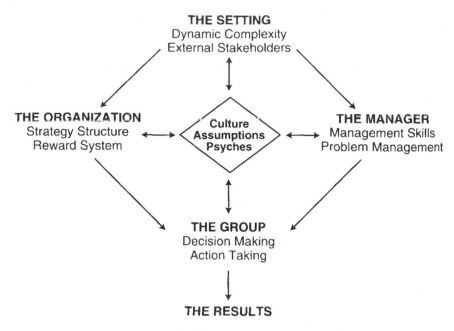

THE SETTING
Dynamic Complexity
External Stakeholders

THE ORGANIZATION
Strategy Structure
Reward System

Culture
Assumptions
Psyches

THE MANAGER
Management Skills
Problem Management

THE GROUP
Decision Making
Action Taking

THE RESULTS

EXHIBIT 7-2. BARRIERS TO SUCCESS.[32]

As globalization bridges the gap between national economies and peoples, empowerment does the same between management and labor.

minorities, becomes the organizational norm based on the competence of the individual. This approach is more open and decentralized. Thus team management is spreading across Asia and Europe. Japanese, who are culturally group oriented, have been slow to empower women and minorities. Meanwhile, in some countries in Asia and Eastern Europe, empowerment is manifesting itself in political restructuring from authoritarianism to democracy and free enterprise, in which managers are freed from government or party controls and are beginning to involve their coworkers in the process of reshaping factories, cooperatives and businesses.

As globalization bridges the gap between national economies and peoples, empowerment does the same between management and labor.

Simons describes empowerment as:[21]

> . . . the ability to feel capable and motivated in pursuing a goal. It is having the self-assurance needed to carry out and fulfill any endeavor. Empowerment can be self-initiated, or the result of attention and support of others.

Kouzes and Posner[33] state that there is one clear and consistent message about empowerment: "feeling powerful—literally feeling 'able'—comes from a deep sense of being in control of our own lives." When we feel we can determine our destiny and have the assurance that the resources and individuals needed to support us are available we can persist in our efforts. Conversely, when an individual is controlled by others, he or she may comply but not excel. Leadership is enhancing the individual's self-confidence and personal effectiveness. Kouzes and Posner have identified five fundamental strategies for empowering others.

1. *Ensure self-leadership by putting people in control of their lives.* When leaders share power and control with others they demonstrate trust and respect in others' abilities, they, in essence, make a covenant with them that is reciprocal and mutually beneficial. Individuals who can affect their leaders are attached to them and committed to the give and take of the shared power of their responsibilities.

2. *Provide choice.* Providing individuals options and discretion in the day-to-day operation of their jobs increases creativity and flexibility as one is freed from the standard set of rules and procedures. Jobs that are broadly designed and defined encourage this. Choice without skill can leave many employees overwhelmed.

3. Thus, *developing competence* is the third essential to empowerment. Leaders must invest in developing individual's skills and competencies. Giving employees opportunities to grow in their area of expertise as well as general business knowledge enables employees to act with the best interest of the corporation and the customer.

4. *Assign critical tasks.* Critical problems in an organization are usually addressed by those who have the most power. However, in innovative corporations like Chaparral Steel, research and development, for example, is brought to the factory floor. "We make the people who are producing the steel responsible for keeping their process on the leading edge of technology worldwide. If they have to travel, they travel. If they have to figure out what the next step is, they go out and find the places where people are doing interesting things. They visit other companies. They work with universities." This empowerment encourages involvement and responsibility regarding tasks that employees can own and make critical excellent judgments about.

5. *Offer visible support.* Leaders who want to empower are highly visible and make conscientious efforts to have employees gain recognition and validation. Making connections and building strong networks and relationships is empowering. A leader introduces employees to others in the corporation or community who may help them along their career path as well. "Strengthening others is essentially the process of turning constituents into leaders themselves—of making people capable of acting on their own initiative." Individuals take responsibility for their own career development, while leaders create a work environment that encourages others to achieve their human potential.

Providing individuals options and discretion in the day-to-day operation of their jobs increases creativity and flexibility

Employees who feel powerless often hoard whatever shreds of power they possess, creating organizational cultures that are often hierarchical and bureaucratic. When leaders share power it builds profound trust and responsibility. Employees view improvements and communication as a two-way street with the leader being as influenced by his or her work force as the work force is of management. Each committed to effectively doing their part.

With a multicultural work force and customer base, leadership provides vision, motivation and reasons for commitment. For contemporary organizations and their workers, knowledge and innovation equal global marketplace power. To that end, the transformation of systems values diverse personnel for their competency, rather than establishing barriers based on race, gender, or handicaps. Today's knowledge and service employees are encouraged to take a measure of control over their work lives.[34] The superintendent of public schools in Charlotte, North Carolina, did just that when he eliminated the positions of ten assistants and had school principals report directly to him. Using objective measures, this administrator proved that by surrendering some control to educators, he improved their productivity. In effect, the superintendent *empowered* principals so they could appreciate the connection between their actions and consequences. The popular manifestation of this trend is *worker participation* that involves employees in ongoing organizational change and development. Examples range from putting employees on the corporate board through devolving power to teams on the factory floor or in offices. Avis, the auto-rental company, empowers workers through 150 influential participation groups. The ultimate application is employee ownership where the workers actually become shareholders, often receiving equity by swapping contract concessions, as happened at Northwest and United Airlines. The National Center for Employee Ownership in Oakland, California, reports that 9,500 American companies already have employee shared ownership plans (ESOPs), representing 10% of the nation's work force, while 5,000 other firms have other programs through which personnel share options and ownership. Although in these, workers usually share only 20% or more of equity, research indicates that a combination of worker participation and/or ownership promotes a 10% growth rate in the enterprise. As Joseph Blasi[35] observes, managers should "create a participatory culture where share ownership becomes the reason to get more involved." That seems to have happened in the British retailing institution, John Lewis Partnership (JPL), where 38,000 employees in its 22 department stores receive a profit-sharing bonus up to 24% of salary.

Worker Transitional Problems

"Diversity is an organizational effort that aims to modify organizations, standards, procedures and management practice that hinder cre-

Employees who feel powerless often hoard whatever shreds of power they possess, creating organizational cultures that are often hierarchical and bureaucratic.

ativity, productivity and advancement of all employees."[36] Global leadership is essential in dealing with problems accentuated by diversity and changes in society that also alter organizational policy and procedures. In attempting to cope with "future shock," the behavior of workers influences changed corporate practices. Some of these social issues in the work force were identified in a recent study conducted by *Training* magazine (October 1994). The percentages cited are from principal responses of 1,194 U.S. organizations, a representative sample of all industries:

❏ Drugs: have a formal policy on substance abuse—3%; have employee assistance programs for recovery from substance abuse—56%; test job applicants for drug use—36%; test employees for drug use with probable cause—35%; conduct/sponsor training programs about substance abuse—28%.
❏ Smoking: have a policy for limiting smoking at work—67%; have policy that bans smoking at work—60%.
❏ AIDS: have an education program on AIDS and HIV infection—21%; have a formal AIDS policy—19%.
❏ Other: have a formal policy on sexual harassment—76%; have a formal affirmative action plan—64%; have a formal code of ethics—54%.

Transitional trauma occurs for many during the work culture shift underway. For some, it is triggered by acquiring new technological skills, or working with automation and robotics or in teams. For others, this form of work culture shock is caused by corporate mergers, downsizing, and reduction in workforce. Midmanagers and midlife workers are often a target in the attempts to cut costs and restructure operations for a more diversified global economy.

In 1994, 10,000 respondents to an "AARP Bulletin" questionnaire indicated they left their jobs because of pressures to nudge or push them out the door. By a 2-to-1 margin, readers replied that their dismissals violated in some way the Age Discrimination Act (ADEA). In addition to the high toll on older workers, they noted the traditional employer-employee compact that rewarded performance and loyalty with job security no longer exists. While some of these displaced, experienced workers go into business for themselves, the majority find it a struggle to get back into the workplace, often settling for less pay, part-time and/or temporary work.

Becoming a temporary or contract worker also has a positive side—it can improve one's quality of life, and permit the individual to decide how much he or she wishes to work. For some an hourly wage without benefits can actually lead to increased annual earnings with more control over one's benefits and retirement investments. In the mid '90s, the National Association of Temporary and Staffing Services reported 1.9 million American workers have temporary jobs, 73% of those in clerical or factory positions. Companies moving toward employing more tem-

Global leadership is essential in dealing with problems accentuated by diversity and changes in society that also alter organizational policy and procedures.

porary or contract workers like the flexibility in times of uncertainty. For high tech firms, especially those who operate on a project basis, they may permanently depend on the temporary service industry. Stellcom Technologies, for instance, employs 100 software engineers who take temporary work assignments, and these average 2,000 hours of work a year (the equivalent of a full-time worker). Within companies and agencies that employ large numbers of temporary workers, whole new management policies, styles and relationships are becoming necessary, further altering the organizational culture.

One reality of the new work culture is that the bond is being broken that tied workers and employers to long-term contracts. Today job security is only to be found within the individual worker who has marketable skills and the ability to learn new ones.

Observers of the contemporary work scene also express concern over what they perceive as the "dehumanization of the workplace." They complain about myopic executives who sacrifice in the name of "reorganization," long-term worker loyalty and gain short-term profits.

Within work cultures, diversity must be managed more effectively and innovatively, whether by an individual or an institution.

Diversity of all kinds is increasing in most countries and organizations.

SUMMARY

Diversity of all kinds is increasing in most countries and organizations. In the U.S. it is expected that all individuals in an organization learn to value diversity. The following statements about diversity make a good summary:[1]

1. Minorities do not want to be tolerated. Neither do other employees. They want to be valued. If they are valued, they can be effective.[37]
2. The "inventor" of racism is not present in any organization, but we all need to learn how to work with one another more effectively.
3. When power is shared, people are able to devote tremendous energy to the work at hand.
4. Human beings/people are the most important asset of any organization. They are the only sustainable competitive advantage for the future.
5. There is a great deal of information on the subject of diversity and much of it is overlapping.
6. There is no simple model for effective diversity training.
7. Diversity training, if effective, impacts positively on an organization's productivity.
8. Diversity training should focus on information, management, processes and results.

9. Diversity training is not a replacement of Equal Employment Opportunity (EEO) or Affirmative Action (AA).
10. Diversity is to be cherished for it enriches life and advances the actualization of human potential.

REFERENCES

1. Moran, R. T. and Stockton, J. L. *Diversity Training, What Works: Training and Development Practices,* Bassi, L. J. and Russ-Eft, D. (eds.), Alexandria, VA: American Society for Training and Development, 1997.
2. Betances, S. "Making Our Society Safe for Differences," *Cultural Diversity Sourcebook,* Abramms, B. and Simons, G. F. (eds.), Amherst, MA: ODT, 1996.
3. Thomas, R. R. "Diversity Is a Business Issue," *Cultural Diversity Fieldbook,* Simons, G., Abramms, B., Hopkins, L. A. and Johnson, D. J. (eds.), NJ: Peterson's/Pacesetter Books, 1996.
4. Moran R. T., Harris, P. R., and Stripp, W. G. *Developing the Global Organization,* Houston, TX: Gulf Publishing, 1993; see also Renesch, J. (ed.). *Leadership in a New Era: Visionary Approaches to the Biggest Crisis of our Time,* San Francisco, CA: Sterling & Stone, Inc., 1994.
5. Toffler, A. *Power Shift: Knowledge, Wealth, and Violence at the Edge of the 21st Century* (1990); and Toffler, A. and Toffler, H. *War and Anti-War: Survival at the Dawn of the 21st Century,* New York, NY: Bantam Books/Doubleday Del Publishing Group, 1994.
6. Howard, A. (ed.). *The Changing Nature of Work,* San Francisco, CA: Jossey-Bass, 1995.
7. Parfit, M. "Human Migration," *National Geographic,* October 1998, pp. 11–14.
8. *Economist,* September 19, 1998, p. 39.
9. Stalker, P. *The Work of Strangers: A Survey of International Migration;* Bohning, W. R. and Schloeter, M. L. (eds.), *Aids in Place of Migration. Geneva,* Switzerland: International Labour Office, 1994. (Also available from ILO Publications Center, 49 Sheridan Ave., Albany, NY 12210, USA.)
10. *Los Angeles Times,* "A Global Pursuit of Happiness," World Report, October 1, 1991, H13.
11. Caranfil, A. G. "Immigration in Europe," *Global Business White Papers,* The Conference Board, No. 14, December 1994.
12. Shusta, R. M., Levine, D. R., Harris, P. R., and Wong, H. Z. *Multicultural Law Enforcement—Strategies for Peacekeeping in a Diverse Society,* Englewood Cliffs, NJ: Prentice Hall, 1995.
13. Sowell, T. *Race and Culture—A World View,* New York, NY: Basic Books/Harper Collins, 1994.
14. Kotkin, J. *Tribes: How Race, Religion and Identity Determine Success in the New Global Economy,* New York, NY: Random House, 1993.
15. Applebaum, E. and Batt, R. *The New American Workplace,* Ithaca, NY: ILR Press/Cornell University, 1994; see also Reich, R. *The Work of Nations,* New York, NY: Vintage Books/Random House, 1992.

16. Wellins, R. S., Byham W. C., and Dixon, G. R. *Inside Teams—How 20 World-Class Organizations Are Winning Through Teamwork,* San Francisco, CA: Jossey-Bass, 1994; see also *Team Performance Teams,* MCB University Press (60/62 Toller Lane, Bradford, West Yorkshire, England, BD8 9BY, UK).

17. Jamieson, D. and O'Mara, J. *Managing Work Force 2000—Gaining the Diversity Advantage,* San Francisco, CA· Jossey-Bass, 1991; see also Coates, J. F., Jarratt, J., and Mahaffie, J. B. *Future Work: Seven Critical Forces Reshaping Work and the Work Force,* Bethesda, MD: World Future Society, 1991.

18. *Fortune,* "Finished at Forty," February 1, 1999, p. 50.

19. To keep up on the trends described, see *At Work—Stories of Tomorrow's Workplace,* available from Berrett-Koehler Publishers (155 Montgomery St., San Francisco, CA 94104, USA; tel: 1-800-922-2929).

20. Reinhold, H. *The Virtual Community,* New York, NY: Harper/Perennial, 1993; *Virtual Reality,* New York, NY: Summit Books, 1991.

21. Simons, G. F., Vazquez, C., and Harris, P. R. *Transcultural Leadership,* Houston, TX: Gulf Publishing, 1993; see also *Managing Diversity* (JALMC, PO Box 819, Jamestown, NY 14702, USA).

22. American Express Financial Advisors. "Diversity: Report to Benchmark Partners," *Cultural Diversity Sourcebook,* Abramms B. and Simons, G. F. (eds.), Amherst, MA: ODT, 1996.

23. *Los Angeles Times,* September 27, 1993, p. B5.

24. Jamieson, D. and O'Mara, J. *Managing Work Force 2000,* San Francisco, CA: Jossey-Bass, 1991.

25. Pueik, V., Tichy, N. M., and Barnett, C. K. *Globalizing Management: Creating and Leading the Competitive Organization,* New York, NY: John Wiley & Son, 1993; see also CPC/Rand Report, *Developing the Global Work Force,* Bethlehem, PA: CPC Inc., 1994.

26. Prahalad, C. K. and Hamel, G. *Competing for the Future: Breakthrough Strategies for Seizing Control of Your Industry and Creating the Markets of Tomorrow,* Harvard Business School Press, 1994.

27. Mobley, M. and Payne T. "Managing," *Security Management,* 1993, p. 35.

28. Noer, D. M. *Healing the Wounds: Overcoming the Trauma of Layoffs and Revitalizing Downsized Organizations,* San Francisco, CA: Jossey-Bass, 1993; also see, "A Recipe for Glue," *Issues & Observations,* Vol. 14:3, 1994, pp. 5–6 (available upon request from the Center for Creative Leadership, P.O. Box 26300, Greensboro, NC 27438; tel: 910/288-7210).

29. CPC Foundation/RAND Corporation Report. *Developing the Global Work Force—Insights for Colleges and Corporations,* Bethlehem, PA: CPC Inc., 1994.

30. Gardenswartz, L. and Rowe, A. *Managing Diversity—A Complete Desk Reference,* San Diego, CA: Pfeiffer & Company, 1993. The same publisher offers numerous diversity games, profiles, and training activities.

31. Nair, K. A *Higher Standard of Leadership—Lessons from the Life of Gandhi,* San Francisco, CA: Berrett-Koehler Publishers, 1994.

32. Kilmann, R. H. "A Completely Integrated Program for Creating and Maintaining Organizational Success," *Organizational Dynamics,* Summer 1989, pp. 4–19.

33. Kouzes, J. M. and Posner, B. Z. *The Leadership Challenge,* San Francisco, CA: Jossey-Bass, 1995.
34. Manz, C. C. and Sims, H. P. *Super Leadership: Leading Others to Lead Themselves,* Englewood Cliffs, NJ: Prentice Hall, 1989; also see, Wick, C. W. and Lean, L. S. *The Leading Edge—How Smart Managers and Smart Companies Stay Ahead,* San Diego, CA: Pfeiffer & Company, 1993.
35. Blasi, J. *The Economist,* June 11, 1994. p. 54.
36. Dorgan, W. "Diversity or Affirmative Action," *Modern Machine Shop,* May 1994, p. 124.
37. Strenski, J. B. "Stress Diversity in Employee Communications," *Public Relations Journal,* August–September, 1994.

Suggested Resources

Relative to the content of this chapter, readers will also find other Gulf Publishing books very relevant:

Human Performance Improvement by W. J. Rothwell, C. K. Hohne, and S. B. King.
The Secret of a Winning Culture by L. E. Senn and J. R. Childress.
The Mindful Corporation by P. Nakai and R. Schultz.
Executive Leadership—Building World Class Organizations by J. A. Osmond.
Revitalize Your Corporate Culture by F. C. Ashley.
Business Abroad—A 10-Step Guide to International Business Transactions by L. E. Koslow.

Managing diversity is a worldwide leadership challenge. It is a global phenomenon that is particularly evident in Europe where there have always been numerous diverse national cultures, but now with an additional challenge—extensive émigré presence in the workforce. In 2001, look for *Diverse Europa: Critical Cultural Considerations and Resources for Doing Business in the European Union* by Dr. George Simons et al. Information may be obtained from Gulf's homepage (http://www.gpcbooks.com/mcd/mcd.html) or Simons' website (www.diversophy.com) or mail (gsimons@diversophy).

WOMEN IN GLOBAL BUSINESS*

Surprisingly, female managers report that the biggest barriers come from within the corporation, rather than from situations actually encountered during foreign assignments.

The growing number of women in work forces around the world, combined with expansion of global companies, should result in an increased number of women in international business. In fact, the number of international businesswomen has grown over the years, but not at a rate consistent with the number of women in the work forces of their respective countries. When it comes to overseas assignments, women face additional barriers. Surprisingly, female managers report that the biggest barriers come from within the corporation, rather than from situations actually encountered during foreign assignments. This chapter addresses the opportunities and challenges faced by women as global business people. From an organizational perspective, companies that use and build upon an increasingly diverse work force including women will have a competitive advantage.

In the world of business over the past few decades, there has been many monumental changes including the removal of impediments to international trade in goods and services, the emergence of global financial markets and access to world capital markets to name a few. Perhaps of equal importance is the emergence of women in the work force worldwide.

The demographics of the work force in most countries are changing. As growing numbers of women enter the U.S. work force, similar trends have been identified in European countries. The percentage of women in the work force worldwide is contained in Exhibit 8-1.

---

*This chapter was written by Elizabeth Moran de Longeaux and Molly Ann Haney. Some material has been adapted from Chapter 10, *The Global Challenge: Building the New Worldwide Enterprise*, Robert T. Moran and John R. Riesenberger, New York: McGraw Hill, 1994.

EXHIBIT 8-1
WOMEN IN THE WORK FORCE *

Country	% of Women Ages 15-64 in Work Force
Australia	64.7
Austria	64.1
Canada	67.8
Denmark	64.9
Finland	64.2
France	62.6
Germany	64.6
Italy	66.6
Japan	63.7
Mexico	42.8
Netherlands	65.9
Pakistan	12.2 (1995)
Philippines	37.5
Sweden	62
Turkey	30.2
UK	62.6
US	56.8

*Labor Force Statistics, 1997, and Employment in Europe, 1998, European Commission, Directorate General for Employment, Industrial Relations

CURRENT STATUS OF GLOBAL WOMEN MANAGERS

Today, women represent more than 50% of the world's population, yet in no country do they represent nearly half of the corporate managers.[1] Although globally women have drastically increased their presence in all industries, the January 1999 edition of *Fast Company*, included a thought-provoking insert called "Fast Fact." The following chart, based on U.S. data, was entitled "This is Progress?"

Facts	Women	Men
CEOs of *Fortune 500* Companies	2	498
# among Top Corporate Officers	83	2,184
Median Salary of Corporate Officers	$518, 596	$765,000

Today, women represent more than 50% of the world's population, yet in no country do they represent nearly half of the corporate managers.

Barriers to women's entry into senior management, otherwise known as the "glass ceiling," exist across the globe, and in some areas of the world it is worse than in others. Today in the United States, women hold only 11% of board seats in *Fortune 500* companies, and in Britain, that number is as small as 5%.[2] Women's representation in management in the United States hovers around 40%, whereas in Europe or Asia, management representation is around 20% to 30%.[2]

Depending on the country, different societal forces have contributed to increasing women's presence in corporations. Women in the United States have benefited from affirmative action and equal opportunity laws that hold employers accountable for promoting women. In France during the 1980s, legislation was passed that made unions the "porte-parole" of women's progress.[1] Women in Europe have also benefited from a history of trail blazing with regards to family-friendly laws.[1] In Eastern Europe, quotas were set regarding the number of women in local management.[1] All of these initiatives have greatly paid off. In Great Britain, for example, the number of women directors doubled from 1993 to 1997.[2] In Germany, women are becoming increasingly present in the political arena. Nevertheless, despite recent progress in most countries, women's advancement in the business arena has been steady but slow. At approximately 50% of the population, women as workers and educated consumers have considerable clout. As we move into the 21st century, companies will need to increasingly reflect this diversity in their work force.

Current Issues

It is surprising to note how very few women have made it to the top of the executive ladder. Statistics show that proportionately there are less women in upper management compared to men. Exhibit 8-2, based on U.S. data, show the breakdown of women in executive and manager-

Depending on the country, different societal forces have contributed to increasing women's presence in corporations.

EXHIBIT 8-2
PERCENTAGE OF WOMEN IN EXECUTIVE,
ADMINISTRATIVE AND MANAGERIAL
OCCUPATIONS—1988 AND 1996*

1988		1996	
Women	39.30%	Women	43.80%
Men	60.70%	Men	56.20%

*U.S. Department of Labor, Bureau of Labor Statistics, Employment and Earnings, January 1989 and January 1997. Source: U.S. Department of Labor, Women's Bureau, "Facts on Working Women: Women in Management," April 1997, No. 97-3.

ial positions. Exhibit 8-3 provides statistics from Catalyst, a New York based non-profit group that works for the advancement of women, about the numbers of women as directors of *Fortune 500* companies.

Exhibit 8-3
1997 Catalyst Census of Women on Board of Directors of the Fortune 500 Companies Key Findings and Trends

Women Directors

❑ In 1997, women held 10.6 % of total board seats on *Fortune 500* companies (643 of 6,081 board seats), up from 10.2 % in 1996.

❑ Women of color represent 12.2% of women board directors (54 directors), 1.4% of total board seats.

Fortune 500 Companies

❑ Eighty-four percent of *Fortune 500* companies (419 companies) have one or more women directors, up from 69% in 1993. Sixteen percent (81 companies) have no women on their boards.

❑ Of *Fortune 100* companies, 96% have at least one woman on their boards. The top 100 more than two times as likely to have multiple women directors as the bottom 100.

❑ Women represent 1% of inside directors (drawn from top management) on boards of *Fortune 500* companies. Twelve women are inside directors, out of 1,199 total inside directors.

❑ One *Fortune 500* company, Golden West Financial Corporation, which has a woman CEO, has achieved parity on its board with five women and five men directors.

Multiple Women Directors

❑ Of the 419 companies with women board directors, 181 have more than one woman. This means that 36% of total *Fortune 500* companies have two or more women directors, up from 17 (35% in 1996). Thirty-one companies have three or more women directors, up from 23 companies in 1996.

❑ Companies established on the *Fortune* list are more likely to have women on their boards than the new *Fortune* companies. There is a statistically significant correlation between companies that remain on the *Fortune 500* list from last year and the number of their women board members compared with companies new to this year's list.

Five Year Trend

❑ In 1993, 69% or 345 of *Fortune 500* companies had women directors. By 1997 this number increased to 84% or 419 companies, and thus represents a 21% increase in the period from 1993–1997.

GLOBAL BARRIERS HINDERING THE ADVANCEMENT OF WOMEN

There are a variety of global issues that confront women in the workplace. A few are highlighted to gain a greater understanding of what women are dealing with and the obstacles still to overcome.

Women are more likely to be pigeon-holed into less challenging positions than men. Women are often placed on a separate, and less promising, career track. Among other skills and talents, upper management positions require broad and varied experience within the company, and preferably profit and loss responsibility. Many potential executives are "pipelined" through certain high-visibility and high-responsibility areas such as marketing, finance, and production, often referred to as "line" positions, in preparation for upper management promotion. According to a recent Catalyst survey, men occupy approximately 94% of the line positions.[3] Women "tend to be in supporting, 'staff' function areas—personnel/human resources, communications, public relations, and customer relations. Movement between these positions and 'line' positions is rare in most major companies. Furthermore, career ladders in staff functions are generally shorter than those in line functions, offering fewer possibilities to gain varied experience."[4] Katrinli and Ozmen conducted a study of thirty-one senior women managers in Turkey, where the proportion of female managers is slowly increasing, but male managers continue to be preferred over female managers. When asked during an interview what their key factors of success were, most women cited "hard work" followed by "being good at my job."[5] When asked whether these key success factors would be the same for men to succeed in Turkey, most of the women responded that there was no difference. An issue women managers face in Turkey is the continuing perception that some jobs are better suited for males than for females. This is a stereotype that can be found across the globe; women are seen as more "human" and therefore better suited for a specific type of job such as human resources, communications, public relations, and marketing. Management, especially in areas such as finance and information services, continues to be often seen as a job better suited for men.

This could be linked to women's role of mother or primary caretaker in the family. The stereotype is that if a woman's focus is on bearing children, she would subsequently be taking time off, and could not be considered an effective front-line executive. In Chile, a woman's marital status can be an important consideration during the hiring process; it is generally featured at the top of a resume with other essentials such as name, address, and phone number, along with a photograph. A young, married woman with no children can be considered a "risky investment" because the perception is that she will soon have children, leave her job, and the company will have to pay for pregnancy expenses. Although times may be changing for Chile, it is still generally expected that women will relinquish their career aspirations to stay at home when children arrive, and for some women this can begin immediately after marriage.

During the 1980s in the U.S., a track called "the mommy track" was designed to facilitate having children and maintaining a professional life. Nevertheless, many women who choose to have children still maintain high career aspirations and get stuck in less challenging and demanding jobs.

Significant pay gaps exist between women and men in the same position. Despite significant progress and a variety of laws designed to prevent wage discrimination, women are still earning less than their male counterparts for the same job. In the United States, "the nation's highest-paid female corporate executives earn 68 cents to every dollar earned by the highest paid corporate executives according to Catalyst, a New York-based nonprofit group that works to advance women in business. The median total compensation of men in the study was $765,000; the median for women was $518,596. Sheila Wellington, president of the Catalyst, said a number of factors contribute to the difference, from age to prior experience to salary negotiation skills."[3] As the highest paid female executives in America, the "cream of the crop" so to speak, the merit system would dictate equal pay for equal performance. However, this fundamental discrimination is widely pervasive and no remedy seems to be in sight.

Despite significant progress and a variety of laws designed to prevent wage discrimination, women are still earning less than their male counterparts for the same job.

SNAP FACTS ON WAGE INEQUITY

- According to the Census Bureau, women earn just 74 cents on average for every dollar men earn. The disparity is greatest for minority women: Black women earn 65 cents and Hispanic women 57 cents for every dollar earned by white men, according to the Census Bureau.
- A college-educated woman makes on average $12,000 less than a college-educated man, according to the AFL-CIO. That means a college-educated woman on average makes $1,800 more than a high school-educated man.
- A woman who is 24 today can expect to lose $523,000 over the course of her working lifetime.
- In 1994, a woman's private-pension benefits were less than half those of men—just $3,000 a year, compared with $7,800.

Career Women News. "Wage Inequity: It's Time for Working Women to Earn Equal Pay!" 1998. www.careerwomen.com

Exclusive corporate cultures. One influential factor still affecting women's advancement in business, and this is true in many areas across the globe, is that most of today's existing work environments were designed by men. Women, functioning in sometimes a more male-oriented corporate culture, are under constant pressure to adapt or transform their styles of working. This, however, is slowly changing. Richstone, chief financial officer at Bull HN Information Systems, stated that "what's becoming a thing of the past are women who think that the way (they're) going to get to the top is by being more male than the males."[6] In Japan, for example, women face a challenge to adapt to the expectation that management requires mixing work and play, often by drinking and bar-hopping until late hours. Women colleagues are nowadays invited to join in on such social activities, although a married woman with a family might find it very difficult to meet, on a consistent basis, such a time commitment. In some South American countries, strong, unspoken norms exist about what is appropriate or inappropriate for a woman to do, regardless of career position; as such, higher level female executives can be excluded from after-work activities and/or can exclude themselves in fear of the backlash in breaching these norms.

In some American corporate environments, younger generations of women have almost eradicated the "male" designated corporate culture by joining in, and instigating, happy hours, golf games, and softball tournaments. In some cases, these women have even redefined the culture itself by adding new twists like cultural outings, etc.

Limited access to information, contacts, and high-level networking opportunities. While the term "old boys' network" was coined long ago, in many companies the institution itself is thriving. The "old boys' network" refers to primarily a group of white male executives who have an informal yet somewhat exclusive club that manifests itself in the upper echelons of management. Women and people of color are generally not included. Communication within these exclusive informal networks can perpetuate gender stereotyping, and bias through jokes, stories, and slurs. Whether it is on the golf course, hunting, having late night drinks, or in the men's room, women are often excluded from this high-level interaction, when it is often these informal networks that can improve chances of promotion and success. Executives and upper level managers like to hire who they know, and the more contact with an individual the better. Unfortunately for women, many of the "bonding" experiences in these types of situations take place in venues that either are not necessarily women-friendly, such as strip clubs, or women are simply not invited out of habit. In Israel, women are almost completely excluded from the senior ranks of the military. This exclusion from what is considered by many in the corporate world as an invaluable learning experience for managing large organizations, limits women as choices as future senior executives.[1]

Women, functioning in sometimes a more male-oriented corporate culture, are under constant pressure to adapt or transform their styles of working.

As a result, women often are not informed of advancement opportunities, are not as visible as a male colleague, and are not given additional opportunities to prove their credibility for promotion. According to Wernick, "managers and executives look for 'signals' from those they will select to advance. Those signals found to be most significant indicate credibility and provide increased access to visibility to decision-makers. Access to information, which is critical to advancement, is often limited to selected groups or individuals within the managerial ranks or workplace."[7] This can be exacerbated when the company does not have a formal executive development program or tracking program that explicitly monitors promotions and pay increases for employees.

Fewer women are asked to take on risky positions. One area where this is particularly evident is for expatriate work, where the position and results tend to be highly visible. Fewer women are asked to fill expatriate positions although just as many women as men request these positions abroad. Adler undertook a study to determine whether MBAs from seven management schools in the United States, Canada, and Europe would like to pursue an international assignment during their career, the overall response was 84% favorable, with little difference between male and female responses. Adler also conducted another survey of 686 Canadian, and American firms to determine the number of women sent abroad. Of 13,338 expatriates, only 3% were female[8] when women actually accounted for 37% of domestic management positions. One other obstacle exists for women who would like to hold international assignments; the biases, in certain countries against women, both native and foreign, is such that it is impossible for women to succeed in that particular country.

Many companies fail to send women overseas on an expatriate assignment in particular areas of the world where the demarcation between male and female roles is clearly defined. Global women managers often talk about the "double-take" or stares they receive in Asia, South America, or the Middle East when they are first introduced. For example in Latin America, women report having been mistaken for the wife, or the secretary during important high-level business meetings and social events. However, most women who were sent abroad say that the first reaction of surprise is quickly replaced by professionalism and respect. Adler interviewed many women who held challenging positions in what are considered non-women friendly countries, and nearly all reported their assignments successful. However, when many women have been nominated for an international business assignment in what the company thought would be a hostile culture, most of these women have succeeded with flying colors. Why? Because expatriate women are not expected to behave according to the same social guidelines as natives of that particular culture, and "that women are especially adept

Access to information, which is critical to advancement, is often limited to selected groups or individuals within the managerial ranks or workplace.

at cross-cultural management skills because they use behavior patterns emphasizing sensitivity, communication skills, community, and relationships. This personal orientation is valuable in globalization. . . ."[9] When the company clearly identifies the woman as the individual in power, and supports her as the clear corporate representative, the message is also sent that discrimination will not be tolerated.

The difficulties that women may encounter when working on a foreign assignment depend to a certain extent on the social and economic context of the country in which they are conducting business, and on the individuals with whom they come into contact. Both the woman international manager and the company she represents can take steps to minimize any negative aspects that might be encountered by considering a few guidelines.

- ❑ **Lay the groundwork.** Do not surprise a client. Before any meeting, regardless of the gender of the participants, provide adequate information about who will be present and the agenda.
- ❑ **Practice what is preached.** If a corporation empowers women managers and treats them equally and seriously in business dealings abroad, it should ensure that women are also treated equally and fairly in the organization. Success begins at home.
- ❑ **Consider women and men for international positions.** Do not rely on the assumption that women will not want to accept the position.
- ❑ **Provide proper cross-cultural training and preparation courses.** Training is vital to women's success abroad. Specific assistance should include what to expect from male superiors, peers, clients and subordinates and how to handle uncomfortable situations as discrimination.
- ❑ **Be realistic.** Women managers abroad suffer from the same culture shock as men. It is important to keep expectations reasonable, build trust and create professional relationships.

Fewer women participate in executive development programs, employer-sponsored training programs, or "fast track" programs. As evidenced through a variety of studies, women are often not given as many opportunities as their male colleagues for education, training, or special high-profile programs. This could emanate from the stereotype that women will eventually leave their jobs to have children, so why invest the money into enhancing their skills, when a male would be a better "investment" opportunity? Without proper corporate intervention to increase women's participation in such programs and opportunities, the subsequent result would be that women remain in their positions with little to no overall growth.

Training is vital

to women's

success abroad.

PERSISTENT GLOBAL CULTURAL STEREOTYPES

Women and men are equal in their managerial abilities and overall ability to succeed. However, the promotion of women to senior positions is often hindered by the existence of biased attitudes or stereotypes. From Asia to the Americas to Europe, some of the unfortunate, and disturbing, *global stereotypes* include, but are not limited to:

❑ Women are fundamentally different and too "soft" to handle ruthless managerial decisions. Women cannot be aggressive enough and will therefore lose business or the competitive edge needed to win.

❑ Women overcompensate when in male environments and become too masculine when managing, alienating employees and often alarming clients.

❑ Women lack quantitative skills and therefore cannot hold technical positions or understand the numbers required in a profit and loss environment. Women possess "soft" skills such as communication and team building.

❑ Women are not as dedicated nor as committed as their male counterparts and therefore are not "executive material." Once a woman becomes a mother, her priorities change completely and she can no longer be counted on as before. Women often opt to quit working and become full time mothers. How can a company promote someone who they know will ultimately leave? Companies cannot afford to have women coming and going whenever they wish.

Women and men are equal in their managerial abilities and overall ability to succeed.

❏ Women are not interested in an international career and therefore should not be considered for international positions. In addition, women can't handle the cultural differences that occur outside of the U.S.

❏ When companies send women abroad their image will be less credible in male-dominated societies.

❏ Other men won't take the woman manager seriously.

❏ Because of current sexual harassment laws, nothing can be said to women without getting it blown out of proportion and all interaction becomes suspect.

❏ Women cause problems by looking for love in the workplace and this will disrupt the workplace and ultimately lead to greater problems.

❏ There aren't enough qualified women to promote. No matter how hard the company has tried, there just aren't any women with the exact qualifications they are looking for.

Such stereotypes are extremely counterproductive to the advancement of women in business around the world, and obscure women's skills.

Stereotypes are extremely counterproductive to the advancement of women in business around the world, and obscure women's skills.

A REALITY CHECK: STEREOTYPES AND THE TRUTH[4]

❏ A 1992 Korn/Ferry Survey of women senior managers helps provide hard facts to combat stereotypes.

❏ Women lack quantitative skills, however, 23% of women compared to 27% of men have spent the majority of their careers in corporate finance.

❏ Although women are always touted as being more nurturing than men, only 18% of women compared to 33% of men stated that "concern for people" was important.

❏ Women are often portrayed to be less willing to work long hours yet women clocked in an average 56 hours per week in 1992, which is the same number of working hours as men.

BALANCING WORK AND FAMILY

Balancing family and the work/life is a major concern of most working women. In the past, women needed to make a clear choice as to whether they wanted to have a career or a family. Now a professional career and motherhood are no longer considered mutually exclusive decisions. Today, this is obvious. Nevertheless, it does recognize that working mothers always have to juggle two full-time jobs. Knight interviewed a series of women who were either middle or senior managers and who had recently become new mothers.[5] All of the women interviewed stated that motherhood had given them a new perspective on their work and that this was, in general, very positive. They also felt that motherhood had given them a new sense of confidence enabling them to let their personalities become apparent in the workplace. Planning was critical to juggle the daily demands of family and work. Nevertheless, many women, particularly in Europe and in Asia, choose to take a break from professional work once they begin a family.

Balancing one's personal and professional responsibilities creates strains. In the United States, for example, there is still a lingering belief that work should take precedence over family life. Some women, having reached a critical point in their career and personal life, make the choice of one over the other, since reconciling them takes a considerable amount of effort. In Europe, it is possible to take time off from work to raise children without the thought that a career is being put into jeopardy.

Many American businesses are addressing the bottom-line implications of employees' needs for affordable and high-quality child and elder care. Wiley Harris of GE Capital Services states that, "Every employee is important to our company's health, and when employees are distracted by family issues, we lose productivity."[10] The American Business Collaboration for Quality Dependent Care (ABC) is a group of 21 large corporations including Kodak, Johnson & Johnson, GE Capital Services, Chevron and IBM. This consortium invested $100 million over a period of six years in 60 American communities to develop, among other things, on-site childcare centers and services for elder care. Specifically in 1989, Johnson and Johnson introduced a program called "Balancing Work and Family" that was designed to address the needs of its changing work force. The company went so far as to add an extra line to its company credo, which now reads "We must be mindful of ways to help our employees fulfill their family responsibilities."[11]

The Family and Medical Leave Act of 1993 was in response to concerns from men and women about being able to care for family members at critical life stages without risk of job loss. Even with the enactment of this Act, the United States continues to compare poorly with other developed countries such as France, Sweden, Canada and Finland where family care is institutionalized. Many women, although able to take the time off without the risk of losing their jobs, cannot do so for monetary reasons.

SELECTED WOMEN MANAGER'S VIEWS

How have several specific women succeeded? Are they going about business differently? The August 5, 1996 edition of *Fortune,* ran an article on "Women, Sex and Power." Contrary to what the title might sug-

In Europe, it is possible to take time off from work to raise children without the thought that a career is being put into jeopardy.

gest, the article focused on seven women who are the best of the best in their fields of business. Among the women were Charlotte Beers of Ogilvy & Mather, Rebecca Marks of Enron Development Corporation, and Jill Barad of Mattel. These women are part of a new female elite who are changing the way women reach the top. More and more women are being featured on the covers of prominent business magazines that are celebrating the success of these pioneers in their fields. In all of these articles there appear to be several attributes that each of these women share.

Taking advantage of opportunities. Rebecca Marks, CEO of Enron Development Corporation, said, "opportunities and challenges define your career—you just have to follow your instincts. Do what excites you. And you don't see the path until you get there."[12] Marks was the first individual to successfully negotiate an important commercial deal after the Middle East peace accords—uniting the efforts of the Israelis and Jordanians to build a natural gas power generation station. "I enjoy being a world-class problem solver," she said. "I'm constantly asking, 'How far can I go? How much can I do?'"[12]

Women are comfortable demonstrating their femininity.

Have confidence in yourself. In the past, many women felt obliged to hide their femininity so as to be seen as managers first and women second. Many women in today's business world no longer view their sexuality as a hindrance and despite the fact that the office is often still male dominated, they are no longer attempting to become more male-like or androgynous in order to be promoted. Women are comfortable demonstrating their femininity. Several interesting examples of "being comfortable" are Charlotte Beers of Ogilvy & Mather who is known to call CEOs "honey" or Jill Barad of Mattel, who often wears hot pink suits. She says, "we never gave up our femininity. We didn't become little men."[12]

Survive and overcome difficult working conditions. Most women, especially of older generations, have had to face discrimination from both men and women alike. Charlotte Beers says, "Early in my career, during my first week at J. Walter Thomson in Chicago, I had a secretary who asked the company for a transfer. She told me, 'No offense, but I want to work for a man who's going to move ahead.'" The story goes that two years later, the secretary, impressed by Beers' stellar career path, asked to come back and Beers, who liked her honesty, accepted.[12] Many successful business women have had to overcome many adverse working conditions and have been able to build their career during these tough moments.

Do things differently. Many women are successful by incorporating aspects of their personality into their work or by daring to do things differently. In the end, many of them drastically change the way business in their field is done. Linda Marcelli, of Merrill Lynch, started selling stocks by setting up personal meetings instead of cold calling. Anita Roddick was an international hit with her "Body Shop" that brought environmental consciousness to a new level.

Have your own leadership style—neither "feminine" nor "masculine." The debate surrounding whether men and women have different leadership styles was raised by Rosener,[13] who found women are more likely to use a transformational management style, pushing their employees to go beyond their own self-interest to see the larger picture. Rosener believed that women executives are succeeding because they are "drawing on the skills and attitudes they developed from their shared experiences of women. . . . They are succeeding because of—not in spite of—certain characteristics generally considered to be 'feminine' and inappropriate in leaders." Women are often described by many to have a more "open" approach to management, relying on consensus building as opposed to the old style of command and control.

However, recent research demonstrates that women and men executives in similar positions demonstrate more similar behaviors than dissimilar. Wajcman, discusses her recent research examining current female and male managers' perceptions and attitudes. Her data show that "women who have made it into senior positions are in most respects indistinguishable from the men in equivalent positions. In fact, the similarities between women and men far outweigh the differences between women and men as groups."[14] Many women are concerned that the debate whether men and women exhibit different leadership styles continues to perpetuate typical stereotypes of women being "soft" managers. As Adler points out, "in study after study, undergraduates, MBAs, and managers (male and female) in the United States have tended to identify stereotypically "masculine" (aggressive) characteristics as managerial and stereotypically "feminine" (cooperative and communicative) characteristics as unmanagerial."[8]

WHAT COMPANIES ARE DOING TO CHAMPION WOMEN

More and more companies are aggressively trying to advance women's issues. Based on research of "women-friendly" companies,[15] several themes were identified that are crucial for a company to become conducive to women. Catalyst conducted research on companies with corporate cultures that promote women.[11] These corporate cultures present greater opportunities for women through:

Many women are concerned that the debate whether men and women exhibit different leadership styles continues to perpetuate typical stereotypes of women being "soft" managers.

❑ **Style:** Most of the "women-friendly" companies studied were said to have an open, participative and creative managerial style. Inclusive language and open communication is the norm.

❑ **Organizational structure:** The structure of these companies is more flexible and hierarchically flatter than other companies. These organizations have also instituted formal and/or informal groups of women that actively provide input and feedback on issues concerning women.

❑ **Company policies:** Emphasis on recruiting and career development programs that value and promote diversity.

❑ **Benefits:** Work schedules include a range of work arrangements that affect both men and women such as flexible work time, part-time work at home, shorter work weeks, paid time off for child or elder care, or a guaranteed job after leave of absence.

❑ **Promotion:** Promotions and salary increases are becoming part of an established executive development program, and are centered on the performance merit system as opposed to seniority. Employee progress can be tracked at all times.

These characteristics of "women-friendly" companies have been proven to provide a more beneficial environment to *men* and women.

In Great Britain, several programs have been created to promote women. Several organizations have created a development program only for women to help them attain the necessary qualifications, career development and guidance within an internal organization. The National Westminster Bank, for example, as early as 1982, allowed women managers to take up to a five-year sabbatical at the birth of a child. Women who choose to do so, must follow training during this period to keep up-to-date. If this condition is met, then they are assured of the same or an equivalent management position when they decide to return to work.

"Women-friendly" companies have been proven to provide a more beneficial environment to men and women.

COMPANY INITIATIVES TO BREAK THE GLASS CEILING

Most companies have put into place specific programs to assist in breaking down barriers impeding women's progression. Most include a combination of flexible work arrangements, mentoring, women's support groups, and leadership development. Various companies have also developed supports and structures designed to advance women.

A Tracking System

Philip Morris' Companies, Inc. has a program in place to monitor the progress of women within their different organizations.[16] The vice-president of Diversity Management, Shirl Harrison, is quoted as saying, "We are tracking and monitoring women in management on a global basis. We have identified the women who are in the different regions, in what positions, and their development needs within our succession planning process. A key component within our management development process is the Philip Morris Leadership Profile, which outlines the characteristics and traits of present and future Philip Morris business leaders. It is a guide for all employees to aspire to which is color/gender-blind and describes in detail what a world-class business leader should be and demonstrate."[16]

A Support Structure

IBM, Kodak, and 3M have women's networks in place to help promote women's careers. Apparently, one-third of all *Fortune 100* companies have such networks aimed at developing skills, career-building and supporting women.

Mentoring Programs

Research has demonstrated that mentoring is a critical part of career success. Mentoring is defined as "a cooperative and nurturing relationship between a more experienced business person and a less experienced person who wants to learn about a particular business and gain valuable insight into some of the unspoken subtleties of doing business."[17] Many experts claim that it is beneficial to have more than one mentor present within an organization and that these mentors should be at different levels. Mentoring comes into play at crucial points in an individual's career and can be an effective source of advice and encouragement.

However, Burke and McKeen found that men and women view mentoring in different ways. They realized that "women view mentoring as a process involving friendship, while men consider it a task-oriented alliance."[8] It is often more difficult for women to find appropriate mentors than it is for men. Many Internet sites have popped up in the past few years offering women the opportunity to network with each other in a nontraditional setting. The U.S. Small Business Administration has set up a specific program, open to all women, specifically focused on helping women who are entrepreneurs or are thinking about becoming entrepreneurs.

Work Still to Be Done

Although women have achieved significant advances since entering the workplace, clearly there is still more work to be done. Women are as qualified and as talented as men. Companies need to take more responsibility to fully integrate women into their environments at all levels of the corporate hierarchy. However, women need to recognize the role they play in shaping their own destiny and taking an active role in designing their future workplace. This entails visualizing a future and working towards the goal of a gender equal workplace. Some issues to consider include:

It is often more difficult for women to find appropriate mentors than it is for men.

❑ *Increasing the flow of information and educating women about current issues.* It is only with concrete facts and information about women's position in the workplace that any calibration of gains can be measured. Catalyst, a non-profit organization focused on women's issues in the workplace, has taken a wonderful role in initiating this process. When women appreciate where they have been, and understand the issues that confront them, they can see and decide where the future lies.

❑ *Demonstrating CEO commitment.*[18] As the corporate leader, the CEO has significant influence on the direction and vision of the firm. "The CEO must raise the issue of diversity, keep it visible and viable, and drive it through every level of the company. All materials flowing from the corporation must reflect that diversity is a core value of the organization. As a consequence, external audiences-customers, stockholders, suppliers, and the community at large-will come to understand that diversity is the corporate philosophy and employment objective of the company."[18]

❑ *Closing the pay gap.* A true merit system distinguishes individuals based on their effort and skills and rewards each person for their work regardless of gender. Men and women work equally hard in the same positions; their pay should reflect this equality.

❑ *Increasing recruitment, providing training opportunities, placing women in high-profile positions.* Companies should step up their efforts to recruit and train qualified women, and ensure that more women get access to "line" positions versus being immediately segmented into "staff" positions.

THE NEXT GENERATION

Given the progress of women to date and the current workplace, much is being done in business schools and basic parenting to encourage the next generation of women to actively participate in business. The workplace is continually demanding highly skilled workers, and a Master's in Business Administration (MBA) is often the degree of choice for companies seeking managerial potential. In fact, an MBA becomes almost a necessity to reach the upper echelons of management at many prestigious consulting, banking, and *Fortune 1000* companies. While enrollments by gender tend to be almost 50-50 female/male in top medical and law programs across the country, MBA programs seem to lag behind that ratio. The good news is that these numbers seem to be increasing as more women consider their futures in the corporate ranks, and schools spend large amounts of time and money trying to attract qualified female candidates. Additionally, programs exist within business schools to foster female networking opportunities within classes and across generations.

Given the progress of women to date and the current workplace, much is being done in business schools and basic parenting to encourage the next generation of women to actively participate in business.

In 1993, the Ms. Foundation for Women began an innovative program entitled "Take Our Daughters to Work Day®" to encourage young adolescent women. Research in the early '90s "indicated that during adolescence girls often receive less attention in school and in youth-serving programs, suffer from lower expectations than do their boy counterparts, and tend to like or dislike themselves based on aspects of their physical appearance."[18] The Day focuses on showing young girls what women are doing in the work world today and to encourage them to visualize the career options in front of them. Web site information states that the Day intends to "focus positive attention on girls' abilities, to urge girls to speak their minds, and to encourage girls to trust their own judgment."[19] Aside from being a day of envisioning possibilities, "Take Our Daughters to Work Day®" enhances girls' self-esteem, boosts confidence, and shows that working women do care about our next generation of women leaders.

National and community initiatives have given increased attention to girls. Organizations such as Women's College Coalition, Girl Power!, and Girls Count provide resources for parents, teachers, and community, policy, and business leaders about young women, and work to educate the public about ensuring gender equality. They simultaneously work to inform young women of academic and career options, and to generate self-esteem and self-awareness. Significant attention is placed on encouraging women to enter the fields of science, math, and technology, heretofore seen as more "male-dominated" educational fields.

Parents play a vital role in shaping perspectives and opinions of girls and, as such, should not consciously or unconsciously set limitations. There are many characteristics that are for one reason or another, designated as male or female; these characteristics should be more gender neutral and inclusive. The Women's College Coalition recommends that parents' "expand career options by offering a diversity of male and female role models. Introduce girls to dynamic women who have successfully combined paid work with family and community involvement. Debunk the myth of Prince Charming. Encourage self-reliance by supporting all that interests, excites, and challenges your daughter both professionally and personally."[20]

Gone will be the days of conferences teaching women skills about juggling, negotiating, becoming visible, networking in the male business environment, the work/life balance.

WHAT THE FUTURE MIGHT HOLD

The obvious long-term goal is gender equality in the workplace: equal job opportunity, equal pay, equal advancement. Once gender parity and equality are achieved, management can redirect its additional time and energy to further enhance corporate objectives. Gone will be the days of conferences teaching women skills about juggling, negotiating, becoming visible, networking in the male business environment, the work/life balance. Dust will gather on the slew of laws designed to prevent discrimination based on gender and policies/programs created to enforce these laws. Men and women will view each other as people first, without regard to gender differences. Short- and long-term changes to consider may include:

❑ *Increased emphasis on strategic alliances between women.* The May 10, 1999 *Wall Street Journal* reported on a new conference "Women & Co.," designed for high level, high powered women executives from across the nation. The conference not only facilitated female specific networking and alliance building opportunities, but also educated the women on current hot topics such as crisis management, the media, dealing with investors, risk management, and selecting CEO's and directors.[21] With the steady increase of women in management, female-female mentoring systems and extended support networks and associations will gain significant power in lobbying for change and making significant inroads in the boardroom.

❑ *More women and men working out of the home.* Advances in technology combined with more family-friendly businesses will allow women and men to easily work out of the home and spend quality time with their children or elder relatives. Email, fax, and tele- and video-conferencing capabilities are just a few of the high tech conveniences that enable all workers to create an office and work productively for their firm in the home. New advances are surely in the pipeline to further facilitate working out of the home. As a result, both the mother and father will have more time to devote to raising the children and sharing family duties.

❑ *More women-owned businesses.* Often when women get discouraged with the traditional workplace, they create their own businesses. If companies are slow to respond to women's needs, we can expect more women-owned businesses that will change the fabric of today's workplace. Women-owned businesses have already doubled as women are recognizing the value of creating one's own work environment, calling the shots, making the hours, and reaping the monetary rewards. Furthermore, with their comprehensive workplace knowledge, these women will design a workplace that is woman-friendly.

❑ *Changed roles within the home.* With more and more couples working full time, duties in the home will become equally divided. Couples will distribute tasks equally including chores, child-rearing, and elder care, and pay more for services such as house cleaning, shopping, laundry, prepared meals, etc. As women continue to make more money, it will be more acceptable and common to see a "house-husband" as the couple together decides the payoff with one breadwinner in the family.

❑ *Heightened development of family-friendly policies.* As companies value their human capital more, policies could include allowing for two-year "sabbaticals" for either parent to raise children, with computerized "update" training and a guaranteed job upon return. "A few employers, including Eli Lilly and IBM, guarantee a job after a three-year leave. Such policies take the heat off parents."[22] Via Internet education, companies could update these employees on current corporate issues or the latest technology in order to ensure that the employee transitions effectively back into the company.

❏ *Acceptance of paid paternity-leave, designed for new fathers.* When companies offer paid paternity leave, they are further encouraging the active role of the father in the family unit. While many women get paid months off after the birth of a child, most fathers are left out of the loop, with only evenings and weekends to help out with the child rearing. While some companies offer time off for the new parent, paid paternity leave is rare.

❏ *Growth of part-time, contract, temporary, or freelance career paths.* If companies do not adequately respond to working parents' needs, the part-time, contract, temporary, and freelance career options will boom. These types of careers give parents the flexibility to combine work and family life, yet without the responsibility of a full-fledged, self-owned business. Many intelligent and educated women chose to stay home with their families because they are forced to choose between work and a family; these types of careers can offer a lucrative middle ground. *The Wall Street Journal* recently reported an increase in the profitable temporary executive business where an individual is hired to do high-powered work for a short amount of time.[23]

❏ *New markets will emerge to support the career woman's work/life balance.* Changes in the work force and consumer demographics inevitably lead to increased opportunity for new markets. This could translate into, increased opportunities in the service industry, retail, food, healthcare, child care, and elder care to meet the needs of working women. Convenience, portability, and ease of use will become more vital as people have less and less time for complicated items.

While some companies offer time off for the new parent, paid paternity leave is rare.

SUMMARY

"I recently went to a day-long meeting, where I was about the only man in attendance. The group included some of the most powerful women in the United States. At the end of the day, I was left with a tossing and turning mind . . . at the ripe old age of 54. That is, I was born a male, white, Anglo-Saxon, Protestant. We are the ruling class . . . to this day. And there's not a damn thing I can do about that. Which means I have a problem. I JUST CAN'T UNDERSTAND. That is, as I listened to these very powerful women talk about the degree to which they had been slighted, particularly if they happened to be Asian-American women or African-American women, it dawned on me that for all my liberalness, I just didn't get it. I did not—and cannot—understand what it means to be systematically slighted and/or ignored. . . . There is an important message here. I can pretend to be very receptive to women's ideas. (I am . . . and I mean it.) But I'm not one of "them." I don't know (K-N-O-W) what it's like to be short-changed. Again and again . . . and yet again.

Which means that the only answer to dealing with these issues (OPPORTUNITIES!) is to have women in positions of great importance throughout the enterprise."[24]

Tom Peters

The problem still remains, how to get women in those positions of great importance throughout the enterprise. Numerous barriers still exist for women across the globe. Women have made incredible advances, yet one of their next great challenges will be to assure proportional representation in senior management positions. But it is perhaps no longer in the hands of women to assure that their voice are heard in business. Demographic projections in the United States, for example, show that new work force entrants over the next 20 years will be 15% white males. The other components of the work force will be women and members of other ethnic, racial and minority groups.[24] A strong business imperative can be made that companies who do not address the needs of their women employees in terms of recruiting, promotion, and career development will suffer several long-term consequences such as:

❑ Not being viewed as an employer of choice.
❑ Undervaluing top performers, therefore not using employees' full potential.
❑ Losing a competitive edge.

In today's competitive world, ignoring the potential of the greatest (in number and in potential) component of your work force is more than just an oversight, it is extremely costly.

Women have made incredible advances, yet one of their next great challenges will be to assure proportional representation in senior management positions.

REFERENCES

1. Adler, N. and Izraeli, D. "Where in the World Are the Women Executives?" *The Business Quarterly,* London, 1994.
2. Guyon, J. "The Global Glass Ceiling," *Fortune,* October 12, 1998.
3. Glanton, E. Womenconnect.com. "Pay Gap Endures at Highest Levels," AP News, November 10, 1998.
4. Glass Ceiling Commission. The Glass Ceiling Fact-Finding Report. "Good Business: Making Full Use of the Nation's Human Capital," 1995, p. 15
5. Tanton, M. *Women in Management: A Developing Presence,* Routeledge. London, 1994, p. 82.
6. Nelton, S. "Men, Women and Leadership," *Nation's Business,* May 1991, p. 19.

7. Wernick, E. *Preparedness, Career Advancement, and the Glass Ceiling,* Glass Ceiling Commission, May 1994.
8. Karsten, M. F. *Management and Gender: Issues and Attitudes,* Connecticut: Praeger Publishers, 1994.
9. Moran, R. T., Harris, P. R., Stripp, W. G., *Developing the Global Organization,* Houston, Texas: Gulf Publishing Co., 1993, p. 304.
10. http://www.pathfinder.com/ParentTime/workfamily/workcare.html
11. Davidson, M. and Burke, R. *Women in Management: Current Research Issues,* London Paul Chapman Publishing, p. 267.
12. "Women, Sex and Power," *Fortune,* August 5, 1996.
13. Rosener, J. B. "Ways Women Lead," *Harvard Business Review,* November 1, 1990.
14. Wajcman, J. *Managing Like a Man,* University Park, PA: Pennsylvania State University Press, 1998.
15. Wilkof, M. V. "Is Your Company and Its Culture Women-Friendly?" *The Journal for Quality and Participation,* June 1995.
16. *Business Week,* "Global Diversity: Reality, Opportunity and Challenge," December 1, 1997.
17. Internet site sysop@advancingwomen.com
18. Glass Ceiling Commission, News Release—Glass Cciling Commission Agrees on 12 Ways to Shatter Barriers," p. 13.
19. www.ms.foundation.org web site
20. www.academic.org web site
21. Beatty. S. "A Power Confab for Exclusive Businesswomen," *Wall Street Journal,* May 10, 1999.
22. Shellenbarger, S. "Work & Family: The New Pace of Work Makes Taking a Break for Child Care Scarier," *Wall Street Journal,* May 19, 1999.
23. "Work Week," *Wall Street Journal,* May 11, 1999.
24. Peters, T., *The Circle of Innovation,* New York: Alfred A. Knopf, Inc., 1997, p. 423.

Further Reading

Millennium Woman—A Guideline to Personal Security and Financial Prosperity for Today's Women, M. O'Shaughnessy, Houston: Gulf Publishing Company, 2000.

The Confident Woman, M. H. Shaevitz, New York: Random House/ Harmony, 1999.

EFFECTIVE PERFORMANCE IN THE GLOBAL MARKETPLACE

According to Toffler[2] we entered the Third Revolution in 1956 when white collar and service workers outnumbered factory workers. In this revolution, knowledge is the ultimate factor of production.

Fifteen people are seated around the table each representing one of our businesses in the Asia-Pacific. . . . The outgoing President of Asia-Pacific formerly ran our business in South Africa. The new president comes from Australia. There are Americans at the table, an Australian, a New Zealander and a Brit . . .and they're attending this business meeting in Beijing . . . home of one of our most recent joint ventures. . . .[1]

To establish global alliances, skills are required. To make these succeed many more skills are essential.

Human performance is dependent on culture and the attitudes it engenders, particularly toward work. The hunting culture, now found only in isolated locations, focused upon survival through the skill of the hunter in the pursuit of food. For the mainstream of civilization, the agricultural work culture followed, and today, in many lands—long hours are devoted to the tilling of the soil and the herding of flocks.

With the rise of the industrial culture, humankind advanced to another stage of its development. Over the past several hundred years, machines, factories, and urbanization have influenced the worker's lifestyle. Industrialization brought unions and safety emphasis, social legislation and security, equal employment opportunity and career development. It also provided workers with more time for education, recreation and actualizing human potential.

According to Toffler[2] we entered the Third Revolution in 1956 when white collar and service workers outnumbered factory workers. In this revolution, knowledge is the ultimate factor of production.

Now we have the opportunity to create the new work culture—the metaindustrial society with its emphasis on information processing and servicing others. We can exercise leadership in the design of the mainstream work culture that will permeate the 21st century; a leadership that will transform the dying industrial culture. In this emerging knowledge culture, electronic communication technologies are converging, uniting, and educating us. This new capacity to share information and knowledge across traditional boundaries is the catalyst for the globalization of trade and markets. Computers, first digital and now neural, are powerful tools to further transcultural communication, aiding in design and manufacturing. Caltech physicist Carver Mead indicates that today's real leaders are those who master ideas and technologies, not land and material resources—they use the global network of telecommunications to liberate human creativity.[3] But to use such technological advances effectively, new global competencies are required, as when innovations in information systems necessitate the crossing the borders of functions and departments, as well as disciplines and nations. To fully comprehend the significance of this phenomenon, we must understand the connection between culture and high performance.

THE PSYCHOLOGICAL CONTRACT

According to Lewis,[4] the individual and the institution to which he or she is affiliated form a psychological contract. This represents unwritten, unexpressed needs and expectations on the part of both parties. For an employee or member, it is highly subjective perspective, and is the glue that binds that person to the organization. In the disappearing industrial work culture, the psychological contract focused on job security in return for loyalty and hard work. Currently, the emphasis is in which employee gives their support in return for opportunities to learn and acquire new skills. Employability, rather than stability, is the centerpiece of the contract.

For expatriate workers, the employer has more influence in terms of provisions for housing, education, welfare, recreation and social events. Because of this, perceived contractual violations may provoke intense reactions from employees overseas. This dissatisfaction may be expressed in a variety of ways from negative communications and damage to company reputation, to misconduct, hostility and even sabotage. Continued exposure abroad to a stressful environment may cause alteration in sleeping patterns, high anxiety, neurotic defense mechanisms and other manifestations of culture shock.

Figure 9-1 shows what must be considered to avoid culture shock and possible breakdown. If one or more of the components in Figure 9-1 is violated, dissatisfaction and negative repercussions are likely to increase. The items listed affect work and home life, and if these expectations are met in the host country, the newcomer is likely to settle into the alien culture, creating both a positive experience and impression. Should this psychological contract be violated, then negative results may be expected.

According to Lewis,[4] the individual and the institution to which he or she is affiliated form a psychological contract.

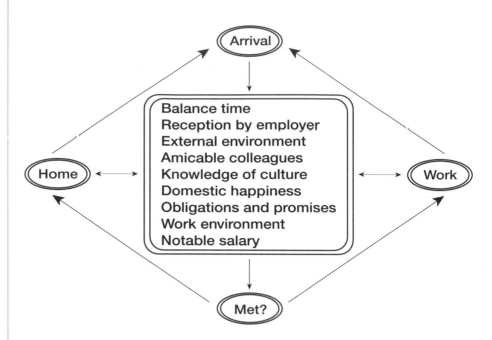

FIGURE 9-1. A PROPOSED FRAMEWORK FOR NEGOTIATING AN
EXPATRIATE'S PSYCHOLOGICAL CONTRACT AND AVOIDING "BREAKDOWN."

DEVELOPING HUMAN RESOURCES

Some cultures inhibit people, constrain their creativity and intellectual activities.

Throughout this book we have underscored the pervasiveness of culture in impacting our lives in general, as well as management and work practice in particular. Some cultures inhibit people, constrain their creativity and intellectual activities. These cultures exclude whole segments of their populations because they are *different*, whether their prescriptions are against ethnic or religious minorities, youth, or women. In such cultures, females, for example, are not permitted to be free and independent human beings; their minds, voices, and desires are locked inside social prisons; their lives are dedicated to the service of males and their families—women's personal rights are minimal, their contributions to the advancements of society and themselves are aborted.

In some developing countries, human development is further curtailed by the misuse of child labor. Rather than a childhood experience of education and play, under-age youth are abused by being recruited into labor intensive occupations, or the military as "child soldiers."

Even in developed nations, schooling of the young is undermined by violence and racism on campus, prejudice toward women, minorities, homosexuals and the disabled. Hate crimes are perpetuated in schools as well as the community. Further, such deviant behavior is also found within institutions of higher education, supposedly dedicated to the pursuit of knowledge and enlightenment. Hence, the importance of starting cross cultural education at all levels, including elementary, so that the young are taught to respect each other and accept differences in people.

GLOBAL PERFORMANCE

Modern society is in transition, and it is impacting work and management performance. The traumas are evident in social, economic, and work life. Examining the cycles and patterns of economic upswings and downswings, Mensch,[5] a German economist, observed in the 1970s that innovations increase dramatically during periods of transition from one era to another. We live in such a period, and witness the innovations in information, silicon, solar, and space technologies that are causing a decline in traditional industries and pointing the way to tomorrow's work culture. Global managers with vision capitalize upon the ongoing changes—that is, they exercise leadership. Vaill[6] uses a metaphor to explain contemporary change, uncertainty, and turbulence that characterize today's organizational life. Vaill states that it is like paddling a canoe or raft in permanent white-water requiring one to shoot the rapids and experience upset and chaos. Leaders, then, learn to read the river, to play in it and even to navigate.

What are some of the trends of which global leaders are aware, and what are some of the right things they do to increase human performance in the international marketplace? Among the nations' executive MBA programs, those catering to working professionals, about 75 percent include an international study trip as part of the curriculum. Often this involves a short assignment abroad where graduate students work with a company overseas as a consultant without compensation under faculty supervision while dealing with real problems.[7]

Global, among other things, means interdependent. The CPC Foundation/Rand Corporation Report[8] found the following factors important for effective performance:

- Generic cognitive skills
- Social skills
- Personal traits
- On-the-job training
- Knowledge in academic major
- Prior work experience
- Firm's recruiting and hiring practices
- Prior cross-cultural experiences
- Foreign language competency
- Attributes of educational institution

The significant findings are:

- Knowledge in one's academic major (domain knowledge) ranks only fifth among ten factors.
- The three highest-rated factors are ones not generally associated with any specific training; generic, cognitive skills, social skills, and personal traits.

Global managers with vision capitalize upon the ongoing changes—that is, they exercise leadership.

❏ Nonacademic training and experience (on-the-job training and prior work experience) are as highly rated as is academic knowledge.

❏ Corporate and academic respondents do not closely agree on the importance of prior cross-cultural experience and foreign language competency.

In Dunbar's study of repatriated global managers and technicians abroad,[9] many reported problems in relation to production levels, management practices, currency fluctuations, obtaining raw materials, quality control, account/finance practices, personnel practices, lack of support staff, unclear goals and objectives, and performance appraisal. They also indicated *more satisfaction* with the overseas assignment when using culturally appropriate interpersonal skills, when assigned to Europe in contrast to a non-Western developing country, when the intrinsic satisfaction with the work experience was somewhat greater than with domestically relocated personnel, and when they had previous cross-cultural experience.

Global managers must be sensitive to the broader implication of his or her actions and decisions upon organizational cultures. Furthermore, such leaders need both a sense of history and of the future. When an organization goes outside its home culture into that of another country, a two-way action takes place. First, the transnational corporation impacts the indigenous culture in healthy or adverse ways. The issue is sensitive in terms of developed and less developed countries, or information-rich versus information-poor peoples. Not every endeavor of advanced countries and their representatives is a benefit to the consuming nation. Colonialism in some less developed areas of the world has been replaced by corporate imperialism or economic exploitation. There are naive multinational executives who think what is good for their corporation, is automatically good for the nation in which they operate. Like the missionary "do-gooders" of the past, they point to what they are doing for those in underdeveloped countries—they bring jobs, technical know-how, training, and capital. Some scholars point with pride to the gradual affluence and industrialization that advanced, technological societies bring by their presence in Third and Fourth World nations. The late futurist Herman Kahn maintained that while the rate of growth in these areas will not be as spectacular as in the First and Second Worlds, it will be significant in raising the people above existing poverty levels, and will help to close the gap between the rich and poor nations.

Second, the indigenous culture impacts the organization and its representatives. There is a broadening of perspective and attitudes about the people, and adaptations are made to the way they do business. This influence can be both positive and negative. On the plus side the transnational organization may learn new managerial or technical practices, as well as different values and goals. On the minus side, the multinational corporation may find itself pressured to conform to local

Not every endeavor of advanced countries and their representatives is a benefit to the consuming nation.

unwritten norms of questionable behavior that can range from bribery to corruption.

BRIBERY AND ETHICS IN A GLOBAL CONTEXT

Corruption and bribery are present in most, if not all, societies. Truth and honesty are noble ideals, but they are also relative. As managers operate globally, they must be aware of the relativism in each culture of accepting a tip, bribe incentive etc. Different criteria and values between Eastern and Western cultures, for example, determine what is acceptable or appropriate.

In developing countries where people struggle to survive, bribes and corruption, especially in the public sector, are endemic to the system, while in industrialized countries, the practice is often more sophisticated, less visible but prevalent. Payoffs to public officials, especially the police, have been reported in the media from Mexico City to the New York Police Department. The following is from an interview with John Noonan,[10] a leading legal scholar, philosopher, and a professor of law at the University of California at Berkeley.

"The Concept Has Roots in Religion"
The concept of bribery dates back to ancient Egypt and Israel and has its roots in religion. In these ancient societies there was at least one type of powerful person you were not supposed to go to with a gift: The judge hearing your case. The judge was the representative of the divine, so you didn't deal with him as though it were a market transaction.

In the later Roman Empire there was some attempt to generalize from judges to other public figures who were not supposed to receive money for their decisions. During this time there was no real enforcement; bribery was realized more as a moral idea than an effective legal norm. Over the ages the bribery ethic came to be enforced, though in the United States you only begin to get serious enforcement against high officials—cabinet officers, federal judges—in this century.

"A Desire to Have Public Purity"
Since the 1960s there has been a quantum jump in bribery prosecutions in America. At one level, that can be explained by centralization of federal power: Just as many other things have come to Washington, so has enforcement of bribery laws.

The usual restraint on prosecuting bribery at the local level has been that everybody is to some extent a part of the system, so they are constrained from being too harsh on others who work in it. But the federal system doesn't have those constraints; it comes down hard on the locals.

Different criteria and values between Eastern and Western cultures, for example, determine what is acceptable or appropriate.

It can smash a whole system of local corruption, and in many parts of the country it has done just that.

Another more speculative explanation is that the jump in enforcement goes hand in hand with a perceptible decline in the desire to enforce sexual morals that began in the '60s. My speculation is that there's a desire to have public purity somewhere—and, if not in our sexual life, then with our public officials. It's interesting that a common language covers both sexual and public virtue. For example, the judge who sells out is considered a prostitute.

"Defining Bribery Is Not Easy"

The push against bribery in the past two decades has produced much legislation, including the Racketeer Influenced and Corrupt Organizations Act and the Foreign Corrupt Practices Act. The latter is unique in the history of the world because it makes bribing someone else's government a crime. What's also unusual is that it applies to the bribe giver rather than the bribe taker.

Defining bribery is not always easy, because many actions fall into a gray area. The cash bribe is the hard-core thing. But once you move away from that you always have questions. If you work at the Pentagon as a procurement official on a weapons system and the contractor hires you to work for him, did he do so because you're a wonderful, efficient administrator or because you gave him a contract? The same holds in political appointments. Did you give a relative of a congressman a job in exchange for a vote or because of his or her administrative skills? It's hard to work out a standard that would be enforceable criminally in such matters.

The Western Ideal Is Accepted "Universally"

Bribery today is universally condemned. The Western ideal has been accepted everywhere, though in many places adherence may be more rhetorical than real.

Eventually I think hard-core bribery will wither away, though gray areas will remain. I suppose that reflects faith in rationality. Bribery is now seen as a bad thing for government, which has become more public—thanks in part to the media. The perception of bribery as an evil, the publicity given it and now the great stress on purity in public office are pushing to eliminate hard-core bribery. It will go the way of slavery.

Ethical Relativism

As indicated earlier, the perception of bribery is culturally relative and it is true that conscience is "culturally conditioned." In some countries, the same action might be considered a tip (to ensure promptness or service), especially when dealing with a bureaucracy. Among government officials in many lands the ethical dilemma has also been labeled, "influ-

Conscience is "culturally conditioned."

ence peddling." Here there is a fine line between legal and illegal or even immoral behavior. The spread of questionable and inappropriate behavior in both business and government within so-called advanced countries has led to a demand by the public for more education in the schools, especially university courses in ethics at business and professional schools. This is especially relevant for law schools because different countries establish their own professional regime to govern lawyers. For example, in the United States lawyers are required to communicate information to clients, while in some countries the attorney for one party may communicate with the lawyer of another with the understanding that the information will not be shared with the latter's clients. In some cultures fees are fixed by professional societies, in others lawyers' fees are to be negotiated directly the client. What is ethical or standard in one culture may not be so in another.[11]

The Cultural Management System

Global leaders function within four basic intermeshing systems of management philosophy and practice: the technical system, the economic system, the political system, and the cultural system. The first three systems are relatively easy to quantify. For example, the use of government statistics, trade association and industry figures, and other quantifiable items are readily available in most countries. The cultural system has received the least consideration, because it tends to be abstract and its influence on management is difficult to specifically describe.

The *macro-environmental* approach in cross-cultural management attempts to identify the impact of education, politics, law, etc. on management practices and effectiveness. The assumption is that management practices depend on these external variables and the differences among organizations in various countries can be explained as a result of differences in environmental conditions. This approach is useful, however, it is incomplete because it seems to imply that the individual passively adapts to his or her environment, and gives the manager little credit for influencing the environment.

Our approach is *behavioral* in the sense that behavioral differences in managers and organizations are a function of cultural influences. The assumption is that a manager's attitudes, values, beliefs, and needs are determined at least in part by his or her culture. Management practices and theories will, therefore, vary from culture to culture. Taking the behavioral approach allows us to respond to these questions: What are the determinants of human behavior? Or, how can I understand why a manager is acting in a particular way?

In the global manager's attempt to understand one's self, as well as to comprehend and predict the behavior of others, he or she uses a multi-layered frame of explanation. If one knows the culture of the other person, then it is possible to make tentative predictions about the person's

Global leaders function within four basic intermeshing systems of management philosophy and practice: the technical system, the economic system, the political system, and the cultural system.

behavior. Furthermore, if one knows the other person's social roles and personality, one can predict behavior with a greater degree of accuracy.

The *basic personality* of a culture is the personality configuration shared by most members of the culture, as a result of early experiences that they have in common. This does not mean that behavior patterns of all members of a culture are similar. There is a wide range of individual differences, but there are many aspects that most of the people share to varying degrees. Unit 3 describes unique cultural aspects of several areas of the world. These local customs and practices can serve as guidelines for managers who must determine appropriate and inappropriate ways of interacting. They illustrate geographic themes and patterns that can be identified to facilitate international business.

This book considers only the nontechnical aspects of business. These pragmatic observations, subject to change with time, circumstances, and the personalities involved, are proposed for facilitating international business. As Edward T. Hall[12] states:

> Deep cultural undercurrents structure life in subtle but highly consistent ways that are not consciously formulated. Like the invisible jet streams in the skies that determine the course of a storm, these hidden currents shape our lives; yet their influence is only beginning to be identified.

CULTURAL CHANGES

In the many countries there has been a rise in the "new ethnicity" and a recognition of pluralism. Social philosopher, Michael Novak[13] explains this as a movement of *self-knowledge* on the part of members of third and fourth generations of southern and eastern European immigrants here. Novak contends that in a broader sense, the new ethnicity includes a renewed self-consciousness on the part of many American ethnic groups, be they Irish, Norwegian, Swede, German, Chinese, Japanese, or Italian. With Hispanic Americans now constituting a major segment of the U.S. population, it is understandable why those Americans with Mexican, Cuban, Puerto Rican, or some other Latin origin, are not only seeking new expression of identity, but also political-social power in the society. The consciousness-raising pride in heritage and accomplishment has been especially evident among the native Indians and black Americans in the U.S. during the last half of this century.

As society becomes more pluralistic, and cultures become more open, people become more aware of both dissimilarities and similarities between themselves and others. They also demand the freedom to be themselves, regardless of cultural context. Minorities of all types seek acceptance and tolerance, rather than discrimination and prejudice.

Becoming more culturally sensitive fosters a living environment in which internal dignity, as well as equity of treatment can coexist. A sense of one's separateness, one's uniqueness, one's ethnic or racial background, need not hamper an individual from becoming a multicultural cosmopolitan. Rather, it may enhance the contribution of a new infusion of diversity toward a *common culture*.

When people are unsure of themselves, uncertain of who they are, and are upset by the transition to a new way of life or work, their performance is affected. Accelerating change threatens our images of self and role. People need assistance in conjuring up new perception of themselves, both individually and institutionally. This is where organizational leaders can help personnel bridge the gap between where technology is and where culture, in general, lags, contributing to identity crises for many persons. We thought we knew who we are, but the old absolutes give way, and we are uncertain. We are people in transition, caught between disappearing and emerging cultures.

Similar representations may be made of *organizations*, because human systems—collections of people—also suffer identity crises. Caught between a disappearing bureaucracy and an emerging "ad-hocracy," the institution may experience reduced sales, poor morale, membership reductions, bankruptcy threats, obsolescence of product lines and services, and increasing frustration with unresponsive management. Organizations, then, are challenged to go through planned renewal and to reproject their public images. However, before undertaking such changes, wise leaders evaluate their organization's culture that can facilitate or hinder the process. Since culture underlies every initiative, an organization needs to pursue a cultural assessment to align the culture with the principles of quality management.

So too with *nations*. When the social fabric unravels or wavers, there are national identities in crisis. After the fall of communism in Yugoslavia, Albania, Russia, and other Eastern Bloc countries, many inhabitants suffered an identity crisis because they had been culturally conditioned by a totalitarian system for seventy years, and found it most difficult to move toward democracy and free enterprise in a few years. Whether one goes to Canada, Pakistan, or China, the peoples of various countries seek to rediscover their collective selves.

Finally, homo sapiens struggles with an identity crisis for the species. We thought we were earthbound, but now we have launched out into the universe. What are the limits of human potential? Is our real home out there? Cosmopolitan leaders can help in promoting synergy between past and future conceptions of ourselves, which so powerfully influence our behavior and accomplishments.

Human response to cultural change and contact with differences, as the late Herman Kahn reminded us, can be constructive or pathological,

Accelerating change threatens our images of self and role.

nonviolent or violent, rational or apocalyptic. Cultural exchange, Octavio Paz observed, requires experiencing the other and that is the essence of change. It alters our psyche, our outlook, and causes some loss of our own cultural beliefs. The paradox is that it may also stimulate a gain or an enlargement of one's perceptions and performance in the adoption of new cultural patterns. Cultural, like biological, evolution demands adaptations for survival and development. Although cultural change is multicausal, "metaindustrial humans" not only create it at the most rapid rate in history, but are also learning to plan and manage change. Culture is a human product subject to alteration and improvement. We are, therefore, discovering innovative ways to improve our performance, even within the new realities of outer space. As we continue to unravel who we really are and become more comfortable with our "selves," then our performance increases and our potential begins to be realized.

Hospital[14] reminds us that in the last few decades an ever-increasing number of people find themselves moving between and among several or more cultures within a life span. This dislocation may occur for political, economic, educational, or professional necessity. Thus, the issue of cross-cultural malaise and trauma keeps surfacing in short stories and novels, while the research literature on the subject expands. One cultural anthropologist claims it takes two generations to make the transition from one culture to another and that those in transit can experience problems after years of apparently successful adaptation.

MANAGING TECHNOLOGY TRANSFER

Another theme in this chapter is technology transfer. Because culture involves the transmission of both knowledge and experience, the arena of technology is one of its most practical manifestations. Technology represents that branch of knowledge dealing with industrial arts, applied science, and engineering—the material objects and artifacts of civilization. When technology results in concepts, inventions, processes, production methods, and mechanisms that are transferred from its use place of origin elsewhere, it becomes a cross-cultural phenomenon. Seurat[15] describes this human characteristic as "the capacity to store and transmit to people the accumulated experience of others." When it is done properly, human progress and prosperity are advanced, but if done improperly, then human life and property may suffer. A laudable goal is to improve the standard of living for those who are to benefit from the transfer.

Technology involves much more than the sale of licenses, franchises, and other forms of agreements for sharing the technology. It may include the transmission of a scientific theory, an engineering capability, or management system—everything from drawings, plans, and manufacturing instructions to tools and instruments, machines and comput-

Culture is a human product subject to alteration and improvement.

ers, facilities and training materials. Technology's scope in an R&D project may range from a pilot to finished production, or from human resource development to turnkey factories. All facets of technology transfer, however, have a cultural dimension. For example, two companies from different countries establish a joint venture for the transfer of unique consumer or industrial products from an industrialized to a developing nation. In the process, their representatives communicate, but with different cultural understandings and systems of law, finance, education, and transportation. One entity may be from the private sector, while the other is from a government-owned company, or combination of both.

The technology transfer is best accomplished when it fosters cultural synergy for all parties. Cultural factors influence project success in every phase of the transfer process—from planning (including setting goals and objectives, defining needs and criteria), to systems analysis (including examination and synthesis of alternatives, selecting optimum targets, and writing specifications), to program implementation (including work definition, scheduling, budgeting, procurement and control systems). Unless global leaders cope with these cultural realities, planning is undermined, goals are fuzzy, sequencing and scheduling are unrealistic, incentives are lacking, misunderstandings abound, and corruption may flourish.

All facets of technology transfer, however, have a cultural dimension.

Technology transfer can be applied to ancient or modern technologies, high or low technologies. Within one's own country, it can span many microcultures as scientists and entrepreneurs seek to move the knowledge beyond its initial application. But often there are cultural barriers to be overcome, and cultural issues to be considered before the transfer can be successfully made.

The mindset of academia and its bureaucracy have prevented the rapid translation of many university innovations and patents from the laboratory to the marketplace. The "entrepreneurial culture" is only beginning to invade the institutions of higher education, especially with the establishment of university industrial parks, incubator programs, and other such devices to bridge the gap between the academic and business worlds.

Technology transfer implies it is suitable from the viewpoint of both the type of technology and the level of development of the recipient. If the technology is too sophisticated or complicated, it may never be used properly. An older technology rather than state-of-the-art may fit into a local situation more efficiently. For example, often simple water pumps in poor countries may be more effective than large water and dam projects. Kumar's research[16] underscores the need to avoid:

❑ Fostering long-term dependency on the part of the receiver of the technology.
❑ Overwhelming the receiver with a technological system that is too complex and sophisticated for use and maintenance.

Instead, Kumar advocates indigenization and transnational cooperation in international economic and community development. He cites the demonstrated successes of many developing multinational and even high-technology firms in serving the markets of their countries. Individuals must be aware that what is appropriate technology for a corporation in a developed country may or may not be appropriate technology for a company in a developing nation.

We have tried to emphasize that cultural inhibitors to the transfer of technology can occur not only between countries, but within the various sectors of one's own economy. "Tech transfer" should be appropriate not only to the needs of less developed peoples, but also to the needs of the planet. That is, the "transferor" must show a regard for the impact of the technology upon the local environment and its ecology. There is a "global commons" on Earth, such as rain forests, that we should all seek to protect, regardless of our place of origin. This is the new concept of *sustainability* relative to harboring the planet's resources. In 1994, for instance in the U.S.A., the National Academy of Science launched a $6 million"Global Commons Project" to provide the nations of the world with new knowledge to promote development while simultaneously ensuring a cleaner, safer, environment.[17]

"Tech transfer" should be appropriate not only to the needs of less developed peoples, but also to the needs of the planet.

EFFECTIVE GLOBAL LEADERSHIP

First, in his or her exercise of leadership, the global manager must continually update and broaden his or her understanding of culture and its impact on our lives. Although there may be no valid management theories that can be universally applied across all cultures, there are many principles and practices of leadership that can be adapted to various countries despite cultural differences. Despite the cultural differences in managerial approaches, it is possible to produce cultural synergy in the pragmatic operations of management.

Elashmawi[18] in his research into global joint ventures, focuses on clashes within multicultural work environments, such as establishing a plant overseas. These offshore enterprises require the hiring, training, and management of local in-country personnel of differing cultural and technical backgrounds. He identifies cultural clashes arising from language and nonverbal communication, time and space orientation, decision-making and information systems, conduct of meetings and training, as well as motivation.

Global leaders have a rare opportunity to contribute to the creation of cyberculture, the new post-industrial way of life, as well as to design the new metaindustrial organizational culture. To succeed in the emerging Information Society means overcoming the cultural conditioning of the past three hundred years of the Industrial Age.[19]

New technologies will turn the Pacific Ocean into a lake of commercial exchange. Bounded by Canada, America, and Mexico on the east, and by Australia/New Zealand, Japan, China, Indonesia, and Malaysia on the west, the Pacific's key trading cities will be Hong Kong, Singapore, Tokyo, and possibly Sydney, Manila, Vancouver, Los Angeles, and San Diego. We envision that by 2010, the Pacific Basin will be a vast, powerful, interconnected economic and cultural community of 4.5 billion people, over half the world's population and 60% of its consumers.

Despite present economic turmoil in the nations of the Far East, there are forecasters who predict the Pacific Basin to be a major 21st century market. Now with Hong Kong returned to China, it remains to be seen whether it will remain a principal financial center as is Singapore and Tokyo. However, with China as the most populated country with rapidly increasing buy/spending power, it already attracts external investment and should continue as a market target.

An undated special report of the Futures Research Division of Security Pacific National Bank in Los Angeles observes:

> The positive forces for economic growth and opportunity in this region are large market and varied work force, abundant raw materials and food supplies, advanced technology created in/by/for the Pacific region, and a developing cultural synergism. We foresee these factors overcoming negative forces in the area such as nationalistic and protectionist sentiments, economic warfare or trade barriers, technological espionage, and other temporary problems.

A common theme is that the Pacific Ocean is becoming a "highway" that links the countries that rim this water body, and that a regional synergy is being forged. The economic synergy centers around abundant markets, human and material resources, enhancing the cultural synergy aided by advanced communications, including information, transportation, and entertainment systems. Its citizens are developing a growing consciousness of community shaped by technology, trade and history.

The countries on the western rim of the Pacific Basin are coming alive to the potential of this unique area. Taiwan's economic planners, for instance, have already launched their own multibillion-dollar, high-technology version of Silicon Valley. They are shifting their economy from labor-intensive to high-technology production.

Further culture specific information of Asian countries is found in Chapter 12.

Atlantic Rim Enterprises

Despite the mania about the Pacific markets, many firms see Europe as their best hope in the near future. In its Western countries, that continent has a concentration of some of the most advanced economies and highest living standards in the world. With the establishment of the EU,

By 2010, the Pacific Basin will be a vast, powerful, interconnected economic and cultural community of 4.5 billion people, over half the world's population and 60% of its consumers.

their economic muscle rivals that of the United States with which they share important cultural and historic ties. The Europeans were the first to invest in the "New World," and the legacy continues for their financial stake in America dwarfs that of Asia.

Further information on this subject is in Chapter 13.

SUMMARY

Global business is a learning laboratory. Peaceful and cooperative free enterprise on an international basis contributes to global economic development, but also reduces the gap in terms of poverty and population. The export/import exchange, particularly of information and new technologies, fosters political and social stability, as well as human resource development.

As Toffler observed, "Nobody knows the future," however, 21st century global leaders can help to influence the new millennium.

REFERENCES

1. Bonsignore, M., chairman and CEO Honeywell Inc., The Conference Board, 1995, presentation at the Strategic Alliances Conference, March 29, 1995.
2. EFI International 1995 Executive Forum Conference, Orlando, FL, February 9–11, 1995.
3. Gilder, G. *Into the Quantum Era of Microcosm: Economics and Technology,* New York: Simon & Schuster, 1989.
4. Lewis, K. G. "Breakdown—A Psychological Contract for Expatriates," *European Business Review,* Vol. 97:6, 1997, pp. 279–293.
5. Mensch, G. and Niehaus, R. J. (eds.). *Work, Organization, and Technological Change,* New York: Plenum, 1982.
6. Vaill, P. *Managing as a Performing Art,* San Francisco, CA: Jossey-Bass, 1989.
7. Groves, M. "Multinational Perspective: MBA Programs are Serious About Giving Students Experience Abroad," *Los Angeles Times,* July 4, 1996, D.4.
8. CPC Foundation/RAND Corporation Report. *Developing the Global Work Force.* 1994.
9. Dunbar, E. "Adjustment and Satisfaction of Patriate U.S. Personnel," *International Journal of Intercultural Relations,* 1992, Vol. 16, pp. 1–16.
10. *U.S. News and World Report,* "Interview with John Noonan," reprinted with permission, copyright 1985.
11. Daly, M. "The Ethical Implications of Globalization of the Legal Profession," *Fordham International Law School Journal,* New York: Fordham University, 1998.
12. Hall, E. R. *Beyond Culture,* Vol. 3 in *The Basic Works of Edward T. Hall,* New York, NY: Bantam/Doubleday, 1989.
13. Novak, M. *Rise of the Unmeltable Ethnics,* New York: McMillian, 1972.

14. Hospital, J. T. *Dislocations*, Baton Rouge, LA: Louisiana State University Press, 1989.
15. Seurat, S. *Technology Transfer—A Realistic Approach*, Houston, TX: Gulf Publishing, 1979.
16. Kumar, K. and McLeod, M. G. (eds.). *Multinationals from Developing Countries*, Lexington, MA: Lexington/D.C. Heath, 1981; Kumar, K. (ed.) *Bonds Without Bondage: Explorations in Transcultural Interactions*, Honolulu, HI: East West Center/University Press of Hawaii, 1979.
17. For information and a free *Forum* newsletter, contact Houston Advanced Research Center, The Woodland Forum (4800 Research Forest Dr., The Woodlands, TX 77381, USA); also Hawkens, P. *The Ecology of Commerce: A Declaration of Sustainability*, New York, NY: Harper Collins, 1993.
18. Elashmawi, F. and Harris, P. R. *Multicultural Management 2000: Essential Skills for Global Business Success*, Houston, TX: Gulf Publishing Co., 1998.
19. Harris, P. R. *New Work Culture: HRD Transformational Management Strategies*, Amherst, MA: Human Resource Development Press, 1998.

Unit 3

Cultural Specifics in Six World Regions

Studies of encounters between cultures, almost always involving asymmetries of power, share a common methodological problem: It is usually the dominant party that writes the (hi)stories of the encounter.

S. B. Ortner, Life and Death on Mt. Everest:
Sherpa and Himalayan Mountaineering,
Princeton, NJ: Princeton University Press, 1999

It is difficult, if not impossible, to describe in the space available all of a society's cultural characteristics. We have tried to give sufficient information to illustrate general concepts, tendencies, attitudes, etc. of major populations; and we have tried to do it with respect.

P. Harris and R. Moran

DOING BUSINESS
WITH NORTH
AMERICANS

United States and Canada

"People may have migrated into North America even before the ice sheets developed more than 20,000 years ago."[1]

College students in Kennewick, Washington unearthed a skull that was eventually carbon-dated at 9,200 years old. The full Paleo-American skeleton, assembled by a forensic anthropologist, provided evidence that the New World's earliest arrivals may not have been direct ancestors of modern day "American Indians." The first North American inhabitants of this continent may have migrated here thousands of years earlier, possibly from southern Asia or even northern Europe. Smithsonian Institution researchers studying other New World human skulls found potential resemblances to archaic Norse populations, as well as the mysterious Ainu, aboriginals from the Japanese islands. Perhaps these early peoples originated from multiple migrations?[2]

Scholars have found evidence that Phoenician merchants, Viking warriors, Irish monks, and Polynesian seafarers reached this Western Hemisphere centuries before an Italian navigator got the credit for this great feat. Of course, the Eskimos, or Inuit, may have already crossed the Bering Sea and settled in North America long before the Phoenicians, Vikings, Irish, and Polynesians arrived.

Recently, archaeologists from the College of William and Mary uncovered an 11,000-year-old spearhead on Jamestown Island, Virginia. The primitive tool was used by Ice Age inhabitants to hunt mastodon and elk. The English landed in Jamestown in 1607.[3]

Although North America geographically includes three nations, we shall generally limit our discussion to the peoples of Canada and the United States—those who live north of the Rio Grande River. Although Mexico is geographically and economically part of North America, *cul-*

CANADA

ALASKA

YUKON

N.W. TERRITORIES

BRITISH COLUMBIA

ALBERTA

SASKATCHEWAN

MANITOBA

ONTARIO

HUDSON BAY

QUEBEC

NEWFOUNDLAND

NOVA SCOTIA

PACIFIC OCEAN

WA

OR

ID

MT

ND

MN

WI

MI

SD

WY

NE

IA

IL

IN

OH

PA

NY

VT

ME

NH

MA

RI

CT

NJ

DE

MD

WV

VA

NV

UT

CO

KS

MO

KY

CA

AZ

NM

OK

AR

TN

NC

SC

MS

AL

GA

TX

LA

FL

ATLANTIC OCEAN

HAWAII

UNITED STATES

PUERTO RICO

turally it is aligned with Latin America, and South/Central America, and therefore is covered in Chapter 11. We begin with an overview of Pan Americas, recognizing that the term "American" can be used by all the inhabitants of that area. However, "American" is more often used to refer to those living in the United States.

PAN AMERICAN MANAGEMENT PERSPECTIVES

This great land body that extends almost from the Arctic to Cape Horn, was named "America" after sixteenth century Italian explorer and merchant, Amerigo Vespucci. Trade was a dominant force in the discovery and development of these unknown territories between the Atlantic and Pacific Oceans. Although all the inhabitants of the Americas have right to the title "American"—and many think of themselves as such—it was the people in that portion called the United States, who popularly appropriated the designation.

The Americas—north, central, and south—have a diversity of cultural heritages, and a synergy of sorts is being forged. It is like a huge laboratory of human relations in which a mixture of cultures from Europe, Africa, and Asia are merging. One tends to think of North America as largely "Anglo-Saxon" types who speak primarily English. However, Canada is bilingual with its second language of French, while the United States is moving in that direction with Spanish. That area south of the Rio Grande River is considered Latin America, because the language there is mainly of Latin origin. Apart from numerous Indian languages, Spanish is dominant in Mexico, Central and South America, while Portuguese is the primary language of Brazil (with some Italian and Japanese being spoken).

For our purpose, Pan America will designate that land mass of some 15 million square miles from the Arctic Ocean south to the convergence of the Atlantic/Pacific Oceans at Drakes Passage. The Americas involve approximately 30 *national* cultures, plus Eskimo (Inuit) and Native American cultures.

For global leaders seeking to function effectively in the Pan American market, it is important to understand the geoeconomic and cultural characteristics that will facilitate business and acculturation. To better comprehend the Pan American market, consider these realities.

Economic Development

International agencies and banks generally consider the North American countries to be rich in terms of annual gross domestic product per capita. Whereas most of Latin America, from Mexico southward, is thought of as developing countries. Despite economic progress in Latin

Trade was a dominant force in the discovery and development of these unknown territories between the Atlantic and Pacific Oceans.

NORTH AMERICA—PROFILE

Population (Approx.)		Land Mass (Approx. Sq. Mi.)	
Canada	30.7 million	Canada	3.8 million
USA	273 million	USA	3.6 million
Total	303.7 million	Total	7.4 million

Major Cultural Influences

❑ Native North American Eskimos (Inuits) and culturally diverse Native American nations; agricultural and nomadic

❑ European—originally Spanish/French/English and later diverse immigration from the continent.

USA

❑ African, including lately, Haitian.

❑ Asian—originally Chinese, Japanese, and Indo-Chinese.

❑ Mexicans, Cubans, and other Latin cultures.

Canada

❑ French, Ukranians, and variety of Commonwealth peoples (e.g., Indians and Pakistanis, West Indies)

Socio-Political Developments

❑ English common law system.

❑ In Canada the struggle of the English/French colonial powers still affects national sense of identity and relations, and government struggles for its own constitution in British Commonwealth.

❑ After a revolutionary war, USA declared independence from England

❑ Egalitarian, democratic, individualistic, materialistic with emphasis on organization and self-development.

❑ Problems of race/minority relations—in Canada, it is principally the human/political rights of the French-speaking group in the dominant English society; in USA, it is principally the rights and integration of African—Americans and Hispanics, as well as other minorities. Protests have been largely peaceful through political/legal action for equal opportunity.

❑ Economically and technically advanced in post-industrial stage of development; into space exploration and development, as well as global leadership.

❑ Religiously pluralistic; majority consider themselves Christian with large Jewish minority.

Education

❑ In the English tradition; public and privately supported institutions of higher education, with unique system of community colleges and technical institutes. In Canada, public support is provided to schools administered by religious organizations, largely Catholic. In USA there is strict separation of church and state, so there are many public elementary/secondary schools and no public support to the parochial and independent school systems. Universal education required by law usually to 12th grade, and many go on to college studies.

America, 16% of their population are still classified as poor (i.e., GDP below $1,500 annually). This helps to explain the economic dependence of the South upon the North in the Americas, and the flow of illegal immigration northward in the search of work. It also points up the problems of these nations with the International Monetary Fund and the World Bank relative to difficulties with repayment of loans, rising inflation, and other economic woes.

Natural/Material Resources

Although both American continents are rich in such resources, the North has developed these resources more extensively. For example, in terms of food production, the United Nations Food and Agricultural Organization (FAO) estimates that only one country in Latin America—Argentina—is considered a developed exporter, such as the U.S.A. and Canada. With reference to energy, the International Institute for Applied Systems Analysis divides the world into seven major energy-related regions—Region 1 is North America with a highly developed market economy, while Region 4 is Latin America, listed as a developing region of potentially rich energy resources.

Human Resources

North America has a combined population of approximately 303.7 million persons with a natural population increase of less than 1%. Latin America has more than 475 million inhabitants and an increase rate between 1–3%; the most populous countries at 3% or more are Mexico, Venezuela, Guatemala, Peru, and Paraguay. Obviously, unless expanding population is brought under control in the South, not only will economic growth there be affected adversely, but continuing social unrest, political, and military turmoil can be expected. Yet, there are human assets in Latin America waiting to be capitalized through education, and training.

In this hemisphere, the interface between its northern and southern inhabitants is a contrast in opportunities and problems. The opportunities for mutual enrichment are through cultural exchanges, scientific collaboration, educational and economic assistance, and efforts promoting peace between the hemispheres. However, the problems proliferate because issues like these cry out for creative solutions from Pan Americans:

❑ Lack of North/South dialogue and synergistic endeavors that benefit the peoples of both continents, such as projects to renew the infrastructures of societies in need, or to provide adequate food and shelter for the poor.

Although both American continents are rich in such resources, the North has developed these resources more extensively. Yet, there are human assets in Latin America waiting to be capitalized through education, and training.

❏ Instability in some Latin states that have yet to become nations, or who suffer from archaic political, justice and economic systems.

❏ Insecurity caused by growing deviant behavior as expressed in anti-social actions such as terrorism and drug trafficking, or the expanding struggle between democratic ideals and totalitarian realities.

❏ Inability to establish a meaningful North/South dialogue and collaborative exchange in the Americas, instead of exploitation and dependence.

Yet for the most part, Pan America is a free enterprise system and market of vast potential. It borders the Pacific Rim on the West, and can benefit from the trade shift from the Atlantic to the Pacific. It can become a laboratory of cooperation.

The popular Latin perception of U.S. Americans is to characterize their northern neighbors as Yankees or "gringos." Most Latins seem to be neutral about Canadians because they are so far north. Canadian contact with their southern neighbors beyond the U.S.A. has been limited. Many Latin Americans have a love-hate relationship about the States. They admire its equality and economic progress, and at the personal level may like many Americans. Many seek to live in the U.S. because of its opportunities. But many Latins also distrust, envy, and fear Americans. Too many North Americans ignore the needs and possibilities in Latin America, and do not pursue collaboration with these neighboring states and peoples. Europe or Asia are more common partners in economic exchanges. However, with the United States, Canada and Mexico implementing NAFTA in 1994 a new era of economic growth, cultural exchanges, developing and expanding markets do much to remove some roadblocks.

According to Mahoney,[4] commenting on U.S., Canadian and Mexican relations:

> The New World came about from the fracture of three empires. The North American Free Trade Agreement now anticipates a new trade and capital communion between Mexico, Canada, and the United States—one that hopes to transcend two centuries of division and, in the Mexican-American case, deep suspicion . . . America and Mexico lived within a labyrinth of solitude, lost not only to each other but to the chance of casting off their traditional roles of the dominant and the dependent. The reawakening at hand is not just with Canada and Mexico, it is with ourselves.

The U.S. has made many efforts to build better relations with its Pan American neighbors. Though such endeavors may have been premature, unsuccessful, or underutilized, they contain seeds for future synergism.

Too many North Americans ignore the needs and possibilities in Latin America, and do not pursue collaboration with these neighboring states and peoples.

Eskimos (Inuits) and Native Americans

From a majority perspective in any society (i.e. as a white, Anglo-Saxon in Canada or the United States) it is difficult to write about indigenous people. However, indigenous people need to be addressed first with respect and in a positive manner, and then we can learn from their culture. History and how it affected their culture is also to be considered.

Members of the majority and others need to be aware of culturally biased words. *The Color of Words: An Encyclopedic Dictionary of Ethnic Bias in the United States,*[5] explains words and expressions used in the United States today that carry ethnic bias. The words listed illustrate the labeling and classifying of people, these classifications are often for "reasons of manipulation or mischief." There are over one thousand words or phrases listed, and the following are some culturally biased examples.

> *Coolie, cooly.* An unskilled Asian laborer or porter. Dating from the mid seventeenth century, the term was applied by Europeans in India and China to a native laborer hired at subsistence wages. In California since the 1860s, Chinese immigrants or sojourners were viewed as a 'race of coolies' who threatened white Californian labor.
>
> *Coon.* A shortened form of *raccoon.* American English, coon is usually dated to 1742. *Coon* has been used derogatorily to refer to a black person, especially a male since the mid-nineteenth century.
>
> *Dink.* Derogatory nickname for an Asian or person of Asian descent, but today usually a Vietnamese, as used by American and Australian soldiers during the Vietnam War. (Ed. Note: "Dink" also describes a social/economic class that has "Dual Incomes, No Kids.")

In parts of the Americas there are two indigenous peoples caught in a culture gap—the Eskimos (Inuits) and the Native Americans. Both have been harmed and helped by the rapid advancement of "white civilization" into their lives. With the introduction of U.S. and Canadian government health and education programs, their life expectancy and educational levels have risen. But so has their frustration, despair, and social deterioration. Many have succumbed to alcoholism and drug addiction, and the level of suicide is exceedingly high. Their problems and potentials are similar on or off reservations; whether in the U.S. state of Alaska or the Canadian Northwest Territories; whether above or below the U.S./Canadian border.

In April 1999, in an attempt to right past wrongs, Canada divided the old Northwest Territory in two and established Nunavut, meaning "our land," giving the Inuit title to 135,000 square miles of their traditional territory. With the creation of Nunavut, the Inuit have won some degree of self-determination. What is remarkable, "is that by conventional measures of political influence like the votes they control or the funds they have access to, (the Eskimos) would have been considered almost powerless."[6] However, using Inuit traditional attributes of patience and compromise they accomplished their goals without long and drawn out court battles and violence.

Weatherford[7] discusses how the misnamed Indians of the Americas transformed the world stating that the contributions of the Native Americans to our economy and culture have been consistently underrated, if not ignored. His conclusion is even more telling—we are allowing the "Indian cultures" to die away without learning what they have to teach us.

The Inuits have given us the snowshoe, toboggan, and kayak among other things, while Native Americans introduced maize, potatoes, sweet potatoes, and manioc. These crops constitute a large portion of today's staple foods. Cotton was also introduced by Native Americans.[8] The Inuit and Native American have much to teach us about the mind, spirit, and body and our relationship to the natural world. The Native American's philosophy of respect, reverence, and cooperation with the earth are finally gaining acceptance in the mainstream.

In reality, tribal or aboriginal peoples everywhere face the same dilemma brought on by accelerating social and technological change. Whether an Inuit in Hudson Bay or a Navajo in northern Arizona, the confrontation with too rapid cultural change leaves the natives bewildered, confused, and almost overwhelmed. The rate of innovation in traditional societies is slow, while it rises astronomically in modern societies in the midst of transition. The traditional culture is past oriented, while the modern society is future-oriented, interpreting history as progressive movement. Unfortunately, Western ethnocentrism even among anthropologists in the past has labeled some of these tribal people in the hunting stage of development as primitive. In fact, these groups are quite developed within their own context, and more in harmony with nature than many people today. They seem to possess a better sense of ecology, energy conservation, food distribution, and overall happiness than many of their so-called civilized counterparts.

In the process of trying to enhance the indigenous peoples of the Americas, one must understand and appreciate the values and assets in such cultures. One is then in a position to create synergy with them relative to their contributions and how both cultures can work together to meet their needs.

The Eskimos (Inuits) and Native North Americans have paid a high price for acculturation. Many of their peoples suffer mental and physical, as well as economic handicaps. But with cooperation and collaboration by their fellow citizens, these proud and resourceful people can create a new place.

We are allowing the "Indian cultures" to die away without learning what they have to teach us. The Eskimos (Inuits) and Native North Americans have paid a high price for acculturation.

Native Americans

Who are the Native Americans? Misnamed "Indians" by Christopher Columbus, Native Americans are the indigenous people who were the local inhabitants of the Americas when the Europeans arrived. These Native Americans' ancestors migrated here from Asia, and possibly Egypt and the Viking homelands. There are obvious cultural differences between the descendants of these aboriginal peoples and modern citizens of North, Central, and South America.

There are approximately 1.8 million Native Americans in the U.S., half of whom live on reservations. The average annual income is below poverty level and their unemployment rate is the highest in the country.

When America was discovered, there were probably less than one million Native Americans living in what is now the U.S. These peoples were scattered and their tribal organizations were largely unrelated. Many early colonists married Native Americans, motivated largely by social and cultural factors. For example, a Native American wife was an asset to a fur trader in teaching him the language and customs of the tribe from which he bought furs. In early New England, however, Native American women had little use in the trading and farming communities, and intermarriage was rare.

The U.S. government, which came into existence with the adoption of the Constitution, began its imperialistic relationship with Native Americans by considering the various tribes as national entities and negotiated with them for land.

There are many fundamental differences between a tribal culture and a dominant culture, say, for example, the United States. Three of these differences include:

❑ In the mainstream culture, time is to be used, saved, and spent. People are paid for their time. Native Americans generally view time as a continuum that is related to the rising and setting of the sun and to the changes in the seasons.
❑ In the mainstream culture, decision-making is based on authority. Some people have authority to make decisions and others do not. Authority in Native American cultures is more horizontal than vertical because of the need to reach unanimity on a decision before any action will be taken.
❑ Most Americans live pretty much for the future. We ask our children what they want to be when they grow up. In contrast, Native American children are not asked the same question, because they already "are"—they are children and they do not have to wait "to be."

Understanding the Native American way of life provides us with a challenge and an opportunity. We can learn to develop skills and to work with Native Americans without destroying their dignity and allow them to change at their own pace. An understanding of Native American history, values, and cultural differences can facilitate communication and business with these remarkable people.

Within the continental United States, many of the Native Americans have passed into the mainstream culture. Today in many states, gaming and casino operations are managed and owned by Native Americans. For those who still live on government reservations, painful progress is made to gain greater control over their own administration of their own affairs, whether this be in schools and services, or within the Federal Bureau of Indian Affairs. With recent financial settlements through the courts over abrogated treaty rights and lost lands, some tribes have established modern corporations to manage their natural resources and to enter into joint ventures with major companies for economic development purposes, even in the field of high technology on the reservations. Native North Americans never had the white man's sense of private property. Tribal culture thought in terms of collective responsibility for the preservation of the land and nature's gifts. Today the ecology and nature movements are catching up to the aboriginal's concern for the environment.

More than half a million Canadians are classified as of native ancestry, and three quarters live on reservations. These are grouped by their government in four categories—status (registered formally under the Indian Act); non-status Indians who have not registered with the government; Metis (descendants of mixed aboriginals and European ancestry); and Inuits (approximately 36,000), a distinct cultural group who generally live north of the tree line and speak primarily their own language (Inuktitut). A 1985 change in Canadian law has caused a dramatic rise in Indian population figures, which includes Indian women who marry Canadians of non-Indian ancestry.

Native North Americans never had the white man's sense of private property. Tribal culture thought in terms of collective responsibility for the preservation of the land and nature's gifts.

MODERN SETTLEMENTS OF OLD CLAIMS

Even equable Canada has its unhappy indigenes: Cree Indians and Inuit fearful of separatism in Quebec; Mohawks farther south in conflict with police over land and smuggling; British Columbia's umpteen tribes which claim—except in a few small areas, they never gave up their rights by treaty and that nearly all of that province's 950,000 km² are rightfully theirs. . . . The "first nations" cannot expect to retrieve title, in the modern sense, to all their land. But they want compensation for it, and recognition of their "aboriginal rights" . . . (I)n remote New Aiyandish, 750 km north of Vancouver, British Columbia's first modern treaty of settlement was concluded. The winners were the Nisga'a, a tribe that has lead the fight for aboriginal rights for more than 100 years. . . .Once ratified, the 6,000 Nisga'a will collectively own 1,992 km² in the Nass river valley. Along with full power of governance, forest and mineral rights, they will get C$121m to help build infrastructure

(continued on next page)

(continued)

in their authorities, and C$190m grants over the next five years as settlement of their claims. . . . Nisga'a argue they will remain Canadians, with the same rights and subject to the same criminal law as others. They have made other concessions in signing this treaty, including losing their exemption from sales and income tax. . . . Most aboriginal leaders are hailing this treaty as a breakthrough that will speed settlement with 51 Indian groups, covering most of the province. . . . Polls in British Columbia indicate that 90% of the general population favor settling such land claims, for the disputes hinder economic investment and development of the region.[9]

Commercial Development on Native American Lands

We shall learn all the devices the white man has.
We shall handle his tools for ourselves.
We shall master his machinery and his inventions, his skills, his medicines, his planning;
But we'll retain our beauty
AND STILL BE INDIAN.

*A young Indian college student,
date unknown*

*Authority in
Native American
cultures is more
horizontal than
vertical.*

Energy companies, searching for commercial quantities of oil, coal, uranium and other natural resources, are present on Native American lands. It is apparent there are differences between the Northern Cheyenne and the oil people who work with them. These differences often make a difference. However, if both groups are respectful and knowledgeable of each other's business motivations, value systems and other aspects of their cultures the possibility of working together for mutual advantage is significantly enhanced. Some energy companies provide education and cross-cultural training for the geologists, landsmen (women) and others who work closely with Native American people in their many phases of intimate contact. These educational seminars involve presentations by Native American leaders, self-assessment exercises, collaborations, team-building exercises and the distribution of articles and books on the various tribes.

It is impossible to provide here an example of the information presented on all the Native American nations. We have profiled one North American tribe to illustrate the rich background and unique aspects one must consider when contemplating investing in tribal resources, forming joint ventures, etc. The following is a condensed profile of the Northern Cheyenne.[10]

HISTORY OF THE NORTHERN CHEYENNE

The name Cheyenne comes from the Sioux word *sahiyela* or *sahiyena* and means "alien speaker." In their own Cheyenne language, however, the name is *Tsitsistas*.

Originally, the Northern and Southern Cheyenne lived together as one tribe. They were first seen by white men in Minnesota in approximately 1640. In the latter part of the 17th century, the Cheyenne began migrating to the Western Plains, where they obtained horses and led basically a nomadic life.

The Cheyenne coalesced into two groups; the Northern Cheyenne who lived in Big Horn and Rosebud counties in Montana and the Southern Cheyenne who lived in the Southern Arapaho in Oklahoma. In the mid 1800s, after several bloody battles with the United States Cavalry, the U.S. government ordered the Northern Cheyenne to the reservation of the Southern Cheyenne in Oklahoma. The Northern Cheyenne, longing for their homeland in Montana, left Oklahoma. Eventually, U.S. troops captured the returning Cheyenne and moved them to army barracks at Fort Robinson, while the army petitioned Washington concerning their fate. When Washington decided the Northern Cheyenne should be returned to Oklahoma, about 150 Cheyenne attempted escape and were shot. The remaining Cheyenne were taken to the Tongue River Reservation in Montana which was established for the Northern Cheyenne.

In 1887, Congress passed a law permitting all Native American Indian tribes to divide their land among tribal members. Each member would receive approximately 160 acres. After holding the land for 25 years the individual could sell the land. Land that was not allocated was owned by the tribe.

The Northern Cheyenne believed that the land that their ancestors had fought and died for should not be divided. Land is mother and is holy. The Indian Bureau informed the Cheyenne that if they divided the land the individuals who owned the land could receive government loans to improve the property. The Cheyenne resisted dividing their land but in 1926 the tribe gave 1,457 members a tract of 160 acres each. The remaining acreage (a little less than half of the reservation) was owned by the tribe. All mineral rights on the land belonged to the tribe. After the 25 years passed there was great pressure on individual Cheyenne to sell their property. Today, less than 2% of the reservation is owned by non-tribal individuals, and 70% is owned by the tribe.

When Washington decided the Northern Cheyenne should be returned to Oklahoma, about 150 Cheyenne attempted escape and were shot.

Government

The Northern Cheyenne are governed by a tribal council that is headed by a president and elected by the tribal members. There are Indian courts with Indian judges and an Indian police force.

In 1933, the Indian Department became the Bureau of Indian Affairs (BIA). The BIA is the *trustee* of reservation lands. Native American land is *entrusted* to the BIA, which is to ensure that the land is used for the best interest of the Native Americans. Historically, the BIA has not always understood the Native American or acted wisely on their behalf.

The traditional Northern Cheyenne view of authority and power was that it was a condition that flowed naturally from one's moral excellence and virtue. Historically, a chief was selected because of his wisdom and honorable actions, and he in turn received the loyalty, respect and obedience of the tribe.

The People

The Cheyenne's world is a mixture of the American world and the European world. Almost everyone speaks English, although many still converse in the Cheyenne language, and in some schools the Cheyenne language is taught.

The Northern Cheyenne and the Plains tribes are fun-loving and enjoy good companionship. They love feasts, happy talk, and story-telling. The efforts of the Northern Cheyenne to preserve their culture are at their heights today. Through education, both in the classroom and through the traditions of the tribe, the Cheyenne are attempting to teach and pass on the Cheyenne ways to their children.

Many non-tribal organizations, for example VISTA Volunteers, have offered programs and assistance to the tribe. Many in the tribe including parents are concerned that the exposure to non-tribal values may create problems or send mixed messages to the young.

The Culture

Historically, the Northern Cheyenne men were hunters who provided for their families and tribe while living on the reservation. Today, that is a financial impossibility for most, and men and women work on or off the reservation in offices and factories. The Northern Cheyenne, and many other tribes as well, perceive their work in combination with their Native American traditions. Work is to be done so that a harmony exists between one's work and the land, nature and one's family; a balance. Tardiness on the job is often a problem because of the different perception of time in the Cheyenne. Non-Native Americans view time as a straight line with a past, present and future, a fast-moving river. Native Americans view time with recurring phases, with one season flowing into the next and one's life leading into another.

Native Americans view time with recurring phases, with one season flowing into the next and one's life leading into another.

In the Native American system, families are extended to include grandparents, aunts, uncles, cousins as well as relatives by marriage. In the Northern Cheyenne tribe the word for mother is the same word for aunt and these aunt-mothers are integral to the child's upbringing.

Traditionally, the naming of a child was an important occasion. The first name took place shortly after birth. If it was a male it was named by the father's family, and a female child was named by the mother's. As a child grew older a new name would be given, sometimes describing a brave or important event in his or her life. These new names might be given when the young man or woman entered puberty.

Powwows, a social custom of the past, still are held several times a year. During the summer, a powwow can bring together many different tribes or unite the Southern and Northern Cheyenne and the Sioux. Historically, a powwow was a sacred event, a prayer for protection to the Great Spirit. Also, traditionally, the powwow was a "giveaway," when horses and goods were shared with others in the tribe. Today, the powwows are for feasting and meeting with old friends and for sustaining old traditions.

Another enjoyable old festivity of the Northern Cheyenne was Distribution Day. In the beginning of government annuities, provisions of beef were distributed on the hoof at distribution centers. A bull was released from a chute and the head of each Native American household chased the animal and killed it with a bow and arrow or rifle. Since this was reminiscent of the old buffalo hunting days, the Native Americans enjoyed it immensely. The women would follow and butcher the animal and pack the meat for traveling back to the reservation. At these gatherings there would be singing and dancing and exchange of gossip and news.

Each Native American culture brings a richness and diversity to the world. An understanding and respect for the differences and similarities can only bring mutual benefit.

CANADA

"The 19th century was the century of the United States, the 20th century will be the century of Canada."[11]

This prediction was made shortly after Wilfrid Laurier, Canada's first French Canadian Prime Minister won the election in 1896. His prediction did not come to pass, but Canada as a country has continued to grow.

Canada is a bilingual and multicultural country, whose more than 30 million people live in 10 provinces, and 2 federal territories, the Northwest Territories (which comprise a third of Canada), and the Yukon Territory in the Far North.

Canada is a nation in the midst of an identity crisis between its two major cultural heritages—English and French—and with a powerful southern neighbor, the United States. Having lost referenda on separate sovereignty for their province, the hardline French-Canadians press for more votes until they win a majority. Earlier attempts at constitutional change in Canada—the Meech Lake and the Charlottetown Constitutional Accords—failed because of the proposed recognition of Quebec as a distinct and different society and culture. There is significant opposition between the federalists and the separatists. Some futurists speculate that if Quebec were ever to become independent, then in time the western Canadian provinces might align themselves with the western U.S. states to create a separate political entity or some new regionalism, while the northeast provinces might do the same with the northeast states. Meanwhile, the country is governed under The Constitution Act.[12]

Canada is a nation in the midst of an identity crisis between its two major cultural heritages—English and French.

Although Canada was established as a political entity in 1867 through the British North American Act, in 1982 has the House of Parliament in the United Kingdom voted to amend it so the Canadian constitution could be brought home and "patriated."

Throughout Canada, the family is the center of society, and homes are often passed along from one generation to another. Nowhere is this more true than in the central province of Quebec, the heart of French Canada. If you have some insights into Latin Europe, you may better comprehend the French-Canadian, which is somewhat unsynergistic and individualistic. People tend to be reserved until you get to know them well. The Roman Catholic tradition dominates. The major industries are mining, forestry, hydroelectricity, and agriculture. Canadians are more aware of their rich cultural diversity and natural resources. The country's economic wealth is centered in forests, petroleum, natural gas, and iron ore. Sprawling democratic Canada has one of the world's highest standards of living and its people are very industrious.

Operating a bilingual business can be a challenge, but French-speaking individuals are an advantage in international commerce. The English spoken in Canada is slightly different from the American version (e.g., British pronunciations, Scottish diphthong sounds like "about"). Proud of their country, sensitive about their relations with the U.S. and comparisons to it, fiercely independent while self-deprecating as a people, Canadians resent being lumped together with the other "Americans" below the 49th parallel. Despite that and the U.S. media/economic dominance, the relations between North Americans is generally good and friendly. There is tremendous potential for synergy between the northern neighboring countries who in many ways are more alike than different.

For those doing business in Canada, it is wise to remember that Canadians are not culturally "just like" their counterparts in the United States. Normally, Canadians are friendly but conservative—more so in the Atlantic and Ontario regions than in the Western provinces; more reserved than their neighbors to the South. Canadians tend to observe formalities and rules of etiquette that might be overlooked in the U.S.

"Canadians haven't forgotten the social contract of *civility*—there is a collective moral authority in Canada that causes people to act with decorum, whether standing in line or observing a forbidden zone. What is often forgotten in the U.S., is observed here, such as suborning one's own desires for the greater good, respect for authority, and distaste for rugged individualism. Canada's Constitution is based on peace, order, and good government. Good manners are ingrained in the society, and cooperation is preferred to competition."[13]

Canadians everywhere know they can count on the federal government in Ottawa, as well as the Northwest Mounted Police to maintain order. Canadians treat government officials in their ten provinces with as much gentleness and deference as they do each other. Media commercials downplay both the work ethic and need to overly achieve, while emphasizing recreational sports and leisure vacations. Canadian literature also reflects cultural themes of failure, pessimism, and mediocrity. Canadians are all too aware of their southern neighbor, determined to define themselves differently.

Patriotic, law-abiding, proud of their dual heritage, Canadians also realize that their nation is vast. With a strong economy, high levels of education and health services, Canadians are confident of their future and welcome foreign business and immigration. Canada is an interesting cultural mosaic. In addition to its main cultural heritage of English and French, there are strong ethnic groups of German, Scandinavian, Asian, Dutch, Ukrainian, Polish, and Italian minorities.

The government operates on the model of the British parliamentary system under a prime minister, the armed forces have been streamlined into a single defense organization, and it does not have a free-market economy for Canada fears foreign domination of its economy. As a part of the British Commonwealth system, many peoples of those countries, such as India and Pakistan, have relocated to Canada. The latest cultural enhancement to the Canadian west coast is coming from Asia. Apart from Indo-Chinese refugees and Japanese investors, the biggest influx is from Hong Kong residents with Commonwealth passports who are talented, affluent and will invest much in their new country.

It is wise to remember that Canadians are not culturally "just like" their counterparts in the United States.

Tips for Doing Business and Negotiating with Canadians

The following is a profile of a Canadian negotiator based on a framework of variables that can substantially influence negotiations.[14]

There are two dominant cultural groups in Canada. Each of these groups has a "typical" negotiating style. The English Canadian culture is the dominant group in the provinces of Ontario, British Columbia, Alberta, Manitoba, Saskatchewan, Nova Scotia, New Brunswick, Newfoundland, and Prince Edward Island. There is also a strong English Canadian minority in the province of Quebec mainly centered in Montreal. The French Canadian culture is dominant in Quebec where the official language of the province is French. There is a strong French Canadian minority in New Brunswick and also in eastern Ontario around the national capital city of Ottawa.

Basic Concept of Negotiation

English and French Canadians tend to confront conflict and focus on points of disagreement as they work through a linear problem solving process. This process involves identifying the problem or opportunity, the objectives of the negotiation, the alternatives, the decision and the plan for action. English Canadians tend to focus on abstract or theoretical values and less on practical facts of key issues that have come out of the negotiation process; whereas, French Canadians tend to prefer a more instrumental and individualistic approach to negotiating. The goal of French Canadian negotiators is to influence the other party, and focus on relationship building.

Selection of Negotiators

English and French Canadian negotiators are usually chosen for a negotiating team based on their knowledge, expertise and previous experience concluding successful negotiations. Individual differences such as gender, age and social class are less important for English than French Canadians. The latter tend to accept greater levels of inequality and ability between different levels of management and are more likely to not send any negotiators if the situation precludes their ability to achieve their individual objectives.

Role of Individual Aspirations

Canadian culture encourages individual aspirations and achievement. Most Canadians are expected to represent the objectives of their organizations ahead of their personal objectives. However, the English Canadians may use more cooperative bargaining strategies, while French Canadians may employ more competitive strategies.

Individual differences such as gender, age and social class are less important for English than French Canadians.

Concern with Protocol

English and French Canadians tend to be at least superficially friendly and informal. English Canadians are less concerned with protocol and usually commence their business with very few preliminaries. French Canadians are more concerned with protocol and ceremony.

Significance of Type of Issue

English Canadians are dedicated to the goal of getting the job done. They seem even less concerned than Americans with building and developing relationships and are both impersonal and task oriented as are the French Canadians.

Complexity of Language

English Canadians, like their American neighbors, are generally low context communicators. The message sent by the words spoken are the intended messages. French-speaking Canadians are high-context communicators, because the spoken word is only one part of the total message.

Nature of Persuasive Argument

Canadians use a rational presentation style with detailed facts and figures organized to support a clearly stated position. A deductive style is favored when parties are expected to be in agreement. This style presents the key recommendations first followed by the key supporting information. An inductive style is preferred when persuasion is necessary. In this case, supporting information is presented first then builds toward acceptance of an argument that is presented last.

Value of Time

English and French Canadians tend to be rigidly bound by their schedules and deadlines. Promptness both beginning and ending meetings is appreciated. If one is made to wait more than five or ten minutes for a scheduled interview, many Canadian business people would assume that a personal slight was intended.

Bases of Trust

Canadian managers seem to believe that trust is an important component in achieving organizational and inter-organizational goals. They believe this even when dealing with negotiators from cultures where trust is not a competitive advantage or may even be a competitive liability.

English Canadians tend to trust the information that is being communicated as long as their counterpart uses a cooperative negotiating strategy that emphasizes the free exchange of information. An agreement will result in a contract that can be enforced legally. If, however, English Canadian negotiators perceive that their counterparts are not using a

Canadian managers seem to believe that trust is an important component in achieving organizational and inter-organizational goals.

cooperative strategy, then trust is damaged because the counterpart may seem to be more interested in achieving individual outcomes rather than joint outcomes.

French Canadians may tend to distrust information more than English Canadians. French Canadians also tend to use more competitive negotiation strategies that place individual objectives ahead of joint outcomes.

UNITED STATES OF AMERICA

The citizens of the United States of America refer to themselves as "Americans," although that term may be claimed by inhabitants of North, South, and Central America. The nation consists of the mainland—the central portion of the North American continent, or 48 States—the state of Alaska in the northwestern tip of the hemisphere; the state of Hawaii, which is located west of the mainland in the Pacific Ocean; and Washington D.C. (District of Columbia) the federal capital the United States. Puerto Rico is a self-governing commonwealth and the U.S. Virgin Islands is a territory. Since the end of World War II, the U.S. has administered 11 trust territories in the South Pacific gradually relinquishing control. Between 1975 and 1980, accords were negotiated with the native islanders to establish the commonwealths of the northern Marianas, the Marshall Islands, and the Federated States of Micronesia; and the Republic of Palau.

The climate is temperate on the coasts, subtropical in the south with extensive deserts and widely different seasons/rainfalls. Many visitors to the U.S. find it difficult to comprehend its immense size and varied topography.

The fourth largest nation in the world, the U.S. was called a "melting pot" culture where people came from many places and melted into the mainstream European cultures of the United States. The "salad bowl" metaphor is perhaps more appropriate as well as accurate and recognizes the contributions of the African, Native, Asian, and Latin cultures with each culture maintaining their unique cultural markers while striving to work and live in harmony. It is true that it is a land of immigrants—from the time of colonists (English/French/Spanish), plus the African slave and 19th century European influx, to the present waves of refugees from Indo-China, Cuba, and Haiti. Growing minorities of Hispanics, blacks, Asians as well as the Native Americans, are rapidly changing the configuration of the population.

The U.S. is a multicultural society. Although the American version of English is spoken with a variety of dialects (18 or more), Spanish is

The U.S. was called a "melting pot"... but "salad bowl" is perhaps more appropriate...

emerging as a second language especially in the Southwest, California, Florida, and Puerto Rico. American speech is as varied as the country's geography. French is spoken also in the state of Louisiana and parts of New England. Recently, there is a strong national movement to adopt English as the country's official language.

A quick overview of the dominant culture reveals the following.

Dominant Traits of American Culture

Goal and Achievement Oriented

Americans think they can accomplish just about anything, given enough time, money, and technology.

Highly Organized and Institutionalistic

Americans prefer a society that is strong institutionally and secure.

Freedom-Loving and Self-Reliant

Americans fought a revolution and subsequent wars to preserve their concept of democracy, so they resent too much control or interference, especially by government or external forces. They believe in the ideal that all persons are created equal, though they sometimes fail to live that ideal fully. They strive through law to promote equal opportunity and to confront their own racism or prejudice. Americans also idealize the self-made person who rises from poverty and adversity. Control of one's destiny is popularly expressed as "doing your own thing." Americans think, for the most part, that with determination and initiative, one can achieve whatever he or she sets out to do and thus fulfill individual human potential.

Work Oriented and Efficient

Americans possess a strong work ethic, though they are learning in the present generation to enjoy leisure time constructively. They are very time conscious and efficient in doing things. They tinker with gadgets and technological systems, always searching for easier, better, more efficient ways of accomplishment.

Friendly and Informal

Americans reject the traditional privileges of royalty and class, but do defer to those with affluence and power. Some Americans are impressed by celebrities created by American mass media. Although informal in greeting and dress, they are a non-contact culture (e.g., avoid embracing in public usually) and maintain certain physical/psychological distance with others (e.g., about two feet).

Competitive and Aggressive

Americans in play or business generally are so oriented because of their drives to achieve and succeed. This is partially traced to their heritage of having to overcome a wilderness and hostile elements in their environment.

Values in Transition

Traditional American values of family loyalty, respect and care of the aged, marriage and the nuclear family, patriotism, material acquisition, forthrightness, and the like are undergoing profound reevaluation.

Generosity

Although Americans seemingly emphasize material values, they are sharing people as has been demonstrated in the Marshall Fund, foreign aid programs, refugee assistance, and their willingness at home and abroad to espouse a good cause and to help neighbors in need. They tend to be altruistic and some would say naive as a people.

Social Institutions

In terms of U.S. social institutions, three are worth noting here. *Education* is viewed as a means of self-development, so participation in the process and within the classroom is encouraged—it is mandatory until age 16 and 97% finish at least elementary school, so the literacy rate is fairly high. There is a public (largely free of cost) and private school system through the university level of education; the latter are either independent or religious affiliated schools.

The average *family* is nuclear, consisting of only parents and children, however, the number of single parent families is increasing. About half of all marriages end in divorce. More than half of American women work outside the home, and women have considerable and improving opportunity for personal and professional growth, guaranteed by law. The society is youth oriented, and usually cares for the elderly outside the home in institutions. It is experimenting with new family arrangements from couples living together without the legal sanction to group communes.

Politically, the government operates on the Constitution of 1787 and the Bill of Rights, which provides a three-branch approach of checks and balances. Currently, there are increasing problems of disillusionment in political leaders, corruption in public offices, and a push toward decentralization or the confederation of states concept (e.g., emphasis on states rights and less government regulation over individual lives).

Although Americans seemingly emphasize material values, they are sharing people....

Challenges to the U.S.

The Americans too are in the midst of profound social change, and even an identity crisis. Among the factors contributing to this maturation challenge are:

❑ Being the world's superpower in a global economy has forced a reassessment of the national self-image. After much success in its war abroad, Korea and Vietnam proved to be costly and questionable conflicts that mass media brought into American homes. The assassinations of some of the country's leaders in the 1960s led to an undermining of the national will, organized public protests, and the need to reexpress national goals. In the 1980s, the American economy was robust, patriotism was high, entrepreneurialism and high-technology ventures flourished, and in the late 1990s the stock market advanced with Internet stocks leading the way. Violence in the streets and in schools continued. Americans were stunned and frustrated by acts of terrorism at the World Trade Center and the federal building in Oklahoma City.
❑ Latinization of the U.S. is affecting the character of the country and its communication.
❑ Social unrest exists, particularly over the increase in violence, racism and a growing underclass. There is concern about two societies—one colored, one white—that view the American experience quite differently.
❑ Transition into a post-industrial society is happening first and faster in the U.S. than in most other countries because of scientific and technological advances. The values and life-styles brought on by the industrial stage of development are being reexamined and new replacements sought for more effective coping in cyberculture.

The impact of such contemporary trends depends on where you are in America, for there are considerable regional differences and subcultures. There is also a big difference between eastern and western life-styles and attitudes. The eastern U.S. is thought to be more establishment, conservative in thinking, over-organized and deteriorating; the western U.S. is seen as more casual, innovative, and flexible.

One aspect for foreign readers to note is that Americans are becoming less isolationist and provincial in their thinking and actions. Mass travel abroad, international communications and business, more foreign students and visitors have affected American perceptions. Furthermore, the impact of foreigners is currently considerable—more outsiders are being

Being the world's superpower in a global economy has forced a reassessment of the national self-image.

transferred to the U.S. for business or professional purposes, and more foreign capital is being heavily invested here. (Corporate acquisitions and property purchases by Canadians, Japanese, Europeans, Middle Easterners and South Africans are considerable, and have even caused some fear and backlash.) Foreign tourism in the U.S. has increased dramatically. The influx of refugees and legal and illegal immigrants has strained existing social systems. But Americans are generally of a cooperative spirit, so they are open to international influences in their society, and usually support endeavors that will promote regional or world synergy. The presence of the United Nations headquarters in New York City is symbolic of this.

Cultural Aspects of the United States

What is America? Is there a mainstream culture shared by the "average" American? Did the salad bowl theory work in practice? Is the United States a pluralistic society? Is it a multicultural society? What is America?

The following list, taken from Stewart[15] and others, is a summary of what can be called U.S. mainstream cultural assumptions and values. The main categories are the mode of activity, social relationships, motivation, the perception of the world, and the perception of self.

Definition of Activity

1. How do people approach activity?
   ❑ concern with "doing," progress, change external environment
   ❑ optimistic, striving
2. What is the desirable pace of life?
   ❑ fast, busy
   ❑ driving
3. How important are goals in planning?
   ❑ stress means, procedures, techniques
4. What are important goals in life?
   ❑ material goals
   ❑ comfort and absence of pain
   ❑ activity
5. Where does responsibility for decisions lie?
   ❑ responsibility lies with each individual
6. At what level do people live?
   ❑ operational, goals evaluated in terms of consequence
7. On what basis do people evaluate?
   ❑ utility (Does it work?)
8. Who should make decisions?
   ❑ the people affected

The influx of refugees and legal and illegal immigrants has strained existing social systems.

9. What is the nature of problem-solving?
   - ❏ planning behavior
   - ❏ anticipates consequences
10. What is the nature of learning?
   - ❏ learner is active (student-centered learning)

Definition of Social Relations

1. How are roles defined?
   - ❏ attained
   - ❏ loosely
   - ❏ generally
2. How do people relate to others whose status is different?
   - ❏ stress equality
   - ❏ minimize differences
   - ❏ stress informality and spontaneity
3. How are gender roles defined?
   - ❏ similar, overlapping
   - ❏ gender equality
   - ❏ friends of both genders
   - ❏ less legitimized
4. What are members' rights and duties in a group?
   - ❏ assumes limited liability
   - ❏ joins group to seek own goals
   - ❏ active members can influence group
5. How do people judge others?
   - ❏ specific abilities of interests
   - ❏ task-centered
   - ❏ fragmentary involvement
6. What is the meaning of friendship?
   - ❏ social friendship (short commitment, friends shared)
7. What is the nature of social reciprocity?
   - ❏ real only
   - ❏ nonbinding (Dutch treat)
   - ❏ equal (Dutch treat)
8. How do people regard friendly aggression in social interaction?
   - ❏ acceptable, interesting, fun

Motivation

1. What is motivating force?
   - ❏ achievement
2. How is person-person competition evaluated?
   - ❏ as constructive, healthy

Perception of the World (World View)

1. What is the (natural) world like?
   - ❑ physical
   - ❑ mechanical
2. How does the world operate?
   - ❑ in a rational, learnable, controllable manner
   - ❑ chance and probability
3. What is the nature of man?
   - ❑ apart from nature or from any hierarchy
   - ❑ impermanent, not fixed, changeable
4. What are the relationships between man and nature?
   - ❑ good is unlimited
   - ❑ man should modify nature for his ends
   - ❑ good health and material comforts expected and desired
5. What is the nature of truth? goodness?
   - ❑ tentative (working-type)
   - ❑ relative to circumstances
   - ❑ experience analyzed in separate components dichotomies
6. How is time defined? Valued?
   - ❑ future (anticipation)
   - ❑ precise units
   - ❑ limited resource
   - ❑ lineal
7. What is the nature of property?
   - ❑ private ownership important as extension of self

Perception of the Self and the Individual

1. In what sort of terms is self defined?
   - ❑ diffuse, changing terms
   - ❑ flexible behavior
2. Where does a person's identity seem to be?
   - ❑ within the self (achievement)
3. Nature of the individual
   - ❑ separate aspects (intent, thought, act, biographical background)
4. On whom should a person place reliance?
   - ❑ self
   - ❑ impersonal organizations
5. What kind of person is valued and respected? What qualities?
   - ❑ youthful (vigorous)
6. What is the basis of social control?
   - ❑ persuasion, appeal to the individual
   - ❑ guilt

In mainstream American society most are concerned with "doing." Americans have a preoccupation with time, organization, and the use of resources. In American social relationships everyone is assumed equal thus removing the need for elaborate forms of social address. Social relationships are characterized by informality and social reciprocities are much less clearly defined. Mainstream Americans are motivated by achievements and accomplishments. American personal identity and, to a certain extent, one's self-worth is measured by what he or she achieves. The world is material rather than spiritual and Americans also see themselves as individual and unique.

However, American culture is in transition. American families are in crisis, especially in the inner cities. Many think that the centerpiece of American life, the large middle class is eroding and under economic threat. Violence is increasing, especially among the young, many of whom lack character education and supervision as parents' attention is directed toward work and earning a living. Under these circumstances, an expanding segment of the population is prone to homelessness, child or spouse abuse, substance abuse, paranoia, crime, hatred, and intolerance. This distressed minority is balanced by a majority of Americans who are relatively affluent and well educated in contrast to the rest of the world population; who are generous in their charity and community service; who are into fitness and wellness regimens; who fight for just causes, such as protecting other species and the environment; who are optimists and futurists. There is growing concern in the U.S. about the increase in violence and racism. According to Shusta et al.[16] violence motivated by hatred because of racial, religious, ethnic, or sexual orientation has existed for generations in the United States as well as the rest of the world. Increasingly, it seems on the rise. The National Institute Against Prejudicial Violence estimated that in 1991 a full 10% of the U.S. population is victimized by some form of *enthoviolence*. That translates into 25 million victims a year.

Subcultures of the United States

By early in the 21st century, whites will become a minority in the state of California. In 1900 the state was 90% Caucasian. The emergence of a polyethnic society is evident in Los Angeles where a cacophony of 160 languages is spoken today. California is now home to up to 2.4 illegal immigrants. The transformation of minorities into majorities is also taking place in Texas, Arizona, New York, Nevada, New Jersey, and Maryland. By 2050, half of the U.S. population will likely be non-white.[17]

The exceptional uniformity that characterized American society in post-World War II period has been supplanted by extreme diversity. The

In American social relationships everyone is assumed equal thus removing the need for elaborate forms of social address. Many think that the centerpiece of American life, the large middle class is eroding and under economic threat.

most integrated national market in the history of the world is splintering into an array of niches. Immigration, legal and illegal, has eroded the homogeneity of the U.S. population and multiplied connections between American society and other societies around the world.[18]

In the United States there are minority cultures of African-Americans, Hispanics, Chinese-Americans, Japanese-Americans, Jews, the physically challenged as well as senior citizens to name but a few. Each of these groups has aspects of their lives, priorities, or values that may differ in part from mainstream America. To work effectively and develop authentic relationships with any subculture, it is necessary to be aware, accept, appreciate, and respect their uniqueness.

Martin et al.[19] state that labels discursively help define identity and are related to power structures. Most identity labels in the U.S. are all in relation to what is not white.

> It has been argued that this lack of attention to white identity and self-labeling reflects the historical power held by whites in the United States. That is, whites as a privileged group take their identity as the norm or standard by which other groups are measured, and this identity is therefore invisible, even to the extent that many whites do not consciously think about the profound effect being white has on their daily lives.
>
> . . . (W)hite privilege and white standards are so culturally embedded that whiteness has been "naturalized." As the racial norm, being white or acknowledging one's whiteness need never be recognized or analyzed by whites because whites generally view themselves as the racial yardstick with which other racial groups are compared.

There are two types of minority groups. Those that are distinguished by the physical; racial groups, and also there are ethnic groups that are differentiated by distinct language, religious, cultural or national characteristics. According to Gudyjunst and Kim[20] there are five characteristics of minority group membership:

> First, members of minority groups are treated differently from members of a majority group by members of the majority group. This inequality usually takes the form of segregation, prejudice, and discrimination. Second, members of minority groups have either physical or cultural characteristics that make them stand our from the majority group. Third, because minority groups stand out, membership in them is not voluntary. Fourth, members of a minority group tend to associate with and marry other members of their group. Finally, members of a minority group are aware of their subordinate status, which leads to strong group solidarity.

Often minority groups are not recognized as legitimate and distinct. Instead they are automatically diminished as less, being judged by their outward physical appearance rather than acknowledging and appreciating their different culture, language, and ethnic characteristics.

Most identity labels in the U.S. are all in relation to what is not white.

African-Americans

The Civil War was fought to liberate their ancestors and give blacks full citizenship. However, for their descendants, the struggle for civil rights and equal opportunity under the law still goes on for African-Americans. A history of inferior status is not dissolved easily or simply. Racism has become more subtle within institutions, housing, or educational opportunities. Despite their accomplishments and the growth of the black middle and upper classes, black teenage unemployment and black deaths from violence within their own communities have also risen. There is much to be done together if all African-American citizens are to share in the American dream. Power is not shared. Economic access is not equal.

Recent global events have convinced most that racism is a significant world problem. The ethnic cleansing in former Yugoslavia, genocide in Rwanda, and the racial epithets spoken yet denied under oath during the O.J. Simpson murder trial by Los Angeles Police Department Detective Mark Fuhrman all obvious examples.

Interestingly, the word racism was never mentioned in Webster's 1939 unabridged dictionary. However, ten years later, the definition does appear in *Webster's Intercollegiate Dictionary* possibly due the effects of World War II and the racist philosophy of Nazi Germany.[21] Whether one focuses on individual, institutional, cultural or symbolic racism it is a phenomenon that is deeply ingrained throughout many cultures.

According to West,[22] race is the most explosive issue in American life today. To begin a serious dialogue regarding race, one must establish the terms for racial issues. As long as the African-Americans are viewed as "them" and the burden falls on blacks to do all the "cultural" and "social" compromising, healthy race relations will not prevail. We can no longer believe that only certain Americans can define what it means to be American, and the rest must simply "fit in."

Minority groups in many cultures have demonstrated signs of rejecting movements towards assimilation and some social scientists question whether, in countries like the United States, for example, there was ever as much assimilation as was widely hoped for or believed. The number of hate crimes is increasing in many societies. There is a rage in many groups that is not being understood or addressed adequately.

This rage is articulated frequently. During the September 15, 1995 popular Oprah Winfrey television program,[23] Lee Mun Wah, the director of the film *The Color of Fear*, showed excerpts from his film. A white American asked, "Why aren't we just humans? I mean why aren't we just brothers?" The African-American responded, "You think that, 'Hey, it will all be fine when we just treat each other like human beings.' And what that says to me is, 'Don't be yourself. Be like me. Keep me comfortable. Connect when I'm ready to connect. Come out to my place. . . .'" You know, I'm not going to trust you until you're as willing

Racism has become more subtle within institutions, housing, or educational opportunities. As long as the African-Americans are viewed as "them" and the burden falls on blacks to do all the "cultural" and "social" compromising, healthy race relations will not prevail.

to be changed and affected by my experience and transformed by my experience as I am every day by yours."

Much research has been conducted on the verbal and nonverbal communication patterns as well as many aspects of African-American life and culture.[24] It is beyond the scope of this book to write in-depth about any culture or the issues faced by people in that society. We hope the references cited in this chapter and in the culture specific chapters will guide readers.

Hispanic Americans

> . . . Hispanics are moving up in every American business area. Their cultural passion and adaptability with emphasis on family, is ideally suited to both the American and global business scene.[25]

As a bridge into the next chapter on Latin America, we end this discussion on U.S. subcultures with a brief examination of an emerging majority. Broadly defined, a Latino or Hispanic, inadequate terminology, is an immigrant to the U.S., or whose ancestors came from Spain or Latin America; most of whom still speak Spanish and reflect the cultural heritage of both Spain and the indigenous peoples of Mexico, Central and South America. This cultural influence is most evident in California, Florida, Nevada, Arizona, Texas, Puerto Rico and Guam. Texans with Mexican ancestry call themselves *Tejanos,* while elsewhere those with such heritage prefer to be known as *Chicanos;* those in New Mexico who trace their roots to Spain, are known as *Hispanos.* From the viewpoint of creating cultural synergy from cultural differences, the Latino expansion and integration into U.S. culture is not just in the southwest and southeast, but also in major urban centers such as Denver, Chicago, and New York, as well as in Miami and Los Angeles, both founded over 200 years ago by Spanish colonists. Many Latinos whose communities here go back to the 16th century consider themselves "native" Americans. It is only 150 years since the U.S. annexed the southwest after the Mexican-American War, and only a century since it occupied Puerto Rico. Today Latinos represent 11% of the U.S. population, having increased by 60% and projected to further expand by 75% in 2015. Census forecasters expect a Hispanic population here of 96 million by year 2050. Spanish-speaking Americans are heterogeneous in terms of skin color, as well as in terms of origin; 65% from Mexico; 12% Puerto Ricans; 12% Central Americans and other Latin countries; 8% Cubans; and 5% Dominicans. They are most diverse in terms of different histories, loyalties, and class. Some come from elite and wealthy backgrounds or ancestors in Mexico, Latin America or Spain, while many others have come as migrant workers, willing to work hard and long to gain low-paying and low-status jobs. Once established, they take advantage of

Many Latinos whose communities here go back to the 16th century consider themselves "native" Americans.

American public education and the ability to move ahead economically and socially.

It is difficult to generalize about Latino-Americans, but they are gaining political power and representation as greater numbers of them vote. Although many are bilingual, they gain a certain cohesiveness through the Spanish language, Roman Catholicism, and family values. They are moving rapidly into middle class status and home ownership. In most states, the number of Latino-owned businesses has doubled and these people prefer working in the private sector. Since 1990, their buying power has risen 65% and is estimated at $380 billion in 1998, and that is likely to triple by 2010. The Latino consumer market—large and growing—has a reputation for brand loyalty. Consider that by year 2000, there will be 6.9 millions Latino school children and most of their parents want them to be taught in English. Spanish-speaking America is the world's fifth largest Hispanic nation. Yet, the dialect of choice for millions of young Latinos is *Spanlish,* which allows them to switch with ease between Spanish and English.[26]

Presently, Latinos lack strong leaders and tend to walk away from abuse and confrontation. Though well involved in baseball, they are not well represented in mainstream American sports, preferring soccer. As they become more assimilated, Latins are slowly entering the mainstream cultural arts. People of Hispanic background bring a distinct, joyous flavor into the American mainstream. They comprise a varied tapestry reflecting Spanish, Indian, African-American, and mulatto heritages.

Tips for Doing Business and Negotiating with Amercans

The following is a profile of an American negotiator reflecting some of variables that can occur in business and negotiations.[4]

Basic Concept of Negotiation
American negotiators view conflict and confrontation as an opportunity to exchange viewpoints and as part of the process in resolution, negotiation and agreement. Americans prefer outlining the issues or problems and a direct approach to determining possible solutions. They are motivated to further the interests of their corporation or government and have a highly competitive nature regarding the outcome or settlement.

Selection of Negotiators
American negotiators are usually chosen for a negotiating team based on their record of success in past negotiations and their knowledge and expertise in the area to be negotiated. Negotiations that are technical in nature require Americans with very specific knowledge and the ability to

Americans prefer outlining the issues or problems and a direct approach to determining possible solutions.

communicate their expertise. Individual differences, gender, age, and social class are not generally criteria for selection, but individual differences in character (cooperative, authoritarian, trustworthy) can determine whether one is chosen for an American negotiating team.

Role of Individual Aspirations

As a rule, Americans encourage individual aspirations and individual achievements. When representing her/his corporation or country, Americans temper their individualism and seek to accomplish and or represent the positions of their company or country.

Concern with Protocol

Generally, Americans are friendly and open. Their etiquette is largely informal and so is their basic concern for protocol. They are relaxed in their business conduct and do not often adhere to strict or explicit codes of behavior and ceremony.

Significance of Type of Issue

The American popular expression of "getting the job done" reflects their desire to assess the situation, and get results quickly. In negotiations, Americans may focus on the tangible aspects of the negotiation without spending too much time on the more intangible aspects such as building relationships during the process.

Complexity of Language

Americans are low-context communicators. The message is primarily in the words spoken and is not overridden by nonverbal communication, the cues of gesture, eye contact, and silence.

Nature of Persuasive Argument

Americans' use of a rational presentation with detailed facts and figures accompanied by logical and analytical arguments is usually the course attempted when persuading one's counterparts.

Value of Time

Every culture has different ways of organizing time and using it. Some cultures are rigidly bound by their schedules and meeting deadlines, while other cultures have a relaxed attitude about detailed plans and schedules. Monochronic time emphasizes schedules, segmentation and promptness. Polychronic time stresses involvement with people and completion of transactions rather than an adherence to a preset schedule. Americans generally have a monochronic time orientation, and for most Americans "time is money." In negotiations, Americans set schedules and appointments and tend to prioritize events and move through the process "controlling" the time allotted them.

Americans generally have a monochronic time orientation, and for most Americans "time is money."

Bases of Trust

In negotiations, Americans generally trust the information being communicated and negotiated is accurate, and they assume that the negotiations will have a desirable outcome. If, however, Americans have had a past experience with a counterpart who has not been trustworthy, they will withhold the trust.

Risk Taking Propensity

Americans are risk takers. In light of their history, their perception of their rugged individualism, and the rewards of capitalism, Americans have embraced risk and are not risk avoidant.

Internal Decision Making Systems

Decision making is becoming more and more decentralized with authority, within predetermined limits, being given to those with negotiating experience. Most of the final decisions must be cleared with senior executives in the organization.

Form of Satisfactory Agreement

Because the American culture is legalistic, Americans prefer and expect detailed contractual agreements to formalize negotiations. A handshake may conclude negotiations, but the attorneys representing both sides will hammer out the legal implications of the agreement.

SUMMARY

In the 19th century a Frenchman, Alexis de Tocqueville, wrote *Democracy in America*. He discovered what he called "habits of the heart," which form the American character and sustain free institutions—family life, religious convictions, and participation in local politics. Bellah et al.[27] examine individualism and commitment in American life. They conclude that rampant individualism within American culture may threaten freedom itself, especially when individual achievement is attained at the expense of the community that provides support, reinforcement, and moral meaning for the individual. Furthermore, within North American society, competition is almost a cultural imperative, but pure selfishness, Bellah argues, does not result in the common good. Yet, he sees new community forces at work within America, such as corporations' becoming more personal and participatory, contributing to the renewal of this society and the creation of a new work culture.

We have reviewed in this chapter the diverse cultures of North America—Native Americans, Canadians and the peoples of the United States. These are complex and cosmopolitan populations worthy of careful study by foreign visitors who wish to succeed.

... within North American society, competition is almost a cultural imperative ...

REFERENCES

1. Gore, R. *National Geographic,* October 1997, pp. 93–97.
2. *Los Angeles Times,* August 13, 1997, p. 1/12.
3. Bundle. B. "Spearhead Relic of last Ice Age," *San Diego Union,* December 14, 1994.
4. Moran, R. T. and Abbott, J. *NAFTA: Managing the Cultural Differences,* Houston, TX: Gulf Publishing Co. 1994, p. xii.
5. Herbst, P. H. *The Color of Words: An Encyclopedic Dictionary of Ethnic Bias in the United States,* Yarmouth, ME: Intercultural Press, 1997, pp. 58–59, 69.
6. *The New York Times International,* "Canada's Eskimos Get a Land of Their Own," April 2, 1999.
7. Weatherford, J. *Indian Givers: How the Indians of the Americas Transformed the World,* New York: Crown Publishers, 1988.
8. Tedlock, D. and Tedlock B. (eds.). *Teachings from the American Earth: Indian Religion and Philosophy,* New York: Liveright, 1975.
9. *The Economist,* August 8, 1998, p. 34.
10. Moran, R. T. and Casey, S. "Profile: The Northern Cheyenne," an unpublished profile, 1983.
11. *The Economist,* "Holding Its Own," July 24, 1999, p. 2.
12. Bracken, S. *Canadian Almanac and Directory,* Toronto: Copp Clark Pittman, 1985.
13. Swardon, A. *The Washington Post Weekly,* "It's Nice to Be Nice," 1995, p.24.
14. The profile of Canadian negotiators was written by Neil R. Abramson, Ph.D., Simon Fraser University, Burnaby, British Columbia, Canada; excerpted from *NAFTA: Managing the Cultural Differences,* Moran, R.T. and Abbott, J. Houston, TX: Gulf Publishing Co., 1994.
15. Stewart, M. *The Age of Interdependence: Economic Policy in a Shrinking World,* Cambridge, MA: MIT Press, 1984.
16. Shusta, R. M., Levine, D. R., Harris, P. R. and Wong, H. Z. *Multicultural Law Enforcement: Peacekeeping in a Diverse Society,* Englewood, NJ: Prentice Hall, 1995.
17. Maharidge, D. *The Coming of the White Minority: California's Eruption and the Nation's Future,* New York: Times Books, 1997.
18. Clough, M. *Los Angeles Times,* July 27, 1997, p. M1/6.
19. Martin, J. N., Krizek, R. L., Nakayama, T. K. and Bradford, L. "Exploring Whiteness: A Study of Self Labels for White Americans," *Communication Quarterly,* 1996, 44,2, p. 125–144.
20. Gudykunst, W. B and Kim, Y. Y. *Communicating with Strangers: An Approach to Intercultural Communication,* 3rd ed., New York: McGraw-Hill Companies, 1994.
21. Katz, P. A. and Taylor, D. A. (eds.). *Eliminating Racism: Profiles in Controversy,* New York: Plenum Press, 1988.
22. West, C. *Race Matters,* New York: Vintage Books, 1993.

23. *The Oprah Winfrey Show,* "The Color of Fear," Burrelle's Information Services, Box 7, Livingston, NJ, 1995.
24. Farley, J. E. *Majority-Minority Relations,* 3rd ed., Englewood Clffs, NJ: Prentice-Hall, 1995; see also Gioseffi, D. *Prejudice: A Global Perspective,* New York: Doubleday, 1993; see also Henderson, G. *Our Souls to Keep,* Yarmouth, ME: Intercultural Press, 1999.
25. Failde, A. and Doyle, W. *Latino Success: Insights from 100 of America's Most Powerful Business Professionals,* New York: Simon and Schuster, 1996.
26. *The Economist,* April 25, 1998, pp.25–27.
27. Bellah, R. N., et al. *Habits of the Heart: Individualism and Commitment in American Life,* Berkeley, CA: University of California Press, 1985.

DOING BUSINESS WITH LATIN AMERICANS

Mexico, Central, and South America

There are commonalities and overlapping cultural themes in Latin American countries such as the influence of the Catholic Church, the value of the family, and the separate and distinct male and female roles.

Many countries in Latin America differ widely in history, socioeconomic status, education, governance, society, and the behavior and values of the people. Nevertheless, there are commonalities and overlapping cultural themes in Latin American countries such as the influence of the Catholic Church, the value of the family, and the separate and distinct male and female roles.

The Latin American region has been inhabited for thousands of years. In 1983, a mummy was accidentally uncovered in Chile, and may be the oldest remains of the human species yet discovered. Scientists claim that the Atacama Desert mummy is more than 7,800 years old, making it about 2,600 years older than its nearest Egyptian counterpart. That ancient seaside settler, along with 95 other mummified people of the Chinchorro culture, were aboriginal hunters and fishermen in what may be the earliest of Latin American settlements. The burial system indicated a well developed social structure. Previously, scholars thought that mongoloid Asian peoples migrated some 30,000 years ago from Alaska down the west coast of the Americas. Other scholars contend that the Asians could not have moved quickly enough to reach the southern hemisphere by the date of the earliest Chinchorro settlement. Thus, archaeologists are unsure from where these early inhabitants came. In any event, we will begin our examination of the diverse cultures in the southern parts of Pan America with their aboriginal descendants, the so-called "Indians." Global managers and developers frequently impinge upon such peoples in the name of economic development with destructive results.

MEXICO

ATLANTIC
OCEAN

HONDURAS

NICARAGUA

GUATEMALA

PANAMA

EL SALVADOR

GUYANA

CENTRAL
AMERICA

VENEZUELA

SURINAME

FR. GUIANA

COSTA RICA

COLOMBIA

ECUADOR

BRAZIL

PERU

BOLIVIA

PARAGUAY

CHILE

SOUTH AMERICA

ARGENTINA

URUGUAY

PACIFIC
OCEAN

ATLANTIC
OCEAN

MEXICO AND CENTRAL AMERICA'S CULTURE DEVELOPMENT

Native peoples, commonly called "Indians" today, make up a high proportion of the populations of many Latin countries, including Mexico and Bolivia. In some parts of the southern hemisphere Indians have integrated into modern civilization. In other localities they have chosen to remain more traditional.

Agencies like the World Bank are now demanding inclusion of programs that protect the rights of 200,000 aborigines before they will fund economic development projects in the Amazon region. In Central America Indians try to survive the ravages and clutches of civil and guerrilla warfare. The Indians are caught between the forces of both left and right. Sometimes the rebels seek haven or recruits among the Indians, while the government troops destroy the Indian villages. The Indians are often caught in the middle of various socio-political revolutionary struggles currently taking place throughout Latin America.

Situated on the Pacific Rim and extending eastward to the Gulf, Mexico is a land of contrast and promise. More than 755,000 square miles in land mass, this country has an expanding population of more than 100 million people. The burgeoning population lives in the central highlands, which constitutes half of the country's total farmland. With 31 states in the United States of Mexico, 20 million people are concentrated in the Federal District capital of Mexico City. Like many developing countries, the young greatly outnumber the old, and the life expectancy is 67 years for males, contrasted to 72 years in the U.S. Other interesting population trends are:

Native peoples, commonly called "Indians" today, make up a high proportion of the populations of many Latin countries, including Mexico and Bolivia.

❑ Thirteen percent are of Indian pure blood ancestry, 10% of European heritage, 75% mixed.
❑ Increasing urbanization.
❑ Decreasing infant mortality, but still a death rate of 35 per 1000.
❑ Rising literacy rate—now 84% of the population, plus a rising educational level.
❑ Rising income per capita, but 18 million underprivileged people, largely in rural areas.
❑ Inadequate diet, medical care, housing and social security continue to plague the nation.

Those planning to work or do business in Mexico must consider several major realities. There is a crushing external debt that the current federal administration is addressing. Pluralism is just beginning to enter the political and religious scene—the dominant one party and one religion system is changing. Mexico, like some of its Latin neighbors, suffers from overpopulation, massive poverty, and an elite upper class that controls much of the country's wealth.

LATIN AMERICA—PROFILE

Population	Land Mass
375 million people	8 million square miles
(without Mexico, see following section)	

National Cultures

25 countries
1 commonwealth (PR)
(12 island countries of West Indies?)
Variety of Indian cultures

Major Cultural Inputs

❏ Native Indians—descended from ancient, highly developed civilizations that flourished prior to European arrival (Mayan, Incas, Aztecs).
❏ European—in most countries largely Spanish with lesser influences of Germans and Italians, except in Brazil where dominant influence was Portuguese.
❏ African.
❏ Asian—ancient Polynesian influence, and some Japanese input in Mexico and Brazil.

Socio-Political Developments

❏ Napoleonic Code of laws
❏ Feudalistic societies of Spain/Portugal imposed by conquerors on developed Indian civilizations.
❏ French/Austrian royalty/empire imposed on Mexico; the latter was center of revolutions in 1821, 1824, 1838 which impacted on South America.
❏ Family oriented with authority centered in the father and often extended to the "father of the nation," a strong dictator.
❏ Universities and republics from the 19th century with great dependence on military institutions/control.
❏ Problems of social class integration—although there was much intermarriage of the races, the powerful elites from an economics/social/political standpoint control and dominate the poor, often peasants of Indian heritage. The disenfranchised have moved beyond political/military protest for social justice to terrorism as a means for changing the status quo.
❏ Economically and technically developing, and in the process of moving from the agricultural and through the industrial stage of development; energy discoveries and development in Mexico can dramatically forge a new relationship with its neighbors.
❏ Although significant growth in spiritualism and Protestantism, the Roman Catholic tradition is still dominant, but undergoing profound role change—instead of traditional support for the oligarchy, many clergy providing leadership in a revolution for social justice.

(Exhibit continued on next page)

Education

❑ In the European tradition, especially Spain/Portugal/France. Ancient and traditional university education with emphasis on the humanities, especially studies in law, medicine, and engineering. *Colegios* are more numerous than American secondary schools and offer the equivalent of junior college. Upper classes tend to send their offspring to private schools and universities, often conducted by the orders of the Catholic Church. Although literacy is increasing, many in the population overall do not receive more than a very few years of primary education; notable exceptions in the larger countries which provide more education. Rigorous examination competition for university entrance. Technical education also on the increase, as well as, use of mass media.

One fourth the size of the U.S., Mexico has a topography that features desert, tropical, mountainous and temperate regions. . . .

MEXICO

MEXICO—PROFILE

Population	101 million
Land..............................	755,985 sq.miles
Education......................	Free and compulsory from ages 6–15
	Literacy rate is 85% female, 90% males
Ethnic groups	Mestizo, 60%
	Indigenous, 29%
	Caucasian, 9%
	Hispanic/Other 1%
Religions	Roman Catholic, 89%
	Other, 11%
Government	Federal system
Political Parties..............	PRI (Partido Revolucionario Institucional),
	PAN (Partido de Accion Nacional) Mexico

One fourth the size of the U.S., Mexico has a topography that features desert, tropical, mountainous and temperate regions with equal parts divided by the Tropic of Cancer. The lofty central plains are the main agricultural region, but only 24 million hectares of the agricultural land is cultivated. Although predominately an agricultural nation, Mexico is rapidly industrializing and is a leading exporter of metals, especially silver. In addition to spectacular growth in manufacturing and tourism, Mexico's hope for a better economic future lies in its recent discoveries and developments in oil and gas. Its energy supplies may rival those of Saudi Arabia. Mexico has a proven oil reserve of 40 billion barrels, and a potential of 220 billion barrels.

With the implementation of the NAFTA, Mexico's relationship with the U.S. is changing, although it has been stormy since the Americans invaded the country in 1846. After the war Mexico ceded almost half of its original territory to the U.S. by the Treaty of Guadalupe (this included Texas, California, Arizona, New Mexico, and part of Utah/Colorado). No border on earth separates two more widely divergent standards of living between two nations. Despite conflicts over illegal immigration, trade, and drug smuggling, the American and Mexican peoples are generally friendly, and the prospects for Mexican and American synergy are promising.

From a business perspective, global managers should understand that:

❑ The 19th century in Mexico was marked by political unrest, the 20th century by economic progress, and in the 21st century Mexico may come into its promise and potential.

❑ Discovered by Hernan Cortez in 1519, Mexico revolted against Spanish rule and achieved independence in 1821. It defeated French influence and interference by 1876, and survived a series of revolutions, achieving political and economic stability by 1940. One political party has dominated since 1930. The federal government consists of an executive, legislative, and judicial branch, and the military does not play a significant role in governance. Government seized and nationalized all Roman Catholic Church properties and reduced the power of that religious organization by anti-clerical laws (culturally, the people are still influenced by Roman Catholic morality and spirituality).

❑ The structure of capital and labor is somewhat different here from other countries in Latin America. The old, landed oligarchy has lost a major share of its property and power. A large rural bourgeoisie has grown among a large group of small landowners who today provide the capital for industrial and financial development. There is a growing salaried middle class, some of whom also cultivate their own land. An agrarian revolution has created a new type of peasant class, benefitting by government land distribution policies, or becoming a major source of U.S. agricultural manpower, as well as the Mexican industrialized workforce. Relative to returns for capital and labor, two thirds go to the corporation and only one third to the employees.

❑ In the '70s, multinational corporations in Mexico (95% American controlled) provided 93% of the payments for imports of technology; and in the '80s, 80% of the technology employed was still foreign. Multinational corporations occasionally obtain slightly lower but safer profits on their investments in Mexico than they do in other

The 19th century in Mexico was marked by political unrest, the 20th century by economic progress, and in the 21st century Mexico may come into its promise and potential.

Latin American countries. Trade balances, employment, family planning, consumer price index, worker wages, and other indicators of economic well-being all continue to be troubling issues for Mexico. Frequent devaluation of the peso and problems with inflation, as well as declining oil prices cause much hardship there.

❑ The North American Free Trade Agreement is the first trade agreement entered into by two industrialized nations and a developing one. The trade agreement is also the first to cover intellectual property, labor rights and the environment.

❑ In the 1990s, corruption among politicians, drug trafficking and questionable elections and a fiscal crisis of major proportions have affected all Mexicans negatively.

Mexico is a country in major transition, seeking to broaden its social and democratic basis, to control tensions between the evolving middle class and the disadvantaged masses, and to contain radical and revolutionary forces within the society.

Mexicans are a relaxed, hospitable, and warm people who may relate more to their Indian than Spanish heritage. They are proud, patriotic, family oriented and hard working. Emotional, with a leisurely sense of time, they are generally comfortable with themselves and others, and are very person-oriented. It is wise for visiting business persons to take time for conversation and socialization. Subsequent sections in this chapter will deal with the cultural dimensions and challenges of doing business in Latin America which generally are applicable to this nation.

Relative to communications, specifically, between Mexicans and their immediate northern neighbors, their former president, Porfirio Diaz, made this classic observation: "Poor Mexico, so far from God, and so near the United States."

Exhibit 11-1 may be helpful in contrasting perceptions between Americans and their neighbors to the south.[1]

Condon[3] has provided some insights to avoid culture-based misunderstandings.

❑ Mexican images and ideals are not only drawn from their Indian heritage, but from Europe (e.g., concepts of freedom and democracy come from France); their views and approach to their Latin neighbors are quite different from North American.

❑ Although the uniqueness of the individual is valued and provides inner dignity, it is not necessarily evident through actions or achievements; slights against personal dignity are regarded as a grave provocation (e.g., Mexicans are comfortable talking about inner qualities like soul or spirit, and may look at North Americans as insensitive because they avoid such subjects).

Mexicans are a relaxed, hospitable, and warm people who may relate more to their Indian than Spanish heritage.

(text continued on page 263)

EXHIBIT 11-1[2]
HISTORICAL STEREOTYPES

Value Affected	Mexican View of N. America	Mexican View of Self	N. American View of Mexican	N. American View of Self
Self control	Cold, insensitive, emotionless	Deal passively with stress, saying *"ni modo"* when something doesn't go to plan	Emotional, volatile, feminine, undisciplined	Rational, calm, masculine, deals actively with stress through discipline in life
Type of civilization	Condescending, contradictory, not credible	Traditional; technically inferior, morally superior	Primitive, in need of instruction on "how to do things"	Advanced, responsible for showing others how to have democracy and free trade
Racial attitude	Indiscriminate racism, can't distinguish high class Mexican from Indian	Social classes have subtle shades; whiter is better; the masses cannot be elevated anyway. North Americans should be able to distinguish between high and low classes and accept high as equals	Indigenous people are inferior, and mestizos combine the worst features of both races. The treatment of the lower classes is unjust, and therefore higher classes deserve no respect	Racially superior, Culturally heterogeneous, but racially homogeneous; racial intermixing not acceptable
Honesty and trustworthiness (hi-low context)	Manipulative, tactless, have ulterior motives against Mexico; can't be trusted	More important to be nice than objective; OK to bend truth or retain info if people's feelings are preserved. (high context)	Dishonest, indirect, sneaky, not trustworthy	Honest, direct, Principled, literal (low context)
Character	Aggressive, at times brutal and abusive	Brave, but overpowered like "niños heroes"	Submissive, weak	Dominant, strong
Time orientation	Obsessively future oriented. Doesn't know how to relax. Unrealistically believes time can be mastered	Lives in and enjoys present, respects past, awaits a future to be determined by god's will: *"si Dios quiere"*	Lives too much in present, while dwelling on past; surrenders own will and ambition to chance; procrastinating	The present is the birthplace of the future; planning, action oriented. "All the flowers of all the tomorrows are in the seeds we plant today"

EXHIBIT 11-1 (CONTINUED)
HISTORICAL STEREOTYPES

Value Affected	Mexican View of N. America	Mexican View of Self	N. American View of Mexican	N. American View of Self
Social classes	Although morally corrupted, economically and perhaps racially superior	Exclusive, but more cultured & civilized at top levels; money not only determinant of status for "*gente decente*" (decent people)	Chaotic, inefficient, unjust; high classes lack character and low classes lack potential	Orderly, efficient, fair; upward mobility is possible to anyone who has money to enter
Religion	Profess a false religion	Repository of higher moral values	Passive Christianity (Catholicism) God's faithful servant	Active Christianity (Protestantism); God's appointed steward
Orientation to nature	Destructive, futilely trying to control what only God can master	Nature merely "is", a creation of God which man can ultimately neither influence nor control	Man cannot control nature; fatalism seen in failing to try. Evidence is economic under-development	Man can and should manage and perfect nature; optimistic due to results of economic progress
National intent	Intervention, imperialism, subversion.	Sovereignty, respect, recognition.	Lacking vision, discipline; needs help to reform flawed political and economic systems.	Good natured missionary, helpful, showing others "the way"
Work ethic	Obsessive materialism, don't know how or when to relax.	Work not inherently redeeming; something that must be done	Lazy, work is bad. As seen in Mexican sayings: "Do not today what you can do tomorrow" and "work is sacred; don't touch it"	Work is the measure of a man. As seen in sayings "never put off until tomorrow what can be done today" and "an idle mind is the devil's workshop"

(*text continued from page 260*)

❑ Respect or "respeto" in Mexico is an emotionally charged word bound up with values of equality, fair play, and democratic spirit.

❑ In conversations, Mexicans tend to maximize differences between persons due to gender, status, or age in contrast to North Americans, who often minimize them (e.g., they defer to one of higher authority). Reality for Mexicans is not just objective but interpersonal, so they may reply in a way that makes the receiver happy although it may not be the fact. They use titles as "señor" or "don" to note social standing. Indigenous people will address whites as "señor" as a sign of respect due them for their race.

❑ Mexicans live with a sense of death, celebrate it in their holidays or feast days, even with disguises, toys, confections, song, and dance. It is treated as a bosom friend or exotic personage, joked about, and played with. They even take flowers and food for their dead during their religious celebration for the dead. Yet in many Latin countries, even dying is a luxury many inhabitants cannot afford. In Mexico a third-class burial can be the equivalent of three annual wages.

Tips for Doing Business and Negotiating with Mexicans

Mexican culture is high-context, valuing beliefs in the divine, the family, personal relations, and individual respect for dignity. In Spanish, Mexicans customize the language by speaking metaphorically through anecdotes, sayings and jokes. Among Latin Americans, Mexicans are the most status conscious—status is related to family, school, wealth, position, and authority. Mexican managers are very individualistic, delegation and team work do not come naturally, but must be learned.[4]

The following is a profile of Mexican negotiators.[1]

Basic Concept of Negotiation Process

Negotiating in Mexico is a complex, long procedure, covering several stages. First, the parties involved must determine if they, as individuals or organizations, can do business together. Establishing a warm working relationship with one's counterparts is essential to the process, and facilitates the negotiation. The stage of getting to know one another is crucial as a foundation for business, because Mexicans will do business with people for "who they are" and not whom they represent. Talking business in the initial stages of a relationship should be avoided.

The stage of getting to know one another is crucial as a foundation for business, because Mexicans will do business with people for "who they are" and not whom they represent.

Many Mexicans resent what they see as a long history of unfair treatment by the North Americans and personal honor or dignity may be a factor within the Mexican negotiating team.

Connections in Mexico are very important and the government has a significant influence in private business matters. Permits are required for just about every business transaction. As a result a government official might elicit a bit of *mordida* (the bite) to complete the transaction.

Selection of Negotiators

Negotiators are selected primarily on status. Family connections, personal or political influence, and education are critical. Hence the importance of *ubicacion* (where one is plugged into the system) becomes evident. Mexican negotiators tend to be high level, male, and well-connected. They expect their counterparts to recognize that and send only corresponding levels of negotiators.

Role of Individual Aspirations

Whether Mexicans are individualists or collectivists seems to depend on the social arena. In business, and with other men, Mexicans tend to be competitive, set on pursuing individual goals and needs for their personal recognition. Often they feel they owe loyalty to their *patron*, but they seek to project a public image of significance and power.

Concern for Protocol

Mexican culture is dominated by courtesy, dignity, tact, and diplomacy. Protocol is important and social competence is as critical as technical competence. Vigorous handshakes even pats on the back are important signs of respect.

Significance of Type of Issue

For Mexicans, relationship-based and personal/internal issues tend to predominate and affect the negotiations and Mexicans emphasize the social and personal aspects of their relationships with the people they encounter, including business people.

Complexity of the Language

Communicative context is formed by body language and emotional cues, not just the words spoken. Mexicans communicate with hand movements, physical contact, and emotional expressions, making Mexicans high-context communicators.

All Latin American cultures embrace closeness. People stand close to each other, sit close to each other, and often touch each other.

Mexican culture is dominated by courtesy, dignity, tact, and diplomacy. Protocol is important and social competence is as critical as technical competence.

Nature of Persuasive Argument

Emotional arguments that are highly dramatic and patriotic are considered persuasive. Along these lines, there is the concept of *proyectismo* (constructing plans without critical analysis and assuming in time all will be accomplished). Perhaps much of this stems from the twin origins of Mexican culture: the Indian, based on magic and superstition, and the Spanish, based on imposition, dogma, and faith.

Value of Time

There is a relaxed polychronic attitude toward time. Although time is a concern, Mexicans do not allow schedules to interfere with experiences involving their family or friends. The culture is more people rather than task-oriented. It is important to be on time for appointments, but one should always expect to wait as a meeting may not end because the next sheduled appointment has arrived.

Bases of Trust

Evaluations of trustworthiness are based initially on intuition and then later on one's past record. Negotiations should occur within a generally trusting atmosphere. Trust must develop through a series of frequent and warm interpersonal transactions, either socially or business oriented. It is not uncommon to invite business partners to family events as part of developing a more intimate relationship.

Risk Taking Propensity

Mexicans tend to be risk-avoidant. They will try to work something out to avoid risk as much as possible. Mexicans tend to be very pessimistic in any situation in which there is some amount of risk.

Internal Decision-Making System

Decision making is highly centralized in government, companies and within negotiating teams. Mexican leaders tend to make decisions without concern for consensus. Individuals with *palanca* (leverage) tend to be well positioned, expressive, and forceful with their opinions and decisions.

Form of Satisfactory Agreement

The only way to be certain that a business agreement has been reached in Mexico is with a written document. Agreements in Mexico fall under the Civil Code, the Commercial Code, or the Law of Commercial Companies.

Kras[5] covers many important and specific management issues faced by U.S. and Mexican managers as they work together.

CENTRAL AMERICA'S STATES

On the western side of the Caribbean Sea is a land bridge between the northern and southern continents of the Americas, which also fronts on the Pacific Ocean. The seven nations located between Mexico and Colombia are usually referred to as Central America—all but Belize are primarily Latin in culture.

If ever there was a need and case for synergy, it is in these Central American states. The nineteenth century federation called the United Provinces of Central America may have been premature, but it provided a cooperative model for the future—if not politically, at least economically. Only by collaboration, can this block of countries overcome their chronic poverty, illiteracy, violence. Perhaps where political and military power-types have failed, local business leaders and global managers may succeed in raising the standards and quality of living for the populace. According to Paige,[6] the only way to understand Central American politics is by focusing on the coffee-growing elites that have long dominated the region. Sandwiched between North and South America, this area cries out for synergistic solutions and contributions from both the Anglo-Latin cultures.

Central America is an area where turmoil imperils hopes for reform. Unfortunately, too often in the past these "banana republics" became comic-opera fiefdoms of U.S. commerce. Despite bustling capitals, millions of people in this strife-torn and suffering region are, for the main part, gentle peasants who have been exploited too long. This strategic land mass is a glaring challenge to the affluent in the Americas. The challenge for Pan American countries includes educational technology used to provide mass education and literacy; cooperatives on a massive scale to improve the peasants' way of life; scientific and technological know-how shared to improve the economies, the health services, and the development of the region; and social justice brought to all levels of society.

Panama, which has never considered itself part of Central America and has been spared the regional strife, might become a laboratory, along with Costa Rica, to create demonstration models that would influence the other states to join in a regional entity for self-improvement. Application of new techniques to promote social peace and reduce internal political violence, as in El Salvador and Guatemala, should become the concern of Pan American social scientists. Simplistic, oppressive, military approaches will not solve the region's problems and tap its vast undeveloped human and natural resources.

If ever there was a need and case for synergy, it is in these Central American states. Only by collaboration, can this block of countries overcome their chronic poverty, illiteracy, violence.

SOUTH AMERICA'S CULTURAL DEVELOPMENT

As the global manager flies over the twelve countries that compose the southern continent of the Americas, he or she is struck by the immensity of this land mass and the potential resources down below, especially in Brazil and Argentina. Nine of these Latin peoples have, in addition to their ancient Indian heritages, a Spanish cultural base, and one nation each has Portuguese, French, British or Dutch cultural inputs. All but Surinam share the Roman Catholic cultural tradition. Most have been enriched by African cultural influxes. Centered between the Atlantic and Pacific oceans, South America has been a multicultural cauldron for mixing Asian, East Indian, as well as European and African cultures in a curious synergy.

South America simultaneously amazes with the beauty of the pre-Columbian art and civilization and the very modern and colorful art works and high-rise architecture, and appalls with the poverty of the masses, the great wealth of the few, the violence, terrorism, and dominance of a powerful military or dictator. We can be encouraged by the progress in education and literacy, improvements in health services and population control, changing images and aspirations of South Americans.

Despite the great diversity in Latin America, there are common themes and patterns. After the development of fairly sophisticated Indian civilizations, there was a period of European colonization and exploitation from the 15th through 18th centuries, followed by wars of independence and attempts at federation during the nineteenth century. Since the early twentieth century, Latin American nations have been engaged in internal and external conflicts. Yet, the last half of this century has seen relative peace between the nations of Central and South America, and significant economic progress.

These countries also share another factor—a Roman Catholic cultural tradition that not only pervades their history, but ways of life and thinking. The Spanish and Portuguese explorers and conquerors brought the missionaries with them to convert and "civilize" the pagan inhabitants. Accompanying the military from South America up through North America were Franciscans, Dominicans, and Jesuits. At first, the clergy protected the Indians and helped through their missions to educate the indigenous populations. Their agricultural and trading centers became the great cities of South, Central, and North America. With the passage

Centered between the Atlantic and Pacific oceans, South America has been a multicultural cauldron for mixing Asian, East Indian, as well as European and African cultures in a curious synergy. These countries also share another factor—a Roman Catholic cultural tradition that not only pervades their history, but ways of life and thinking.

of time and increase in wealth, the Church became part of the establishment, despite the notable successes of priest revolutionaries, like Father Miguel Hidalgo, who espoused the causes of nationalism of the peasants. As a major land owner itself, the Church has not only supported the oligarchy, but opposed population control, divorce, and social change. But recently, in opposition to the continuation of feudal conditions and serfdom for peasants, a group of socially-minded clergy have provided a viewpoint in support of change.

With the encouragement of Pope John XXIII's Second Vatican Council in the 1960s, the promotion of social justice became a Roman Catholic priority in Latin America. A series of episcopal conferences confirmed the efforts, while Latin American bishops such as Leonidas Proaño of Ecuador, the martyred Oscar Romero of El Salvador, and Dom Helder Camarra of Brazil, became forces for change in their dioceses and nations. Some priests and religious leaders became militant and even joined the guerrillas or Marxists. Others suffered harassment, beatings, torture, and death in their defense of the poor and human rights.

The growth of the militant theology and activities in the Latin American Church caused Pope John-Paul in his visits to the Western Hemisphere, to protest social inequities, and yet warn the clergy of the need to concentrate on their spiritual mission. In any event, no modern manager operating in Latin America can afford to ignore the Church as a cultural force. Cooperation and collaboration for social improvement in Latin America can be significantly advanced when business cooperates with institutions for human development.

Rodriquez[7] examined the conversions underway in Latin America from Catholic to Protestant beliefs. The new brand of Christianity on the rise is "Evangelico," principally Pentecostal, with a fundamentalist view of scriptural teachings. In the 20th century, Protestants have now risen to 50 million on that continent. With a conversion rate of 400 per hour, demographers predict Latin American will be evangelical before the end of the 21st century! The "born again" movement matches the transition toward industrialization and urbanization. The religious cultural shift is away from the more tolerant, feminine orientation with its tragic sense of life and death, toward self-reform, spiritual empowerment, and taking responsibility for improving your own life now, not just in the "hereafter." Rodriquez reports that a powerful tool for this religious revolution is satellite television beamed southward from what is left of Protestant America's "Bible Belt." Four hundred years of authoritarian Christianity may be overturned in a single generation, and Latin American peoples will never be the same again!

Four hundred years of authoritarian Christianity may be overturned in a single generation, and Latin American peoples will never be the same again!

LATIN AMERICAN CULTURAL THEMES

The continent of Central and South America is made up of many nations and cultures. The Spanish heritage and language dominates except in Brazil where the Portuguese language and culture dominates with a significant influence also being made by Pan Asians. Other European influences (German, Irish, Italian), as well as African influences, are evident across the Americas. Some countries, such as Colombia and Mexico, have strong manifestations of ancient Indian cultures.

Global managers realize that all the countries and peoples south of the U.S. border are not basically the same. Communication and business practice must be adapted to local circumstances. Generalizations regarding Latin America are dangerous. Many of the countries differ greatly in socio-economic status, educational levels, governance, and composition of the population. However, Lanier's[8] insights about Latin America may prove helpful.

Social Customs

Shaking Hands. This is the same as in Europe. If there are several people in the room enter with a little bow and then go around to each person and shake hands. The "hi everybody" is considered rude and brash. "So long, see you tomorrow" is equally poor. The *abrazo* (embrace) is a greeting used with individuals one knows well.

Pleasantries. Nobody rushes into business. As a foreign business person, take your time and ask about your colleague's family's health, or the weather, or perhaps the local sports team.

Thank-you notes. Send thank-you notes promptly after any courtesy. Flowers are often presented as a thank-you.

Time. Latin Americans are often late according to North American standards but expect North Americans to be on time. Their offices close about 6 and dinner usually begins at 8. As a guest, do not arrive exactly on time, but up to about a half hour late.

Party Traditions. Traditionally, women congregated on one side of the room and men on the other, but that is changing.

If you visit a Brazilian's home, *cafezinho* (demitasse) will be served for you and you should do the same for guests in your home.

For large formal affairs, invitations are written by hand. Flowers are often sent before a large affair. At a smaller party you should take them to your host or hostess.

Generalizations regarding Latin America are dangerous. Many of the countries differ greatly in socio-economic status, educational levels, governance, and composition of the population.

Privacy. There are closed doors, fences, and high walls around homes. Knock, and wait to be invited in. Don't drop in on neighbors. This is not a custom. Personal security is very important.

What About Questions? Some North Americans get to know people by asking questions. However, in Latin America it is safer to talk about local issues of interest. Questions are often interpreted as prying.

Space. Latin speaking distance is closer than North American speaking distance. Instead of handshakes men often embrace.

Class and Status. People may not be served on a first-come, first-served basis. Their place in society may determine the order of preference.

Doing Business. The pace in Latin America is traditionally slow especially when negotiations are under way. Decisions are made at the top. Brazilians, for example, do not like quick, infrequent visits. They like relationships that continue. This implies a long term commitment to Brazil.

Deals are never concluded over the telephone or by letter, but in person.

Don't call anyone by his or her first name unless the person has invited you to do so. When in doubt, be formal.

Dress conservatively and use business cards of good quality and in the local language.

Themes and Patterns

Themes are basic orientations that are shared by many or most of the people. They are beginning points for understanding, and sometimes form a pattern of behavior.

Personalismo. For the most part, a Latin's concerns are family, personal friends, hobbies, political party, and possibly athletics such as the local bullfight. But transcending all these is the concern for oneself. So to reach a Latin, relate everything to him or her in personalized terms.

Machismo. It means "maleness" and is an attitude that men have towards women. The macho is aggressive and sometimes insensitive and machismo represents power. Machismo is made up of virility, zest for action, daring, competitiveness, and the will to conquer. How is it translated into daily business life? A man must demonstrate forcefulness, self-confidence, visible courage, and leadership with a flourish. The machismo concept is implanted early in childhood and varies from country to country. Saving face and honor are important concepts for men. Never criticize family or friends. Yet, the female may actually control the home, children, and husband.

Desires to Get Rich Quick—Fatalism. There is instability in many Latin American economies and as a result there is a boom or bust attitude. Many desire to make it rich by speculation, manipulation or gambling. As a result, Latin business people are not as interested in stable growth as U.S. business persons. Related to this is the Latin American tendency

The pace in Latin America is traditionally slow especially when negotiations are under way. Decisions are made at the top.

to let chance guide their destiny. Most are convinced that outside forces govern their lives. They are willing to "accept the inevitable" Don Quixote who followed his quest whether or not it appeared hopeless seems like a foolish man to many Americans. To most Latin Americans he is heroic. He was "bowing to fate," "taking what comes" and "resigned to the inevitable."

Good Manners and Dignity. Latin Americans are much like Europeans in this respect. They are more formal, and more elaborate. They shake hands on meeting and departing. In Latin America, the work one does is directly related to the social class one is in.

One is born "high" or "low." Latin Americans are by and large stratified societies. Latin Americans are born with a sense of place but the two-class society, very rich and very poor, is giving way to a growing middle class.

Aristocratic values plus late industrialization and strong central governments have combined to create an imbalance in manpower needs of South America and the supply. Large numbers of South American workers have no industrial skills, while there is an oversupply of professional and white collar workers, but an acute shortage of managers.

Hospitality. Latin Americans are warm, friendly, and hospitable. They like to talk, and want to know about a visitor's family and interests.

Authoritarianism. Signs of respect can be determined in both tone of voice and manner that denote grades of inferiority and superiority in a hierarchical society.

The *patron* is the man of power or wealth who sustains loyalty from those of lesser status. He can be the employer, the politico, the landowner, and in other cases the money lender or merchant. Authoritarianism does not allow for questioning. The *patron* knows everything and is all powerful. To play these roles, one has to be respectful in a subservient position. As the middle class continues to grow in size and strength, authoritarianism is less prevalent.

Latin America is going through a social revolution in which agricultural and traditional societies are giving way to modern industrial nations. The impact of Roman Catholicism is strong in the Latin cultures but lessening as a force in the daily lives of people especially in the urban areas. The profound social and economic changes underway are altering many of the above customs and influences, especially among the younger generation. World communications, international exchanges, and contemporary realities are transforming Latin America. Its global managers of Latin America are sophisticated in the ways of international business, and may not illustrate, at least on the surface, the typical social or cultural characteristics of the region.

Gordon,[9] offers these conclusions from his research that may help to improve cross-cultural communications throughout the Americas:

In Latin America, the work one does is directly related to the social class one is in. Latin Americans are by and large stratified societies.

Syllogistic Nature of Meaning

Be alert to covert assumptions that may act as the context for interpreting the meaning of an overt message from another of a different cultural background. The message is only the raw material for interpretation, and one should attempt to consider the silent assumptions.

Situation-Associated Assumptions

Link particular assumptions for interpretation with a situation, not just with words, gestures, or voice tone used in the message sending. The concept of situation, whether speaking Spanish or Portuguese, or operating through an interpreter, is to seek out the objectives of the situation; the time and space patterns of the activities involved; the roles of actors in the situation; the rules governing the interaction in that local Latin American situation. The word *familia,* for example, connotes much more to a Latin American than the American sense of family.

Dissonant Cross-Cultural Assumptions

Dissonance occurs in communications if the sender tries to impose his or her cultural assumptions upon the foreign assumptions behind the interaction. The problem in U.S.-Canadian interfaces is that both too often assume they are quite similar, whereas the subtle cultural differences may escape each other. North American business people can make many incorrect assumptions about their Latin American counterparts.

Values, Conflict, and Communication

The real difficulties in cross-cultural communications may be occurring because value systems are in conflict. While northern and southern Americans at a Pan American conference, for instance, may agree on general goals, the conflict might be anticipated in the means to achieve such goals; that is, the time, place, division of labor, sequence of actions, etc. When one does not consider the other's values, then emotions may rise and disagreements increase.

Trivial Actions and Profound Effects

In cross-cultural negotiations, the seemingly trivial aspects may lead to an accumulation of misunderstandings that have profound impact upon the relationship. North Americans, for example, when guests in a Latin home or office may overlook mundane details to their own detriment and a fruitful intercultural encounter. If one does not have sensitivity in "small matters," it can lead to misinterpretation of intent or motives.

Making Allowances for Foreigners

Although members of a host culture may make normal allowances for guests' alien behavior, some of the foreigner's behavior may not be forgiven for the native does not comprehend the other's context and reason for

The word familia, *connotes much more to a Latin American than the American sense of family.*

In cross-cultural negotiations, the seemingly trivial aspects may lead to an accumulation of misunderstandings that have profound impact upon the relationship.

such unacceptable actions. More often the North American gets into difficulty by not making allowances with self because of foreign status, as well as not attempting to conform to behavior norms of a given situation.

Vicious Circle Effect

Minor communication breakdowns can escalate and be exacerbated so that the natives make judgments about the visitor's desires and motivations that may indeed be false, and create negative images in the mind of the host. This may lead to social isolation of the foreigner, making it more difficult for the visitor to understand the host culture and people. To move behind a superficial level of communication, this vicious circle must somehow be broken by the foreigner or he/she becomes a prisoner of isolation.

Blind Leading the Blind

Amateur observers of a foreign culture may provide ethnocentric distortions of reality produced by systematic misinterpretation of the cross-cultural experience. Thus, a business person from North America about to be assigned in Latin America may seek out a colleague for input about the culture because that other person had already done business there. A manager should check out the feedback of a single colleague with objective data (e.g., books and reports) and then only make tentative judgments before living in the host culture for some time.

For successful Pan American exchanges and collaboration, Gordon's research indicates that each party in the cross-cultural encounter must learn: (a) to recognize symptoms of miscommunication in oneself and the other; (b) to separate fact, interpretation, and conclusion; (c) to derive silent assumptions about major premises in the interpretive process from the foreigner's minor premises and conclusions; and (d) to request information from the host country citizen in such a way as not to bias or inhibit the response.

CHALLENGES FOR PAN AMERICAN COOPERATION

The prospects for Pan American synergy in the 21st century are encouraging. The last half of the 20th century has seen some remarkable progress in the Americas. Inflation is still a major problem, coordination of economic policies is distant, but barriers to trade are being reduced and governments are committed to cutting fiscal deficits. There has also been relative peace between the nations of this Western Hemisphere, despite internal upheavals within various Latin American states.

There have also been some noble efforts toward economic cooperation that lay the groundwork for real collaboration in the future. It takes time for such diverse cultures to learn the value and skills of joint endeavors. But the ground for synergy has been broken in such undertakings as the Organization of American States, the North Atlantic Treaty Organization, the Central American Common Market, the Andean Pact, the Alliance for Progress, and North American Free Trade Agreement. In the global marketplace of the 21st century, emerging business opportunities will be found in Latin America. A strong synergistic indicator is MERCOUR (Mercado Comun del Sur). MERCOUR is a type of common market made up of Argentina, Brazil, Paraguay, and Uruguay with Chile as an associate member. NAFTA is an open market of almost 400 million people, while MERCOUR seeks to do something similar for its 240 million inhabitants. Meanwhile, a revival is underway in the older ANDEAN Group composed of Venezuela, Columbia, Ecuador, and Peru. All such cooperative arrangements seek to collaborate in common economic and trade policies that are more market friendly while reducing protectionism.[4]

Underlying all of Latin America's difficulties is the need for integral development in the areas of education, health care, and opportunities for self-development.

One hopeful sign is the shift away from unilateral foreign aid to sharing of resources through multilateral institutions, such as the World Bank and the Inter-American Development Bank. Lately, the concerns of the various American nations have shifted more to the social arena with the establishment of such entities as the Inter-American Commission on Human Rights. Those with vision will set goals to close the Pan American poverty gap within the next fifty years.

Underlying all of Latin America's difficulties is the need for integral development in the areas of education, health care, and opportunities for self-development. The interdependence of North and Latin America, and the need of one part of the hemisphere for the other is obvious. Economic development is now more horizontal in the Americas, and not just vertical.

Another reason for optimism about the future of relationships in the Americas is the accomplishments and prospects of the Pan American Development Foundation. It is a nonprofit, private voluntary agency established in 1962 through leading citizens of the Americas and the General Secretariat of the OAS. Its objective is to help the lowest-income people in Latin America and the Caribbean to participate productively in the socioeconomic and cultural development of their societies. PADF activates the involvement of the local private sector, especially the business community, through the formation of national development foundations in the various countries.

"Synergizing" the Pan American potential presents a macromanagement challenge:

❑ To better manage the national resources of all states in the hemisphere by more effective collaboration of public and private sectors in each country, and between north/south regional relations.
❑ To manage the transfer of technology and information for mutual development of North and Latin American peoples.

"LATIN AMERICA DECIDES, IF YOU CAN'T BEAT 'EM, JOIN 'EM

Even in the loopy landscape of South American economies, Ecuador is an extreme case. Last year it defaulted on some of its debt, roughly 70% of its banks have been taken over by the state, inflation exceeded 60 percent, and the local currency—the sucre—is running at 25,000 to the dollar. . . . On January 9th, President Jamil Mahuad announced that the United States dollar would be the new coin of the realm. The sucre would be used only for small change. Ecuador thus joins a growing list of more than two dozen countries, the largest of them Panama, that use the dollar as their official currency, as well as the people in 50 other countries who unofficially put their trust in American money, according to the International Monetary Fund."

—Anthony DePalma
New York Times, January 23, 2000,
p. WK4

❏ To contribute to economic and social development of Latin America through the exercise of corporate social responsibility by multinational enterprises on both continents.

SUMMARY

In the last two chapters, we have sought to provide global managers an overview of the Western Hemisphere in terms of its diverse national cultures and their development, as well as some problems and opportunities for synergy. To improve the quality of life for all the hemisphere's inhabitants, effective and ecologically controlled use of resources on these twin continents is a major management challenge. Trained and experienced managers in transnational enterprises throughout the Americas may be able to accomplish in the decades ahead what politicians, dictators, revolutionaries, and soldiers have failed to accomplish in the past centuries—Pan American cooperation and collaboration for the common good.

To improve the quality of life for all the hemisphere's inhabitants, effective and ecologically controlled use of resources on these twin continents is a major management challenge.

REFERENCES

1. Moran, R. T. and Abbott, J. *NAFTA: Managing the Cultural Differences,* Houston, TX: Gulf Publishing Co., 1994.
2. Table based upon selected observations from *Good Neighbors* by John Condon, *Distant Neighbors* by Alan Riding, *The United States and Latin America: Myths*

and Stereotypes of Civilization and Nature, by Frederick B. Pike, *Occupied America,* by Rodolfo Acuña, *The Labyrinth of Solitude,* by Octavio Paz, and *The Psychology of the Mexican,* by Rodolfo Diaz-Guerrero

3. Condon, J. *Good Neighbors: Communicating with Mexicans,* 2nd ed., Yarmouth, ME: Intercultural Press, 1997.

4. Elashmawi, F. and Harris, P. R. *Multicultural Management 2000,* 2nd ed., Houston, TX: Gulf Publishing Co., 1998.

5. Kras, E. *Management in Two Cultures,* Yarmouth, ME: Intercultural Press, 1995.

6. Paige, J. *Democracy in Central America,* Cambridge, MA: Harvard University Press, 1998.

7. Rodriquez, R. *Los Angeles Times,* August 13, 1989.

8. Lanier, A. *Living in Latin America,* Yarmouth, ME: Intercultural Press, 1988.

9. Gordon, R. *Living In Latin America,* Skokie, IL: National Textbook 1976 (available through Intercultural Press, Yarmouth, ME 04096). To further comprehend Latin American culture, you may find *Spain Is Different* (1992) by Helen W. Ames useful. To view the video series on Argentina, Brazil, Chile, and Mexico, entitled *Doing Business in Latin America* (1996), consult Big World, Inc. at Intercultural Press, Yarmouth, ME 04096.

DOING BUSINESS
WITH ASIANS
Australia, China, India, Indonesia, Japan, Malaysia, Philippines, South Korea, Vietnam

Asia is a continent bounded by Europe and the Arctic, Pacific, and Indian oceans. Sometimes referred to as the Far East, its almost 2 billion inhabitants are dispersed over 16 million square miles. It is an area of increasing importance to global managers as a trade shift occurs from the Atlantic to the Pacific. One world leader referred to the next century as "The Century of the Pacific"; if that forecast is valid, then the information in this chapter takes on increasing importance. By the year 2020, China's GNP will exceed the United States' GNP by 40%.[1]

However, there are regional realities to be confronted before such optimistic scenarios can be realized. In the early '90s, many Asian countries achieved spectacular economic growth as their affluence and middle class population increased. By 1998, many of these same nations were facing social instability as a result of an "economic meltdown" caused by an undermining of their financial, banking and even political systems. Matlock[2] states:

The claim that Asia's recent economic success resulted from a specific Asian virtue has suffered a severe blow since the monetary and economic setbacks. . . . What brought rapid economic development to the "Asian tigers" was the same thing that brought it to countries elsewhere: capitalism, hard work, frugality, and limited government. There was no Asian miracle; if economic development was more rapid in some Asian countries than it had been in the West, that was because modern technology and communication have accelerated the process of change and because these countries were playing catch-up. It takes longer for pioneers to clear the way than for late starters to follow a well-marked trail.

By the year 2020, China's GNP will exceed the United States' GNP by 40%.[1]

ASIA

CHINA

SOUTH
KOREA

JAPAN

INDIA

TAIWAN

VIETNAM

PHILIPPINES

INDONESIA

MALAYSIA

AUSTRALIA

NEW ZEALAND

SELECTED PACIFIC BASIN COUNTRIES

The Pacific Rim has a diversity of peoples and cultures in various stages of economic and technological development. A fourth of humankind lives in the rapidly developing People's Republic of China, while approximately half the human race lives in Asia. Asia is so large in terms of geography, human and natural resources, and disparate business practices that total coverage is beyond the scope of this unit. But the insights shared in this representative sample of Asia will help global managers to be more sensitive and appreciative of their Asian counterparts. A review of Australia follows, which is a country in Asia, but not culturally Asian.

Schnitzer, Liebranz, and Kubin[3] have assembled an introduction to our main topic. Exhibit 12-1 summarizes the principal cultural differences of Asians in general with those of Americans. Readers are encouraged to expand this listing based on their experience and readings.

EXHIBIT 12-1[3]
A COMPARISON OF
GENERAL CULTURAL DIFFERENCES

Asian Countries

❑ Equity is more important than wealth.
❑ Saving and conserving resources is highly valued.
❑ Group is the most important part of society and is emphasized for motivation.
❑ Cohesive and strong families and ties often extend to distant relatives—even the nation and its leaders. Relationship society with strong network of social ties.
❑ Highly disciplined and motivated workforce/societies.
❑ Education is an investment in the prestige and economic wellbeing of the family.
❑ Protocol, rank, and status are important.
❑ Personal conflicts are to be avoided—e.g., few lawyers.
❑ Public service is a moral responsibility.

United States of America

❑ Wealth is more important than equity.
❑ Consumption is highly valued, awareness for conservation is growing.
❑ Individual is the most important part of society and the person is emphasized for motivation, although team emphasis is growing.
❑ Nuclear and mobile family. Experimentation with new home/housing/commune living communities of non-relatives. Fluid society that de-emphasizes strong social ties.

(continued on next page)

A fourth of humankind lives in the rapidly developing People's Republic of China, while approximately half the human race lives in Asia.

EXHIBIT 12-1[3]
A COMPARISON OF
GENERAL CULTURAL DIFFERENCES (CONTINUED)

United States of America (continued)

❑ Decline in the "protestant work ethic" and hierarchy.
❑ Education is an investment is personal development/success.
❑ Informality and competence is important.
❑ Conflict is energy, to be managed—many lawyers.
❑ Distrust of big government and bureaucracy.

AUSTRALIA[4-10]

AUSTRALIA-PROFILE

Population	19 million
Ethnic groups	European 94%, Asian 5%, Aboriginal 1%
Religions	Christianity 73%, (Roman Catholics 26%, Anglican 24%, others 23%), non-religious/other denominations 27%
Education	Compulsory (age 6 to 15) Literacy—99%
Land	2,966,151 miles^2
Government	Commonwealth of Australia
Political Parties	Australian Democratic Labor Party, Australian Democrats Party, Australian Labor Party, Liberal Party of Australia, National Party of Australia, Socialist Party of Australia
Per Capita Income	$20,370
Exports to US	US$ 2.6 billion
Imports from US	US$ 2.2 billion

The original inhabitants of Australia were the Aborigines, who some think arrived more than 40,000 years ago by raft across the waters separating the continent from the Indonesia archipelago.

Historical Overview

The original inhabitants of Australia were the Aborigines, who some think arrived more than 40,000 years ago by raft across the waters separating the continent from the Indonesia archipelago. Portuguese, Spanish, Dutch, and English explorers observed the land throughout the 1600s, but it remained undisturbed for the most part until the next century. In

1770, Captain James Cook explored the east coast and claimed it for the British. The first fleet of British settlers arrived in Sydney in 1778 under the command of Captain Arthur Philip, who founded penal colonies in Sydney, Brisbane, and Hobart. Thus, the first settlers in Australia were primarily convicts or soldiers, usually of British or Irish origin.

With the discovery of gold in 1851, the number of immigrants increased dramatically, generating high growth and trade. This environment resulted in unprecedented wealth and stability into the 20th century. In 1901, the six established colonies—New South Wales, Tasmania, Western Australia, South Australia, Victoria, and Queensland—agreed to federate as the Commonwealth of Australia, under British law. The first federal parliament was opened at Melbourne in May 1901. The seat of government was later transferred to Canberra, a city designed by American Walter Burley Griffin in May 1927. Australia gained complete autonomy from Britain in both internal and external affairs when the Statute of Westminster Adoption Act passed in 1942.

Australia first established ties with the United States during World War II. Since that conflict over 50 years ago, Australia has played an active role in world politics and maintained friendly relations with the US. The ANZUS security treaty, signed in 1952 between Australia, New Zealand, and the United States, continues to be supported despite opposition from New Zealand on nuclear issues. Under this treaty, several joint meetings and activities operate simultaneously.

Political elections in the last half of the 20th century have confirmed the dominance of the Labor Party and their candidates for prime minister.

Australian Governance

Australia is the sixth largest country in the world, and only a bit smaller than the continental United States. It is also the only country in the world to make up an entire continent.

Australia is known officially as the Commonwealth of Australia. While it remains a sovereign nation, it officially recognizes the monarch Queen Elizabeth II. Currently, a debate is underway whether the country should become an independent republic or maintain its ties with the British monarchy. The queen has formal executive power, which is exercised by the monarch's appointed representative, the governor-general, who in turn acts on the advice of the Federal Executive Council, led by the prime minister. The prime minister is appointed by the governor-general. The Federal Parliament consists of a House of Representatives, which has 147 members, and a Senate, which has 76 members. Australia includes six federal states, Canberra, the national capital, and three territories. Each state has a governor, representing the monarch, and its own legislative, judicial, and executive system. Although the

Australia is the sixth largest country in the world. It is also the only country in the world to make up an entire continent.

states enjoy great autonomy, national law overrides all state laws where there is conflict.

The People and Their Homeland

The current population is Australia is approximately 19 million inhabitants and is growing at a rate of .96% a year. More than 85% of all households live in urban areas, mostly along the coastal regions. Sydney, Australia's largest city, accounts for 6 million people alone. Close to 40% of all people live in Sydney and Melbourne combined. Approximately one-third of all Australians are younger than 20 years, accounting for a very young population.

More than 94% of all Australians descend from European ancestry. Typical origins include Dutch, Estonian, French, German, Greek, Italian, Latvian, Lithuanian, Polish, and Yugoslavian.

People from Asian origins comprise 4% of the population and include Polynesian, Vietnamese, and Cambodian nationalities. The remaining 1% of Australians are the Aborigines, the original inhabitants of Australia.

Aborigines have a very distinct culture, which, at one time, was almost completely destroyed by Caucasian Australians. However, these people are now recognized as an important part of Australian history, and many attempts are being made to preserve and cultivate this culture. The Aborigines hold a distinct spiritual link to the land on which they live. This relationship guides their entire lives as they remain in harmony with the land. The family is the center of Aborigine society, which is a very complex one. However, ceremonies, traditions, and social obligations help the Aborigines feel like they are one with each other and the land.

Education, free to all, is compulsory from age 6 to 15. Money for schools comes from federal funds, which are administered by the respective state government officials. Children who live in the outback can receive schooling via two-way radio. About one-fourth of all Australian children attend private schools. All states have public universities, which a significant portion of the population attend. The school year has four quarters, with three vacation breaks in April, July, and October. Most Australians have completed eleven years of schooling, indicating that they have finished compulsory education and high school. The literacy rate is 99%.

Approximately 73% of Australians claim to be Christians. Of this percent, 26% are Roman Catholics, 24% Anglicans, and 23% some other denomination. Other religions and nonreligious parts of society account for the remaining 27%. Religion does not play a dominant role in the typical Australian's daily life.

Approximately one-third of all Australians are younger than 20 years, accounting for a very young population.

Health care is provided free of charge to all Australian citizens. This program is called Medicare, and is funded by a 1.25% income tax. Although medicare covers all public health-care costs, private health care options also exist. For example, patients treated by private doctors in either private or public hospitals pay for private health insurance. Approximately 65% of all hospitals are public. The rate of infant mortality is 5.4 per 1,000. Life expectancy ranges from 77 years for men, to 83 years for women.

English is the official language of Australia, but many immigrant groups continue to speak their native tongues at home. The Aborigines, who once commanded over 250 working languages, teach only the remaining 50 or so which survived. Because of this loss, the government has started placing a greater emphasis on the revival of Aborigine languages. In the Aborigine culture, there is a stress on learning the Aborigine language first, and the English language second. They also have their own radio system, which broadcasts programs and music in many Aborigine languages. As a result, many Aborigine families are now beginning to speak traditional languages at home.

The English that Australians speak is quite similar to "Queen's English" or British English; however, many Australian expressions sprinkle the vocabulary, resulting in a very colorful language. For example, the following phrases and words are heard commonly: no worries, mate, (no problem, guy); rubbish (trash or garbage); over the road (across the street); rubber (eraser); mate (male friend); biscuits (cookies); chemist (drugstore); and bonnet (the hood of a car). Furthermore, colloquialisms dot the language, including the following: spot on (right on), bingle ("fender-bender"), dinky-di (something genuine), and like a possum up a gum tree (to say someone is moving fast). It is also typically Australian to shorten words, such as uni, (university), kindi (kindergarten), and teli (television) or add an "ie" to the end, e.g. barbecue is barbie, and mosquito is mozzi. Because some Australian slang might insult other non-Australian English speakers and vice versa, it is important to speak standard English (without using expressions and colloquialisms). The Australians also tend to be very direct in their statements, which results in many strangers, including Americans, feeling attacked when told, for example, "you don't know what you're talking about." The foreigner will gain much respect, however, if he/she counterattacks and does not try to seek approval or run from the argument.

Customs and Courtesies

❑ Australians are generally easy going and friendly. Most Australians greet friends with either a firm, friendly handshake or a "G'day," but

The Aborigines, who once commanded over 250 working languages, teach only the remaining 50 or so which survived. As a result, many Aborigine families are now beginning to speak traditional languages at home.

do not appreciate zealous visitors who constantly overuse the latter. More formal greetings might include a simple "hello, how are you?" style of greeting, but do not have the formal British reserve of their ancestors.

❏ It is customary for men to shake hands at the beginning and ending of a meeting, but women are not required to do this. Instead, they are more inclined to give each other a kiss on the cheek in greeting and leaving. It is quite acceptable for visitors to introduce themselves in social environments, without waiting to be introduced by someone else. If friends see each other from a distance, the customary greeting is a wave, not yelling, as this type of behavior is considered impolite.

❏ In an Australian business setting, it is appropriate to offer your business cards, but do not be surprised if you do not receive one in return, because many Australian businesspeople do not carry them.

❏ When introduced in initial greetings, Australians may address someone with their full name or say "Sir" as a sign of respect. However, Australians are quick to switch to an informal first-name basis, and visitors may do so if an Australian initiates this cue.

Australians are generally easy going and friendly. Most Australians greet friends with either a firm, friendly handshake or a "G'day."

There are some basic rules of etiquette in Australia that should be respected by all visitors. These include:

❏ Men should never wink at a woman, even if they are friends, as this is considered inappropriate behavior.

❏ Yawning in public is quite rude; if someone must yawn, him/herself should cover the mouth and excuse themselves.

❏ Men should not behave too physically with each other as this may imply unmanliness.

❏ The American gesture for "2," forming a "v" with the index and middle finger of one hand is considered vulgar.

❏ The "o.k." or hitchhiking sign used frequently in the US is also considered very rude.

❏ Sniffling several times when one has a cold is not polite; one should be excused to blow the nose in private.

❏ Avoid using the term "stuffed" or "rooting" (for the home team), because both of these terms have vulgar connotations.

❏ Eye contact is important, especially in business meetings.

❏ Like the British, respect is given for lines of people, or queues; therefore, never cut in line, go politely to the end, and wait your turn.

❏ Sportsmanlike gestures of any kind are appreciated because good sportsmanship is highly respected.

❏ Guests of honor usually sit next to the host on the right side.

❑ Finishing a drink, turning the glass upside down, and setting it on the pub counter is a sign that you can outdrink anyone else in the house in some Australian pubs.

❑ When addressing audiences, stand erect and use modest body language.

Australians are outgoing, very relaxed, and have a good sense of humor, even in tense situations. Most use their hands and non-verbal gestures to emphasize and clarify their speech. They are quite open about expressing their feelings, although men still are not very emotional due to the stigma of appearing feminine.

Australians speak frankly and directly; they dislike pretensions of any kind, and will not shy away from disagreement. They generally dislike class structure and differences, which may result in someone sitting next to a cab driver if alone. Close friendships are valued highly here and have a somewhat different connotation than friendship in the United States. Australia is a clean country and the citizens respect these standards. Fines are quite high if one is caught littering.

Australians tend to dress like Americans and Europeans, i.e. quite informally. Business attire, on the other hand, is very conservative. Men typically wear a dark suit and tie, while women wear a dress or skirt and blouse. Regardless of occasion, clothing is never tattered or sloppy and is respectable in public. Wearing clothes with holes or in the wrong size is considered inappropriate. Women tend to wear pants much less than in the United States, and many people wear hats in the summer as protection from the sun.

Australia is located in the Southern Hemisphere, the seasons are the exact opposite of North America. Light clothing is worn in the warm summers, but heavier clothing and rain gear is needed for the winter months. In fact, warmer clothing, i.e. sweaters, may even be needed inside private homes because many are not centrally heated.

Australia is a land of warm, friendly, and informal people, who enjoy life and "work to live," not "live to work." Due to their British background and influence, they share a culture and language that is very similar to the United States. This experience has resulted in a very close Australian-U.S. relationship, which covers the spectrum of commercial and cultural contacts to political and defense cooperation. Companies wishing to conduct business in Australia will find relatively few obstacles in sight, especially since the successful conclusion of the General Agreement on Tariffs and Trade Uruguay Round of trade liberalization. However, it is important to remember that while Australians speak English and seem to behave exactly like Americans, differences in language and culture do exist and should be both respected and appreciated. This respect will result in cementing an already friendly relationship with Australians, as well as leading to success in business.

Australians speak frankly and directly; they dislike pretensions of any kind, and will not shy away from disagreement. They generally dislike class structure and differences. . . . While Australians speak English and seem to behave exactly like Americans, differences in language and culture do exist. . . .

PEOPLE'S REPUBLIC OF CHINA

Deng Xiaoping realized that economic progress required infusions of Western technology and skills. . . .

For many centuries, China was the world's foremost nation, then development ceased. Napoleon told us "let the giant sleep," and it did until Nixon aroused it from its slumbers. Radical change has since ensued, and the pace will gather momentum. There has also been a major shift in the world economy to countries in the Pacific Rim, including Taiwan, Hong Kong, Thailand, Malaysia, Singapore, and Indonesia. Additionally, there is a new economic superpower which has no flag, no state, and is not easily recognizable. This is the fifty-odd million "overseas Chinese"—the lords of the Pacific Rim. They are the new superpower who have built multinationals, registered in various countries named, and form the tip of the iceberg. Their businesses are different from those of the West. They are held together not by binding legal contracts, but by family connections and mutual trust, a system which evolved over the past two millennia.[11]

Background Briefing

With the death of Mao Tse Tung in 1976, China's new leader Deng Xiaoping realized that economic progress required infusions of Western technology and skills, opening possibilities for investors who would move China economically forward. On January 1, 1979, full diplomatic relations between the People's Republic of China (PRC) and the United States of America were established. On March 1, 1979, embassies of the U.S. and the PRC opened in Peking and Washington, respectively. The first U.S. ambassador to the PRC was Leonard Woodcock, former United Auto Workers' president. Since that time a great deal of water has flowed along the Yangtze River and the number of businesspeople and others visiting mainland China has steadily increased.

There has been some progress in modernization and economic liberalization along with some setbacks. On July 1, 1997 the People's Republic of China assumed control of the British crown colony of Hong Kong. The Communist government installed its own regime and installed some curtailments on human rights. Under these circumstances, the issue is whether Hong Kong will continue to be an economic powerhouse and a regional center for trade and tourism. Its inhabitants have been exposed to the advantages of the free enterprise system, even electing their own Legislative Council. The key question is whether its sophisticated business leaders and entrepreneurs will continue to flourish under centralized planning, and help in the economic and socio-political transformation of mainland China. Meanwhile, in 1998 another European enclave has been returned to the "motherland," namely, the former Portuguese colony of Macao. In both places the Chinese culture dominates, but it has been influenced by Western cultures of Britain and Portugal because of their long presence in each former colony. According to Patten,[12]

> "If China is able to master the daunting problems now facing it (failing state industries, the social pressures of rising expectations, pell-mell urbanization), it will need more than Hong Kong's wealth; it will also need to heed Hong Kong's experience. . . . Hong Kong is at one and the same time China's window on the world, bridge to the world, shop front for the world, and paradigm for the world of what the whole of China could become."

A trading partner that enjoys U.S. most-favored-nation status, China offers great opportunities for U.S. business expansion. The Chinese government recently eliminated quotas, licensing, and other controls on more than 30% of commodities subject to restriction, and tariffs have been cut on more than 4,000 product categories. The country boasts the fastest growing economy in the world. China's major cities are highly desirable target markets densely populated by consumers with large disposable incomes. The country has 95 cities with populations exceeding one million. Cities that are especially promising are Beijing, Shanghai, and Guangzhou.[7]

Historical Perspective

The Chinese have always held themselves in high esteem. The name of their country translates as "center of the world" for they saw themselves, their country, and culture as the center of human civilization. They expected that all other peoples and nations would pay tribute to the Chinese. However, one of China's most predominant characteristics is its tradition of isolation. China is one of the oldest advanced civiliza-

The name of their country translates as "center of the world" for they saw themselves, their country, and culture as the center of human civilization.

tions. For more than 2,300 years China enclosed itself behind the Great Wall and forced traders and merchants to remain outside these walls.

The long history of Western imperialism in China is one of great humiliation for the Chinese. In 1949, following the establishment of the People's Republic of China, the Chinese Communist Party attempted to change basic attitudes, values, and behavior of the Chinese people. The purpose of Mao Tse-tung and his reformers was to give the country a new direction, building a traditional feudalistic society into a modern socialistic one.

A fundamental tool in effecting these changes in basic Chinese values was the development of a people's democracy where each individual from the peasant farmer to high government official would take part in decision making at all levels on a regular basis. To accomplish this, work crews, communities, factory organizations, and schools were organized into study teams as a part of the daily business to investigate the socialistic principles upon which the government was established. In attempting to make these changes, four major areas were identified as obstacles to overcome:

In 1949, following the establishment of the People's Republic of China, the Chinese Communist Party attempted to change basic attitudes, values, and behavior of the Chinese people.

1. The difference in economic and political development of urban and rural areas.
2. The reduction of economic and political inequality between the industrial and peasant workers.
3. The reduction of inequality between manual laborers and the elite.
4. The reduction of inequality between the sexes.

Since 1949, two major events in Chinese history occurred: the Great Leap Forward in the late 1950s and the Cultural Revolution in the late 1960s. During these two periods, economic efficiency and social order were forsaken as the country embarked on major new programs that were designed to eliminate "revisionist" elements and to illustrate to the people the significant importance of their role. By mid 1985, the late Deng Xiaoping[14] inaugurated campaigns for modernization and economic reform, even encouraging entrepreneurialism and replacing senior party leaders with younger officials. To deter democratization, sad and traumatic events of suppression occurred in 1989, including the riots in Tiananmen Square that have been described as the "great leap backwards." The Chinese political leadership is only beginning to comprehend that in a civil society, the rule of law and democratic institutions lead to a productive and stable polity.

Negotiating in China

China is a group-oriented society and any negotiation must cover the interests of many different parties. In meetings, Chinese will examine a counterpart's attitude and speech and apply it to the problem solving.

Technical competence is critical, and some negotiators have requested more seasoned technical people join their negotiating team midway through negotiations.

The Chinese rank among the toughest negotiators in the world, but they are reputable and honorable. In addition, China is probably one of the most difficult countries to understand and adapt to. Lucian Pye[15] makes the following points regarding Chinese negotiators from discussions with American negotiators. The points are valid today for anyone interested in working in China.

❑ Emphasis is placed on trust and mutual connections.

❑ Chinese stick to their word.

❑ They are interested in long-range benefits.

❑ They respond well to foreign representatives who say they "specialize" in the PRC.

❑ They are sensitive to national slights and still addicted to propagandistic slogans and codes.

❑ Many Americans are convinced that the Chinese consciously use such slow-down techniques as bargaining ploys because Chinese can exploit a natural American tendency for impatience.

❑ During first encounters, the Chinese usually seem to be bound by their traditional non-legalistic practices.

❑ Businesspersons may come to appreciate that they operate only at the tolerance of the Chinese.

❑ Chinese seem to have a compelling need to dwell on the subject of friendship, convincing many American businesspersons that reciprocity in this spirit was a prerequisite for doing business with China.

❑ Once Chinese decide upon who and what is the best, they show great steadfastness.

❑ Chinese sometimes put pressure on visiting businesspersons when discussing the final arrangements by suggesting that they have broken the spirit of friendship in which the business relationship was originally established.

❑ In negotiations with Chinese, nothing should be considered final until it has been actually realized.

❑ Chinese do not treat the signing of a contract as a completed agreement. They conceive of the relationship in longer and more continuous terms and will not hesitate to suggest modifications immediately on the heels of an agreement.

❑ So as not to lose face, Chinese prefer to negotiate through an intermediary.

❑ Initially, a business meeting is devoted to pleasantries—serving tea, chit chat, fencing, waiting for the right opening to begin serious discussions.

❑ An early key signal of the intensity of Chinese interest in doing business with you was the caliber of the Chinese assigned to the sessions.

The Chinese rank among the toughest negotiators in the world, but they are reputable and honorable.

❑ Chinese posture becomes rigid whenever they feel their goals are being compromised.

Business Courtesies

When a foreign visitor has an appointment with a Chinese official, one will generally be introduced and offered some tea and cigarettes. The offering of a cigarette in the PRC has become a common expression of hospitality. Prior to your entrance, your Chinese host will be briefed on who you are and why you are there. There may be initiated polite questions about your trip and the U.S., generally in the area of pleasantries, and perhaps even about your family. If your call is merely a courtesy call, it may not go beyond this. If this is more than a courtesy call, it would be appropriate to begin discussion of a business nature at this time. The Chinese host will generally indicate when it is time for a person to leave.

It is also important to reciprocate invitations if they are given by the PRC. For example, if a banquet is given in the honor of the American team, they should reciprocate by giving a banquet for the Chinese team. Small company souvenirs or American picture books often make good presents, but expensive gifts should not be given.

It is also important to reciprocate invitations if they are given by the PRC.

Some Business Cautions

The Chinese are sensitive about foreigners' comments on Chinese politics. Even a joke about the late Chairman Mao, or any of their other political leaders, is extremely inappropriate. It is suggested that it is best to listen, ask questions related to your particular business for being in the PRC, and leave it at that.

❑ The Chinese are punctual, and you should arrive promptly on time for each meeting.
❑ The Chinese do not like to be touched or slapped on the back or even to shake hands. A slight bow and a brief shake of the hands is more appropriate.
❑ In China, the family name is always mentioned first. For example, Teng Hsiao-ping should be addressed as Mr. Teng.
❑ During one's stay in the PRC, a visitor could be invited to a dinner in a restaurant by the organization that is sponsoring the visit. The guest should arrive on time or even perhaps a little early. The host would normally toast the guest at an early stage of the meal with the guest reciprocating after a short interval. During the meal, alcoholic beverages should not be consumed until a toast has been made. It is a custom to toast other persons at the table throughout the meal. At the end of the dinner, the guest of honor makes the first move to depart. The usual procedure is to leave shortly after the meal is finished. Most dinner parties usually end by 8:30 or 9:00 in the evening.

- It is customary to use business cards in the PRC, and it is recommended that one side be printed in Chinese. Americans or foreign businesspersons traveling to Beijing via Hong Kong can easily have these cards printed in a matter of hours in that city.
- The Chinese generally believe that foreign businesspersons will be highly qualified technically in their specific areas of expertise. The Chinese businessperson does not need to show his or her intellectual expertise or to make an impression on the foreign guest. The foreign businessperson who is a true professional will have discreet but lavish attention showered on him or her while in China.
- The Chinese businessperson traditionally places much emphasis on proper etiquette. It is recommended that the qualities that foreign businesspersons possess going to the PRC are dignity, reserve, patience, persistence, and a sensitivity to and respect for Chinese customs and temperament.
- The Chinese generally give preference to companies with long-standing relationships with state trading companies. Newcomers and new business organizations have to adjust to the Chinese style of arranging and negotiating contracts.
- Very often, several visits to the PRC are necessary to consummate any business transaction. The foreign businessperson should realize this. It has been found by many American businesspeople that three, four, and five business negotiating sessions are often required to finalize the negotiations.
- Traders coming to sell products in China must be prepared to spend a much longer time than buyers, and may find themselves waiting for appointments day after day. This is when one must exhibit patience, and perseverance, as well as a sensitivity to Chinese customs and way of doing business.

Guidelines for Doing Business in the PRC

- The foreign businessperson should not focus on the individual Chinese person, but rather on the group of individuals who are working for a particular goal. If a Chinese individual is singled out as possessing unique qualities, this could very well embarrass the person.
- The visitor should also behave in a non-condescending manner. The people from the PRC have had their experience in the past with Western imperialism and superiority.
- Generally, in discussions with Chinese, the foreigner should avoid "self centered" conversation in which "I" is excessively used. The Chinese view with contempt the individual who strives to display personal attributes.
- The Chinese are somewhat more reticent, retiring, reserved, or shy when compared with North Americans. They avoid open displays of

It is customary to use business cards in the PRC, and it is recommended that one side be printed in Chinese.

affection and the speaking distance between two people in non-intimate relationships is greater than in the West.

❑ Chinese are not a "touching" society, and in this respect, they are very similar to North Americans; nor do they appreciate loud, boisterous behavior.

❑ Telephone calls and fax machines are a vital part of business. But Chinese think that important business is only conducted face to face.

John Frankenstein states:[16]

Business savvy and cultural sensitivity are needed for success, and preparing a manager adequately for his stay in China could make the difference between merely servicing and succeeding.

Finally, it is wise for global managers to remember that in all developing nations—from Asia to Africa—Westerners should never denigrate traditional beliefs and practices that are still fundamental to the culture.

INDIA

INDIA—PROFILE

Population	1 billion
Ethnic Groups	72% Indo Aryan, 25% Dravidian, 3% Mongoloid/Other
Religions	Hindu, Muslim, Christian, Sikh, Buddhist, Jains
Languages	15 major languages with English as link
Education	52% literacy
Land	1,269,219 mi^2
Government	Federal Republic
Political Parties	Congress (I), Lok Dal, Janata, Communist (CPI), (AIADMK), others
Per Capita Income	US$ 380
Exports to U.S.	$3,500 million
Imports from U.S.	$6,700 million

Cultural Characteristics of Business in India[17]

Through the organized efforts of Mahatma Gandhi and other Indians infused with a sense of nationalism, British rule ended in August 1947. In January 1950, the Indian Constitution was promulgated, and the country became a sovereign democratic republic.

Chinese are not a "touching" society, and in this respect, they are very similar to North Americans; nor do they appreciate loud, boisterous behavior.

The government of India is based on the British parliamentary system with a bicameral legislature and executive and judicial branches. India is governed by a council of ministers led by the prime minister (appointed by the president). The ministers and prime minister are responsible to the House of People, the Lok Sabha, which is elected by universal adult franchise. There is an upper House called the Rajya Sabha, i.e. the Senate. Bills submitted by the Prime Minister have to be passed by both the Lok Sabha and the Rajya Sabha before being signed by the President. The bills only become law on the President's signature. The President may return the bills to the legislature for changes that he or she may suggest.

The powers of the government are, in fact, vested in the Prime Minister, who is generally the leader of the majority party in Parliament and usually the lower House, Lok Sabha. Nevertheless, the President is the commander-in-chief of the armed forces and also has the right to fire the Prime Minister in cases of national emergency or lack of confidence. The President has very little executive power.

The government owns and runs many enterprises, such as the airlines, railroads, insurance industry, power facilities, and irrigation projects. However, since 1990 the government has embarked on a program of liberalization. The country has made a move from an import substitution-oriented economy to an export-oriented economy. The government also has the controlling power in the production of metals, steel, chemicals, and engineering equipment. Eighty-five percent of the nation's banking assets are government controlled.

Money supply is managed by the Reserve Bank of India, which is the country's central bank. The unit of currency is the rupee. The Reserve Bank acts as banker to the government, the commercial banks, and some of the financial institutions. The banking system is deeply involved in the industrialization of the country through financing of both fixed assets as well as working capital.

Commercial banks may be classified into five categories: 1) The State Bank of India and its subsidiaries, 2) nationalized banks, 3) foreign banks, 4) non-nationalized Indian scheduled banks, and 5) private banks.

The government policies in recent years have resulted in a turnaround that can only be termed remarkable. Compared to early 1990, when the government had less than $500 in foreign currency reserves to pay for imports, the Reserve Bank is today flush with $20 billion in reserves. India's economy is very weather-dependent as 50% of the country's national income is derived from agriculture and allied activities. The weather also affects the health of the laborers.

In terms of business, the public sector banks, namely the State Bank of India and nationalized banks, occupy a dominating position. The State Bank of India is the biggest commercial bank in the country, and it also carries out some of the functions of the Reserve Bank of India. Some of the larger banks also provide merchant banking service.

The government owns and runs many enterprises, such as the airlines, railroads, insurance industry, power facilities, and irrigation projects.

Since 1950, India's economy has been directed by a series of five-year plans that set goals and allocate resources. Major areas addressed by the plans include electric power generation, irrigation, gas and oil exploration and production.

The industrial economy of India has a public sector and a private sector. The public sector companies are government-run industrial and commercial undertakings, while the private sector is composed of profit-oriented business organizations run increasingly by professional managers. The country has made rapid industrial growth in recent years with capabilities increasing in almost every sphere of industry. Exports have become much more diversified from just agricultural products to textiles, tea, iron ore, spices, and light engineering products.

Foreign trade has become an important part of the Indian economy. Imports include fuel, petroleum, fertilizers, iron and steel, chemicals, machinery, transportation equipment, paper, and gemstones.

There are positive aspects to doing business in India. English is the major language, and there is a large pool of managerial, skilled and semi-skilled labor. There is also a good and developed capital market and a large domestic market. Over the last 10 years, Bangalore, a beautiful city in south central India, has emerged as the Silicon Valley of India. In fact, two thirds of all custom software programming for the U.S. is done in India.

The government updates its trading policy annually and publishes statements accordingly. Corruption, bribes, or payments for "fixing" exist in everyday life and are something that must be dealt with and accepted to get things accomplished. In India, business is based on personal contacts and it is crucial to know the right person in order to get contracts.

India is bounded northwest by Pakistan; north by China, Tibet, Nepal and Bhutan; east by Myanmar (formerly Burma); southeast, south, and southwest by the Indian Ocean.

India is rich in coal, hydroelectric power potentials, industrial raw materials (iron and manganese), and manpower. Like their resources, economic development has occurred in only a few isolated sectors of the economy which many attribute to the constraints of tradition and culture.

There is not enough work for all their people, so poverty is prevalent. With a large adult population labor-saving modern equipment must be balanced with a surplus of labor force. Over the last twenty years, India has implemented intensive population control programs, but none were successful. The high birth rate has been attributed to early marriage, the emphasis placed on bearing sons by the Hindu religion, the security of having children to take care of parents in old age, and the low level of education achieved by the rural masses.

Climate and culture contribute to the high incidence of disease and influence the patterns of work. The hot weather season brings constant dust that results in various infections and eye irritations and limits out-

India is rich in coal, hydroelectric power potentials, industrial raw materials (iron and manganese), and manpower. Like their resources, economic development has occurred in only a few isolated sectors. . . .

door physical activity. The cold, damp, rainy season brings on colds, malaria, and rheumatism. Their practice of vegetarianism contributes to malnutrition and protein deficiencies. The people of India have a general syndrome known as "weakness" brought on by their constant exposure to epidemic diseases such as cholera and typhus, and the malnutrition factor. This syndrome is usually seen more frequently among the wealthy and educated.

India has a great variety of languages, customs, beliefs, and cultures, almost all of which are difficult for a westerner to comprehend. There are 16 official languages (English is one of them) and more than 1400 dialects. Because of a lack of internal transportation the resulting isolation of people has facilitated the growth of separate cultural regions. Language reflects these regional differences and is a problem in achieving national unity. Most languages find their origin in an ancient Indian language call Sanskrit.

Hinduism is not only the principal religion of India, it dominates the culture and relationships. Sometimes it is a source of ethnic conflict. It determines a woman's role in society. Although the Hindu woman's legal position has greatly improved over the years, she is still bound by ancient traditions of behavior that emphasize her absolute dedication, submission, and obedience to her husband and his wishes. This may not be so strictly adhered to in the big cities and westernized circles where women are increasing in the workforce, especially in the professions (doctors, engineers, lawyers) and in government. Her status in the household is low until she has given birth to a male child. Female children are seen as a burden and future debt due to the dowry paid at marriage to the husband's family.

Family and friends have an importance far beyond that to which the West is accustomed. Extended family living is the norm. A friend's role is to "sense" a person's need and to do something about it. To speak one's mind is a sign of friendship.

Astrologers play an important role in India, as the people believe that nothing is accidental and the universe and all living components have a fundamental order.

Social Customs

☐ Social freedom between the sexes is not appreciated very much in India. A stranger should not speak to a woman if he is not acquainted with her or her family.

☐ A stranger will not be expected to help a woman out of a car, boat, etc. as her husband might resent it.

☐ For a young woman to take the hand of a man who is not her husband is objectionable.

Because of a lack of internal transportation the resulting isolation of people has facilitated the growth of separate cultural regions. Language reflects these regional differences and is a problem in achieving national unity.

Hospitality is

universal in India,

and Indians are

tolerant of the

social faux pas of

a foreigner.

- ❏ Bold, emancipated women may dare to indulge in dancing with their husbands, but to dance with anyone who is not her husband would be improper.
- ❏ Use of first name for address should be, as mentioned before, avoided. It is customary to add to the names of the Hindus the affix "ji" as a mark of respect. For instance, Ravi in polite speech becomes Raviji. Here Ravi is the first name but, by adding affix "ji," you are calling the person with respect and, in this instance, use of first name will not be improper.
- ❏ In Bengal, mister is replaced by "Babu." Thus, Ravi Babu = Mr. Ravi.
- ❏ In much of India, in correspondence or invitation cards, the classic Sanskrit prefix "Shriman" for men and "Shrimati" for women are used.
- ❏ The method of greeting depends upon the social status of the persons meeting. A son greets his father usually by bowing down and touching his feet.
- ❏ An American businessperson in India will be considered an equal and, among equals, the usual method used will be to press one's palms together in front of the chest and say "namaste" meaning "greetings to you."
- ❏ Among the other classes of people, educated in western style, shaking hands is acceptable.
- ❏ Hindu women who have been educated usually would not mind shaking hands with men when introduced. However, it is safer not to extend one's hand to a Hindu woman until she takes the initiative and extends her hand first. It is safer to stick with "namaste." This actually is the universal form of greeting in India.
- ❏ Indian food varies from province to province. Hindus in most cases are vegetarians and beef is prohibited for a Hindu. Meat of other kinds is eaten by the Hindus. Tandoori chicken from the north is one of the most popular chicken dishes in India.
- ❏ Among respectable Hindus, the drinking of alcoholic beverages of any kind is considered most degrading. It can be said that traditional Hindus are a nation of water drinkers. While entertaining at home, it is purely with non-alcoholic beverages like tea, coffee, etc. However, in upper middle class and upper class homes alcoholic drinks are not uncommon.
- ❏ Western food is available in all the good hotels. A variety of desserts made out of fruits or milk are also available. Betel leaf (paan in Hindi) is usually taken after a meal to aid the digestion and freshen one's mouth.
- ❏ Hospitality is universal in India, and Indians are tolerant of the social faux pas of a foreigner. The duty of entertaining guests is laid down in religion as of prime importance. A well mannered Hindu will not eat without asking his guest to join him. It is said that satisfaction of a guest will assuredly bring the housekeeper wealth, reputation, long life, and a place in heaven.

- One is not required to take a gift if invited for supper but, if one did, it would be accepted graciously.
- Do not be surprised if you have your meal only with your business partner and not the whole family. Wives and children usually help from the kitchen to make sure that the guest is treated well.
- At home, eating without knives and forks and spoon is not uncommon. People eat with their hands at home.
- If dining with the whole family, wait until everybody is at the table before you start eating. Let the host start eating first before you do or start when you are asked to go ahead.
- Do not get upset if your host asks you several times to have some more food. Simply refuse politely if you don't want more. It is Indian custom to ask repeatedly to make sure their guest does not get up hungry from the table.
- Indian businessmen, in many situations, wear "dhotis." The "dhoti" is a single piece of white cloth about five yards long and three to four feet broad. It is passed round the waist up to half its length, and the other half is drawn between the legs and tucked at the waist. For the upper part of the body they wear long shirts. Due to hot climate most of the year, long overcoats are worn only on special occasions. Sikhs from Punjab wear turbans, which have a religious significance.
- Well-to-do Hindus who wish to appear aristocratic wear long coats like the Rajahs. The long coat, known as "sherwani," has been standardized and is the dress recognized by the government of India for official and ceremonial wear.
- The Hindu lady is extremely loyal to her sari. While most of the modernized Hindu males have adopted the European costume in their outdoor life, Hindu women have kept the sari. The modern sari compares favorably with fashionable clothes of western women.
- For the businessmen visiting India, shirt, trousers, tie, and suit will be proper attire. The Indian climate is hot; therefore, a very light suit in winter is recommended. If a person is in the north during winter, he will find it a little cooler and, again, a light sweater and a jacket will be sufficient.
- Women in public places should avoid wearing shorts or revealing dresses, as it draws unneeded attention.
- The dominant religion in India is Hinduism, which is more than a religion—it is a complete rule of life. India also has Muslims, Parsees, Jains, Buddhists, Sikhs, Christians, and Jews. Hinduism represents approximately 87% of the population. The customs and manners of the Hindus are strongly influenced by religion. Hinduism involves a variety of beliefs, practices, and gods. The rules of Hinduism may be interpreted in many ways, depending on the community. While Hin-

Indian businessmen, in many situations, wear "dhotis." The "dhoti" is a single piece of white cloth about five yards long and three to four feet broad.

duism for thousands of years has had a rigid caste system, where classes determined what a person did in his or her life, things have changed since independence from the British in 1947.

India is a land of contrasts—from ancient practices, like sacred cows and transportation by bullock carts, to modern lifestyles, such as Air India jets and high-technology industrial parks. Yet the remnants of the past influence the present—Hindu myths and philosophy, British infrastructure and practices, European colonial enclaves. The noble teachings of Mahatma Gandhi on non-violence and tolerance are frequently ignored today. Hindu nationalism dominates the government to the exclusion of Moslems; the subcontinent is divided into three antagonistic countries; war threatens with Pakistan over Kashmir; India moves ahead with guided missiles, atomic weapons, and a space program; globalization has led to increased foreign investment into Indian enterprises. Thus, it is difficult for the visitor to understand such contradictions and progress, no less the myriad cultures and languages to be encountered there.

One important thing to remember when going to India: The Indians are very tolerant and will completely accept the fact that you are unfamiliar with their customs and procedures. There is no need to conform to Indian behavior.

India is a land of contrasts—from ancient practices, like sacred cows and transportation by bullock carts, to modern lifestyles, such as Air India jets and high-technology industrial parks.

NON-VERBAL COMMUNICATION AND SOCIAL TIPS

- ❑ Grasping one's own ears expresses repentance or sincerity.
- ❑ Beckoning is done with the palm turned down; pointing is often done with the chin.
- ❑ Backslapping is not a sign of affection.
- ❑ The namaste gesture can be used to signal you've had enough food.
- ❑ American men should not touch women in public, nor talk to a lone woman in public.
- ❑ The left hand is considered unclean. Use the right hand for eating with the fingers or for giving or accepting things.
- ❑ Do not lick postage stamps.
- ❑ Eat willingly with your hand if the occasion calls for it.
- ❑ Don't ask personal questions until you become close to someone.
- ❑ Use titles such as doctor and professor.
- ❑ Whistling is considered impolite.
- ❑ Public displays of affection are inappropriate.
- ❑ Bargain for goods and services.

INDONESIA

Characteristics of Business in Indonesia

Straddling the equator and drenched in rain, Indonesia is a treasure house of natural diversity. Its vast stretches of rain forest—the largest outside the Amazon—contains perhaps the richest and most unusual collection of plants and animals on earth, from elephants to tree kangaroos.

But the world's fourth most populace nation with 200 million people has crammed 60% of them into the Java area. Yet, this tropical crossroads is replete with natural resources still to be fully used. For example, with almost two-thirds of its land covered with forest, the country has become the world's largest exporter of plywood. But logging and farming strip 4,700 square miles annually, adding to fire and pollution problems. While oil and gas exports have driven economic growth, the nation is also a major exporter of zinc, nickel, and copper. Poor infrastructure has limited resource exploitation.[18]

"Bkinneka tunggal Ika" translated "unity through diversity" is the national motto of Indonesia. This nation of islands represents a rich variety of local customs and traditions found among its diverse people.

Indonesia is an archipelago situated across the equator between the continents of Asia and Australia. It is the largest archipelago in the world, with 13,677 islands of which 6,044 are inhabited. It stretches 3,330 miles from east to west, and 1,300 miles from north to south. There are four main island groups in Indonesia. The Greater Sunda

"Bkinneka tunggal Ika" translated "unity through diversity" is the national motto of Indonesia.

Islands are composed of Java, which has population of 80 million; Sumatra, which is the sixth largest island in the world; and two other large islands. The other three groups of islands include the Lesser Sunda Islands, the Malukus, and West Iran.

Formerly known as the Dutch East Indies, Indonesia remained the territory of the Netherlands until 1942 when it was occupied by the Japanese. Although Indonesia gained its independence in 1945, it continued to struggle with intermittent guerrilla warfare until 1949 in order to gain total independence from the Dutch. In 1949, the Dutch transferred sovereignty of nearly all of the land of the Dutch East Indies except West Iran, which is now known as the Netherlands New Guinea. The new country became known as the Republic of Indonesia in 1950, and in 1963 West Iran also became part of the nation. General Suharto, a leader of the counter-coup, was formally made President of Indonesia in 1966. In 1998, because of social unrest, corruption, and financial deterioration, his 32-year rule ended. Corruption and nepotism finally disillusioned the populace lead by young students. Suharto was forced out of the presidential office to be replaced by B. J. Habibie who is distrusted because of ties to the previous discredited regime.

During the 1980s, there was apparent economic progress in Indonesia. However, as the decade of the '90s closed, the Indonesian economy was in ruins with pervasive corruption, millions sinking back into poverty and hunger, exceptional natural disasters, chaos in the explosion of long-suppressed pluralistic politics and a society threatening to fragment along ethnic and religious lines. In August 1999 East Timor voted for independence. The Indonesian military quickly moved in forcing many to seek refuge on neighboring islands. While many politicians seek to curb the grip of the Chinese minority over the country's commercial life, the price of rice rose because of El Niño and the people starve. Such "hunger breeds racial bigotry, a search for scapegoats, and fear of authoritarian backlash."[19]

Indonesia is the largest Islamic land in the world. Generally, people do not strictly adhere to the rules of the Koran, rather the village law or Adat prevails in Indonesian rural and urban areas. Even though Indonesia is a Moslem country, women have never been veiled, nor have they been secluded like other Moslem women in the Middle East. On many of the islands, women vote and hold leadership positions. However, women have been guaranteed full and complete rights, although Indonesia is a male-dominated country. Education of women is a problem with women comprising only 30% of the students at the university or college level. Thus, with this disparity in education, the Indonesian woman's position is behind that of her male counterpart.

Cultural Characteristics

The family is the basic unit of Indonesian life. It is a highly complex system with many interlocking relationships in the vast network of an

Indonesia is the largest Islamic land in the world.

extended family system. For most Indonesians, the family is the first priority. There are many young people in Indonesia, with nearly 70% of the total population under 30 years of age. The customary law or Adat permits polygamy, but it is not practiced by many persons. In December, 1973, a bill was passed requiring free consent for girls with the minimum age of 16 and for boys with the minimum age of 19 in the sharing of property acquired in marriage. In the case of divorce, the children are often assigned to the custody of both parents.

A basic concept in Indonesian daily life both in a social and a business context is the importance of avoiding making someone feel *malu*. The word literally means ashamed, insulted or embarrassed. Criticizing or contradicting a person in front of others will cause you to lose face and the person will feel *malu* as a result of your action.

Also important to Indonesians are the concepts of unity and conformity. They do not strive, as many Americans do, to become individualistic.

Behavior Modes

A common courtesy that should be respected is not raising one's voice or demonstrating externally intense emotions. Head-on confrontations are embarrassing to most Indonesians. Thus, they prefer to talk indirectly and ambiguously about areas of difference until common ground can be found. *Sembah* or *hormat* is the art of paying respect to one's superiors who are generally persons of higher rank or position either by birth, by economic status, or by age. One form of demonstrating sembah or hormat is by not questioning one's superiors.

In Indonesia, there is a subtle but very hierarchical approach to interpersonal relationships that is related not only to family and to the village, but also to the larger community and to the government. Leadership is very paternalistic and consensus is the mode followed by all persons. Young persons defer to old people, though in the cities this is changing somewhat. Indonesians are known for their friendly hospitality.

It is suggested that foreigners working in Indonesia never refuse an offer for food or drink, but at the same time to not appear greedy; it is customary not to finish it completely.

Gestures and Greetings

There are certain gestures that should be avoided while in Indonesia. For example, never touch the head of an older Indonesian as it is thought to be the place where the spirit resides. Kissing and embracing in public should also be avoided because it is considered rude and coarse. In addition, personal questions should not be asked as this may be interpreted by Indonesians as an invasion of privacy. The use of the left hand for eating or for passing of gifts should be avoided because it is considered the unclean hand. Pointing is also considered rude in Indone-

A basic concept in Indonesian daily life both in a social and a business context is the importance of avoiding making someone feel malu. The word literally means ashamed, insulted or embarrassed.

sia, and therefore should be avoided. Handshakes are becoming customary in Jakarta among Westernized Indonesians. However, in general, there is no physical contact especially for different genders and ages. The traditional greeting is a nodding of the head and a gracious smile.

Business Interactions

Indonesians are extremely indirect in business contexts. Therefore, it is very important to circumvent a subject before the critical issues are mentioned. Everything is negotiated in Indonesia, and the people love to bargain. With the exception of department stores, there are few fixed prices. Once a person is respected as a bargainer, a merchant will offer far more reasonable prices.

Indonesians do not like to be pressured or hurried. Time in the United States can be wasted, spent, utilized, and saved. In contrast, time in Indonesia is viewed as a limitless pool. There is a phrase in Indonesia describing this concept that translates as "rubber time," so that time stretches or shrinks and is therefore very flexible.

The national language of Indonesia, Bahasa Indonesia, was officially adopted in 1928. At the time of this decision, Bahasa Indonesia was a regional language spoken by only 5% of the total population of Indonesia. To achieve a higher ideal of the unity of the Indonesian people, the major sub-races such as Javanese (14%), Sudanese (14%), and others pushed aside their regional feelings and adopted the idea of a common language.

Indonesians are extremely indirect in business contexts. Everything is negotiated in Indonesia, and the people love to bargain.

JAPAN

JAPAN—PROFILE

Population	125 million
Ethnic Groups.................	Japanese (99.4%) Other, mostly Korean (0.6%)
Religions	Shinto and Buddhist, 16% belong to other faiths
Education	99% Literacy
Land	143,000 miles^2
Government	Constitutional Monarchy
Political Parties	Liberal Democratic (LDP), Japan Socialist (JSP), Democratic Socialist (DSP), Japan Communist (JCP), Clean Government (CGP), New Liberal Club (NLC), Social Democratic Federation (SDF)
Per Capita Income	US$ 41,019
Exports to U.S.	$65,500 million
Imports from U.S.	$121,600 million

"Japan Perplexes the World." These are the first four words that Karel van Wolferen,[20] a European journalist who has worked in Japan more than twenty-five years, wrote about Japan. He states that Japan does not work as it appears, and there is even more reason to be concerned about the economic power of the Japanese than some realize.

Because Japan is going through profound economic and social change within a generation, its cultural specifics must be viewed in that context.[21]

Japanese markets are indeed hard, but not impossible to crack, as McDonald's, Coca-Cola, IBM, and many others have demonstrated. Informal protection, in the form of close linkages between supplier and customer, is a handicap to outsiders. As *The Economist* (December 12, 1987) observed:

❑ The Japanese are not a rational people in the sense economists use that term—they will sacrifice their interests as consumers for the nation as a whole; they will make spending decisions on the basis of who is selling, not on the basis of what is sold; in short, they would rather pay more for something than less for it.

❑ The Japanese are prone to value quality and reliability to a degree that Westerners find hard to understand, and then insist on high standards of after-sales service. They also place a premium on long-term relations with customers and suppliers, or trustworthiness.

❑ The Japanese society is more "cartelized" than America, so that people at the same level in different organizations know each other from school days and are comfortable doing business with one another—with a minimum of explanation and a maximum of cooperation.

Yet, realities of their participation in the international market are causing changes in such cultural preferences, especially among the new generation.

Cultural Characteristics of Business in Japan

Asia is a polyglot of nations and cultures, so it is difficult to generalize about its diverse peoples and their mindsets. Japanese behavior may seem puzzling and a source of both confusion and wonderment. For North Americans perched on the Pacific Rim, Japan is the epitome of the East and its enigmas.

Japanese feudal society lasted until the 19th century when Commodore Perry's voyage forced open Japan to the West. Typically a series of changing images about the Japanese people and culture emerge, and can be grouped around stages. The first is pre-World War II, when the Japanese were admired for their ambitious effort to catch up to European and American industrialization. At this stage and the next, many viewed Japanese diplomatic endeavors as devious.

For North Americans perched on the Pacific Rim, Japan is the epitome of the East and its enigmas.

During World War II, the image shifted as Americans and others were abashed by the daring Japanese attack upon Pearl Harbor, and puzzled by continued loyalty to their Emperor even in defeat. Finally, in the present post-war period, many find it hard to believe that these victims of atomic devastation and military occupation could bounce back and become a leading superindustrial nation.

The following cultural characteristics apply to doing business in Japan.

Language and Communication

❑ Indirect and vague is more acceptable than direct and specific references—ambiguous terminology is preferred.

❑ Sentences frequently are left unfinished so that another make may a conclusion.

❑ Conversation transpires within ill-defined and shadowy context, never quite definite so as not to preclude personal interpretation.

❑ The language is capable of delicate nuances regarding states of mind and relationships—while rich in imagination, it can be clumsy for science and business.

❑ There are layers of soft language with various degrees of courtesy and respect. The female is especially affected by this; "plain" or "coarse" language is considered improper for her.

❑ The listener makes little noises of tentative suggestion, understanding, and encouragement—"hai" may mean more than "yes" and imply, "I'm listening," or, "I understand."

❑ There is a formal politeness for official negotiation and ordinary business communication, while an informal approach may be used while socializing. Frequently, while entertaining, the real business and political deals are concluded.

Dress and Appearance

❑ Neat, orderly, and conservative for managers; ordinary workers and students frequently wear a distinctive uniform and even a company pin, which managers also may sport (holdover from feudal days when a kimono carried a lord's symbol). The ancient, classical dress, the kimono, is becoming less common even in the privacy of the home, and is retained for ceremonial events. Western formal dress is used for important state occasions.

❑ Traditional native dress is sexless although the shape of the garment is different. The colors are often neutral with women sometimes tending toward flowery patterns.

❑ Japanese wear contemporary clothes and hair styles. Also they appear to be physically larger than their parents.

❑ Colors have different significance in Japanese culture (e.g., white for sorrow, black for joy).

The language is capable of delicate nuances regarding states of mind and relationships— while rich in imagination, it can be clumsy for science and business.

TIPS FOR BUSINESS INTERACTIONS WITH THE JAPANESE

❏ Japanese will try to achieve sales and profits without harming face and harmony and creating a poor standing in the business community.

❏ Third party or indirect introductions are important and can create trust between individuals who come together through a mutual friend, go-between or arbitrator. This person may be involved until the conclusion of the negotiation.

❏ Whomever you approach in the organization, do so at the highest level; the first person contacted is also involved throughout the negotiation.

❏ Avoid direct communication on money; leave this to the go-between or lower echelon staff.

❏ Never put a Japanese in a position where he or she must admit failure or impotency.

❏ Avoid praise of your product or services; let your literature or go-between do that.

❏ Use business cards with your titles, preferably in both Japanese and English.

❏ The logical, cognitive, or intellectual approach is insufficient; the emotional level of communication is considered important (e.g., as in dealing with a known business associate vs. a stranger).

❏ Formality prevails in senior staff meetings with interpreters present. The more important the meeting, the more senior executives present.

❏ Wait patiently for meetings to move beyond preliminary tea and inconsequential talk.

Eating is more ritualistic, communal, and time consuming. The interaction is considered as important as the food.

Food and Eating Habits

❏ Eating is more ritualistic, communal, and time consuming. The interaction is considered as important as the food.

❏ Tokyo is said to have a restaurant, bar, or cabaret for every 110 members of the population with many international foods represented. Fast food establishments are everywhere.

❏ Traditional diet emphasizes rice and fish.

❏ The youth tend toward popular Western foods and accouterments for eating.

❏ Avoid bringing your wife to a business dinner, even if a Japanese host invites her out of politeness.

❏ Learning to drink alcohol in public without offense is one of the important accomplishments that a young Japanese would-be executive must learn.

Time and Age Consciousness

❏ Japanese are punctual yet they expect you to wait for group decisions that take time.
❏ In negotiating a licensing agreement, it may take three years for a decision, but once made, the Japanese may be ready to go into production within a few weeks (unless this point of decision is followed by quick action, the Japanese may criticize the Westerner for "endless delay and procrastination").
❏ Respect seniority and the elderly.
❏ Young managers, recruited from the universities after stiff examinations, are expected to stay with a company until they are sixty years of age, conforming, doing what's expected of them, and showing respect and deference. Then the crucial decision is made as to whether the sixty year-old manager is to become a company director; if he or she makes it, he or she can stay beyond the normal Western retirement age and may work into his or her 80s. The remainder of the managerial group not so selected become department or subsidiary directors and are expected to retire at 55–60, though even then they can be retained in a temporary capacity.

Reward and Recognition

❏ There is a tendency away from individual reward and toward recognition to the group or organization.
❏ Great emphasis is placed on security, as well as a social need for "belonging."
❏ Money, if passed to a Japanese businessperson, should be in an envelope.
❏ For social visiting, a guest is frequently given a present or small gift, such as a hand towel beautifully wrapped; however, on the next exchange of visit, you are expected to offer a gift in kind.
❏ Personal relationships score high with Japanese and future relationships depend on how you respond in the first encounter.
❏ Cut and dry relationships with business contacts are inadequate and must be supplemented by a social relationship for maximum effect. This is usually entertaining the client for a "night on the town," and not at one's home. Part of the Japanese manager's reward is a generous budget for entertaining. When away from home on business, the Japanese businessperson expects to be entertained lavishly (theater tickets, etc.) but repays this kindness manifold.

Relationships

❏ Cohesive and crowded in a California-size nation—this accounts for rituals of bowing, politeness, etc. in crowded urban areas.

Personal relationships score high with Japanese and future relationships depend on how you respond in the first encounter.

- Familial and group oriented, instead of individualistic.
- Youth epitomize the culture in change—energetic, productive, yet anxious for change; gaining a new sense of "I/my/me-ness" while the pattern for others is "we-ness."
- Group leadership regarded more than individual initiative—tendency toward clannishness based on family or group connections, know your place and be comfortable with it.
- Drive toward agglomeration, combines, clustering of organizational relationships.
- Sense of order, propriety, and appropriate behavior between inferiors and superiors.
- International relationships—close emotional and economic ties to U.S. but suspicious of aggressive Americans; they mistrust China, yet they are emotionally allied and identify with the Chinese.
- In business relationships, there are two Japans—officialdom and the intellectuals (e.g., politicians and businesspersons). In both, decisions tend to be group mulling for consensus, give and take inconclusiveness, and the traditional authority pyramid.
- Symbiotic relationship between government and business—cozy but not constricting.
- Social and self control disguise highly emotional quality of Japanese character and relationships; mesh of binding social relationships weakening and hard to comprehend.
- Even riots, especially among the more rebellious youths, can be orderly, well-conducted public events staged within a mutually accepted framework of a dangerous game.
- In context of social relations, Japanese tend to be clean, polite, and disciplined; but publicly with strangers, can be pushy and inconsiderate (e.g., the tourist).
- Sensitive to what others think or expect of the individual and have a sharp sense of right and wrong; yet find it difficult to deal with the unexpected and strange and so may laugh inappropriately.
- The general gap between the generations is very wide. In business, it is somewhat bridged for the young manager who is assigned an elder, who is an upper middle manager, fifty-five years old or more. This senior person is rarely the direct superior of the young manager, but is expected to know him or her, meet regularly, and be available for advice and counsel, and to assist in transfers and discipline, when necessary. This respected elder manager is always consulted on promotions and other personnel matters concerning that young person's career. He or she is the human contact for the organization with the young manager, the listener and guide who provides a significant human relationship.

In business relationships, there are two Japans—officialdom and the intellectuals (e.g., politicians and businesspersons). In both, decisions tend to be group mulling for consensus. . . .

Myths about Dealing with Japanese Business Organizations

- ❑ Your company has more know-how and they must learn from us, not vice versa.
- ❑ The on-the-job training of American managers abroad can be combined with their simultaneous roles as trainers of our Japanese staff.
- ❑ The American "Asian expert" is the best person to handle our company relations with Japan.
- ❑ To overcome our lack of knowledge of the Japanese language, all we need is an interpreter to get on with building our Japanese subsidiary and developing amicable rapport with other Japanese companies and government agencies.
- ❑ The best place to recruit capable Japanese managers for our subsidiary in Japan is in the United States among Japanese now studying or seeking jobs.
- ❑ To transfer Japanese to the home office in the U.S. for management training and study tours will allow for sufficient transfer of our management practices into their situation.
- ❑ The Japanese need our management skills, so the best way to transplant them is by direct investment.
- ❑ In some companies, a Japanese management recruit is sent to a company training institute for orientation in spiritual awareness, consciousness, and company pride. Even laborers are sometimes sent to Buddhist temples for several days of Zen meditation, interspersed with lectures on religion and company policy.
- ❑ The typical Japanese company attitude is for total employee involvement in return for company gymnasium facilities, free medical care, commuting allowances, subsidized lunches, cut rate groceries, bachelor quarters, low-rent apartments for married employees and sometimes help from their marriage brokers and counselors.

The Japanese character is diverse with a sense of poetry and of the ephemeral; there is a concern for the transitory, inconclusive qualities of life, for nature, and its observation.

Attitudes and Beliefs

- ❑ The Japanese character is diverse with a sense of poetry and of the ephemeral; there is a concern for the transitory, inconclusive qualities of life, for nature, and its observation. It is actively curious, energetic and quick, with a sense of delicacy and wistfulness.
- ❑ These great lovers of success are extremely adaptable—basically, they do not resist change, and are open to new technology.

- Fundamentally, the Japanese have little concern for theology or philosophy, and seemingly substitute the family in this regard. Although realists, they are like their island homeland—a floating world that changes course.
- The dominant religious thrust is the convergence of Shintoism and Buddhism (married Shinto, buried Buddhist). Christianity has had limited impact. The crusading Soka Gakkai sect is also a political party that fights inequalities of the social structure, while enshrining the idealistic, self-denial, and the espousal of the underdog.

Business Attitudes

- Increasing concern for acquisition of second generation management skill, not simply technical, knowledge of products, or manufacturing, but sophisticated management theory and concepts transferred to the Japanese environment. This is forcing changes in the way of dealing with foreigners. A more competitive climate is developing for foreigners that permits direct investment.

Fundamentally, the Japanese have little concern for theology or philosophy, and seemingly substitute the family in this regard.

JAPANESE LIFETIME EMPLOYMENT IS NOT AS SIMPLE AS IT SEEMS:

- Not all workers are considered permanent. A substantial body of employees (perhaps 20%) are not subject to this job security. Some positions are hired and paid for by the hour; women are generally considered in the temporary work category, and some who retire at fifty-five may be kept on in that temporary capacity: adjustments in work force can be readily made among these "temporaries."
- Pay as a rule is on the basis of seniority and doubles every fifteen years.
- Retirement is a two-year salary, severance bonus, usually at fifty-five. Western pension plans are beginning to come into companies slowly and are low in benefits.
- Permanent employees who leave an employer will have a very difficult time being permanent again for another employer.
- The whole concept of permanent employment is left over from feudal arrangements of the past, and is now being undermined by super industrial developments.

Values and Standards

The Japanese personality generally is self-confident and flexible, demonstrating a sense of order, propriety, and appropriate behavior.... Japanese value congenial, known surroundings and seek to create an atmosphere of well-focused energy and disciplined good cheer.

❑ The Japanese personality generally is self-confident and flexible, demonstrating a sense of order, propriety, and appropriate behavior; there is a tendency toward diligence and thrift, balanced by a fun-loving approach which, at times, seems almost frivolous and extravagant.

❑ In outlook the Japanese are cautious and given to stalling tactics, as well as being insular, manifested by the ingroup tendency.

❑ The rigid, ossified Japanese class system by which each person has his or her place as superior or inferior is disappearing.

❑ Japanese value peace and economic progress, ensured somewhat by the fact that only 1% of the nation's gross national product is devoted to defense spending.

❑ This culture highly regards new ideas and technologies, swallowing them up until they are Japanized (internalized) after careful, detailed examination; there is a subtle shift of emphasis from copying to creating underway.

❑ Japanese society values training and education, especially of the young. It also values a spirit of intensity and craftsmanship manifested by a quality of deep penetration and pride in work no matter how humble.

❑ Japanese value congenial, known surroundings and seek to create an atmosphere of well-focused energy and disciplined good cheer.

❑ A basic standard of Japanese life is work and play hard—work particularly for the good of the family or company family, and maintain controlled competition and cooperation in the process.

❑ The yen is mightier than the sword.

❑ Japanese fear foreign military involvement.

❑ The radical, revolutionary portion of Japanese youth have an entirely different set of values from the majority—they can be vicious and violent, yet espouse a spirit of self-denial, self-correction, self-dedication to what they consider a high cause. Even criminal gangs will publicly apologize in press conferences to the public when they cause too much violence and disruption in society.

❑ Generally, the Japanese are moved to heroically inspired deeds, rather than charity or noblesse oblige.

❑ The goals of Japanese society seem to be steady employment, corporate growth, product superiority, and national economic welfare, which is considered more important than profits; the goals of the individual seem to be "more" for the organization and for self, in that order.

❑ Corporate social responsibility is a standard built into the Japanese system: increasingly Japanese companies are giving a percentage of profits to promote education, social welfare, culture and protection of the environment.

❑ Another organizational standard is to provide psychological security in the job, in return for loyalty to the company; there is a concept of mutual obligation between employer and employee. Strikes are only beginning to creep into the work culture.

❑ The seniority standard is slowly giving way to merit promotion.

❑ The Japanese value decision by consensus. Before action is taken, much time is spent on defining the question. They decide first if there is a need for a decision and what it is all about. The focus is upon what the decision is really about, not what it should be; once agreement is reached, then the Japanese move with great speed to the action stage. Referral of the question is made to the appropriate people, in effect indicating top management's answer to the question. The system forces the Japanese to make big decisions and to avoid the Western tendency toward small decisions that are easy to make (minutia). For example, instead of making a decision on a particular joint venture, the Japanese might consider the direction the business should go, and this joint venture is then only a small aspect of the larger issue. By emphasizing the importance of understanding alternative solutions, the Japanese seem to avoid becoming prisoners of their own preconceived answers.

Another standard of Japanese work life seems to be *continuous training*.

❑ It is performance focused in contrast to Western promotion focused; in scope, it involves training not only in one's own job, but in all jobs at one's level.

❑ The emphasis is on productivity and the real burden of training is on the learner—"What have we learned to do the job better?"

❑ On the whole, they believe the older worker is more productive, and output per man-hour is invariably higher in a plant with an older work population.

❑ The industrial engineer teaches how to improve one's own productivity and process.

❑ Generally, there are no craft unions in Japanese industry and little mobility among blue collar workers; what mobility exists is among office workers and professionals.

❑ Education is seen as a preparation for life, rather than life itself; those with "graduate education" are generally too old to start in the Japanese work system, and when employed they come in as specialists.

The Japanese are a remarkable and unique people. Their subtle, complex culture in particular, illustrates the differences and diversity of Asian cultures in general. The Japanese have learned and successfully applied many lessons from Americans.

Generally, there are no craft unions in Japanese industry and little mobility among blue collar workers....

MALAYSIA

MALAYSIA-PROFILE	
Population	24.8 million
Ethnic Groups	Malay 59%, Chinese 32%, Indian 10%, Other 1%
Religions	Muslim, Buddhist and Hindu
Education.......................	Compulsory 7 Years (6–13 Years) Literacy 83.5%
Land..............................	127,320 miles^2
Government	Constitutional Monarchy
Political Parties...............	Main parties are: National Front, United Malaysia National Organization (UMNO), Malaysian Chinese Association, United Traditional Bunnipictra Party, Malaysian Indian Congress
Per Capita Income	US$ 4,360
Exports to U.S.	US$ 10.8 billion
Imports from U.S.	US$ 18.8 billion

Budi surrounds the ethical system of the Malay people. Its basic rules are respect and courtesy, especially towards elders, and affection and love for one's parents. . . .

Cultural Characteristics of Business in Malaysia

At the end of British rule in 1963, the Federation of Malaysia consisted of 13 states, 11 of which are part of peninsular Malaysia and the 2 states of Sabah and Sarawak are characterized by flat coastal plains rising to steep mountain ranges. Malaysia's major exports are rubber, tin, palm oil, timber, and petroleum; the major imports are machinery, transportation equipment, and consumer goods.

Kuala Lumpur is the capital of Malaysia and is the location of the federal parliament and the prime minister. In addition, each of the 13 state governments has parliaments and prime ministers and 9 have sultans. The present government policy promotes Malay participation in business and the dispersal of industry to less developed areas. The government is a parliamentary democracy under a constitutional monarchy.

Cultural Concepts

The fundamental concept of *Budi* surrounds the ethical system of the Malay people. *Budi* illustrates the ideal behavior expected of a Malay. Its basic rules are respect and courtesy, especially towards elders, and affection and love for one's parents, as well as a pleasant disposition and harmony in the family, the neighborhood, and in the society. There are two forms of *Budi: Adab*, which means that the individual has a responsibility to show courtesy at all times; and *Rukun*, which means that the individual must act to obtain harmony either in a family or in society. Malays place the utmost importance on relationships with relatives, friends, and colleagues.

Malays do not seem to value the pursuit of wealth for its own sake. They do, however, believe in hard work and self-reliance. Life is viewed as a passing thing, and family and friends take precedence over self-centered interests, such as the accumulation of profit and materialism. The Malays' love for children is reflected in the gentle and tender manner in which they raise them.

Gestures and Greetings

There are several forms of nonverbal communication that one observes while in Malaysia that will be helpful. Familiarity with greetings and certain gestures to avoid will lead to a more successful business trip. The following are a few examples:

❑ When meeting a Malay, the elder person should be mentioned before the younger, the more important before the less important, and the woman before the man.
❑ In rural areas, it is customary for men and women to shake hands with each other. When meeting a man, a Malay woman may *salaam*, which is bowing very low while placing the right palm on the forehead, and then covering their hands if they believe that a person is unaware of the social etiquette pertaining to handshaking. The traditional Malay greeting resembles a handshake with both hands but without the grasp. The man offers both hands to his friend, lightly touches his friend's outstretched hands, and then brings his hands to his breast. This simply means that "I greet you from my heart."
❑ In Malaysia, instead of pointing to a place, object, or person with the right index finger, which is considered impolite, it is more common to point with the thumb of the right hand with the fingers folded under.
❑ In calling for a taxi, one uses the fingers of the right hand, moving them together with the palm facing down in a waving or "come here" gesture, which is opposite to the typical American beckoning of a taxi.
❑ A gesture to avoid is patting a child on the head. The head is considered to be the center of the intellectual and sacred power, and is therefore holy and should not be touched.

Religion

Islam is the predominant religion in Malaysia and exerts a great influence not only on the method of worship but the Malay's way of life. Foreign business representatives hoping to function effectively in Malaysia must understand Islam to comprehend the culture. Whereas

Malays do not seem to value the pursuit of wealth for its own sake. They do, however, believe in hard work and self-reliance.

Americans' religious practices are generally confined to Sundays, Malays' religious practices are part of daily life.

A Muslim is guided by the prescriptions of the Koran that details the rules of behavior that include all social and business activities. Muslims are expected to recite the creed, "There is no God but Allah, and Muhammad is his Prophet." They must pray five times a day and worship Allah as the only true God. Providing charity, helping the needy, fasting during the month of Ramadan, and if possible, making a trip to Mecca are additional practices that the Muslim Malays are expected to perform. They should also refrain from eating pork or drinking alcoholic beverages. In the main portion of the Mosque, the Muslim place of worship, Malay women sit apart from the men and are not allowed at any time to mix casually or to eat with them.

Malays deeply respect traditional customs but, in some cases, these customs do not complement their religion. In these instances, the practices of Islam have been adapted to fit more effectively with the traditional customs. These traditional practices and beliefs are called *Adat,* the Malay word for custom. The importance of these *Adat* are illustrated by their proverb, "Let the child perish but not the *Adat.*"

Nature and Human Nature

In some Western cultures an underlying belief exists that humanity can overcome nature. In the Islamic faith, the Malay position concerning human relationship to nature is one of being subject to or living in harmony with nature. At times, a Malay feels subject to the elements because of a fatalistic attitude and belief of the supremacy of God's will. A Malay also believes that he or she is part of the natural world that reflects his or her belief in animism—the notion that plants and animals have a spiritual dimension.

A Malay pays little attention to what has happened in the past and regards the future as both vague and unpredictable.

A Malay pays little attention to what has happened in the past and regards the future as both vague and unpredictable. Planning for the future or hoping that the future will be better than either the present or the past is simply not their way of life.

Malays, generally, are not very ambitious. In the past, the chances of a Malay succeeding in worldly terms were small and did not depend on the efforts of the individual. Furthermore, if in fact one did succeed, there were laws that prohibited the accumulation of wealth by Malay peasants. From the perspective of the Islamic faith, there is a strong sense of fatalism as indicated by the common expressions such as "God willing" or "If God wants me to be something I will, if not, God's will be done." These factors favor a lack of motivation for worldly success, which is replaced by a motivation to develop deep and lasting relationships with friends and relatives. Traditionally, Malays have felt that in receiving material success, they might lose the highly valued respect of their family and friends.

Trust, Respect, and Leadership

Trust for a Malay is fundamental to a successful interpersonal relationship. An individual's capability for loyalty, commitment, and companionship are the key characteristics upon which the Malay generally bases trust. The process for developing trust is internal and personal. In some Western cultures, the basis for trust is external and professional, centered around a level of expertise and performance.

Initially in a relationship, Malays show respect through formalities. However, as a relationship progresses, formalities are slowly dropped until an informal atmosphere is reached. This slow transformation can confuse some businesspersons. Malays respect a compromising person who is willing "to give and take." In Malay negotiations, the person who compromises is the most respected person and will often receive more than anticipated.

In Western organizations and institutions, status is usually attributed to someone demonstrating leadership capabilities. In Malaysia, the process is somewhat reversed. Malays are born into a certain social position or status, and if the status is very high or important, then they are expected to demonstrate leadership capabilities. For a Malay, the most important quality of a leader is confidence and the ability to understand people. A leader in Malaysia is also expected to be religiously devout, humble, sincere, and tactful. Even if a person is not worthy of respect, the position might demand that he or she receive it. A Malay feels most comfortable in a hierarchical structure with a clearly defined role, and emphasis on room for growth in interpersonal relationships.

Work Ethic

In Malaysia, work is viewed as one of many activities. A large percentage of time in a Malay's life is spent developing deeper relationships with family and friends in ways that would appear as idle time to many. An example of this perspective is the treatment of the elderly. An elderly person in Malaysia is regarded as a wise counselor who plays an important role in society.

Malaysia is composed mainly of fishing and farming villages with only a few large cities. This factor has important ramifications concerning their educational and technical abilities. In general, many Malays do not go to college and those who do often major in liberal arts as opposed to business or engineering. Therefore, Malays may lack specialization and technical sophistication.

Politics and Power

Of fundamental importance to anyone working in Malaysia is an understanding of the pluralism in that country. To succeed in Malaysia,

An individual's capability for loyalty, commitment, and companionship are the key characteristics upon which the Malay generally bases trust.

one must understand some of the differences, similarities, and difficulties between the Malays and other Bumiputra, Chinese, and Indians.

After much tension and rioting, a twenty-year development plan favoring the Malays was initiated in 1970 between Malaysia and China. The plan contained two principal economic objectives. First, to check the dominance of Chinese economic control by requiring a definite percent of the labor force to be Malay. Second, the plan stated that the foreign share of the Malay market would be reduced from 60% to 30% by 1990. In spite of the efforts toward modernization and education, results have not been completely satisfactory. Even though there will be a decrease in the Malay market allocated to foreign investors, there is still room for expansion of the present foreign-controlled market.

The fact that a near balance of power exists between Malays and Chinese requires close cooperation between the two cultures. However, due to the differences in customs, culture, and values, there has been a great deal of tension between the two groups, at times producing unstable environments. The unpleasant relationship between the Malays and the Chinese appears ongoing, perhaps due to the strong cultural differences between the Chinese Buddhist and Islamic practices of the Malays.

Foreign businesspersons in Malaysia are challenged to apply synergistic skills to their relationships. This will foster not only cooperation between themselves and the Malays, but will contribute to collaboration among the country's diverse inhabitants.

The unpleasant relationship between the Malays and the Chinese appears ongoing, perhaps due to the strong cultural differences between the Chinese Buddhist and Islamic practices of the Malays.

PHILIPPINES

PHILIPPINES—PROFILE

Population	71.8 million
Ethnic Groups	Christian Malay 91.5%, Muslim Malay 4%, Chinese 2%, Other 2% (Polynesian and Spanish cultural influences.)
Religions	Roman Catholic 84%, Protestant 6%, Muslim 5%, Buddhist 3%
Education	6 Years Compulsory (7–12) Literacy about 94.6%
Land	116,000 miles^2
Government	Republic
Political Parties	Democratic Filipino Struggle, Power of EDSA, National Union for Christian Democrats (NUCD), National People's Coalition (NPC)
Per Capita Income	US$ 1,160
Exports to U.S.	$7,417 million
Imports from U.S.	$10,445 million

Cultural Characteristics of Business in the Philippines[23]

For years, the most striking feature of the Philippines was the dogged competition between tragedy and farce. While its neighbors became bywords for economic dynamism, the Philippines became famous for the excess of its rules, for the shanty towns of Manila, for telephones that never worked, and for lights that kept going out. The government's budget is on course with a surplus, and the infrastructure bottlenecks that throttled growth for so long are gradually being tackled. At last, the Philippines look ready to emulate sustained rapid growth enjoyed by much of the region until recently.[24]

In this multicultural society, Filipino or Philipino is the principal language, but English is spoken as well as Chinese.

Hospitality, friendliness, and sincerity are prominent aspects of the Filipino culture. An ambience filled with gaiety is the result of over 300 years of the Spanish influence. Filipinos are predominantly of Malay stock, with Chinese and American cultural influences. The Philippines' 7,000 islands cover approximately 116,000 square miles in the South China Sea. The eleven largest islands comprise over 95% of the total land area and population, with Luzon being the largest island, and Mindanao being the second largest. Although Manila, located on Luzon, is the most well-known area, Quezon City was declared the capital of the Philippines in 1948. However, most government activity still remains in Manila.

Great contrasts in terrain and climate exist throughout the Philippines. Northern Luzon is mountainous, the southern islands are comparatively dry, while other parts are dense jungle areas. In addition, throughout the islands there are a number of volcanoes. The Philippines are located within the tropic zone with the low areas having a warm, humid climate and only slight variations from the average temperature of 80°F. The monsoon season lasts from June to November, and periodic typhoons pass over the island causing immense floods and damage to crops and homes.

The foreign policy of the Philippines is based on a close alliance with many other Asian countries. The major alliance of which the Philippines is a part is ASEAN—the Association of South East Asia Nations.

Western businesspeople have generally reported that the Filipino government is inefficient and that having contacts in high places of government is essential in cutting through the bureaucratic red tape. The people basically work on the "mañana" system, because they seldom complete things on time despite deadlines. However, in their own fashion, things do get done. "Almost, but not quite" is the foreigner's conclusion.

Utang na loob, literally meaning "debt on the inside," is another trait of some Filipinos. A Filipino remains indebted for a favor for a long period of time, perhaps several generations. One maybe asked to respond to a favor that was bestowed upon an ancestor many years ago.

Hospitality, friendliness, and sincerity are prominent aspects of the Filipino culture. An ambience filled with gaiety is the result of over 300 years of the Spanish influence.

The Philippines' economy is based on agriculture, forestry, and fishing, which employ more than half of the total labor force and account for more than 50% of all exports. The agricultural sector consists of the production of food crops essentially for domestic consumption (rice and corn), and cash crops for export. The country's major exports are sugar, copra, copra meal, coconut oil, pineapple, tobacco, and abaca. The Philippines is also one of the world's leading producers of wood and wood products. Although fishing contributes to the Philippines' economy, the fertile fishing area has not been developed to its full potential. The Philippines are rich in mineral resources with nickel, copper, and other mineral deposits among the largest in the world. However, only a small portion of these have been surveyed and exploited. Government programs have recently been initiated to strengthen the industrial development and have included protective import duties and taxes. Until 1970, the U.S. was a leading trading partner of the Philippines. However, trade with Japan has now surpassed that of the U.S. because of considerable tourist and business investments. The Philippines' commitment to free enterprise and friendly relations with Japan and the U.S. continues.

The Philippines' population has more than doubled since it received independence from the United States in 1946. With a population numbering approximately 72 million, the Philippines has one of the highest birth rates in the world. People have come to the Philippines from many Southeast Asian countries, such as Indonesia, Malaysia, and China. The blend of these cultures has formed the Filipino race. The most significant alien ethnic group residing in the Philippines are the Chinese who have played an important role in commerce since the fourteenth century, when they first came to the Philippines to trade.

The present culture strongly reflects Hispanic influence. The education system was influenced by the relationship of the Philippines with the United States from 1898 to 1946. Education is highly valued and there is free, though not compulsory, education through the secondary level. The literacy rate is approximately 94% with a large portion of the nation's budget being spent on education. The Philippines prides itself on its educational system.

The standard of living in the Philippines varies, with only a few families owning a large percentage of the rural and urban real estate. These wealthy few control profitable businesses and the universities, and they live in luxury. Reform, especially in land ownership, progresses slowly.

The Filipinos are a conforming people who rarely create disturbances. Thus, they are willing to go along with conditions rather than trying to change them. Their belief in *pakiksama*, which literally means the ability to get along with people, emphasizes the Filipino attitude of conceding with the majority rather than strongly standing up for his or her personal opinion. Confrontation is avoided. The consequences of an insult or crime are quick, poetically just, and often violent.

True feelings of the Filipinos are often hidden behind an agreeing facade, and the foreign businessperson in the Philippines should attempt to read these hidden signals that are given. Also, as in the case of many developing countries, a foreign businessperson should be aware that an informal business sector operates underground parallel to the formal sector.

Cultural Concepts

Filipinos generate warmth and friendliness. The everyday greeting for acquaintances and friends is a handshake greeting for men and occasionally a light pat on the back for men, while some women may kiss each other on the cheek. Older people should be shown respect and should always be allowed to take the lead. Filipinos place great importance on the family. The well-being of the family supersedes every other desire, therefore questions concerning the family are very important. The Filipino male does not strive to accumulate money and power for his own sake, but rather to better his family position, although there are some ambitious men and women. Large extended families, including cousins and friends, reflect the great interdependence of the family in the Philippines.

Family corporations, where the management is composed of the nuclear family and all the stockholders are relatives, are numerous. Naturally, nepotism is prevalent. Trust is not easily given to those who do not belong. The *palakasan* system refers to going through connections instead of through the proper channel. Having the right connections can facilitate a deal or employment.

Hiya or shame is an important social force for Filipinos, and the idea is instilled in their children at an early age. To accuse a person of not having this hiya trait is a gross insult because it indicates that a person is unable to feel shame as well as all other emotions. Therefore, it is very important never to criticize another person in public or in front of his friends because it shames him or her, and is thus the greatest of insults.

The negative ramifications of hiya are that the Filipinos avoid change, innovation, or competition simply because if the result is failure, it would cause him to shame his family. Consequently, the Filipino family and the Filipino businessperson will "save face" at any cost.

Success in the mind of the Filipino is often a function of fate rather than individual merit, and therefore, most people are content in their social position only because they feel fate has placed them there. Expressions such as "never mind," "it doesn't matter," or "it was my fate" are common reactions to problems such as typhoons, epidemics, and crop failures. Another demonstration of their belief in fate is that the Filipinos frequently gamble and play games of chance.

Due to the Spanish influence, the Filipinos are a somewhat emotional people, and very sensitive. They are loyal friends and demand the same

The palakasan *system refers to going through connections instead of through the proper channel. Having the right connections can facilitate a deal or employment.*

kind of loyalty in return. This aspect is reflected in social situations, as well as business interactions. They are reluctant to share or to do business with a person unless there is a mutual sincerity. This has been a great obstacle in the past, as Filipinos have described American businesspeople as being overly aggressive and insensitive to feelings.

The Filipinos are hospitable and enjoy entertaining. When accepting invitations, one should inquire if the starting time is "American time" or "Filipino time." In the case of American time, one should arrive at the hour requested. However, if the arrival time is on Filipino time, it is not necessary to arrive until an hour or two later than requested. However, for sit-down dinner with a limited number of guests, one is expected to be on time.

The concept of individualism is valued by the Filipinos. If a foreign businessperson fails to treat a Filipino as an individual, the foreigner will be refused help. It is important to take time to talk with adults and children and not be judgmental. The Filipinos will make every effort to maintain their reputation as being a hospitable people. In return, foreign businesspeople should be polite and respectful towards the Filipinos.

Although a moral double standard for males and females is still prevalent in the Philippines, the country prides itself on being one of the few Asian countries with a large percentage of women in government and politics. Also, women as well as men inherit property in contrast to other Asian countries.

Nonverbal Communication

There are several nonverbal communication techniques used in the Philippines, and the following are some examples that can be helpful in a business context. The raising of the eyebrows indicates an affirmative reply, namely a "yes." A jerk of the head downward means "I don't know," while a jerk upward means "yes." Like the Japanese, the Filipinos rarely say "no" as we do. They resist confrontation and may say "yes" verbally while putting their head downward, namely a nonverbal signal for "I don't know." To indicate "come here" one would extend the hand out with the palm down moving the fingers in and out as in a scratching motion.

Religion

The Philippines is the only predominantly Christian country in the Far East, primarily due to the Spanish influence. Over 84% of all Filipinos are Roman Catholic, which affects their culture and daily activities. The second largest church in the Philippines is the *Iglesia ni Cristo* or Church of Christ. There is a growing revival of fundamentalism in the country.

The Philippines is the only predominantly Christian country in the Far East, primarily due to the Spanish influence.

A significant minority striving for human and religious rights is the one and a half million Filipinos who are Moslems. In southern areas of the islands, Islamic practices and militants dominate.

The Idea of Right and Wrong

Although the concepts of morality and ethics are much the same in the Philippines as in the United States, there are certain contrasts. According to American tradition, also present in these islands, right and wrong behavior reflects the relationship between an individual and the Almighty God. Theoretically, punishment or rewards are according to divine judgment. The individual may see certain behavior as sinful, and thus feel guilty if he has sinned. To most Filipinos, however, religion is less specifically related to daily behavior. What is "correct" behavior is more likely to be defined by tradition and related to the family and other reciprocal obligations. Failure to measure up in terms of family expectations and traditions produces feelings of shame.

As in most developing nations, including the Philippines, corruption is prevalent in the public services, government, and business. It is not uncommon for many complications in business and government bureaucracy to be speedily resolved by the payment of a favor. Such practices are the result of long historical and cultural development, rooted in the Spanish tradition in the Philippines.

The Filipinos have produced an extraordinary synergy among their diverse cultural groups. They are a people open to cooperation and collaboration.

The Filipinos have produced an extraordinary synergy among their diverse cultural groups. They are a people open to cooperation and collaboration.

TIPS FOR WORKING WITH FILIPINOS

- Filipinos see no reason why conflict should be courted when silence or evasive speech will preserve peace.
- Filipinos' excessive attention to recognition sometimes results in preoccupation of form over substance, and people tend to say what they do not mean to maintain appearances.
- Filipino food may be eaten the "kamayan" way or with the hands.
- The business card, as far as Filipinos are concerned, is a handy reference and could be exchanged at the end of a meeting. Filipino businesspeople do not consider it a breach of etiquette if one fails to produce it at the first instant.
- In a business negotiation, every detail, however significant, should be negotiated to avoid misunderstanding and renegotiation.
- A Filipino business partner has to be cultivated. Only when a relationship is developed can this result in a reliable business relationship. Filipinos place greater importance on personal relations than on a written contract.

SOUTH KOREA

It took South Korea only three decades to transform itself from a farming nation to an industrial giant.

Korea was virtually unknown to the rest of the world until the great struggle and war in the 1950s. At that time, it became a focus of world attention in a clash between the East and the West. Korea became a battleground of communist and democratic ideologies. Thus, today it is a divided country, with the U.N. maintaining a buffer zone of peace between the communistic system in the North and a democratic totalitarian military regime, elected in 1993, in the South.

South Korea's economic transformation is the wonder of the world, and some see its future role as comparable to Japan.[25] It took South Korea only three decades to transform itself from a farming nation to an industrial giant. Its quality products and energetic workers are exported around the globe, along with eager-to-learn technicians. South Korea has begun to open its market in a bid to join the big league of global competition, but some say it is difficult to shed its protectionist ways.[26]

South Korea has renewed its cities and is building satellite cities around Seoul, as well as renewing the country's west coast. While northern relatives stagnate under totalitarianism, this dynamic society produced first-class Olympic games and facilities in 1988. It has experienced a relatively peaceful election transition toward a more democratic government. Its population is restless for more democracy, improved working conditions and benefits, and progress toward national reunification with the North. The Korea Development Institute reports that the country, like Taiwan, is restructuring toward a domestic-driven economy, especially with citizens having more disposable income. There is a growing demand for domestic goods and services, along with the desire for improved housing and tourism abroad. Yet, most South Koreans feel they have sacrificed too long, live in relative poverty, and complain of inequities. The workforce is no longer docile and cheap. Doing business there requires great care and sensitivity. The Korean people are responding to the economic crisis of the late 1990s with "disciplined determination and entrepreneurship."[27]

Religion

The underlying ethic of Korea is Shamanism, but the people have also been strongly influenced by Buddhism and Confucianism. Shamanism is the religion of ancient Koreans for whom the elements of earth, mountains, rivers, etc. were sacred. Buddhism was introduced in Korea in the fourth century and has the longest history among the organized religions in Korea. Confucianism also has been a strong force, and the most influential of the newer native Korean religions is Ch-ondo-gyo, which was founded in the mid-nineteenth century on the belief that every person represents heaven.

Christianity was introduced in Korea in 1783 by Korean diplomatic delegates who came in contact with the Bible in China.

Cultural Concepts*

A vital concept to understand in Korea is *kibun*, which is one of the most important factors influencing the conduct and the relationship with others. The word literally means inner feelings. If one's *kibun* is good, then one functions smoothly and with ease and feels like a million dollars. If one's *kibun* is upset or bad, then things may come to a complete halt, and one feels depressed. The word has no true English equivalent, but "mood" is close. In interpersonal relationships, keeping the *kibun* in good order often takes precedence over all other considerations.

In business situations individuals try to operate in a manner that will enhance the kibun of both persons. To damage the kibun may effectively cut off relationships and create an enemy. One does not tend to do business with a person who has damaged one's kibun. Much of the disturbance of kibun in interpersonal relationships has to do with lower class persons disturbing higher class persons. Thus, for example, a teacher can scold a student in the class and no individual feels hurt, so no one's kibun is especially disturbed.

A vital concept to understand in Korea is kibun, which is one of the most important factors influencing the conduct and the relationship with others. The word literally means inner feelings.

---

*Much of the culture specific material on Korea has been excerpted with permission from Dr. Paul S. Crane'e excellent book, *Korean Patterns* © 1974 by the Royal Asiatic Society.

Proper interpersonal relationships are all important among Koreans, and there is little concept of equality in relationships among Koreans. Relationships tend to be vertical rather than horizontal, and each person is in a relatively higher or lower position. It is essential for one to know the levels of society and to know one's place in the scheme of things. In relationships, it is often necessary to appear to lower oneself in selfless humility and give honor to other people. To put oneself forward is considered arrogance and worthy of scorn.

Confucianism's emphasis on hierarchy has also influenced relationships. Confucian thought is that one should rank the public higher than the private; one's business or government duties come before one's personal consideration.

Protocol is extremely important to Koreans. When meeting others, if you do not appreciate a person's actual position and give it due recognition, then one might as well withdraw on some pretext and try to avoid future contacts. A representative of another person or group at a meeting is treated with great care because the substitute may be sensitive to slights, either real or imagined, and report it back to his or her colleagues. This is very difficult for Westerners to understand, but a Korean who fails to observe the basic rules of social exchange is considered by other Koreans to not even be a person—he or she is an "unperson" or "unable." Koreans show very little concern for an unperson's feelings or comfort, and in short, such an unperson is not worthy of much consideration; however, every effort must be made to remain within the framework of polite relation.

Protocol is extremely important to Koreans.

Deference or Respect to Elders

Elders in Korean society are always honored, respected, pampered, appeased. To engender the anger of an elder means serious damage, because age allows an older person to influence the opinions of others, regardless of the right or wrong of the situation. Like children, elders must be given special delicacies at meals, and their every wish and desire is catered to whenever possible. The custom and manner in which elderly people are sometimes sent to elder care facilities in the United States is extremely barbarous and shocking to the Koreans. Every home in Korea, no matter how poor, allocates the best room in the house to the honored grandfather or grandmother.

Etiquette

Koreans are considered by others to be among the most naturally polite people in the world when the proper rules of etiquette are followed. In personal relationships with strangers or associates, Koreans tend to be very strict in observing the rules of etiquette. To touch another person physically is considered an affront to his or her person, unless there is a well-established bond of close friendship or childhood ties.

In modern Korean society many businesspersons now shake hands as a sign that they are modernized. However, they will very often bow at the same time that they shake a person's hand. To slap someone on the back or to put one's arms around a casual acquaintance or to be too familiar with someone in public is a serious breach that may effectively cool future relations.

To embarrass someone by making a joke at his or her expense is highly resented even if done by a foreigner who does not understand the customs.

After a few drinks, businessmen often become very affectionate, but at the same time apologize for being a bit drunk. The next day they will tell their colleagues that they are sorry for imposing on one's good nature while being a little tipsy.

When appearing in public to speak, one bows first towards the audience and then towards the chairman of the meeting. Businesspeople should learn the proper bowing procedures and etiquette of Koreans. Korean businesspersons do not seem to worry about keeping time, being on time, beginning on time, or leaving on time to the same extent that Western businesspersons do. However, this is changing now and there is more of a tendency to follow the same time schedule as in the West.

Introductions

It is not the custom among the Koreans to introduce one person to another. Instead, one would say to another, "I have never seen you before" or "I am seeing you for the first time." The other person repeats the same thing, and then usually the elder of the two persons in age or rank says, "Let us introduce ourselves." Each person then steps back a little, bows from the waist, states his or her own name, or the elder initiates a handshake. They are then formally introduced. Names are stated in a low, humble voice, and then calling cards are exchanged. One may learn the new person's name and position at leisure. Do not say, "Sorry, I did not get your name. Would you tell me again?" Business cards are very necessary in Korea and should be used by foreign or Western businesspeople at all times.

The use of names in Korea has an entirely different connotation than in most Western countries. To the Confucian, using a name is presumptuous and impolite, as a name is something to be honored and respected and it should not be used casually. In Shamanism, to write a name calls up the spirit world and is considered bad luck. One's name, whether it is written or spoken, has its own special meaning and is that person's per-

Business cards are very necessary in Korea and should be used by foreign or Western businesspeople at all times.

sonal property. To call someone directly by his name is an affront in most social circumstances.

In Korea there are approximately 300 surnames, but more than half are Kims, Lees and Parks. When a Western businessperson uses a Korean's name to his face one can usually observe a slight wince around the eyes of a Korean. It is almost always there. A Korean is addressed by his title, position, trade, profession, or some other honorific title such as teacher. As opposed to our U.S. training of saying, "Good morning, Mr. Kim," a polite good morning is better or "Good morning, teacher" is acceptable. Many Koreans live next to each other for years without even knowing their full names. A Korean's name is usually made up of three characters—the family's surname is placed first, and then the given name, which is made up of one character. It is used by all members of the same generation. By knowing this name, a person's generation in the family tree can be recognized.

Privacy and Propriety

Privacy is a luxury that few can afford in Korea, and Koreans have learned to make imaginary walls about themselves. A visitor calling on a person on a hot day may find this person with his feet on the desk, fanning himself. The visitor coughs to announce his arrival, but he does not knock. This person does not "see" the person he has come to visit, nor does this person "see" the visitor until he has risen. Then they "see" each other and begin the formality of greeting. To have privacy, a Korean withdraws behind an imaginary curtain, or does what he or she has to do, not seeing or being seen by those who, by the literal Western eye, are in plain view. It is considered discourteous to violate this screen of privacy once it is drawn about a person. A discreet cough is intended to notify the person behind the screen that an interruption is impending.

Table manners are based on making the guest feel comfortable. The attitude of a servant is proper for a host with his guest. Traditionally, at meals, the hostess is at the lowest place, the farthest from the place of honor, and often will not even eat in the presence of a guest. Before beginning to eat, the host will often make a formal welcome speech stating the purpose of the gathering and paying his respects to his guest. Often food is served on small individual tables, each with many side dishes of food, a bowl of soup, and a bowl of rice. Korean food tends to be highly seasoned with red pepper, thus a careful sip of the soup is advisable before taking a large mouthful. To lay the chopsticks or spoon on the table is to indicate that you have finished eating. To put them on the top of a dish or bowl means that you are merely resting. A guest may show his appreciation for the meal by slurping soup or smacking one's lips. The host will continue to urge his guest to eat more, but a courteous refusal can be accepted. A good healthy belch after a meal is a sign that one has eaten well and enjoyed it.

"Clearly, South Korea did get something important right in its drive for growth. . . . High savings, lots of investments, industries determined to compete in world markets, an educated and eager work force and pro-business policies were more to the point."
The Economist December 9, 1995, p. 12

Gift Giving

Koreans give gifts on many occasions, and the appropriate etiquette surrounding the giving of gifts is often a problem to Western businesspeople. In this context, every gift expects something in return, and one rarely gives an expensive gift without a purpose. The purpose may be to establish an obligation, to gain a certain advantage, or merely to create an atmosphere in which the recipient will be more pliable to the request of the donor. To return a gift is considered an affront, but in some instances it may be better to return the gift than to accept it with no intention of doing a favor in return. Some Koreans have a special ability to work their way into the affection of foreigners and form personal relationships that may later prove embarrassing and/or difficult to handle when some impossible or very often illegal and unlawful request is made. In Korean, "yes" may merely mean "I heard you," and not agreement or intention of complying. To say "no" is an affront and could hurt the feelings, and thus is poor etiquette. Many Koreans often say "yes" to each other and to foreigners and then go their own way doing quite the opposite with little sense of breaking a promise or agreement.

Business Attitudes

In business, praise is a way of life, and without subtle praise, business would come to a halt. One must begin on the periphery in business relationships and gradually zero in on the main business in narrowing circles. To directly begin a discussion of some delicate business matter or new business venture is considered by Koreans to be the height of stupidity and dooms the project to almost certain failure. Impatience to a Korean is a major fault. A highly skilled businessperson moves with deliberation, dignity, and studied motions, and senses the impressions and nuances being sent by the other businesspeople.

To Korean businessmen, Western businesspersons often appear to make contracts on the assumptions that all the factors will remain indefinitely the same. In Korea a written contract is becoming as important as in the West. A change in the economy, the political situation, or personal reasons of one of the contractors may invalidate the completion of the contract without any sense of misdeed.

Because there are many similarities between Korean and other Asian cultures, cross-cultural skills that are effective in this society have application elsewhere. For example, there is a large minority population of Koreans in Los Angeles and their native language is the third largest spoken in that California city. In many ways Korean is also a synergistic culture, except for the political division of the peninsula. Fortunately, North and South Korea have begun a positive dialogue to permit further exchanges among divided families: this may eventually lead to improvement in their political and economic relationships.

In business, praise is a way of life, and without subtle praise, business would come to a halt.

VIETNAM[29]

VIETNAM—PROFILE	
Population	81 million
Ethnic groups	Kinh (Ethnic Vietnamese) 90%; Tay 2%; Thai 2%; Hoa 1%; Kho-me 1%; Muong 1%; Nong 1%; Others 2%;
Religions	Buddhism 86%; Christianity 7%; Caodaism 3%; Hoa Hao 2%; Islam 1%
Education	Compulsory 12 years (from age 6) Literacy 94%
Land	127,545 miles^2
Government	Socialist Republic of Vietnam, a Communist state
Political Parties	Communist Party of Vietnam
Per Capita Income	US $340
Exports to U.S.	US$286.6 million
Imports from U.S.	US$388.5 million

The French dominated Vietnam until World War II when the Japanese occupied parts of the country.

Historical Overview

For more than a thousand years from 111 B.C. to A.D. 939, Vietnam was ruled by the Chinese as a Chinese province called Giao Chia. Even after throwing off the Chinese, Vietnam had to resist numerous Chinese attacks. Because of the long duration of Chinese power, Vietnam was heavily influenced by their neighbors and kept close political and military ties. As the population expanded southward, Vietnam came into conflict with a number of dynasties. However, the people succeeded in overthrowing the Hindu Kingdom, Khmer empire, and Le dynasty until the Nguyen dynasty took over the whole country. becoming the first to rule Vietnam in 1802.

The Nguyen dynasty remained in power until the French brought Vietnam directly under its rule in 1867. They effectively divided the country into 3 parts: forming protectorates in Tonkin and Annam in the North and Central area of Vietnam and the directly administered Cochin China in the South.

The French dominated Vietnam until World War II when the Japanese occupied parts of the country. After Japan was defeated, the Allies divided the country into two parts: the North and the South. France gained power in the South, while China chose a new emperor in the North, Boa Dai, who stepped down in favor of Ho Chi Minh, founder and leader of

Vietnam communism. Ho Chi Minh was very powerful throughout this period and proclaimed on September 2, 1945 the independence of the Provisional Democratic Republic of Vietnam (DRV). He proceeded to invade the French-ruled South which led to another war the French ultimately lost in 1954 at Dien Bien Phu.

After terms for an agreement were signed in Geneva in 1954, Ngo Dinh Diem became the Prime Minister of the South and following a referendum in 1955, proclaimed himself President of the Republic of Vietnam. He refused to hold 1956 elections under the new peace agreement. Therefore, the North approved a strategy for the communist-based National Liberation Front (NLF) to oppose Diem. In 1959, the DRV actively supported the NLF and its movement into South Vietnam, prompting the U.S. to expand military support for Diem in 1961. The war turned into an American war following an incident involving U.S. warships. American troops and supplies were sent in to fight against the Viet Cong guerrillas (Southern communists fighting the South Vietnamese government), and North Vietnamese troops (Viet Minh). The war spread to Laos and Cambodia. President Johnson extended the war to North Vietnam, increasing troops from 25,000 in early 1965 to 500,000 in 1968, and bombing extensively the areas held by the Viet Cong.

When the communists launched the Tet offensive in 1968, U.S. public opinion showed diminished public support and the opinion that the war could not be won. Peace talks in January 1973 included a cease-fire in the South, the withdrawal of U.S. forces by the beginning of 1975, and the eventual peaceful reunification of Vietnam. However, in December 1974, combined PRG (Provisional Revolutionary Government formed by the NLF in the South) and North Vietnamese troops attacked the South which ultimately led to the fall of Saigon in April 1975.

Effective control of Vietnam was placed in the hands of Hanoi, which renamed the city of Saigon to Ho Chi Minh City in 1976. In an attempt to neutralize opposition, thousands of officials were summoned to "reeducation camps." All three Indochinese countries, Vietnam, Laos, and Cambodia, came under the communist government. Thousands of families fled these countries at that time.

In 1976, the communist National Assembly met and changed the name from the Democratic Republic of Viet Nam to the Socialist Republic of Vietnam. Furthermore, the communist party, known as the Vietnam Worker's Party, changed its name to the Communist Party of Vietnam (CPV). The U.S. refused to acknowledge the new government and severed all diplomatic relations. After the war, troops under Cambodia's Pol Pot government attacked Southern Vietnam. This led to an all-out Vietnamese invasion of Cambodia in December 1978, installing a new government loyal to Hanoi. In the same period, the Chinese launched an unsuccessful attack against the Vietnamese and ultimately withdrew from Vietnam.

Effective control of Vietnam was placed in the hands of Hanoi, which renamed the city of Saigon to Ho Chi Minh City in 1976.

Since then, Vietnam has focused on internal matters. In 1986, Nguyen Van Linh, Communist Party General Secretary, introduced the concept of "doi moi," or renovation. This term includes private enterprise and the approval of 100% foreign ownership of firms and joint ventures, openness to overseas Vietnamese, an interest in tourism, and greater individual freedoms. It took 3 years, however, for the South to start implementing these reforms, along with the withdrawal of Vietnamese troops from Cambodia in 1989. Since then, the government has been fully committed to the idea of "doi moi," as is evidenced by new investors from Japan, Taiwan, Hong Kong, and Australia. These countries already know they won't have to wait long for the emerging, thriving Vietnamese economy. Australia has targeted Vietnam its "Asian Business Success Program" while billboards with ads for Minolta and Hitachi dominate intersections in Hanoi and Ho Chi Minh City. For the rest of the non-Asian countries who didn't jump at the early opportunities, competition will be even stiffer now.

It was also the 1989 peace treaty with Cambodia that opened up diplomatic talks with the U.S. and the countries of Western Europe. In fact, the treaty was the turning point for Vietnam. Within months diplomatic ties had been fully reestablished with China and the previously mentioned countries. Washington opened a diplomatic office in Hanoi in 1991 to coordinate the search for American MIAs (soldiers missing in action). After cooperation from the Vietnamese in the search for MIAs, the U.S. lifted some economic sanctions in 1992 and 1993. President Clinton then lifted the trade and investment embargo in February 1994 to the delight of U.S. businesses who started investing heavily. By August 1994, the U.S. had established itself as a significant investor in Vietnam.

The Vietnamese people heralded the end of the trade embargo as the end of the "American War" as they refer to the Vietnam War.

The People and Their Homeland

The Socialist Republic of Vietnam is located in Southeast Asia, bordered by Laos and Cambodia to the west, China to the north, and the South China Sea to the east and south. The climate is humid in both the summer and winter seasons, with temperatures in Hanoi ranging between 13°C (55°F) to 33°C (91°F). Monsoon rains are present throughout the year, contributing to the average rainfall of 60 to 80 inches.

The new constitution adopted by the National Assembly on April 15, 1992 declared the omnipotence of the Communist Party. The National Assembly, consisting of 400 members who are elected to 5-year terms by universal adult suffrage, holds all legislative powers. The president, elected by the Ninth National Assembly, is also the head of state and commander-in-chief of the armed forces. The president then appoints a prime minister with the approval of the National Assembly, who in turn forms a government consisting of a vice president and a council of ministers. The National Assembly must approve all appointments.

The climate is humid in both the summer and winter seasons. Monsoon rains are present throughout the year, contributing to the average rainfall of 60 to 80 inches.

The country is divided into provinces, which are under tight control of the central government. On a local level, citizens are elected to a people's council, which runs the local government.

The Vietnamese economy is based on the agriculture, forestry, and fishing industries, which employ 73% of the work force and account for 60% of all exports. The agricultural sector consists of a staple crop of rice which, in 1993, provided 12% of export earnings as well as other cash crops of rubber, coffee, tea, cotton, and soybeans. A ban was imposed on logs and timber in 1992, in order to preserve the heavily depleted forests. Fishing is also very important: seafood including shrimp, crabs and cuttle fish are exported as are petroleum and coal.

Vietnam's principle trading partner is Singapore. Other major trading partners include France, Germany, Japan, and Hong Kong.

Education, which is free to all, begins at age 6 and continues to age 18. University education is also free, but there is tough competition for admittance. The literacy rate is 94% and approximately 10% of the nation's budget is spent on education.

The state operates a system of social security, in which health care is provided to everyone, free of cost. However, in 1991 there was one practicing doctor for 3,140 inhabitants, and facilities are often inadequate, especially in rural areas. Infant mortality is 47 per 1,000; life expectancy ranges from 63 to 67 years.

The official language in Vietnam is Vietnamese, but there exist also distinct northern, central, and southern dialects. Furthermore, many minority groups speak their own language at home, but Vietnamese is taught in all schools. The most popular foreign languages to study include English, Russian, and French. Most government officials understand some English.

The Vietnamese have lived 1,000 years under Chinese domination. Then came French colonialism from 1867–1954. After this period, the civil war ensued for 30 years which included the war against the United States. This has left the Vietnamese people with a strong sense of national pride. They are more future-oriented than past-oriented, which explains their inability to understand Americans' fixation with the American War. Because the American War was relatively short compared to Vietnam's past, and because two wars have been fought against China and Cambodia since then, the Vietnamese do not harbor animosity towards Americans and the American War. They view it already as past history. In fact, most Vietnamese are very curious towards all American things and are interested in conducting business with Americans.

Great change is taking place now in Vietnam and with it, struggles to get ahead. People in the urban areas are generally happy, due to improved basic services, and a more open political and cultural environment. However, people in the rural areas, which constitute 75% of the Vietnam population, are very unhappy and frustrated currently. This malaise is due to a dearth of cultural opportunities, lack of electricity and other basic services, and neglect of the poor. Party officials still take

They are more future-oriented than past-oriented, which explains their inability to understand Americans' fixation with the American War.

advantage of the peasants, who do not hold much weight in voting matters. For Vietnam to obtain prosperity, the inequalities that exist between urban and rural citizens must disappear.

Customs and Courtesies

In Vietnam, people shake hands when greeting and saying good-bye to someone. Also common is the use of both hands, which indicates respect. A slight bow of the head also shows respect. Elderly people in rural areas may also nod their head upon greeting someone, and women are more inclined to bow their head than to shake hands.

In Vietnam, names begin with the family name followed by the given name. For example, in the name Nguyen Van Duc, Nguyen is the family name and Van Duc is the given name. Although they address each other by given name, the Vietnamese add titles that show their relationship to the other person. These titles tend to be used more personally in one's family than professionally. Among co-workers, the younger of the two might call the other "ahn" or older brother. To say hello to someone using the given name and title, they would say "Xin Chao" or hello. However, "Xin chao" could have one of six other meanings, because Vietnamese is a tonal language. Therefore, it is important to stress the proper syllable where needed. International visitors who can properly say "Xin Chao" are met with delight by the Vietnamese. In business settings, business cards may be exchanged in greetings.

The following gestures should be noted when in the company of the Vietnamese:

❏ Do not touch the head of a young child as it is considered a sensitive spiritual point.
❏ Do not use your index finger to call someone over since it is considered rude.
❏ When calling someone, wave all four fingers with the palm down.
❏ Men and women do not show affection in public.
❏ Members of the same sex may hold hands in public. This is normal.
❏ The Vietnamese use both hands to give an object to another person.

The Vietnamese place a great deal of importance on visiting people. Therefore, one should not just "drop by" someone's house without first being invited. They also show a strong sense of hospitality and prepare well in advance of the guest's arrival. Gifts for the hostess are not required but greatly appreciated. A small gift for the children or elderly parent is also much appreciated. Acceptable gifts include flowers, tea, or incense.

The traditional Vietnamese family is an extended one, including parents, unmarried children, and married sons with their families. The extended family still predominates in rural regions; however, there is a

The traditional Vietnamese family is an extended one, including parents, unmarried children, and married sons with their families.

trend toward singly-family homes in urban locations. Families maintain strong ties with each other and provide financial and emotional support as needed.

Vietnam is the world's 13th largest country, so Americans and others who think only of the Vietnam War and communism should think again. Because the policies of doi moi were introduced in the mid-1980s, the government has shown a strong interest in becoming a market economy and opening itself to outsiders. Furthermore, with the reestablishment of diplomatic relations with the U.S. and other major economic players, business opportunities have increased dramatically over the past year. Those companies who take advantage of conducting business in Vietnam now will be rewarded with a high growth market of consumers that is estimated to reach 600 million by 2010.

SUMMARY

Asia is a demonstration model of the complexity and multidimensional aspects of culture. Perhaps it is enough to convince global managers of the important distinctions that exist between the people of this region and ourselves in critical matters like physical appearance, language, religion, family, social attitudes, and other assumptions that influence business practice and relationships. The new market opportunities in the Pacific Basin alone should motivate us to seek culture specific information whether we are dealing with Australians who are seemingly similar or with Thais who are so obviously different.

Observed in an editorial, (*The Economist*, December 9, 1995):

> The experience of countries like South Korea, Taiwan and Thailand suggests that there is indeed a connection between prosperity and democracy.

The social situation in Asia is normally peaceful, but also very dynamic, often volatile. Traditional societies are in transition. However, in these ancient lands and cultures, trade has always been the way to promote commercial exchange and prosperity.

Asia is a demonstration model of the complexity and multidimensional aspects of culture.

REFERENCES

1. *The Economist*, October 1, 1994.
2. Matlock, J. W. *The New York Times Book Review*, "Chinese Checkers," September 13, 1998.
3. Schnitzer, M. C., Liebranz, M. L., and Kubin, K. K. *International Business*, Cincinnati, OH: South-Western Publishing, 1985.
4. *The Europa World Yearbook*, 1994, Vol, 1, London: Europa Publications, Ltd. 1994.

5. Passport System, "A Guide to Communicating in the Global Marketplace," *Getting Through Customs,* Australia, 1993.
6. Background Notes—Australia, U.S. Department of State, Bureau of Public Affairs, Office of Public Education, Feb. 1994.
7. "EIU Country Profile—Australia," *The Economist Intelligence Unit,* Kent, England: 1994-95.
8. Axtell, R. E. *Gestures: The Dos and Taboos of Body Language Around the World,* New York: John Wiley and Sons, 1990.
9. Axtell, R. E., *Dos and Taboos of Hosting International Visitors,* New York: John Wiley and Sons, 1990.
10. Copeland L. and Griggs, L., *Going International: How to Make Friends and Deal Effectively in the Global Marketplace,* New York: Random House, 1985; see also Renwick, G. W., Smart, R., and Henderson, D. I., *A Fair Go for A—Australian and American Interactions,* Yarmouth, ME: Intercultural Press, 1991.
11. Drucker, P. *Managing in a Time of Great Change,* Oxford, UK: Butterworth-Heinemann, 1993.
12. Patten, C. *East and West—China, Power and the Future of Asia,* New York: Times Books/Random House, 1998.
13. United States Postal Service, "Focus on . . . The People's Republic of China," *Passport* 1997, Vol.3:1, p.3.
14. Pinyin—On January 1, 1979, China adopted officially the "pinyin" system of writing Chinese characters in the Latin alphabet. This is a system of romanization invented by the Chinese that has been widely used for years in China on street signs, as well as in elementary Chinese textbooks. Pinyin is now to replace the familiar Wade-Giles romanization system. The following are examples of the Wade-Giles and pinyin systems:

Wade-Giles	**Pinyin**
Kwangchow/Canton	Guangzhou
Peking	Beijing
Mao Tse-tung	Mao Zedong
Teng Hsiao-ping	Deng Xiaoping
Hua Kuo-feng	Hua Geofeng
Chou En-lai	Zhou Enlai

15. Pye, L. *Chinese Commercial Negotiating Style,* Cambridge, MA Oelgeschlager, Gunn & Hain Publishers, 1982.
16. Frankenstein, J. *Asian Wall Street Journal,* August 26, 1995.
17. Moran, R. T. *Venturing Abroad in Asia,* London: McGraw-Hill, 1988, adapted with permission.
18. "Indonesia," *National Geographic,* February 1996.
19. "Indonesia's Agony and the Price of Rice," *The Economist,* September 19, 1998.
20. Van Wolferen, K. *The Enigma of Japanese Power,* New York: Alfred A.Knopf, 1985.
21. Hall, E. T. and Hall, M. R. *Hidden Differences—Doing Business with the Japanese,* Garden City, NJ: Anchor/Doubleday, 1987.
22. DeMente, B. *Made in Japan,* Yarmouth, ME: Intercultural Press/National Textbook, 1987.

23. Verluyten, S. P. "Doing Business in the Philippines," preliminary version of paper. University of Antwerp RUCA-TEW, Belgium, November 1992.
24. *The Economist,* "Staying Ahead in the Philippines," November 16, 1996, p. 18/33.
25. Amsden, A. *Asia's Next Giant: Late Industrialization in South Korea,* Cambridge, UK: Oxford University Press, 1989; see also Kang, T. P. *Is Korea the Next Japan?* New York: Free Press, 1989.
26. Wantanabe, T. "Old Habits Die Hard in the Mermit Kingdom," *Los Angeles Times,* February 14, 1997, p. 1
27. Ungoon, G. R., Sters, R. M., and Park S. *Korean Enterprise: The Quest for Globalization,* Boston, MA: Harvard Business Press, 1997.
28. *The Economist,* July 1999.
29. Researched and written by Laurel Cool based on the following references:
    - "Socialist Republic of Vietnam," *Culturgram 1995,* Provo, UT: Brigham Young University, 1995.
    - *The Europa World Yearbook,* 1994, Vol. 2, London: Europa Publications, Ltd., 1994.
    - "EIU Country Report, Third Quarter, Vietnam," *The Economist Intelligence Unit,* Kent, England, 1994.
    - Haub, C. "After Decades of War, A New Economy is Emerging," *Consumers of Southeast Asia Market: Asia Pacific,* Ithaca, NY: W-Two Publications, 1994.
    - Walsh, D. "Another Tiger?" *Consumers of Southeast Asia,* Ithaca, NY: W-Two Publications, 1994.
30. Intercultural Press, Yarmouth, ME has three videos that may be helpful for this chapter: *Doing Business in Southeast Asia* (1997), *West Meets East in Japan* (1992), *Chinese Cultural Values—The Other Pole of the Human Mind* (1996).
31. Readers interested in China may wish to consult *The China Quarterly,* Oxford University Press, Walton St., Oxford OX2 6DP, UK; and *The Chinese Space Program,* Brian Harvey, Wiley/Praxis, The Whitehouse, Eastergate, Chichester, West Sussex PO20 6UR, UK.

Recommended Reading

Dunung, S. P. *Doing Business in Asia—The Complete Guide.* San Francisco, CA: Jossey-Bass Publishers, 1998.
Elashmawi, F. and Harris, P. R. *Multicultural Management 2000—Essential Cultural Insights for Global Business Success.* Houston, TX: Gulf Publishing, 1998.
Herbig, P. A. *Handbook of Cross-Cultural Marketing.* New York, NY: The International Business Press.

13

DOING BUSINESS WITH EUROPEANS

Great Britain, France, Germany, Russia, and Eastern Europe

The winds of economic, social and political change are sweeping throughout the whole continent, both in its western and eastern portions.

Europe is a continent previously clearly divided into two geopolitical spheres. Business practices varied according to whether the capitalist or socialist system was used. The demise of communism has blurred the demarcation but complicated the situation by adding more nations and cultures to an already highly diverse mixture of peoples. Thus, it is difficult to generalize about Europe.

Europe is also a dynamic and very exciting place to do business in the 21st century. The winds of economic, social and political change are sweeping throughout the whole continent, both in its western and eastern portions. Travelers, traders, and those planning to relocate there should seek out the very latest sources of information.

Since 1957, the European Community (EC) member nations have striven together to improve their standard of living and to foster closer relations among their countries.

While the 14-member European Union progresses, there is a trend on that continent to preserve local cultures and languages. While we all may be aware of the long struggle of Basques in Spain and France to keep their language, customs, and institutions, these are less known developments:

❏ In France, Radio Kerne broadcasts in Breton, a Celtic language spoken for more than 2000 years. It is part of a movement to save the culture of Brittany. Moreover, this language of the Druids is now on the Internet with its own website.
❏ Since 1997, other minority languages, once banned in the name of equality, may now be taught, such as Occitan, Corsican, and Alsatian.
❏ In other countries, the same trend is evident—in Spain, Catalan is the official government language of Catalonia; Gaelic has not only

ARCTIC OCEAN

BARENTS
SEA

ATLANTIC
OCEAN

SWEDEN

FINLAND

RUSSIA

NORWAY

UNITED
KINGDOM

LATVIA
LITHUANIA
BELARUS

DENMARK

POLAND

GERMANY

UKRAINE

FRANCE

ROM.

BLACK
SEA

ITALY

SPAIN

AEGEAN
SEA

GREECE

EUROPE

MEDITERRANEAN
SEA

returned to Ireland, but to Scotland and Wales; broadcasts in Frisian and Limburgs may be heard in Northern Italy and The Netherlands; in Finland, the news can now be heard in Saami.

Thus, the 41-nation Council of Europe has created a Bureau of Lesser-used Languages, which finances projects, such as an Internet browser in Welsh, cartoon books in Alsatian, etc. Concerned about democracy and human rights, The council's position is that this revival has economic benefits as it stimulates local food, dress, music, and crafts, as well as language courses and networks, both personal and electronic.

Beginning in 1993 a formal agreement allowed goods, people, services, information, and capital to move freely among the EU countries. Currently, the twelve members consist of Belgium, Denmark, France, Germany, Greece, Ireland, Italy, Luxembourg, the Netherlands, Portugal, Spain, and the United Kingdom. But all is not smooth sailing as different and competing visions are emerging. However, most of following issues have been solved or are in the process of resolution.

- ❑ Technical—differing national standards and regulations, conflicting business laws, and protected public procurements.
- ❑ Free flow of goods, once they have cleared customs in the EC, as if national boundaries did not exist.
- ❑ Free movement of workers, so that citizens of one state may seek employment in another without discrimination relative to type of job, remunerations, or other employment conditions.
- ❑ Freedom of establishment, so a citizen or business from one state has the right to locate and conduct business elsewhere in the EC.
- ❑ Freedom to provide services to persons throughout the EC.

The efforts toward European integration and standardization have successfully lead to greater political and currency unification.

Some of the benefits of the new EC policies include:

Industry

- ❑ Direct cost savings from removal of internal border controls.
- ❑ Increased competition.
- ❑ Economies of scale in production.
- ❑ Greater expenditures on research and development.
- ❑ More efficient use of labor.

Economy

- ❑ Lower prices.
- ❑ Increased consumer demand.
- ❑ Decreased unemployment.
- ❑ Increased growth throughout the EC.

Beginning in 1993 a formal agreement allowed goods, people, services, information, and capital to move freely among the EU countries. The efforts toward European integration and standardization have successfully lead to greater political and currency unification.

To take advantage of the single market opportunities, global corporations are establishing EC-based companies, and the Japanese are most prominent in this strategy. Many foreign enterprises are acquiring or merging with European industrial units, and the cross-cultural challenges increase at both the national and corporate levels. Global managers assigned to Europe will have to be more competitive, as well as better trained and culturally sensitive. They also must deal with various economies and monetary systems, particularly the results of the establishment of the euro in January 1999.

EUROPEAN MANAGEMENT SYNERGY

Cultural identity and not nation-state should be the basis of Europe's future. Cultural identity is only possible if it is based on a certain level of economic development.[1]

As Europe moves beyond national borders and cultures toward regional cooperation, a new European identity is developing, but the cultural identity of each of the countries in the EC needs to be preserved, and such preservation is the basis for Europe's future. Latin verve and British pragmatism need to be viewed as a strength of the EC rather than a divisive element. The distinct cultures and enormous differences in values and outlooks among member countries must be addressed to remove impediments to deeper unity. However, among the EC's burgeoning bureaucracy of approximately 20,000, no organized research is ongoing to study the impact of cultural diversity in the EC.[2]

Nowhere is this collaboration more evident than in the field of management. Managers readily cross national boundaries not only on mutual business, but for professional development together. The three great management learning centers have multicultural participants—INSEAD (Fontainebleu, France), International Management Institute (Geneva, Switzerland), and Management Centre Europe (Brussels, Belgium). Furthermore, European managers attend courses and workshops in each other's universities, and read one another's management journals and business publications.

Perhaps the transnational aspects of European management is best demonstrated in matters of partnerships, joint ventures, and acquisitions. For example, the Republic of Ireland not only boasts of its more than 200 British industries, and many new American and European firms, but of the young, well-educated work force available for service. The "internationalization" of European "manpower" has been progressing throughout this century, caused by the growth of the multinational corporation. Since World War II, an estimated 30 million workers—mostly from underdeveloped countries in southern Europe and North Africa— have flowed into northern Europe. European business

As Europe moves beyond national borders and cultures toward regional cooperation, a new European identity is developing. . . .

people have always excelled at multilingual skills. However, these trends are some of the reasons why cross-cultural training is increasing within European management development.

Commenting on the unsettling phenomenon of large-scale, non-European resettlement the *Los Angeles Times* (February 6, 1989) observed:

❑ Twice as many Britons speak Urdu, Punjabi, or Gujarati as Welsh, the native language of Wales in the U.K.
❑ 700,000 Arabs in France will be eligible to vote in the next presidential election.
❑ Road signs now appear in Spain in Arabic to accommodate the one million Moroccans who vacation there in the summer.

Such changes can alter a society's image of itself, and unravel the social and religious traditions of centuries.

THE EUROPEAN VIEW[3]

When one considers Japan and the United States, a certain set of beliefs, customs, values, practices, and feelings come to mind that delineates how Americans and Japanese look at life and behave. When one thinks of Europe, it is not as easy to come to such a firm grasp of what it means to be European. Yet, each country or continent has a common set of concepts.

A perspective on Europeans was stated by Paplexopoulos in Bloom, Calori, and de Woot.[3]

> Business in the United States is concerned with quantities, numbers, and performance far more than with people. . . . In Europe, it seems to me, one insists more that humans are, and should be, at the center of our thought and philosophy.

Europeans have an inherent interest in the quality of life, at all levels of society. There is a predominant humanist belief that people are to be served by progress and not the reverse.

Europeans generally have an inordinate sense of reality. When one reflects upon the wars and disruptions in Europe in this century alone, one can understand how Europeans know that tragedy can be just a breath away, and that perhaps only this moment is real.

Historically, Americans have had to conquer the elements to develop their country. In contrast, Europeans most often have had to fight their fellow men. This has taught Europeans about survival. European perception of Americans is that they are generally naive, partially because Americans give the impression that they believe everything they say. European heritage is such that they think in the context of centuries whereas Americans historical sense is in terms of decades.

Europeans have endured. They have a sense of history and security. They have survived plagues, the great wars, border and government changes. They have lived through many ambiguities and have the threads of ancient customs and traditions in the fabric of their cultures. They know the fragility of their civilization. On the one hand is the sense of survival, but the balance is that disaster is often not far off.

However, this perspective can have a disadvantage in that Europeans may be less willing to take a risk on a new idea or new venture with a possibly good future. The concept of simply making money is not the foundation of a company; the long-term survival of the company is as important. Some Europeans like to hedge their bets, backing several projects in different fields in hopes that one may pay off.

According to Bloom et al.[3] the European perspective is not as easy to define as Japan or the United States but it does exist. The following are the characteristics that are representative of European culture:

- An almost cynical realism schooled by history.
- A belief that individuals should be at the center of life.
- A sense of social responsibility.
- A mistrust of authority.
- A feeling that all people have weaknesses and sometimes one has to "muddle through" life.
- A desire for security and continuity.
- A belief that maximum profit is not the primary aim of business.

Noorerhaven[2] points up that relationships between the individual and authority in Europe are accented by differences in educational and political attitudes within the continent.

Schooling

- Teachers in The Netherlands and Scandinavia have far less "distance" between themselves and their pupils than their counterparts in Mediterranean countries.
- In one of the world's most egalitarian societies, Dutch children are taught to keep low profiles, and that being "first" at something is not necessarily a virtue. Whereas in Mediterranean countries, such as Greece and Italy, children tend to be nurtured as special, unique, and implicitly superior individuals. In Britain it is acceptable to finish first, but only if one can do it without seeming to work harder.

Politics

- Countries like Britain and Denmark, with long traditions of relatively non-intrusive government, but with respect for the law, have tended to resist proposals for new regulations from EC's executives in Brus-

The concept of simply making money is not the foundation of a company; the long-term survival of the company is as important. In one of the world's most egalitarian societies, Dutch children are taught to keep low profiles, and that being "first" at something is not necessarily a virtue.

sels. Yet, once agreement is reached, they have the best record of implementation.

☐ On the other hand, Belgium, where bureaucracy is oppressive and evading law/regulations is a national sport, ranks among the quickest to propose new EC rules, but has the worst record for implementing adopted regulations.

The three large markets in the EC are Great Britain, Germany, and France, so we have selected these target cultures for analysis as a representative sample. The first because it is the "mother country" of all English-speaking nations, and the third because it is the center of French cultural influences throughout the world and the home of many international agencies, such as UNESCO. Also included is information regarding Russia, the Commonwealth of Independent States, and Eastern Europe.

GENERAL TIPS FOR DOING BUSINESS IN EUROPE

Europeans gauge the forethought and commitment of a foreign firm by the way it treats its sales representatives.

☐ Customer service is the key to success. The standards of Europe in this regard are not up to that of the United States, especially in matters of rapid repairs and home service.

☐ Publish price lists in terms of local currency.

☐ Deploy Americans to Europe on the basis of a two-year minimum commitment to establish meaningful customer relations; the staying power of expatriate personnel is a subtle indicator—whenever possible, hire locals and then train them.

☐ Lease office equipment and computers in Europe because of the electrical differences in power outlets.

☐ Ensure that sales personnel know their products. Europeans are sophisticated buyers of foreign merchandise.

☐ Europeans gauge the forethought and commitment of a foreign firm by the way it treats its sales representatives. They perceive the sales person as a key role to be judged on long-term performance; select such representatives very carefully.

☐ Europeans do not like change, so it is important for the foreign company to project stability and long-range commitment; yet they are attracted to "new" products, processes, and services.

☐ When able to properly serve the primary market in Europe, remember geographic distances are not great. Assess the secondary markets (Spain and Portugal, Greece, and the Eastern European countries), and respond carefully to all inquiries from such areas.

☐ Beside cultural, language, and political differences in Europe, be prepared to cope with technical differences (e.g., length of stationery and forms that do not fit standard copying machines, ink that does not reproduce well, different abbreviations).

- ❑ European nomenclature and honorific titles are to be observed in oral and written communication (especially spellings in English that differ between British and American versions).
- ❑ Europeans value personal contacts and mementos, so the token gift may create a favorable impression or participation in a trade fair which is part of centuries-old tradition.

GREAT BRITAIN

GREAT BRITAIN—PROFILE

Population	59 million
Ethnic Groups	British (Anglo-Saxons), West Indian, Pakistani, and some Middle Easterners
Religions	Church of England, Roman Catholic, Presbyterian
Education	12 years compulsory Literacy 99%
Land	94,226 mi^2
Government	Constitutional Monarchy
Political Parties	Conservative, Labour, Liberal, Social Democratic, Communist, Official Unionist, Democratic Unionist, Social Democratic
Per Capita Income	$19,810
Exports to U.S.	$36,425 billion
Imports from U.S.	$32,659 billion

Cultural Characteristics of Business

The United Kingdom constitutes that area of the island consisting of England, Wales, and Scotland. Presently, it also includes six counties of Northern Ireland known as Ulster. Although secondary languages or dialects such as Welsh, Scottish, and Irish are spoken in various regions, English is the principal language of Great Britain.

The English language has almost become a universal means of communication, especially in business and international travel, and is a tribute to the hearty race of Anglo-Saxon-Celts living on two small islands off the eastern coast of Europe. Even though the sun is setting on the British Empire, their global influence in the past, and to some extent in the present, is staggering to conceive. Not only their language, but their customs, laws, and life-styles penetrated remote corners of the world and held sway over several continents from North America to Asia.

European nomenclature and honorific titles are to be observed in oral and written communication. . . . The English language has almost become a universal means of communication, especially in business and international travel.

While the United States is indebted to many nations for its cultural heritage, the English-Irish-Scotch combination provided the main thrust to its society. Through the unique format of the British Commonwealth of Nations, the United Kingdom with its royal family and social institutions had an impact on most races and many cultures. The British were even the stimulant for the export of Irish immigrants, missionaries, politicians, and prisoners throughout the world. There are leaders today in Australia and Argentina, as well as Africa and the Americas, of Irish heritage whose ancestors left "Hibernia" with British encouragement. Furthermore, the British spearheaded the European effort in both World Wars I and II.

Today, the British have been forced to retreat, in many ways, to the confines of their island kingdom. And they have been followed by the multicultured inhabitants of the commonwealth who used their privilege of British passport to resettle in the "mother country." Added to this influx from the "colonies" are the transfers of many affluent Middle Easterners to England seeking property, education, health services, and recreation. It would appear that the phenomenon of the medieval crusades has been reversed. In any event, what was once a largely white, homogeneous society is becoming quite heterogeneous. Ulster is racked by armed struggles (economic, political social) between Catholic and Protestant (Orangemen) communities. Paramilitary operations by extremists from both sides have been the source of conflict and violence; human rights were transgressed and terrorism was exported to the very heart of Great Britain itself.

Currently, the British government is in a period of negotiation, seeking to promote some form of agreement and reconciliation with all parties, including the Irish Republican Party (IRA) and the Republic of Ireland in the south. Despite recent difficulties, the British still go about business in a very civilized, unflappable way. After all, this courageous people did withstand Nazi bombings and blitz fifty years ago.

The material in this section is presented using the case study method for analysis, learning, and application.

What was once a largely white, homogeneous society is becoming quite heterogeneous.

Case Study: Americans in Great Britain

Scenario—
❑ Background of the characters   ❑ Critical incidents
❑ Briefing of the boss   ❑ Issues for analysis

Background of the Characters

Jeff is a transatlantic commuter and an employee of Easting, Inc. Two years ago he was appointed the corporate executive liaison officer for the British Isles, responsible for supervising the company's subsidiary there, Aquaphone, Ltd. He was quite satisfied with his rise in the new-style aristocracy of American business. He would jet four times a year to London and stay at the Claridge Hotel. He was especially excited by the employee rallies that he addressed at Fairfield Hall, Croydon. He liked this peculiar British practice, which gave him an opportunity to provide the personnel with a pep talk so that he could counteract the cynicism in workers, a blight across so much of British industrial thinking. He hoped to instill enthusiasm, the lack of which is the biggest curse of their industry. Jeff was not only competent but highly motivated in the spirit that the "business of America is business."

Up until now he seemed to have been reasonably successful on this assignment. He seemed to get along well with the man in England who reported directly to him, Dudley Letts-Jones. In fact, whenever Dudley visited corporate headquarters in Pittsburgh, Jeff and his wife made a point of entertaining their guests at the Rolling Hills Country Club where they were members. Jeff was surprised that it took Dudley two years to invite him to his club.

After special studies in management and technology, Dudley had drifted into industry with the help of some old school buddies. He was a natural leader and soon moved into executive positions. At the time Easting acquired Aquaphone, Ltd., Dudley was a managing director and the American multinational eventually promoted him to president of their subsidiary. His wife, Dolores, was not too happy over these developments. She jokingly reminded him that his first duty was to home and family, and warned that she might be forced to act like Mrs. Terese Patten. Mrs. Patten accused Avon, an American-owned firm, of enticing her 33-year-old husband away from her because he seemed "married to the job."

Dudley was typically British-generous, enterprising, inventive, loyal with an instinct to compromise. A perfect English gentleman, at times, he appeared to conceal character under a veneer of dandyism. On occasion, his high-pitched nasal mumblings were useful for evading precise conversation on delicate issues. However, recently Dudley was frustrated. He felt financially constrained by the devaluation of the pound and the taxes of a Socialist-welfare government. He had to sell his weekend country house, couldn't take the usual family vacations to the Continent or Bermuda, and was hesitant to replace his aging Bentley. His absolute assurance had been shaken. The advantages of the past for his class had eroded.

Angus McKay, an engineer, after working for a series of English firms in Scotland in minor management and technical positions, he got his first big career break when Easting took over the company with which he was employed. Now he is general manager of the

Aquaphone plant in Leith and reports directly to Dudley-Letts Jones. He welcomes the periodic visits of Jeff Donovan for he says he "likes to work for Yanks—they're just like Scotsmen." Besides he has American relatives who work in the factories of New England and the coal mines of Pennsylvania.

Angus welcomes the American invasion of Scotland because he believes the London government has given exclusive advantage to English concerns, and neglected the development of Scottish industry. Before the American take-over, he complained of having to make do with obsolescent equipment in cramped conditions. He thinks Jeff has done a good job of replacing nineteenth-century ideas, pay rates, and equipment. He has urged Easting to take advantage of the favorable treatment afforded to them in Scotland, and points out that they are not restricted in locating new factories. Labor and rent are cheap and plentiful, and local authorities most accommodating. Already the Scottish Council for Development and Industry has been most helpful to Aquaphone, Ltd.

With the introduction of American management know-how and advanced technology, production has soared to over 200 million pound sterling. Angus notes that as of last year Americans owned 95% of the office machine industry, 92% of the household appliances trade, and 66% of the computer output in Scotland. This bothers him a bit. He is still a fierce Scottish nationalist and wonders if they are exchanging one master for another. He knows that the profits he helps to earn go largely back to the U.S. and that their position is vulnerable to changes in American commercial policies, research, and development.

Briefing of the Boss

Jeff would never forget the day he got the assignment to Great Britain. His boss called him into his office and began the conversation in a unique way: "The English have a great tradition of service to the empire; they choose their very best young men for an overseas posting to broaden their experience before returning home to a major career assignment. Jeff, I am giving you such an opportunity in the field of international business in the British Isles." Jeff had found the following points to be most significant:

❑ Don't ever assume that the British are just like us because we seem to speak the same language and seem to share a common heritage. Centuries of civilization and empire building have given them an inner pride and composure. Yet, their current position in the world's economic and geopolitical scene has diminished, but they still have their network of commonwealth nations, and exercise considerable global influence. We have a lot to learn from the British experience in international affairs.

❑ Furthermore, you must learn to respect the accomplishments of British technology. When they founded the thirteen colonies here, they were already pioneering the Industrial Revolution. We benefited from their technological advances from then to now, most recently from radar to atomic power. Yes, Britain is suffering today from financial reverses, but the British as a people respond best to adversity, as World War II demonstrated. North Sea oil, tourism, and other developments may yet create a situation in which we more than welcome their friendship.

❑ The United Kingdom is a polyglot of ancient cultural influences—Angles, Saxons, Normans, Vikings, Celts, Picts, Romans, and others. Today this so-called homogeneous isle is becoming more pluralistic with the influx of immigrants from the commonwealth nations—Indonesians, Arabs, Africans, Asians. Nationalism is being manifested in Scotland, Wales, and North Ireland, sometimes with bloody or devastating economic results. Even the languages of these small islands range from standard English to Cockney, Scottish, Yorkshire, Norfolk, and Welsh versions. You have to be sensitive to such forces when you do business in the United Kingdom and rid yourself of stereotypes.

❑ Great Britain is a country of paradoxes, and if you are going to be successful there, you have to understand what makes the British tick. To get inside their life space or mindset, you have to analyze their national character, culture, and current environment. Normally, you will find them reserved, polite, and often friendly. For all their simulated modesty, the British can be tough and blandly ruthless when necessary. They are masters at intelligence gathering, political blackmail, and chicanery, as a reading of the book *Intrepid* will illustrate. Despite how quaint and eccentric they may appear to you at times, don't sell them short. They are a game people who built an empire with a handful of men and women. Although England and Wales are only the size of Alabama, and the population density is close to the size of France, the British once ruled 14 million square miles and more than 500 million souls.

❑ One may decry the patronizing manner of imperial splendor and their rank consciousness, but their idealism explains their effortless superiority in world affairs and their inward, invisible grace as a people. It produced a tradition of public service and an education and class system that was dedicated to the needs of the Empire. It also spawned a credo that natural leaders are those who are "high-born."

Great Britain is a country of paradoxes, and if you are going to be successful there, you have to understand what makes the British tick.

These are some of the underlying forces that influence the people you are about to do business with in Britain. We Americans are a free-ranging people who have never experienced the feudal system. Such ancient experiences even affect modern British labor relations in a very staid society that is slow to change. There, militant trade unionism developed to combat the class system curtailments of the workers. It arose with the Industrial Revolution that devalued the ancient crafts and replaced them with factory work. It even led to a radical socialism that advocates the public ownership of production, distribution, and exchanges, challenging the whole free enterprise system. Truculence and a bloody-minded reluctance to toil for the "boss class" added to the natural conservatism of British labor. It produced a class-war outlook in which profit is regarded as a dirty word and productivity is not popular currency. So tread carefully in matters of labor relations, lest you stir up deep passions. Don't think you can just translate your experience on the American labor scene to the United Kingdom.

They value free time and are content with fewer possessions (at least they were before the advent of our mass media, consumer advertising blitz). They are careful to preserve status and convention on the work scene, even with regard to tea and the pace of work. The American view of money making and profits, efficiency and cost effectiveness has been almost thought to be irreconcilable with the British approach.

Our whole approach to search for management talent, for example, puzzles the British who formerly waited for such candidates to apply to the company, or to surface through old school ties. You are going to have to introduce American management recruitment, assessment, and development into our new subsidiary, as well as a system of job evaluation.

Finally, our corporate policy is one of tactfulness and identification with a host country abroad in which we operate. We seek to adapt our company policies and ways to meet the legitimate concerns and grievances of indigenous people beyond our borders and in whose nation we operate. In the case of the United Kingdom, I do not think we can rely on the traditional special relationship of past Anglo-American friendship and cooperation. We must continue to develop a synergistic relationship.

Critical Incidents in London and Edinburgh

As he flew British Airways back to New York, Jeff was uneasy. Those parting words of his boss some two years previously were coming back to haunt him. He thought he had the United Kingdom situation well in hand. With the changes he had introduced, Aquaphone, Ltd., had increased sales and profits, better working conditions, and avoided significant labor strife. Yet, something had happened on his latest visits to London and Edinburgh that disturbed him and had portent for his corporation's relations with its subsidiary.

It started first with Dudley Letts-Jones. This English executive had always been most proper and gentlemanly with him. He seemed to accept and adequately implement the management changes Jeff proposed, and even came up with some worthwhile innovations of his own. Dudley did not have the lackadaisical outlook of some of his British colleagues. The issue that concerned Jeff was the matter of *over staffing*. Jeff felt that Aquaphone could manage with fewer production workers, fewer researchers, and fewer maintenance personnel. In fact, he had proposed to Dudley goals for reducing personnel in each category by 20%, 30% and 40% respectively. He was surprised when Dudley balked at his obvious attempts to promote improved cost effectiveness and efficiency.

The Englishman fumed, and said,

> Three percent of our top management here have quit in the last few months to work for British-owned firms. They are irked by decisions like this that are made in Pittsburgh without regard or insight into our unique situation.

Jeff suspected that he did not make matters better when he pointed out that the interests of shareholders demanded such economies. In fact, he may have made the situation worse when he paraphrased Bill Keafer, vice-president of Warner Electric Clutch and Brake of Illinois, who had contrasted the performance of American and British workers: "With the same machinery the American turns out three times as much as his British counterpart. Even though we pay our workers twice as much as yours, even though we are four thousand miles from Europe and we're just two hundred years old, we each make the same product and undersell you all over the continent."

Dudley had silently accepted this rebuff and the new proposals on staffing. Yet, Jeff was startled a few days later when Dudley finally invited him to be his guest for lunch at the Imperial Club. Jeff wondered how long it would take him to be admitted to the inner sanctuary of the English gentlemen. Dudley had greeted him graciously and after a hearty meal of chops and ale, it dawned on Jeff that Dudley was still upset. Dudley fortified himself with quite a few glasses before this outburst ensued.

> Do you realize, Jeff, that since 1850 the U.S. has brought over 200,000 of our patents to produce products that you then sell to us. Furthermore, you hire away to America or in your companies here our best brains among our professions, scientists, and technicians.
>
> The past two bloody World Wars have put us in your debt. It drained the core of my country's strength and manpower. While we fought to preserve democracy in Western Europe and even the Pacific,

The past two bloody World Wars have put us in your debt. It drained the core of my country's strength and manpower.

as well as Africa and the Middle East, we also squandered in these bloody struggles the patrimony that twelve generations or more of Englishmen had built. I know you Yanks came into both conflicts to help us, but our expenditure in proportion to population, in terms of lives and money, was many times that of your country. Britain may have seemed to have been a major force in defeating Germany in both wars, but America emerged as the real victor in both conflicts. We mortgaged most of our possessions in the Western Hemisphere to stop the Nazis. While the wealth of our nation declined, yours went up. While the cream of our male leaders and even our civilian population were devastated, yours were relatively untouched. While our factories deteriorated, our gold pledged for loans during World War II, your American traders prospered and your nation left rich beyond your dreams. When we were compelled in 1940 to deposit our securities with the U.S. for a loan to survive, other European nations got similar aid in the postwar years under the Marshall Plan for nothing."

Jeff had been startled by this line of talk from Dudley and wondered about the point of it. Yet, it was uttered with a quiet intensity and feeling that he had never before sensed in his British colleague. It could not just be written off as the effect of too much alcohol. Especially, when Dudley had continued:

You set policies in the U.S., and then expect British plants to follow instructions based on American experience and requirements.

> During my lifetime, England has lost a territorial empire, while America has gained a commercial empire. I have watched my country decline drastically in natural resources and productivity, while we pursued an insane internationalism. How do you think I feel when I witness Arabs and other foreigners like yourself buying up the British Isles! I almost resent having to be employed by an American-owned subsidiary! Many of your American business chaps over here are vulgar, noisy, and brash. Your high pressure salesmanship is causing Britons to buy what they don't need and can't afford.

The conversation was loaded with implication, and Jeff did not quite know how to deal with it, or where to begin. He tried to be empathetic and agreed that some Americans were pushy, but then got back to his favorite theme of industriousness. He suggested that the British economy was improving and people could afford more if the English got over its obsession with "full employment." But Dudley continued:

> Jolly good, I don't mind you in your country defending your way of life and doing business, but don't impose your way of life on us in Great Britain and then get upset with us if we try to preserve our way of life. You set policies in the U.S., and then expect British plants to follow instructions based on American experience and requirements. I loathe the absolute conviction of your corporate headquarters on the absolute virtuousness of their policies and the perfectness of their products. You treat us like a branch factory. There are a lot of us who feel that American executives like yourself are here mainly to watch over

us. In fact, the whole form of the American take-over of business here begins to look like "commercial apartheid." What bugs me is that some of our own young technologists almost take the line, "God bless the Yanks and his relations, and keep us in our proper stations." Many of our business and government leaders have a sickening anxiety to please the Americans.

Jeff was taken back by the new direction of Dudley's responses. He has always tried hard to be fair and just in his relations with his British counterpart. Was he responsible for this ventilation of pent-up emotion? But Dudley was not finished:

Your firms force us into a dependency relationship. The power is firmly in American corporate headquarters, so that no matter how competent or effective we may be here in Britain, we have little input into your corporation policy and finance plans that affect our business here. We often have to make parts for American products that our government then contracts to buy, such as aircraft. To make matters worse, in some of the American subsidiaries, Britons are being replaced in key positions by Americans, and we are not even allowed to be shareholders. You hog all the capital! As things are now going, Britain is becoming a U.S. industrial satellite. I would like to see my country next July declare a Declaration of Economic Independence from the U.S., or else apply to become the 51st state!

And thus ended the tirade. Jeff thanked Dudley for his candor, said he would report back to headquarters on its implications, and get back to him to explore if anything could be done, at least by Easting, to improve their British relations.

But Jeff's troubles were not over on this United Kingdom jaunt. For when he took the Edinburgh Express up to visit the Leith plant, he hoped to relax with the genial Scot, Angus McKay, and get in a few rounds of golf. Their first few meetings went well, and by the third day when they shared a pleasant salmon dinner, Jeff thought all was in order. But then the very next morning, Angus got to the issue of expansion of research and development. He started on it quite bluntly, despite a lilting Scottish burr:

It sticks in my gullet that because of the War, American research and development flourished, while ours declined, putting your firms in a position to follow-up and exploit many of our patents. If we are going to have a genuine business association, our people need the opportunity to develop their research capabilities. Right now most of the significant investigations and studies are being done in the U.S. But you don't pick our brains enough here, so that we have an interchange of ideas and an intermixing of effort in every phase of activity, especially research and development. If we are to have a cooperative technology and relationship, there need to be mechanisms for more cross-fertiliza-

If we are going to have a genuine business association, our people need the opportunity to develop their research capabilities.

tion. I have some bright lads here who are bogged down in production, and I can offer little scope to utilize their research competencies. Now, don't get me wrong, Mr. Donovan, I am not complaining. But I think it is to Aquaphone's advantage to keep such talent here before some other American firm woos them to the States. You Americans have done much to build up the economy of Scotland, which we appreciate. We are very grateful that twice as many American firms have invested here as in England. I am just proposing a new direction for Aquaphone's further expenditures in Leith.

Jeff thanked him for his suggestion and asked Angus to prepare a detailed memorandum on his idea for research and development expansion, along with costs and personnel to be involved. He promised to push it in the United States, but had private reservations on how receptive top management would be to this particular proposal. Then he flew home to ponder the new challenge he was facing in the British Isles.

Issues for Analysis

1. Contrast the life space of the three principal characters in this critical incident and examine how their cultural values affected their perceptions and communications.
2. Review the briefing of the boss for what information it provides to you on the British character, culture, and way of doing business.
3. Review the critical incident in London with Dudley. List some of the learnings you received that help you to better understand why he reacted as he did. If you were Jeff, how would you report the situation to headquarters and what would you recommend?
4. Review the critical incident outside of Edinburgh with Angus. Is it a real issue for many American firms? If you were Jeff, how would you handle it and what would you recommend? What are the implications of Scottish nationalism for Americans doing business there? How would you deal with such issues, whether there or in Wales or North Ireland?
5. As you go back over this case, what applications could you make to your own situation when doing business in Britain? (Do consider the differences in British people, the social class system, the national inferiority feelings, the constraints on American executives who are not on the scene for long time periods, as well as the limitations of their own cultural backgrounds, etc.) Are there other implications from this case about doing business in Europe?

6. Does this case provide any clues on these current problems in Britain?
   - Social class unrest and conflict.
   - Obsolete social institutions and legislation.
   - Labor conflict with frequent strikes and high unemployment.
   - Differences in British/American perspectives during communications.

FRANCE

FRANCE—PROFILE

Population	58.8 million
Ethnic Groups	Celtic and Latin Teutonic, Slavic, North African, Indochinese, Basque
Religions	Roman Catholic 90%, Protestant 2%, Jewish 1%, Muslim 1%, Unaffiliated 6%
Education........................	Compulsory ages 6–16
	Literacy 99%
Land................................	213,000 mi^2
Government	Republic
Political Parties................	Socialist (PS), Communist (PCF), Left Radical (MRG), Rassemblement Pour la République (RPR), Union for French Democracy Republicans (PR), Center for Social Democrats (CDS), Radical (RAD)
Per Capita Income	$26,290
Exports to U.S.................	$5,964.9 million
Imports from U.S.	$20,636 million

Cultural Characteristics of Business in France

... the French constitute the most brilliant and the most dangerous nation in Europe and the best qualified in turn to become an object of admiration, hatred, pity or terror, but never of indifference.

Alexis de Tocqueville

... Britons and Americans value France because it is so stubbornly different. ... France has changed for the worse in the past three decades, and that its citizens are obsessed with *l'exception francaise* or France's exclusive place in the world. While the conservative French still resist change, the majority of their countrymen have accepted fast food chains, shorter lunches and summer vacations, less time for mistresses and the conveniences of supermarkets, as well as urbanization. . . . The average Frenchman is concerned about an elite of bureaucrats, businessmen, and politicians who seemingly run the country to benefit themselves amidst corruption and public scandals.

New York Times, August 1, 1999

Idealism

The French tend to believe that the basic truths on which life is based derive from principles and immutable or universal laws. They are concerned with the essence of values. The motto of the French Republic is "Liberty, Equality and Fraternity." To the French, values such as these should transcend everything else in life. They behave in an individualistic manner. *"Chacun defend son beef-steak"* (everyone protects his own steak). Sometimes they are frustrated and find it difficult to live by these ideals in everyday life, yet the hunger for these altruistic ideals is still present and deeply ingrained in most French people.

Social Structure and Status

The French are very status conscious. Social status in France depends on one's social origins. Outward signs of social status are the level of education, a beautiful house with a well-designed, tasteful facade (not a gaudy one), knowledge of literature and fine arts, and the social origins of one's ancestors.

Social classes are very important in France as well. The French social classes are the aristocracy, the upper bourgeoisie, the upper-middle bourgeoisie, the middle, the lower-middle, and lower classes (blue-collar workers, peasants). Social classes categorize people according to their professional activities (teachers, doctors, lawyers, craftsmen, foremen, and peasants), as well as, their political opinions (conservative, left-oriented).

Social interactions are thus affected by these social stereotypes. It is extremely hard for a French individual to be rid of social stereotypes. They affect personal identity. Unlike an American who can theoretically attain the highest levels of social consideration by working hard and being professionally successful, the French find it difficult to do so. If professionally successful, the French can expect to climb one or two stages of the social ladder in a lifetime, but often nothing more.

Cooperation and Competition

The French are not basically oriented towards competition. To them, the word competition has a very narrow meaning—practicing a sport at the highest level of international excellency. For example, the French

The motto of the French Republic is "Liberty, Equality and Fraternity." To the French, values such as these should transcend everything else in life.

consider superstar athletes such as Greg LeMonde, Michael Jordan, or Tiger Woods as involved in competition. The average French person does not feel affected by competition, which can be dangerous to the country's economic welfare. A few years ago during a New Year's Eve television speech, then-President Giscard d'Estaing tried to educate the French and make them face the fact that competition really should affect their lives. He said competition is not just what the French soccer team experiences during the Soccer World Cup. The economic welfare of the French people actually depends on how competitive French goods are on international markets. He tried to awaken the French to the notion of competition, so that they would motivate themselves to work harder and be more productive.

When confronted with individuals with a competitive drive, the French may interpret them as being antagonistic, ruthless, and power-hungry. They may feel threatened, and overreact or withdraw from the discussion. Yet, the pyramidal structure of the French educational system exposes French children and adolescents to competition very early.

Personal Characteristics

French people are friendly, humorous, and sardonic. Americans may also be friendly, but they are so friendly that they are seldom sardonic. Americans need to be liked. The French need to be admired. Americans tend to like people who agree with them. French people are more likely to be interested in a person who disagrees with them. Because they want to be liked, Americans try to impress others. On the other hand, the French are very hard to impress, and impatient with those who try. A French person when trying to get a sense of a person, looks for qualities within the person and for personality. An American looks at the person's achievements. French people tend to gain recognition and to develop their identity by thinking and acting against others, while Americans increase their self-esteem by acting in accord with the actions and expectations of others. French people are more inner-oriented, and base behavior and evaluations upon feelings, preferences, and expectations.

Trust and Respect

A French person trusts an individual according to their inner evaluation of the personality and character. An American trusts a person according to past personal achievements and upon other people's recognition and ranking of that person. Because social stereotypes are so vivid, an average French person cannot earn respect from members of other social classes merely through work accomplishments and performance.

Carroll[4] reports on a foreign student living with a French family who closed the door to his bedroom after dinner. The student did not understand that closed doors are considered rude and that the visitor was expected to socialize with the family. Furthermore, when their shutters

When confronted with individuals with a competitive drive, the French may interpret them as being antagonistic, ruthless, and power-hungry.

to the outside are closed, this is not a sign of the "distrustfulness of the French," but a desire for privacy from the passer-by.

Style of Conversation

Many Americans use superlatives like most, best, and largest. The reason may be the importance of competition as a social value for the Americans, along with the importance of quantified measurements in assessing standards of excellency. American conversations usually include numerous pronouns such as "I" or "my." French interlocutors seldom put themselves forward or try to make themselves look good in conversations. If they accidentally do, they will usually add, "Je ne cherche pas à me vanter mais . . ." ("I do not want to boast but . . ."). Boasting is often considered a weakness, a sign of self-satisfaction and immaturity. In conversations with the French, some may ask their French counterparts questions about themselves. The French will probably shun such questions, and orient the conversation towards more general subjects. To them, it is not proper to show characteristics of self-centeredness.

The French often criticize institutions, conditions, and people they live with. A disagreement can be considered stimulating to a French person, while Americans may perceive it as an argument and be embarrassed. It is not uncommon to see two French people arguing with each other, their faces reddened with what seems to be anger, exchanging lively, heated, and irreconcilable arguments. Then later, they shake hands and comment, "That was a good discussion. We should do it again sometime!" The French tend to think that such arguments are interesting and stimulating. It is also a meaningful outlet for tension.

Humor

The French enjoy and appreciate humor. However, the French tend to use humor in more numerous situations than Americans do. They also often add a touch of cynicism to their humor, and may not hesitate to make fun of institutions and people.

Consistency and Contradictions

Americans prefer consistency and predictability, and expect role-conforming in their relationships. The French, on the other hand, abound in contradictions and are not overly disturbed by them and relish the complexity of them. They profess lofty ideals of fraternity and equality, but at times show characteristics of utmost individualism and selfish materialism. On the political scene, they seem continuously restless, verbally criticizing the government and capitalism, yet are basically conservative.

Attitudes Toward Work

Attitudes of the French toward work depend on whether they are employed in the public sector or in the private sector. In the French bureaucracy and in public concerns, there is little incentive to be pro-

A disagreement can be considered stimulating to a French person, while Americans may perceive it as an argument and be embarrassed.

ductive. Quotas are rarely assigned, and it is virtually impossible to lay off or dismiss employees on the basis of job performance. Massive strikes have caused difficulties when companies have attempted to reform or modernize.

In the private sector, the situation is different. It is true that French workers do not respect the work ethic as much as many American counterparts do. They are usually not motivated by competition or the desire to emulate fellow workers. They frown on working overtime and have four to five weeks of vacation a year. However, they usually work hard in their allotted working time. French workers have the reputation of being productive. Part of the explanation for such productiveness may lie in the French tradition of craftsmanship. A large proportion of the French work force has been traditionally employed in small, independent businesses where there is widespread respect for a job well-done. Many French people take pride in work that is done well because traditionally they have not been employed in huge, impersonal industrial concerns. They often have a direct stake in the work they are doing, and are usually concerned with quality.

Authority

French companies contain many social reference groups that are mutually exclusive. Tight reins of authority are needed to ensure adequate job performance. The lesser emphasis on delegation of responsibility limits accountability and contributes to a more rigid organization structure. As a consequence, decision making is more centralized in French companies, and it may take longer before decisions are reached and applied. This may be a source of frustration for American executives (especially lower- and middle-management executives) who are working with French executives from a comparative management level. Americans may resent the amount of time that is necessary before their recommendations are considered and dealt with by top management. Americans are accustomed to executives having a higher degree of responsibility. The flow of communication is improved if American executives have direct access to two or three top executives of a French company. This is where the actual decision-making power is.

The highest executives of large French companies also differ from their American counterparts in their conception of authority. The top two men of a French company are less accountable than their American counterparts, generally because the French are judged on personal attributes as well as performance. It takes poor performance for them to be challenged in their functions by a board of directors or by subordinates. Patterns of authority are more stable in French industry. Therefore, because they do not need to justify their actions to the same extent, the very top French executives tend to be more autocratic in their managerial style.

Executive functions, also, have more overtones of social leadership. In their professional activities, these very top industry executives are auto-

Decision making is more centralized in French companies, and it may take longer before decisions are reached and applied. Because they do not need to justify their actions to the same extent, the very top French executives tend to be more autocratic in their managerial style.

cratic leaders, but in addition, they have a high social, and even political, status.

It is interesting to compare French and American business magazine interviews of executives. Along with professional experiences and activities, top French executives usually mention details concerning their personal lives such as former professors who had an impact on them, enriching social and personal experiences, books that influenced their outlook on life, and what their convictions on political and social issues are. On the other hand, top American executives will more likely emphasize the progression of their career in terms of professional achievements.

Organizational Structure and Decision-Making

The organizational structure of French companies tends to be more rigid than that of American companies. The French put less emphasis on control of individual performance. The Americans, on the other hand, tend to favor a flexible organizational structure with greater delegation of responsibility, and greater control of individual performance.

Americans attach much importance to achievement. Therefore, decision making in U.S. companies occurs at levels where the results allow managers to reach quantifiable goals. The decision-making process is more centralized in French companies. Important decisions are made by only the top executives.

Motivation

Most Americans put high value on professional accomplishments. Their self-esteem derives largely from these accomplishments, and so does their social status. They are motivated to work hard to earn money, because job and social security depend on such efforts. As a result, most Americans are very ambitious and expend considerable energy in their work.

However, there is a major difference between the motivations of Americans and French people concerning work. Although the French appreciate the Americans' industriousness and devotion to their work, they do not believe it is worthwhile. To the French the *qualité de la vie* (quality of life) is what matters. The French attach a great importance to free time and vacations, and are seldom willing to sacrifice the enjoyment of life out of dedication to work.

Conflict

Americans do not like conflict, especially interpersonal conflict. They feel uncomfortable, and are concerned about what others think when they are involved in conflict. Because most Americans are pragmatic, they think of conflict as a hindrance to achieving goals.

However, the French, partly because they live in a more closed society with relatively little social mobility, are used to conflict. They are aware that some positions are irreconcilable, and that people must live with these irreconcilable opinions. They, therefore, tend not to mind conflict, and sometimes enjoy it. They even respect others who carry it off with style and get results. The French are also less concerned about negative reactions from those with whom they are in conflict.

Mesbache[5] discovered that French managers reported difficulties in adjusting to life in other countries. In a study of 31 French managers from 16 French companies, he reported problems caused by emphasis in the French culture on pride in their past cultural heritage, causing them to be too critical of people who do not benefit from that same cultural tradition. In their self-descriptions, the French managers felt handicapped by their conditioning to a formal way of thinking, and by lack of actual knowledge of other cultures.

TIPS FOR WORKING IN FRANCE

- ❏ A firm and pumping handshake is considered uncultured. A French handshake is a quick shake with some pressure in the grip.
- ❏ A French woman offers her hand first.
- ❏ Punctuality in business and social invitation is important. If invited to a person's home for a social occasion, it is polite to bring a gift of flowers or wine, but not roses or chrysanthemums because they are used at funerals.
- ❏ At mealtime a French person enjoys pleasant conversation, but not personal questions or the subject of money.
- ❏ Snapping the fingers of both hands and slapping an open palm over a closed fist have vulgar meanings.
- ❏ Great importance is placed on neatness and taste.

The French are also less concerned about negative reactions from those with whom they are in conflict.

FEDERAL REPUBLIC OF GERMANY

GERMANY—PROFILE

Population	81.7 million
Ethnic Groups	German, Danish, Turkish minorities
Religions	Roman Catholic 45%, Protestant 45%
Education	99% Literacy
Land	137,828 mi²
Government	Republic
Political Parties	Christian Democratic Union (CDU), Christian Socialist Union (CSU), Free Democratic (FDP), Social Democrats (SPD), Communist (DKP), Green Party, Party of Democratic Socialism (PDS)

(Profile continued on next page)

Per Capita Income	$28,860
Exports to U.S	$24,458 million
Imports to U.S	$43,121.5 million

> Where were you the day the Wall came down.
> *Business Week*, November 27, 1989

> Laughing clubs are being organized in Germany to combat the trend toward seriousness. Statistics show that on average Germans only laugh six minutes daily. There are now 22 laughing clubs around the country with about 350 members.
> *The Prague Post*, September 17, 1999

The integration of the Western free enterprise/ democratic tradition and the Eastern totalitarian/ socialistic tradition of the past fifty years moves steadily forward.

For Europeans the day November 9, 1989 was a date that will live long in their memories. The elimination of the Berlin Wall marked the end of an era. The beginning of a new era dawned on October 3, 1990 when Germany was reunified. We present this information on the Federal Republic of Germany and some on Eastern Europe, realizing that the political and economic situation is changing very rapidly. As a reunited whole, Germany has evolved into a democratic, market-oriented system. The integration of the Western free enterprise/democratic tradition and the Eastern totalitarian/socialistic tradition of the past fifty years moves steadily forward. However, cultural values, mindsets, as well as customs, and courtesies do not change quickly and endure even when political events change.

After forty years of life apart, how long will it be until the former "east Germans" and the "west Germans" become simply Germans? To simplify outrageously, the *weiss* think the *ossis* have spent too long living in their own little world and are naive, unsophisticated, and lack self-confidence. They are not good as managers or entrepreneurs because they have no experience in a market economy and are far from being grateful for the benefits unity has brought.

The *ossis* think the *weiss* are arrogant and that relentless competition has made them hard as nails. Furthermore, the westerns have secured the best jobs in the east making the *ossis* resentful.

Such stereotypes must be revised because studies show:

❑ Unemployment in the east hit women workers disproportionately. However, since 1990, 150,000 east German women have started their own businesses.

❑ Western managers who have worked with easterners say they show more enthusiasm and flexibility than their counterparts in the west.

❑ Easterners attach more importance to work than they do leisure.

❑ Easterners consider themselves to be more independent, interested and warmhearted compared to westerners.[6]

Cultural Characteristics of Business

Located in the northern part of Europe, the Federal Republic of Germany occupies an area of approximately 137,828 square miles and is about the size of Montana with a population estimated at 81 million. Northern Germany is relatively flat, however, the elevation rises gradually in the south. The climate is considered temperate.

Germans have a reputation for being industrious, hard working, reserved, and perhaps even cold. They are meticulous and exact, and often militaristic in the preciseness of their actions. On the other hand, some of the world's greatest composers, writers, and philosophers are products of a German heritage.

The Germans are not an outward people; they tend to be very private. Though their daily routine brings them into close contact with many different people, they are close to only a very few. The German language is a key to understanding this. The Germans make a strong distinction between an acquaintance *(Bekannte)* and a friend *(Freund)*. German will only use *Freund* when he or she really means it, otherwise it is a *Bekannte*. Close family ties are also cherished.

Because Germans are exact, bus, train, and plane schedules all run on schedule. The manager's day is also well planned. The Germans are not a spontaneous people. Their attitude is to organize the time allotted to its greatest efficiency, rather than take an attitude of wait and see what happens.

The Federal Republic was only a part of an earlier and far more extensive Germany. The basic legislation establishing the present form of government is the Grundgesetz (basic law) of 1949 in which a constitutional federal democracy was formed. After the Second World War, the Allied forces divided Germany into two countries, moving the capital from Berlin to Bonn during this period. It was felt it would be difficult to have Berlin continue to serve as the capital, because it was not only a divided city, but also it was completely surrounded by the communist East Zone, the German Democratic Republic (East Germany). In 1990, the two Germanies were reunified and Berlin is again the capital.

There are two main governing bodies in Germany, the Bundestag (Parliament) and the Bundesrat (Federal Council). The Bundestag, the larger of the two, comprises elected representatives from the ten states and possesses legislative power. The Bundestag consists of approximately 615 deputies who are elected for a 4-year term. It consists of approximately 68 members, who have nonvoting status, although it can exercise the veto power in matters concerning Laender (the 15 states) interests. Germany has a president; however, the position is of honor

Because Germans are exact, bus, train, and plane schedules all run on schedule. The manager's day is also well planned.

and formality, not one of power. The real power lies in the office of chancellor *(Bundeskanzler)*. The chancellor is either the leading representative of the party with a majority of seats in the Bundestag, or the leader of the largest party in a coalition government.

The Christian Democratic Union, the major party, operates with the Christian Socialist Union. Although each party maintains its own structure, the two form a common caucus in the Bundestag and do not run opposing campaigns. The CDU/CSU is generally conservative on economic and social policy.

The SDP is the second major party in Germany and stresses social programs. In foreign policy, it emphasizes ties with the Atlantic alliance but seeks improved relations with Eastern Europe. The SDP has a powerful base in the larger cities and industrialized Laender.

Though some of Germany's past can be seen in the old cities and buildings, much of Germany is very modern. This is especially true of the major cities and industrial areas, which were almost destroyed during World War II. Germany has risen from the rubble to become the third largest industrial giant in the Western world, following the U.S. and Japan.

There are three things that heavily influence the structure of business in Germany today. These points are the European Community (EC), codetermination, and government involvement. Germany is one of the original members of the EC. Much of German business practices and laws are directly tied to the regulations and directives from the EC.

The principle of collective good is important in the idea of codetermination *(Mitbestimmung)*. Codetermination allows for worker input into the management of the firm. Any firm with more than five employees should have a worker's council *(Betriebsrat)* that represents the employees and helps them solve various grievances with the firm's management. Any coal or steel firm of more than 2,000 workers is required to have 50% of the company's supervisory board composed of workers. There is also a specially chosen labor representative to represent labor on the management board of the company. This all illustrates an attempt to include a most important part of the economic structure, the worker.

Unions are very strong and provide workers with many more rights than some foreign counterparts. For example, they can become involved in decisions on dismissal. The process of codetermination gives management and workers the opportunity to work together to shape or define the firm's goals, objectives, and responsibilities. Employees are represented in five trade unions of professional organizations: German Trades Union Federation, German Salaried Staff Union, Christian Trade Union Federation, German Civil Servant's Federation, and the Union of Executive Employees.

The Germans are among the highest paid workers in the world and enjoy a high standard of living. They are able to afford the luxuries and extras of life. An important part of this concept is the vast welfare state that supports the German worker. This includes liberal pensions, bonus-

Three things...

heavily influence

the structure of

business in

Germany

today... the

European

Community (EC),

codetermination,

and government

involvement.

es, medical and dental care, and five to six weeks of paid vacation. Though taxes are heavy, this system has relieved the typical German from many financial worries.

Germany is committed to a free enterprise economy, but government and business work very closely together. The former communist system of East Germany is being transformed into an economy where there is more voluntary participation of business with government in planning the economy. This means there is greater cooperation to decide what is best for Germany as a whole.

Another important factor in the economy is the extent of government control/participation in industry. The state holds control or equity participation in hundreds of firms. In the public service arena, the railroads and postal system are now privatized with the state owning most of the shares. The state also owns a trade monopoly in alcohol.

An area that is perhaps the fastest growing in Germany, as well as throughout Europe, is joint government and private business ventures. This means a partnership between private business and firms controlled by the government. With denationalization ongoing, this increase in joint partnership ventures is another indication of "collective interest" being an important part of the German business and economic community.

Trade plays a very important role in the German economy to sustain growth and the German standard of living because sufficient natural resources are very limited. By far the largest percentage of trade is within the EC.

Social Customs

Germans are very knowledgeable and capable business people. They pride themselves on having quality products to offer on the world markets. They are formal in their business dealings, not only with foreigners, but among themselves as well. For the foreigner, it is best to be conservative and subdued, unless you are given the indication to be more informal. The Germans do not like loud people, especially in business, and have little respect for the pushy or brassy businessperson. To them such behavior reflects a weakness in the person or company.

In Germany, you must be very careful of what you say, either in print or verbally. If the other party can show that something was promised or intimated, even though a contract was not signed, you can still be held liable for that promise. This is a reason why the Germans tend to be so exact in their dealings and somewhat more distant in their business relationships.

The handshake is an important part of the German greeting. They shake hands often, not only on the first greeting of the day, but also at the conclusion of a conversation. Firm handshakes are preferred. Generally the older person, or the person of higher authority, will extend the hand first. The woman extends her hand first, unless the man holds a higher position. A verbal response also accompanies the handshake.

Germany is committed to a free enterprise economy, but government and business work very closely together.

Men should bow slightly. This is mostly a slight bow from the shoulders and neck as the man leans forward a little as he greets the other person. If one is entering a room filled with many people, the person should proceed around the room shaking everyone's hands. Again, a friendly "good morning" or "good day" is appropriate.

In Germany, there are two forms of address, the polite and the familiar. The familiar form *du,* similar to "thou" in English, is used only for relatives, very close friends, children, and animals. The polite form *sie* is used on all other occasions, including the business environment. Any foreigner addressing a German should use the polite form. Many Germans have known each other for years and still use the polite form. A German may initiate the usage of the *du* form, although this is a rare occurrence.

Not only should you use the polite form of speech, but you should also refrain from using first names; *Herr* and *Frau* are more appropriate. In addition, women should always be called Frau regardless of their marital status.

The Germans are title conscious and proper etiquette requires addressing them by their title. Also, those who have attained their Ph.D. are addressed by the term *doktor*; i.e., "Herr Doktor Schmidt" or "Frau Doktor Braun." Women are called by their first names. The wife of Georg Meyer will not be Frau Georg Meyer, but rather Frau Ursula Meyer. A friend or associate should introduce the newcomer to the group, as Germans prefer third-party introductions.

In some countries, it is quite common to entertain a client for dinner at a fashionable restaurant. In Germany, particularly with large corporations dealing in multimillion-dollar contracts, the superiors will not allow their subordinates to accept the invitation. Many German firms would consider this to be a conflict of interest and one could easily lose his objectivity—*Verpflichtungen*. A good rule to follow is to conduct business during business hours.

The Germans like to discuss things and enjoy a good discussion on the topics of the day. Religion, politics, and nuclear power are freely discussed, but conversations relating to one's private life should be avoided.

Gestures

The Germans are generally restrained in their body movements. They do not wave their arms and hands a lot as in other cultures. It is impolite to talk to someone with your hands in your pockets. It is also considered rude to sit with the bottom of your shoes facing another person. For this reason, German men cross their legs at the knees, rather than with an ankle on the other knee. Most body movements could best be characterized as conservative. Whether sitting or standing, it is generally in a more upright and rigid position.

The Germans like to discuss things and enjoy a good discussion on the topics of the day.

Language

German is the official language in Germany, although in border areas, other languages are spoken more often. There are hundreds of dialects and local variations spoken throughout the countryside, although dialects are generally only spoken in less formal situations with friends. *Hochdeutsch,* or the "high" German, is found in all magazines, newspapers, television, etc. In a business context, your counterpart will avoid the usage of dialects. English is the major foreign language taught in Germany. Most business people are conversant in English.

Religion

The Roman Catholic Church (45%) and the German Protestant Church (45%) account for just about all religious affiliations. Both churches are very powerful and influential in Germany. Other denominations are grouped together in what the Germans call Sekte (sects). Church activity in general has dropped over the years. There is not the clear separation of church and state as in the U.S. or other European countries.

GENERAL TIPS FOR DOING BUSINESS IN GERMANY

- ❑ Guests usually stand when the host enters the room and remain standing until he offers them a seat again.
- ❑ References to baseball, basketball, or American football are usually not completely understood.
- ❑ Do not talk with your hands in your pockets.
- ❑ Do not prop your leg or legs on desks, chairs, or tables.
- ❑ A handshake is the most common form of greeting, but it should be firm only with men.
- ❑ Chew gum only in private.
- ❑ Do not point at your head.
- ❑ Use cosmetics and jewelry sparingly.
- ❑ Do not talk about personal finances.
- ❑ Do not brag about your personal achievements.

EASTERN/CENTRAL EUROPE

Where or What Is Eastern Europe?

> Time has finally run out for Communism. But its edifice has not yet crumbled. May we not be crushed beneath its rubble instead of gaining liberty.
>
> *Alexander I. Solzhenitsyn*

There are hundreds of dialects and local variations spoken throughout the countryside, although dialects are generally only spoken in less formal situations with friends.

For all the money and attention devoted to ex-communist countries, no one has yet worked out where they are. That is to say, plopping the whole lot into an area called "Eastern Europe" is convenient, but falls foul of geography, reason, and fairness. Geography, because the five central Asian republics (Kazakhstan being the largest) have no claim to being *eastern* and the Caucasian ones are in limbo between Asia and Europe. Bureaucrats take a long breath and speak in one gulp of central and eastern Europe, the newly independent states. But this disguises reality, the real problem that contemporary national borders do not reflect. People and history should be the criteria as much as borders.[7]

Among the disappearing institutions to which Solzhenitsyn refers was the East Bloc or COMECON, which once included in this economic "alliance," the Soviet Union and its satellite nations. Predictably, the former Union of Soviet Socialist Republics (USSR) outweighed the other countries, accounting for two-thirds of the total market and absorbing the resources of member states who were also bound by military allegiance to its Warsaw Pact. Freed of the Communist yoke, the nearly 380+ million behind the Iron Curtain said "goodbye" to such arrangements, and turned westward for capital, resources, and training. Although the newly liberated nations of Eastern and Central Europe will look to develop markets in Western Europe, North and South America, Asia and Africa, their principal trading partners are likely to be each other and the emerging "Commonwealth of Independent States" (CIS).

After decades under rigid Communist control, East Germany (now united with West Germany), Poland, Czechoslovakia, Hungary, the disintegrating Yugoslavia, Romania, Bulgaria, and Albania, as well as the CIS itself, are in the midst of slow, painful, traumatic changes toward greater democratic reforms and market economies. In the process, all these victims of centralized socialistic planning are left with exhausted labor reserves and high unemployment, ill-prepared and unproductive workers, out-of-date machinery and plants. In addition to severe shortage of food and consumer goods, these nations are devastated by a frightful legacy of environmental pollution, ecological and economic ruins, as well as a collapsing infrastructure. The failed totalitarian utopia and ideology left them a damaged citizenry on the verge of social collapse. Zbigniew Brzezinski, former U.S. presidential adviser, reminds us not to mourn the passing of this empire called "evil" because it produced more deaths than any other country, through purges, exile, mass deportation, genocide, and state terrorism. No wonder its citizens became cynical, and rejected the "dictatorship of the proletariat."

Much has happened in "Eurasia" during the last two editions of this book, and in the next sections we will describe the "way it was for the last 70 years—a system of "top-down" control over society's entire structure by a single bureaucratized party called the *nomenklatura*. For that was the environment in this vast area which still affects "mindset"

People and history should be the criteria as much as borders.

of this generation even after the demise of the Soviet Union and the onset of the second Russian Revolution.

Now the whole political, social, and business situation is in profound transition. Representatives there from free-enterprise nations and companies are more welcome, but they face a whole new series of challenges and opportunities. The pace of change in these lands differs from Hungary and Poland, which are in the vanguard, to Albania, which still clings to the hard-line Communist approach.

The underlying reasons for the alterations in these nations are economic—authoritarian government with its centralized planning and administration is not working, and the economies of all the nations are in severe trouble. Reforming Communist societies economically, however, has led their peoples increasingly to demand political reforms—mainly toward more democratization and nationalization.

However, the essential problem for the people in Eastern Europe's nine nations is *cultural conditioning*. Having been conditioned for decades to a totalitarian system run by a Communist elite, the workers are not easily coaxed into making individual decisions and participating, into exercising initiative and imagination. Even when given freedom, creativity has been long stifled by mindless conformity.

Eastern Europe's Changing Business Culture

The East European market for West Bloc suppliers is basically open for agricultural products, new industrial, electronic and chemical products. The future may be for consumer products and high technologies as well as significant foreign aid.

In the recent past, the Communist Party of the East European countries dominated the countries' political and economic life. All major government and economic decision-making posts were filled by party members. The guiding party doctrine of democratic centralism ensured that decisions made at the top were not questioned by the lower echelons. This led to a situation in which a few people at the peak of the pyramid made almost every significant decision, and local initiative was practically nonexistent.

The export and import monopoly of the ministry of foreign trade and its foreign trade organizations prevented industrial ministries and producing enterprises from having any meaningful contact with world market demand and supply. The main idea governing the institution of a state monopoly was to prevent capitalist countries from influencing the course of economic activities in the east European countries. Now, western investment and trade are sought.

An organization that may be helpful for newcomers in East European countries is the Chamber of Commerce and Industry. This organization is not directly involved in foreign trade deals, but carries out numerous functions aimed at promoting East European foreign trade. This organi-

The East European market for West Bloc suppliers is basically open for agricultural products, new industrial, electronic and chemical products. An organization that may be helpful for newcomers in East European countries is the Chamber of Commerce and Industry.

zation can set up contacts with officials in the Foreign Trade Organization and in other organizations. The national chamber of commerce coordinates the activities of the chambers of commerce from all branch offices in large cities throughout each country. Among the main functions of the chamber of commerce is developing contacts with foreign business organizations. To promote trade and economic relations with particular countries, several joint chambers of commerce have been set up. They invite and act as a host to foreign commercial delegations visiting the country, as well as sending their own delegations abroad. They help arrange foreign exhibitions in the particular country and organize participation of their own countries in international trade fairs abroad. The chamber handles operations involved in patenting foreign inventions in East European countries and East European countries' inventions abroad, as well as the registration of trademarks in East Europe.

In the 21st century, the nations of Central Europe identify increasingly with Western culture—they seek admission to the European Community and the North American Treaty Organization, as well as other international organizations. Old European institutions are finding new missions and roles. With the reduction of Soviet militarism, NATO is transforming itself into an organization of peacekeepers. Half a century after its founding, NATO's expanded its mandate to extend freedom, human rights, civility, and the rule of law in Europe. In an end-of-the century world of failed states and repeated atrocities, NATO has decided it must sometime have the courage to act to uphold a moral standard, one that the laws of war have long but often vainly identified.[8]

Many of these peoples caught in the conflict of the former "Cold War" suffer from a national identity crisis. In the former Czechosolvakia, the problem was settled peacefully by dividing into two entities—the Czech and Slovak Republics. In Yugoslavia, the opposite happened—civil war, ethnic cleansing, and human rights abuses, and currently negotiations forced upon the parties by the international community. The cultural conflict is both religious and ethnic in nature, and has gone on for centuries.

Until the current reforms, it should be noted that members of these Eastern Europe Chambers were members of the Communist Party, and some used it as a cover for government intelligence organizations. Now the system is under transformation, which may go on for decades. The trends, depending on where you are in Eastern Europe, are toward reviving the private sector, so that business people cannot only own property, but get access to labor, capital, machinery and raw materials. Increasingly, managers and executives are being pen-nitted direct negotiation with foreign business representatives and investors. In opening up the huge, inefficient public sector, governments have undertaken a number of reform experiments, such as:

The trends, depending on where you are in Eastern Europe, are toward reviving the private sector, so that business people cannot only own property, but get access to labor, capital, machinery and raw materials.

- Demonopolization and down-sizing to hundreds of smaller production entities.
- Production subsidies, like those given to consumers, but to losing state companies.
- Legislative changes making it easier to transform state-owned to private or cooperative-owned enterprises.
- Price setting by the market instead of the government.
- Creation of a more flexible and open banking system that lends money on the basis of fiscal soundness instead of planner's whim.
- Innovations to attract Western investment and credit, and foster joint ventures (e.g., Western debt-holders permitted to cancel part of their foreign debt holdings in return for equity share in state firms).

The slow shift is seemingly away from ideology and the planned economy toward a non-capitalist market economy—production, price, and the like come from the market, not government, but the factories responding to the orders are somehow communally owned and democratically managed by a board of experts. Many Eastern European countries, such as Poland and Russia itself, are attempting to transfer ownership of state properties to share-owning workers. Property ownership is a key concept undergoing redefinition.

Global managers with vision see new market possibilities in Eastern Europe, and seek to develop links there with representatives from governments, parties, unions, businesses, churches, environmentalists, and students. Aware of the cultural and intellectual heritage of the region, as well as its potential, they network and encourage entrepreneurs, provide training and services, promote diversification and outside investment. Exchanges of managers and students between free enterprise nations and organizations with counterparts in Eastern Europe are fostered. Trade and education can be powerful means to facilitating reform, and the countries to start with are Hungary and Poland as these media reports demonstrate.

After the devastation of WWII, Eastern Europe has suffered through years of political and economic upheaval and mismanagement.

> Poland and Hungary, which have reformed their economies most, are booming, have low inflation, and falling interest rates. And their economies increasingly face west, not east. Most of their trade is now with the European Union, the biggest foreign investor in their economies. They are, moreover, on a fast track to EU membership, conceivably by 2005; and they will one day join the euro. . . .
>
> Poland and Hungary are reforming more effectively. By and large, they have restructured their state firms before selling them off. Poland has dealt with banks' bad debt and is now privatizing them. Hungary's banking market is mostly foreign-owned and highly competitive. Both countries have enjoyed several years of strong growth. Poland's economy grew by 5% in the 12 months to the third quarter of last year; Hungary's did even better, with GDP growth of 5.6%.[9]

After the devastation of WWII, Eastern Europe has suffered through years of political and economic upheaval and mismanagement. Western assistance, in the form of investment and joint ventures, that feature a mix of generous terms and innovative marketing are enabling a new wave of hopeful deliberate growth. A cultural and economic revolution is underway, as well as an ideological reformation in which the concept of "socialism" is being redefined and reapplied. The 21st century provides a rare chance to produce cultural synergy and peaceful prosperity in this region for those bold enough to participate in the improvement process.

Making Distinctions Between Peoples and Systems

For effective international trade and relations, global managers must distinguish between a people and culture that one may admire, and a political and economic ideology or systems that one may not. The myriad cultures of Eastern Europe from Poland through Russia have produced admirable civilizations and talented citizens. Although one may prefer an open, free enterprise system over a closed, totalitarian form, a successful global manager still seeks synergy and peaceful relations with the inhabitants of the latter who may voluntarily or by force of circumstances live that way.

The countries of Eastern Europe are in profound transition to a market-oriented economy.

Stereotyping all Communists is not only ethnocentric, but unwise business strategy. The countries of Eastern Europe are in profound transition to a market-oriented economy. Many former communists are in leadership positions in business and politics. Some have genuinely embraced democratic, free enterprise concepts and practices; others among them fiercely resist such changes. The challenge for global leaders is to encourage the former, while supporting those non-communists who seek their country's revival within a larger European partnership.

A case in point was Armand Hammer, a physician who became chairman of Occidental Petroleum Corporation in Los Angeles. Probably no Western businessperson had done more to develop large-scale economic cooperation between the United States and Marxist countries. Hammer was a classic entrepreneur who first went to the Soviet Union in 1921 with medical relief. That intercultural experience helped to transform him into an importer and exporter who in the process became a multi-millionaire. After 60 years of dealing with communist leaders from Lenin of the Soviet Union to Deng Xiaoping of the People's Republic of China, Hammer had high praise for the leaders personally, as well as for their peoples and their national achievements.

Hammer forecast the culture of free enterprise would take root not only in Russia and its neighboring republics, but also in all of Asia, even the People's Republic of China. The old, passive and submissive mentality of populations formerly under totalitarian regimes is dying as inhabitants regain their dignity and enthusiasm for work.

To acculturate the peoples of Eastern Europe to real democracy and a market economy is a massive re-education challenge. George Soros has made the case for this.[10] Through his private Soros Foundation, this billionaire funds practical projects in this region and China by dissenters, journalists, educators, and entrepreneurs seeking to bolster battered economies in their transition from socialism to free enterprise systems. In 1991, at the start of the infamous Soviet coup, his foundation gave photocopiers to Russian President Boris Yeltsin and helped print fliers to rally Moscow citizens to support the embattled reformers behind the barricades at the Federation's "White House." Since then, this founder of the mutual Quantum Fund spends 80% of his time traveling to urge, cajole, and influence leaders and policy to stop spiraling chaos and economic collapse of the Commonwealth republics and their Eastern Bloc neighbors through a new type "Marshall Plan" with a central bank to further credit and trade in the region.[11]

Perelman and Bereny[12] maintain that academic initiatives, including those of the U.S. Treasury secretary and the International Monetary Fund, make a mistake by focusing upon education of the old Soviet managerial elite. Instead the emphasis should be upon broadly cultivating entrepreneurial job skills, as well as basic market and consumer literacy among the masses of people victimized under the former Communist empire. They advocate the following for former Soviet bloc countries, temporarily impoverished as they come out of their "dark age":

❑ Promote economic re-education of whole workforces as was done by General Electric at Hungary's Tungstram plants to cut costs and improve productivity.
❑ Encourage distance education by telecommunication, instead of relying on traditional scholastic methods bound by buildings and transportation of students.
❑ Enhance commercial enterprise to discount sales of products and services needed in Eastern Europe for re-learning about capitalism and how it works, rather than depend on the grant approach.

Instead of charity and philanthropy for these emerging democracies, Perelman and Bereny advocate seeking lucrative market opportunities for prodigious learning in Eastern and Central Europe like franchise business with training, such as McDonald's Hamburger University. They suggest that the Commonwealth itself devote part of their foreign sales of oil and gold to this reeducation process.

RUSSIAN FEDERATION
AND THE COMMONWEALTH
OF INDEPENDENT STATES (C.I.S)

For over half the 20th century, a geopolitical and cultural entity existed called the Union of Soviet Socialist Republics (USSR) founded in 1922. This huge area included 140 national groups—some European and some Asian in culture; some Christian and some 50 million Islamic in religion. The loyalities of inhabitants in this vast region have always been first to their tribe, clan, or village, Despite many negative impacts, centralized planning and socialism did produce many accomplishments in terms of improved health, education, industrialization, and spectacular advances in the space program. Yet within 74 years, this totalitariam superpower began to collapse and implode despite the best efforts of then-president Mikhail Gorbachev to promote renewal through *glasnost*. The Cold War with the West was lost, and the Eastern Bloc of nations disintegrated. Today, some former socialistic states seek membership in the European Union and the North Atlantic Treaty Organization (NATO).

Rising from the ruins of the Soviet empire is the Russian Federation under the democratic reformists, lead first by President Boris Yeltsin. We include here a profile of Russia, the centerpiece in the emerging Commonwealth of Independent States (CIS).

RUSSIA—PROFILE

Population	145.8 million
Ethnic Groups	Russian 82% and 126 different ethnic groups (27 million), Tatar 3.8%, Ukranian 3%
Religions	Russian Orthodox 18%, Atheist 70%, Muslim 9%, Other 3%
Education	Compulsory 10 years (from age 7)
Land	6.59 million mi^2
Government	Federation, Bicameral Parliamentary system
Political Parties	Russia's Democratic Choice, Liberal Democratic Party of Russia, Communist Party of the Russian Federation, Agrarian Party of Russia, Independents and others
Per Capita Income	$2,410

Changing Business Cultures of Russia and the C.I.S.

The former Soviet empire stretched from the Gulf of Finland to the Pacific, then containing 31 autonomous republics and regions with some 450 million inhabitants, 112 recognized languages and 5 different alphabets. With the demise of the Union of Soviet Republics on December 8, 1991 came a collapse of centralized government services and support from Moscow, a socialist type economy, and a push for increased sovereignty or independence. The Russian Federation came into being with a Duma or lower house of parliament dominated by ex-communists and reform obstructionists, while the upper house of regional leaders sought to curb Kremlin control. Russia has attempted to provide leadership among former satellite states of the U.S.S.R. by forming the Commonwealth of Independent States (C.I.S.). It is a noble attempt to form an alliance that would promote cooperation among the members while allowing for national diversity. So far the strategy has not worked because of the continuing chaos and economic crises within Russia itself. With a breakdown of old systems, there has been a vacuum with no relevant pre-communist institutions that could be revived quickly. A struggle for power and reform goes on in Russia between those seeking free enterprise and more democracy, and those ex-communist who favor centralized planning and controls. The renewal of Russia's financial, legal and economic systems languishes while a new infrastructure has yet to be constructed.

Remnick[13] has observed that as the great monolith disintegrates, the initial excitement of the populace has been replaced by widespread dejection and lethargy. At the turn of the century, Russia is no longer a superpower and military threat. The rapid turnover in leadership, the rise of new strongmen and affluent elite, the increase in crime and corruption, the misuse of new freedoms, the economic stagnation—all combine to make its disenchanted citizens lower their expectations and struggle for survival. Yet Remnick writes of positive signs of Russian renewal; increased privatization, great freedom of religion and the arts, decline in inflation, and growth in entrepreneurialism. Realistically, it will be well into the 21st century before Russia can transform itself into a more open, democratic, and free enterprise society.

Meanwhile with an entire culture in profound transition, it is a challenge for the outsider to understand the situation, whether as an investor, businessperson, or tourist. One can be impressed by Russia's historical progress, cultural heritage, artistic contributions, magnificent edifices, and impressive outer space accomplishments. Some contemporary issues to consider about Russia and its people are:[14]

❑ Declining exports and increasing imports that many cannot afford, plus market forces that officials cannot control.
❑ As millions of workers go unpaid, some for more than a year, government credibility has hit a new low. Strikes, beggary, penury, stress, and alcoholism have risen rapidly.
❑ Intelligent Muscovites are talking seriously for the first time in five years about a financial and political crisis that may have to be settled by force.

With a breakdown of old systems, there has been a vacuum with no relevant pre-communist institutions that could be revived quickly. The renewal of Russia's financial, legal and economic systems languishes while a new infrastructure has yet to be constructed.

- The chaos of currency speculation and devaluation, plus staggering foreign debt could pave the way for a creeping coup, constitutional or otherwise.
- If things continue to disintegrate, the fear is that Russia will swing to facism, antisemitism, or extreme nationalism and economic protectionism.
- With the "new capitalism" failing to deliver, the masses have become disillusioned with privatization that seemingly only benefits the "new aristocracy"—notorious tycoons or oligarchs who prosper through "crony capitalism" and deposit their profits abroad.
- Foreign investors who are used to reaping big profits are now wary as the country seeks to restructure its debt obligations.

Instability and Transformation

Some immediate problems facing the Commonwealth are:

- Accelerating disintegration of the economy and need for new economic systems and enterprises.
- Deepening crises in food/consumer goods production and distribution, as well as housing.
- Breakdowns in fuel and transportation systems.
- Extensive job dislocation and rising unemployment.
- Political fragmentation and power-seeking by the republics, such as the independence movement in Chechnya.

The transition to a market system within the Commonwealth and among its neighboring republics has many positives upon which to capitalize, such as:

- Incredible human resources of literate peoples with a millennium of unique traditions and contributions to the arts and sciences from music and the ballet to space technology and physics.
- Vast natural and material resources, much of which is yet to be developed.
- Sound educational system that provides high-level instruction in mathematics and sciences.
- Co-dependent economies that foster cooperative alliances, as in a compact signed among five Central Asian republics of Kazakhstan, Kirghizia, Tadzhikistan, Turkmenia, and Uzbekistan.
- Growing interest in preserving and protecting the environment and preventing disasters like nuclear accidents.
- Widespread movement toward divesting state industries to private enterprise, and state landholdings to private ownership.
- Majority of the population demonstrating for conservative public decisions made in a democratic way, desiring order and discipline, but not totalitarianism.

The transition to a market system within the Commonwealth and among its neighboring republics has many positives upon which to capitalize.

OBJECTIVES OF THE C.I.S.[15]

☐ Repeal all Soviet laws and assume powers of old regime.
☐ Launch radical economic reforms, including freeing most prices.
☐ Keep the ruble, but allow new currencies.
☐ Set up European community-style free trade.
☐ Create joint control of nuclear weapons.
☐ Fulfill all Soviet foreign treaties and debt obligations.

☐ Increasing interest in protecting individual and human rights, while moving in the direction of democracy and economic pragmatism.
☐ Resurgence of religion and religious tolerance.
☐ Expanding entrepreneurialism, even among academics and scientists.

In addition to the Russian Federation, the other key Commonwealth player is the ancient Ukraine with its beautiful capital of Kiev. This major republic encompasses a land mass of 233,100 square miles with 52 million inhabitants. Native Ukrainians make up 74% of that population, with 21% ethnic Russian. Although entirely dependent upon Russia for oil, gasoline, and natural gas, this new country is known as the "breadbasket" for producing food in the previous Soviet Union, 56% of its corn; 54% of its sugar beets; 25% of its wheat; 21% of its milk and meat; and 26% of its potatoes. The Ukraine also provides 47% of its iron, 23% of its coal, and 30% of its chemical industry equipment. The importance of this republic in the new economic alliance is evident not only in these statistics, but in the fact that it manufactured a fourth of the USSR's agricultural machinery and construction equipment.

Trade and Business Opportunities

Breaking into the C.I.S. markets takes an enormous amount of perseverance and hard work by foreign firms. The companies that have succeeded developed long-range strategies and approached market opportunities aggressively

Although the C.I.S. can offer foreign companies and universities much in terms of scientific, technical, and engineering talent, as well as processes, its greatest need from the West and Japan is for capital investment, plus management systems and development. A good case in point is KamAZ, an auto and truck manufacturing giant founded in 1969 at Kama in Central Russia that developed hundreds of subsidiaries in the Ukraine, Kazakhstan, and Bashkiria. During the "detente" period of the '70s, it benefited from a multinational consortium of American, West German, French, and Italian firms that provided millions of dollars worth of equipment and 1,000 foreign experts. By the '80s, production of rugged, sophisticated trucks and engines had risen to 250,000 units

Although the C.I.S. can offer foreign companies and universities much in terms of scientific, technical, and engineering talent, as well as processes, its greatest need from the West and Japan is for capital investment, plus management systems and development.

annually. But with the communist state pocketing the profits, no modernization, and an acute shortage of equipment, the huge enterprise with 170,000 employees and a "company city" of 500,000 began to suffer from deterioration. In 1989, "perestroika" led to more privatization as workers approved lease-holding and empowered management to negotiate for them to take over the state-owned business. Under the innovative leadership of its general manager, Nikolai Beth, a joint stock company was established with shares purchased by its own personnel and 1,200 other plans and organizations. In the '90s, the KamAZ products are winning prizes at international rallys and competitions, but the worker-owners link their higher living standards and social protection with growth of production and quality improvement. Their corporate future depends upon penetrating foreign markets with their reliable, heavy-duty trucks, as sales in Saudi Arabia, Senegal, and Egypt prove. For that to happen, KamAZ seeks international partners in trading firms and automove firms throughout the world. The saga of the transformation and requirements of this one Russian business is both symbolic of what is happening throughout the republics in the C.I.S., and the opportunities for cultural synergy by businesses from mature market economies.

In the past few years more than 1,300 joint venture agreements were entered into by Western and Russian companies and institutions. Corporate giants have proven that successful projects could be accomplished even with the old regime, as Pepsico, Coca Cola, Dow Chemical, Marriott, and American Express have demonstrated. Most suffered from the Soviet bureaucracy and their regulations, but some, like McDonald's, are achieving superbly. If fledgling democracy and free enterprise are to prosper in the Commonwealth, then business innovators must reach out and take risks for long-term technological and commercial undertakings, such as the following:

❑ KMPG-Peat Marwick formed a joint venture in 1991 with Moscow's Institute of Post Graduate Management Training in Construction, the Civil Engineering Institute, and Perestroika Joint Venture. Together they established the International Construction Management Center (ICMC) to provide management training and technical assistance to 40,000 Commonwealth managers in construction and related industries. This was accomplished after KMPG had established a successful presence in nearby Eastern European countries. The ICMC also hopes to link Western businesses, suppliers, financiers, and governments to construction opportunities in the area.

❑ Novogorod Business School is the second to be opened with the help of the Soviet-U.S. Society of Business Training. Set up in 1991 in the ancient town of Novogorod in northwestern Russia, the two-year, American-style curriculum includes two months of education in the U.S. so that graduates may receive an MBA from Portland University in Oregon. The first such school has already been situated in Khabarovsk.

❑ Center for U.S.-U.S.S.R. Initiative, which presumably will undergo a name change, is working with the Foundation for Social Invention in Russia to promote exchanges of Moscow business people to establish contacts with their counterparts on the East Coast of America.

Negotiating Style and Protocol

During the transition from centralized planning to market economies within the C.I.S., foreigners can expect much confusion, frustration, and uncertainty. However, most of the inhabitants are anxious to find international partners and learn about Western business practices. No longer having to answer to a centralized government and wanting to move as quickly as possible toward "free enterprise," C.I.S. business negotiators may be more flexible and accommodating than their Soviet predecessors. The following insights should provide valuable guidelines when conducting business with the C.I.S.

Russian officials expect to conduct business with only the highest-ranking executives. On the initial visit, the Western firm is advised to send its top personnel to ensure a favorable first impression. Any person representing a Western company in the C.I.S. should be at least a regional or East European manager. Russians are not impressed by "representatives." Final negotiations on larger deals should be handled by a top executive to demonstrate to the Russians the importance the Western firm is placing on this business. The chairperson or deputy chairperson might even consider entering the negotiations at some decisive stage.

There are two stages to negotiating with the Russians. During the first stage, they try to get as many competitive offers as possible, and play one supplier against another before making a final decision. Nothing may happen for a while after the Western firm has submitted its bid. Then, the Russians may notify the firm that it is still interested and resume negotiations. Potential suppliers are expected to provide detailed technical explanations of their products, so that the Russians can evaluate precisely what is being offered.

Having collected several competitive offers, the Russians are adept at creating competition among the suppliers. Quotations from competitors are revealed to force bidding suppliers to cut their prices.

The second phase of negotiations begins when the supplier has been chosen. This phase is usually shorter than the first one, but it still takes time to settle all the various points in the final contract.

Russian negotiators often negotiate with the weakest competitor first. After concessions are obtained from the weakest, the other companies are notified they also must accept them.

Another maneuver used by Russian negotiators is to first fix the final price the supplier is willing to take for its product. Once this price is firmly fixed, the Russians may make additional demands for such extra services as free training of technicians or equipment maintenance, which were not originally included in the producer description and price. Experienced companies make it a standing rule to begin contract talks

Russian officials expect to conduct business with only the highest-ranking executives.

by discussing the articles of the purchasing agreement before any discussion begins on final price.

It should also be made clear at the beginning on which points the supplier is willing to make concessions and on which it is not. The longer an executive postpones talking about demands that are of major importance to his/her company, the more forcefully the Russians may oppose them later.

Each agreement made with the Russians should stand on its own accord. Granting a price discount or making concessions to the Russians to win future business simply does not work. A common Russian tactic is to ask for a bulk price for a product, and then to apply the lower price per-unit from the bulk price to a smaller lot. It is implied, and sometimes even promised verbally, that more purchases will follow. However, the Russians will honor only written agreements.

It is important to let the Russians know exactly where your firm stands on all issues. The Russians do not respect negotiators who make large concessions, because they think the firm's position is padded to grant them for special effect. The firm should be prepared to stand by its position, and to drop negotiations and cut its losses if necessary. This will impress the Russians far more than slowly acquiescing to their demands.

Although the "old" Soviet system may no longer exist, attitudes and cultural perceptions are much more resilient. Remember these people are very protocol conscious. The following are some cultural clues that may advance synergistic relations:

❑ *Consumers* are only beginning to get accustomed to higher quality for higher prices. In addition to a plentiful and consistent supply of quality food, they seek modern conveniences and entertainment. Having been subjected to substandard clothing and outdated styles, they hunger for Western adornments that are colorful, stylish, and practical in their climate. However, business dress is conservative (e.g., suit and tie).

❑ *Business contacts*—new Commonwealth and individual republic ministries are gradually taking over the functions of the Ministry of Foreign Trade. The latter's renamed Russian Market Institute can provide useful data and quotations. Instead of cultivating the Foreign Trade Officers as in the past, outsiders will have to network and seek direct contacts with new factory owners and entrepreneurs. Emerging there and in the U.S. are consulting firms/publications to facilitate business in Eastern Europe.

❑ *Currency challenges*—innovative ways must be developed to convert the volatile ruble and other new monetary units into international hard currency, such as by barter, exchange of services, or third-country transfer.

It should also be made clear at the beginning on which points the supplier is willing to make concessions and on which it is not. Although the "old" Soviet system may no longer exist, attitudes and cultural perceptions are much more resilient.

- *Attention to details*—because of the Soviet cultural conditioning for the past seven decades, visitors can expect local officials to give much attention to such matters as seating arrangements and invitations, business cards printed in both Cyrillic and one's own language or English, whether the representative is a top executive, and the caliber of a technical presentation both in writing and orally. Continuity is an important factor, so the visiting team should designate one person as project manager or spokesman in all business dealings. Remember that these peoples are trying to overcome prior totalitarian conditioning to be dependent and compliant to authority, not to exercise personal responsibility or initiative.

- *Communication* is facilitated when the foreigner can speak the local language, but many Russians, Ukrainians, and other republic representatives are comfortable speaking in English or German, while the elite may prefer French. The use of interpreters has both positives (like in clarifying meaning or building interpersonal relations) and negatives (perceptual slanting by the translator or lack of technical understanding). Orally, Russians may greet foreigners with "gospodin" (Mr.) or "gospozha" (Miss or Mrs.), and ask acquaintances for their "imya" (first name) or "ochestvo" (patronymic). The later is formed by adding "-vitch" or "-ova" to the person's father's name as a token admission of familiarity. Normally, custom uses first names for close friends and family.

- *Time sense* is quite different here, and the locals dislike the quick tempo of Western business or the attitude that time is money. They use the slower tempo to good advantage, especially in negotiations or business socializing. The inhabitants here quote old Russian proverbs like, "If you travel for a day, take bread for a week," or "Patience and work, and everything will work out." Part of this stoicism and slowness is due to inadequate telecommunications and transportation. Within this colossus of a country, even simple technological advances like fax machines can save much time and facilitate communication.

- *National psyche*—Russians have long suffered from a sense of inferiority (for which they overcompensate); in the days of the aristocracy, the Czar's court turned to things French and German to show how civilized and sophisticated they were. Having been often cut off from outside contacts, the Russians also have manifested xenophobia periodically. Totalitarianism made many citizens feel like prisoners in their own society. The younger generation is more educated, more open, and more cosmopolitan, as well as more disillusioned and cynical.

Russian Body Language

To the Western observer, the Soviet may appear stiff. Gestures are usually kept to a minimum, and expressions may seem blank and uninterested. Smiles are rare, except between people who are very close. This

Time sense is quite different here, and the locals dislike the quick tempo of Western business or the attitude that time is money.

is the public image Russians seem to convey. In private, Soviets are much more expressive, and the modest reserve that they project in public breaks down under more personal surroundings.

Russian officials are generous hosts with food and beverage. Dinners are long and elaborate, and toasts are frequently and generously made to good business relationships and mutual friendships. The visiting foreign businessperson should be prepared to encounter some friendly "imbibing competition stemming from the Russian prowess for drinking.

TIPS FOR NEGOTIATING

❑ Be conscious of the emphasis the Russians place on dealing with high-ranking executives.
❑ Russians will enter all negotiations well prepared in research so it is advisable to be accompanied by at least one member of your technical personnel.
❑ Continuity is an important factor, so one person should be identified as the project manager throughout all negotiations.
❑ Be prepared to devote a lot of senior executive time, because of the chaotic situation and lingering bureaucracy.
❑ Take advantage of the many cultural opportunities and historical sites—then praise your hosts when you enjoy such experiences.

SUMMARY

Although cultures and business practices change, we have provided sufficient information for the global manager to be more effective in Europe, both East and West. Culture specific information about England, France, Germany, Russia, and the Commonwealth of Independent States are but a sampling of that continent's complex cultural groupings and national entities. Such material may help avoid the trap of overgeneralized assumptions about Europeans, so as to create more synergistic relationships there with management and other leaders in industry and commerce. The information is the initial step in developing a personal file of business intelligence about countries and cultures in which one is expected to perform well; such information should be continually verified for validity in specific times and places, as well as with different individuals and organizations.

At the beginning of the 21st century, profound economic, social, political, and cultural changes in Europe, East and West, call for transformational leadership if free enterprise and democracy are to flourish there, while human rights are respected and protected.

In private, Soviets are much more expressive, and the modest reserve than they project in public break down under more personal surroundings.

With new freedoms and opportunity to practice democracy, as well as to suffer its pitfalls, the millions in the Commonwealth of Independent States are changing rapidly. What has been said in this section now may prove to be invalid tomorrow. During the transformation underway, the only certainties in this vast area are change and diversity.

REFERENCES

1. VandeVelde, F. *The European,* April 1996, pp.11-17.
2. Tyler, M. "The United States of Europe," *The Los Angeles Times,* May 20, 1996, pp. 1–A8; see also Cannon-Brookes, P. "New Europeans," *European Business Review,* 1997, Vol. 97:1.
3. Bloom, H., Calori, R. and de Woot, P. *EURO Management,* London: Kogan Page Ltd., 1994.
4. Carroll, R. *Cultural Misunderstandings: The French-American Experience,* Chicago, IL: University of Chicago Press, 1987.
5. Mesbache, A. "American and French Managers' Self-Perceived Abilities for Effective Functioning in Another Culture: A Comparative Study," unpublished doctoral dissertation. San Diego, CA: United States International University, 1986. Available through University Microfilms International.
6. *The Economist,* "A Survey of Germany," November 9, 1996, insert.
7. *The Economist,* November 16, 1998, p. 49/50.
8. Cohen, R. "NATO Shatters Old Limits in the Name of Preventing Evil," *New York Times,* October 18, 1998, WK3.
9. *The Economist,* "Converging Hopes," February 13, 1999, V350, p. 74.
10. Soros, G. *Underwriting Democracy,* New York: Iree Press, 1991.
11. *USA Today,* November 14, 1991, p. 88.
12. Perelman, L. and Bereny, J. *Wall Street Journal,* October 14, 1991.
13. Remnick, D. *Resurrection—The Struggle for a New Russia,* New York: Random House, 1997.
14. *The Economist,* July 19, 1998, pp. 19–21; see also *New York Times,* August 23, 1998, p.WK6.
15. *Business Central Europe,* available through the *Economist* Newpaper Ltd., P.O. Box 14, Harold Hill, Romford RM3 830, UK (Fax 44 1708 381 211).

Recommended Reading

Ames, H. W. *Spain Is Different,* Yarmouth, ME: Intercultural Press, 1992.
Bateman, M. (ed). *Business Cultures in Central and Eastern Europe,* Oxford, UK: Butterworth Heinemann, 1997.
Broome, B. J. *Exploring the Greek Mosaic—A Guide to Intercultural Communication in Greece,* Yarmouth, ME: Intercultural Press, 1996.

Fisher, G. *The Mindset in Ethnic Controls*, Yarmouth, ME: Intercultural Press, 1998.

Hill, R. *We Europeans*, 3rd ed., Yarmouth, ME: Intercultural Press, 1997.

Holden, N., Cooper, G. and Carr, J. *Dealing with the New Russia—Management Cultures in Collision*. Chichester, UK/New York, USA, 1998.

McDaniel, T. *The Agony of the Russian Idea*, Princeton, NJ: Princeton University Press, 1997.

Plasser, F. and Pribersky, A. (eds.). *Political Culture in East Central Europe*, Aldersho, UK: Avebury Publishers, 1996.

Platt, P. *French or Foe: Getting the Most Out of Living and Working in France*, Yarmouth, ME: Intercultural Press, 1998.

Torino Group-European Training Foundation. *Redesigning Management Development in the New Europe* (see website, http://www.etf.eu.int or Email for report, info@etf.eu.int).

DOING BUSINESS WITH MIDDLE EASTERNERS

The Middle East commonly refers to the lands from the eastern shores of the Mediterranean and Aegean Seas to India. It is an area where geography and ecology are important architects of history, a meeting place of three continents, a focal point in the development of civilization. After the Ice Age, its topography was gradually transformed from a climate that supported grasslands and waterways into vast steppes and desert.

MIDDLE EAST OVERVIEW

In ancient times, the Middle East was referred to as Mesopotamia, during a period in the second millennium B.C. when Libya was rich in olives, wine, and livestock, while Egypt was a marshland teeming with wildlife and reed forests.[1] It was here that agriculture and irrigation were first developed along the Nile Valley. Although the first settlers in the Tigris-Euphrates Valley were Sumerians, its peoples became largely Semites and spoke a Semitic language from which evolved the major languages spoken by today's Middle Easterners, such as Aramaic, Syriac, Hebrew, and Arabic. Here the first cities were founded and flourished with exotic names like Ur, Babylon, and Gaza. This ancient land became the center of civilization—its cultures produced farming, pottery making, written records, art, monumental architecture, urbanization, religions, legal codes and complex political and trading systems.

From its very beginning as a site for human settlement now, the Middle East has been marked by *diversity*. The waves of immigration into the area for thousands of years have extended from the first Sumerians possibly from Central Asia to the latest Filipino or Indian migrant in

This ancient land became the center of civilization—its cultures produced farming, pottery making, written records, art, monumental architecture, urbanization, religions, legal codes and complex political and trading systems.

search of work. In the last part of the 20th century, more than 3 million Asian and Indian laborers were imported into the area to help build a modern infrastructure. Although there is much today that is shared in common by the majority of Middle Easterners, such as the Arab culture, language, and religion, there are also distinct ethnic minorities in every country of the region. Since the seventh century, Islam is the principal binder among the peoples of this area. Non-Arabs, such as the Iranians, are linked to their Muslim brothers and sisters throughout the world.[2]

Islam began in 570 A.D. with the birth in Mecca on the Arabian peninsula of Muhammad the Prophet. This great leader was a combination of general, statesman, social reformer, empire builder, and visionary. Islam as both a religion and philosophy owes its origin to Muhammad's teachings, which he encapsulated in the *Qur'an,* the scared Book of Muslims, as precious to them as the Holy Bible is to Jews and Christians. Islam means the act of giving one's self to God or Allah. The "Koran" contains the discourse of Allah revealed to his prophet Muhammad. Yet, as a religion, Islam has diversity in terms of different interpretations of its teachings by Sunni Muslims in Algeria and Saudi Arabia, or the Shi'is Muslims in Iran and Iraq where most believers are Shiites. No visitor or business person to the Middle East can hope to comprehend the country without understanding the powerful religious and cultural force of Islam. Its primary tenets are summarized in Exhibit 14-1.

No visitor or business person to the Middle East can hope to comprehend the country without understanding the powerful religious and cultural force of Islam.

EXHIBIT 14-1
PILLARS OF ISLAMIC BELIEF

Profession of Faith (Shahadah)—open proclamation of submission that "there is no God but Allah and Muhammad is the messenger of God"—mosques chant this five times a day.

Prayer (Salah)—at prescribed hours, worship or ritual prayer five times daily individually if not preferably in groups—the bowing or kneeling for this is toward Mecca; the Muslim doing this must be pure, hence newly washed and not dirty; Fridays is the traditional day of rest when the congregational prayers for men at midday should ordinarily be performed in the mosque.

Almsgiving (Zakah)—the Koran teaches that all believers must give to the needy, and today this is normally a personal act ranging from 2% to 10% of one's yearly income.

Fasting (Sawm)—throughout the thirty-day lunar month of Ramadan, a Muslim abstains from food and drink, while practicing continence in other respects, from dawn to sunset; in some Muslim countries, such as Saudi Arabia, the obligation is legally enforced.

Pilgrimage (Haj)—at least once in a lifetime, a Muslim is expected to perform this act of piety by going as a pilgrim during the month of Haj

(Exhibit continued on next page)

to Mecca, if one is financially and physically able; merit is great for those who go there and perform the rites and ceremonies for 8–13 days.

Note: Some Muslims believe in a sixth pillar, **Holy War** or Al-Jihad, which offers the reward of salvation—that is, effort to promote Islamic doctrine among non-believers, not necessarily by actual war as occurred in past ages. All observant Muslims are expected to practice hospitality toward strangers, even "infidels," as well as to enhance family relationships.

Islam produced a great civilization that made enormous contributions to art, architecture, astronomy, literature, mathematics, medicine, and other intellectual pursuits.

The word "caldron" describes this region because since recorded history the Middle East has been embroiled, and its inhabitants agitated.

The historical perspective is helpful when visiting Muslim lands. At its height, Islam's empire was larger than that of Rome at its zenith. Islam produced a great civilization that made enormous contributions to art, architecture, astronomy, literature, mathematics, medicine, and other intellectual pursuits.

Furthermore, if we seek to discern Islam in its Middle Eastern origins, we can then gain insight into many other Muslim cultures outside the region. For example, the Muslim culture and way of life is global in scope. Parts of Europe have large Muslim populations, including Albania, Bosnia, France, Spain, and Russia with its neighbors in the Commonwealth of Independent States. In North America and especially Asia entire nations are Muslim (e.g., Bangladesh, Pakistan, and Indonesia) as well as in Africa (e.g., Gambia, Morocco, and Nigeria). Throughout the world, there are 42 Muslim majority nations—Iran, Sudan, and Mauritania are officially Islamic States ruled by Islamic law. In the next chapter the continent of Africa is discussed which alone contains 11 countries with majority Muslim populations, only one of which, Egypt, is considered in the Middle East. Religious diversity is also evident in all Middle Eastern nations because of varied religious minorities, Christians and Jews of many persuasions or sects, as well as myriad other believers.

The word "caldron" describes this region because since recorded history the Middle East has been embroiled and its inhabitants agitated. When the indigenous tribes were not in conflict with one another, their crossroad location became the battleground for warring invaders or "Crusaders." From the 16th century, the Muslims of the Middle East were under the domination of the Ottoman Turks until the last two centuries, when the control of the West began to be exercised there. In this century alone we have witnessed a series of wars extending from European colonial occupiers or "protectors" to two American and Allied invasions in the '90s triggered by controversy between Iraq and Kuwait leading to the Gulf War and United Nations' sanctions against the former. Further, the "re-creation" of the nation of Israel in 1948 convulsed and divided the Arab world, leading to the emergence of fanatic fundamentalists and terrorists among both Muslims and Jews. Sometimes the conflicts are within countries where Muslim extremists oppose established governments, as in Algeria and Egypt. At other times, the fighting occurs because local militants with outside assistance oppose occupiers, as in the West Bank and Gaza, and often there have been outright civil wars, as in Yemen and Somalia. Currently, the hope for the region is that the battles between Israel and her Muslim neighbors give way to peaceful negotiations and conflict resolution, such as with Egypt, Jordan, the Palestine Liberation Organization and Syria. However, some see the biggest clash in the area as being between Western-style modernization, fueled by interaction with oil-seeking external powers, and traditional Muslim values. Economic factors almost beyond their control are sweeping the Muslim nations into the global marketplace. The 1994 opening of a McDonald's restaurant in Islam's holiest city of Mecca, Saudi Arabia, epitomizes the rapid changes underway.[3] In general, the Middle East today can be described as a region in the midst of profound cultural, social, political, and economic transition!

To complete this introduction on the Middle East, a review of the major areas or countries in the region is provided. Typically, the areas are grouped into four geographic regions—North African States, Gulf States, Central Arab States, Iran and Israel—a combined population of more than 250 million people. Despite traditions extending back several millennia, most of the nations there are relatively new; with the exception of Egypt and Iran, the others came into their present being in the 20th century, largely since the First World War. Depending on time period, political conditions, and geographical perspective, the number of states in the Middle East varies. Currently, there appears to be 14 nations in this designated area—Bahrain, Egypt, Iraq, Iran, Israel, Jordan, Kuwait, Lebanon, Oman, Qatar, Saudi Arabia, Syria, United Arab Emirates, and Yemen if it stays united. Depending on the final outcome of Israel/PLO negotiations regarding Palestinian autonomy another state may emerge in the 21st century.

Technically, Turkey is not a part of the Middle East, though popularly its inhabitants are called "Middle Easterners." Although largely Muslim, the Turks are a non-Arabic country whose dominant language is Turkish. Its more than 58 million people include ethnic minorities who do speak Arabic, Kurdish, and Greek.

The dream of Arab unity in the Middle East periodically manifests itself. In modern times, leadership in Pan-Arabism was initially manifested by Christian Arabs in Lebanon and Syria. Recent attempts at political formation of a "United Arab Republic" have been unsuccessful in the long term. Economic integration of six Persian Gulf countries resulted in the founding of a Gulf Cooperation Council. An Arab League also promotes better communication systems for the region using the language of Arabic, and is manifested in the Arab Regional Satellite System (ARABSAT). As oil discovery and development became the dominant economic thrust of the area, Middle Eastern oil-producing nations joined together in the Organization of Petroleum Exporting

The dream of Arab unity in the Middle East periodically manifests itself.

Countries (OPEC) and founded their own Organization of Arab Petroleum Exporting Countries (OAPEC). In the 20th century, regional governance has ranged from authoritarianism to democratic experiments, interspersed with Muslim regimes ruled by the *mullahs* or religious leaders, as currently in Iran. In 20 countries constituting the Arab World, 7 consider themselves republics, including Mauritania calling itself an "Islamic Republic" and Syria the "Bath Socialist Republic"; 7 others are monarchies; 4 have one-party rule or dictatorships; the UAE is a federation of sheikdoms, while Somalia has no government at the moment. Politically, the Middle East still is in evolutionary transition as a result of modernization, particularly with reference to economic and educational development. Economically, the Middle East has yet to integrate itself through trade pacts and tariff agreements. Oil plays a significant role in the economics of the Middle East and in the politics of many western countries.

Finally, the impact of the Western cultural invasion in Middle Eastern societies, has caused explosive dislocations. Westernization has brought progress at a high price—weakened parental authority and family cohesion, broken homes and sexual promiscuity, materialism for the masses and affluence for the elite, urban ills and traffic congestion.

The outcome of this social unrest seemingly has been twofold. First, Islamic fundamentalists cry out against what they perceive as "Western decadence and immorality." They reject modern democratic values, such as individual freedom, the right to know, rights of women, and other practices that are standard in industrialized nations. Some traditionalists seek to establish a government based on Islamic law. Second, some Middle Eastern governments have responded to fundamentalists with harsh and authoritarian security actions, branding them "terrorists." This happened in Algeria where attempts by the populace to democratically elect an Islamic government were suppressed by the government in power. The Middle East is a region with leaders who are long lived. Colonel Muammar Qaddafi (Libya), President Hafez al-Assad (Syria) Saddam Hussein (Iraq) and Yasser Arafat (Palestine—not a recognized state) have ruled their countries for approximately thirty years. The death of King Hussein (Jordan) took an important Arab representative out of the balance of leadership power in the Middle East.

CHARACTERISTICS OF ARAB CULTURE

For outsiders, the key to better comprehension of the contemporary Middle East is understanding Arab culture.[4] We repeat that not all Middle Easterners are Arab, as Iranians, Turks and Israelis will remind you. According to Feghali,[5] Arab countries can be identified as members of League of Arab States that was formed in 1945 to promote cooperation between Arab countries. Members include 22 sovereign states: Algeria,

Djibouti, Egypt, Libya, Mauritania, Morocco, Somalia, Sudan, Tunisia, Iraq, Jordan, Lebanon, Palestine, Syria, Bahrain, Kuwait, Oman, Qatar, Saudi Arabia, United Arab Emirates, Yemen, and Comoros Islands. While Arab countries are considered Middle Eastern, not all Middle Eastern countries are Arab. To say that member countries have similar cultural attitudes, behaviors and communication is very misleading. For example, the African countries of Sudan, Somalia and Mauritania speak tribal languages rather than Arabic and have cultural practices that favor their African heritage.

Not all Arabs believers in Islam, as Christian Arabs will confirm. But Arab peoples are the majority, and most of them are Muslim—both of these worlds overlap. As a rule of thumb, Arab is an ethnic reference to a Semite, while Muslim signifies religious belief and grouping. One who is sensitive to such cultural differences can create cultural synergy not only in this region, but also in interactions with those throughout the world whose way of life is strongly influenced by Islam or Arab culture.

The connotation Arab refers to a group of people whose behavioral pattern is unique because of their culture, language, religion, and even their nationalism. They all do not look or dress alike, so avoid stereotyping. Alison Lanier[6] reminds us that Arab is *not* a race, a skin color, a nationality, or even a Muslim. By original definition in the pre-Islamic period, an Arab was an inhabitant of Arabia, a member of the nomadic Bedouin tribes. During the Islamic Expansion Era, Lanier informs us that Arabs carried their religion, language and culture throughout the Middle East and beyond, intermarrying with the conquered peoples from Persia to the Pyrenees. Thus, today Arabs are not so much an ethnic group as a community with a state of mind. Arab leaders once explained the concept as "Whoever lives in our country, speaks our language, is brought up in our culture, and takes pride in our glory is one of us." The confusion about the meaning of Arab has meant that Arab often is used interchangeable with Middle East or Muslim. For example,

Arab is not a race, a skin color, a nationality, or even a Muslim.

> On January 18, 1993, *NBC Nightly News* anchor Tom Brokaw reported a U.S. bombing attack on Iraq. Going live to correspondent Tom Aspell in Baghdad, Brokaw asked about the reaction of "the Muslim world" to the bombing. Aspell replied, "The reaction in the Arab world is. . . ." Such subtle incidents contribute to a lack of differentiation and broad stereotyping of groups in this world region.[5]
>
> What are some generalities to know about this distinctive Arab culture? Simply, that is a varied tapestry of religious as well as socio-political configurations, causing Arabs to constantly recast and revise themselves as circumstances around them also change.[7]

Arab Values

In traditional societies, the paramount virtues are considered to be dignity, honor, and reputation—foreigners at all costs should avoid causing an Arab to lose face, or to be shamed (and in the case of a woman, to lose her virginity before marriage). Loyalty to family as well as courteous and harmonious communications are emphasized. Arab priorities are first to one's self, then kinsman, townsman or tribesman, and those who share the same religion and country in that order. Scholars wonder how long this community can maintain their traditional characteristics of generosity, gallantry, courage, patience, and endurance. Contrast this image of an Arab with the false stereotypes created by American films and television about such peoples.

Arab Personal Distance

As anthropologists observe, Arabs seek close, personal relationships, preferably without great distance or intermediaries. Thus, olfaction is prominent in Arab life, so as part of their complex behavior system, they consistently breathe on others when they talk. For the Arab good smells are pleasing, a way to be involved with each other. To smell a friend's breath is desirable, and to deny another your breath is to act ashamed. Body and food odors are used to enhance human relationships; the former even is important in the choice of a mate. Not only is their "olfactory boundary" used to relate or separate, but Arabs may experience "olfactory crowding" when a smell is unpleasant. This cultural difference also extends to an Arab facing or not facing another person; to view another peripherally is impolite, so to sit or stand "back-to-back" is rude. While Arabs may be very involved when interacting with friends, they may not seek close distance in conversations with strangers or mere acquaintances. On such social occasions, they may sit on opposite sides of a room and talk across to one another. Yet, they are generally a warm and expressive people, both verbally and nonverbally. Arabs are active participants with each other, but resist being crowded in enclosed spaces or by boundaries.

Arab Sociability

Cordiality is at the core of this culture, and is evident from feasting at a lamb banquet to drinking their strong black coffee. It extends also to business meetings when the first session is devoted to getting acquainted with little regard for schedule or appointments. The communication pattern is both oral and aural—the emphasis on listening also explains why so many prefer to learn from audio cassettes and radio. The traditional greeting is to place one's right hand on the chest near the heart as an indication of sincerity and warmth, though "modern" Arabs may precede this with a long, limp handshake. The custom is for men to kiss one another on both cheeks. For those Arabs who are Muslims, there

Arab priorities are first to one's self, then kinsman, townsman or tribesman, and those who share the same religion and country in that order.

are Islamic teachings that affect social relations, such as taboos against eating pork, drinking alcohol, gambling, and prostitution.

Arab Women

The Arab patriarchal culture places the male in the dominant role, while protecting and respecting the female. In an Arab household, for example, the man is overtly the head with a strong role and influence— the mother "behind the scenes" is often the authority on family matters. Publicly, the woman defers to her husband, but privately she may be more assertive. Paradoxically, Islam does not advance the thesis of women's inherent inferiority, only her difference; it does not perceive biological inferiority and affirms potential equality between the sexes. During an interview, Dr. Fatima Mernissi[8] stated:

> The whole Muslim system is based on the assumption that the woman is a powerful and dangerous being. All sexual institutions (polygamy, repudiation, sexual segregation, etc.) can be perceived as a strategy for containing her power . . . a defense against her disruptive power of female sexuality.

The "Koran," for instance, does not say that woman must be veiled, only that they must be modest in appearance by covering arms and hair, considered very sensual. Scholars see the use of the veil as symbolic with sociological meaning. The veil's use depends upon time period and circumstances. Some Arab countries are without dress restrictions for women as they may wear the latest fashion, while others, which are more traditional, may require a long cloak covering of black gauze or chiffon. The cultural contrasts within Arab societies on this matter are considerable. In some Arab cultures most females are illiterate, while in others they are well educated; in some they are not allowed outside their home alone nor permitted to drive an automobile, while in other states, woman may hold jobs and drive cars. In many Arab countries, women are not allowed to vote, while in others they have that franchise; in most Arab societies, marriages are arranged, while in a growing number, freedom of marital choice is respected. Within an Arab world in turmoil, one may observe both resurgent Islamic fundamentalism and an emerging feminist movement.

Foreign women visiting Arab countries must exercise great sensitivity as to what is acceptable or unacceptable in the local situation. Whether there as a tourist or on business, female visitors have to attune themselves to what is considered locally as proper behavior and attire for their gender. Ladies from outside the culture who do not heed this coun-

The Arab patriarchal culture places the male in the dominant role, while protecting and respecting the female. Within an Arab world in turmoil, one may observe both resurgent Islamic fundamentalism and an emerging feminist movement.

sel may have unhappy experiences. Whether female or male, those who would engage in successful commercial or professional exchanges within the Arab world should be aware of some proprieties.

A Case in Synergy

Over the centuries, the relations between Christianity and Islam have been marked by both conflict and cooperation. A 21st century model for the latter is the Center for Muslim-Christian Understanding at Georgetown University. The CMCU was founded in 1993 on the belief that dialogue and the study of each other's traditions is a necessary step on the path to mutual understanding of Muslims and Christians, Easterners and Westerners. To date, the Center remains the only academic institution in the United States dedicated to exploring the 14 centuries of cultural, historical, political and theological interactions of Christians and Islam.

The Center presents a view that the Islamic world cannot be defined by broad generalizations and not by its extremists, but rather by its interplay of enormously rich cultures and ideas. The violence of some Islamic militant groups cannot be denied, but the news media have often inflated their power and importance with sensational reporting. "You cannot judge one-fifth of the world's population by a small minority. What is ignored is that according to the Qur'an, terrorism is un-Islamic. The social ideals of Islam are, in fact, compassion, mercy, justice, fundamental rights and liberties, and the equitable distribution of wealth."[9]

You cannot judge one-fifth of the world's population by a small minority. What is ignored is that according to the Qur'an, terrorism is un-Islamic.

There will be further insights presented subsequently about Arab culture, but one should realize that it is a way of life in profound change—socially, economically, politically, and even religiously. Practices may vary depending on the degree of a locality's economic progress, as well as the extent of modernization and education.

CULTURAL ASPECTS— EGYPT AND SAUDI ARABIA

By focusing on two similar but distinctly different cultural targets, Egypt and Saudi Arabia, one may gain insight into the cultural dimensions of the other remarkable peoples in the region.[10] Both countries are part of the Arab world, but Egypt originates from an ancient civilization, while Saudi Arabia is a 20th century creation.

EGYPT

EGYPT—PROFILE

Population	63 million
Land..............................	386,662 mi²
Ethnic Groups	Arabs 95%, Bedouins, small minority
Religions	Islam 90%, Coptic Christians, small minority
Education.......................	Literacy rate 57%
Government	Republic with one Legislative House (People's Assembly)

Modern archeological studies continually provide insights into Egypt's Old Kingdom and the findings eventually translate into museum exhibits and popular media presentations. This is the civilization that built the first great nation-state and flourished for five and a half centuries before its collapse. It is a culture that produced *hieroglyphics*, one of the world's first written languages, and humanity's first macroprojects—construction of monumental pyramids dating from 2630 to 2250 B.C. Whether tombs of pre-dynastic kings or latter Pharaohs, these magnificent structures reveal a culture whose leaders and builders were obsessed with preparing for the afterlife. In the mineral-rich Eastern desert of Upper Egypt, the hub was Thebes with its awesome funerary temples and rock-cut tombs. The building of pyramids and tombs became a central force for organization and mobilization of townspeople, a means for creating a national state, a magnet for early Middle Eastern trade. Then as now, the Nile River with its network of hand-dug canals tied the country together geographically. By 2200 B.C. climatic crises arose when Nile flooding became undependable and drought seized the land.

The People and Their Homeland

Most of Egypt is high dry plains, rugged hills and mountains, stretching along the Red Sea Coast to the valley of the Nile. The population of the old Kingdom was less than 2 million, while today's Egypt has nearly 63 million inhabitants, obviously, this is too many people for a land mass of 386,000 square miles that is largely desert. This most populous of Arab states has one of the highest population densities in the world. Cairo, for instance, has approximately 15 million people for a city originally designed for 3 million. Its citizens are mostly a Hamitic people practicing the Sunni form of the Muslim religion.

The building of pyramids and tombs became a central force for organization and mobilization of townspeople, a means for creating a national state, a magnet for early Middle Eastern trade.

In northern Egypt there is a mixture of peoples from the Mediterranean and other Arab countries, while the south consists mainly of black African Nubians. In addition to thousands of the latter, this relatively homogeneous people also includes two other minorities—a few million Coptic Christians and more than fifty thousand nomadic Bedouins. The major language spoken is Arabic, with some French and English, reflecting the heritage of previous colonialists.

While upwards of 20 million Egyptians are literate, 64% male and 39% female, almost twice that number are illiterate. Despite the government provision of free education through university, only some 6 million benefit from this learning opportunity at some level. Egypt's educated are sought by other Arab nations as professors and teachers, scientists and technicians, managers and engineers, specialists and craftsmen.

Geographic Features and Cities

In northern Egypt there is a mixture of peoples from the Mediterranean and other Arab countries, while the south consists mainly of black African Nubians.

Although a Middle Eastern nation, Egypt is located on the African continent at a crossroads for the Mediterranean Basin, Africa, and Asia. Less than 5% of the country is cultivated, with the climate permitting several crops a year, but the potential exists for increased agricultural production.

Beside its great north-south Nile River, other notable geographical features are:

❑ The Suez Canal linking the Mediterranean Sea on the north with the Gulf of Suez and Red Sea on the southeast—it divides the Eastern or Arabian Desert from the Western or Libyan Desert (the Great Sand Sea).
❑ The northeastern Sinai Peninsula, a desert area that abuts Israel and the Gulf of Aqaba.
❑ The Aswan High Dam in the southeast with its Lake Nasser extending down into the Nubian Desert and the southern border with Sudan.

Egypt has ten major cities—Cairo, Alexandria, Giza, Shoubra, El-Kheima, El-Mahalla, El Koubra, Tanta, Port Said, and El Mansoura. There are projects underway to develop new urban areas, such as Sadat City on the road between Cairo and Alexandria, and Nasser City in the desert near the International Airport. To better disperse population now concentrated in 5% of its territory, Egypt has undertaken massive opening and reclamation of new lands along its Mediterranean coast and in the Sinai. In addition, with the assistance of U.N. and U.S. aid, a master plan is reconstructing the Suez Canal area within the inner/outer regions. However, the capitol, Cairo, is Africa's and the Middle East's most populous city, blending the cultures of both ancient and modern, East and West, Islam and Christianity. Its origins can be traced to nearby El Fustai, founded by Arabs in A.D. 641, but Cairo reached its height of world influence during the Mamluk era when architectural gems were built (1217–1517 A.D.).

Political and Social Conditions

The foundations of governance were laid by twenty dynasties when Pharaohs and kings reigned from 3000 to 715 B.C., extending their rule as far as Lower Nubia, Palestine, and Syria. Invasions in that period brought in temporary rulers and settlers from Asiatic Hyksos, Libyans, Persia, and Nubia. Since 333 B.C., Egypt's heritage reflects the presence of a series of conquerors—from Alexander the Great and the Roman Empire, to Arabs and the Turkish Ottoman Empire, to the establishment of a British presence (1882–1952) during which a monarchy was formed in 1922 under King Fouad I. Because of worsening economic and social conditions, military officers staged a coup d'etat in 1952 under the leadership of Lt. Colonel Gamel Abdel Nasser. On June 18, 1960 this junta declared Egypt a republic, a date now celebrated annually as National Day. This became a turning point for Egyptians who then felt more independent, spearheading a resurgence of Arab nationalism throughout the Middle East. In 1971, a new constitution was adopted for the Arab Republic of Egypt that guarantees the individual rights of its citizens. Subsequently, two presidents have lead the country—former General Anwar Sadat who was assassinated, and currently former General Hosni Mubarak. With the death of King Hussein of Jordan, President Mubarak will have a more influential role in the Middle East peace talks. There is a National Assembly with four political parties.

During the closing four decades of the 20th century, Egypt has struggled internally to restructure its socio-economic system, including re-apportioning wealth and some land reform. Moving away from earlier experiments with socialism, contemporary Egypt espouses democracy and a market economy, providing incentives for both domestic and foreign investment. Yet, this is a developing economy, plagued by uncontrolled population growth, poverty and insufficient food. With 94% of the people Muslim adherents, it is understandable that civil law is influenced by *Shariah* or Islamic Law. But it is a economic degradation among the masses that fuels Islamic militants seeking to establish a Muslim government, often leading to terrorist acts against both the leadership and foreigners.

There are many external pressures that explain why Egypt has wasted its limited resources on military expansion and regional conflicts. Supposedly, the leader of the Arab world was expected to provide the primary opposition to the establishment of Israel. Since President Sadat signed and put into effect a Peace Treaty with Israel (March 25, 1979), Egypt for many years was the target of Arab economic reprisals, as well as recipient of significant foreign aid from the United States. Reconciliation and synergy are increasingly the goal with its neighbors. Jordan and the Palestinian Liberation Organization have also signed agreements with Israel, and Syria/Lebanon consider the prospects. To curb attacks

Moving away from earlier experiments with socialism, contemporary Egypt espouses democracy and a market economy, providing incentives for both domestic and foreign investment.

of Islamic militants in the area, President Mubarak hosted a summit in Cairo at the beginning of Ramadan 1995. Prime Minister Yitzhak Rabin of Israel, PLO leader Yasser Arafat, and the late King Hussein of Jordan joined him in the elusive pursuit of peace and prosperity for the Middle East. In a collective communique, "the four parties condemned all outbreaks of bloodshed, terror, and violence in the region and reaffirmed their intentions to stand staunchly against and put an end to all such acts."[11] Ironically, Rabin was assassinated by a Jewish fundamentalist in 1995.

The Middle Eastern nations have more to gain economically and socially by peaceful cooperation than from continuing conflict. That is the lesson of history over thousands of years in the area.

The Economy

The change and diversification underway is evident in exports—a shift from traditional cotton and rice to rising petroleum production and tourism. Europe, followed by the United States, is a growing importer of Egypt's exports. With the gradual dismantling of bureaucratic regulations, foreign investment increases as does reclamation projects. Although processing cotton is still the main industrial output, other industries are growing from electronics and chemicals to mining and construction. The currency is the Egyptian pound divided into 100 piasters or 1000 millimes. Seeking to maintain parity with the U.S. dollar, the Central Bank weekly sets the premium exchange rate.

In addition to the general business protocols discussed later for the region, local customs for doing business include:

❑ Law 43 and subsequent amendments liberalize foreign investment, providing incentives, particularly with reference to new technologies, as well as exemptions (from nationalization, custom duties, some regulations and taxes, etc.), plus guarantees for repatriation of capital.
❑ Since 1974 there have been significant changes in the business environment to encourage the private sector of an economy still dominated by the public sector.
❑ The 10 million people that comprise the available work force are well trained and regulated for the region. Egyptian skilled labor and entrepreneurial talent is sought by other nations in the area. Basic Labor Law 91 protects worker rights and sets work policy; foreign firms may be exempt from some of these regulations.
❑ For potential traders and investors, the most significant developments have been in the banking system that now allows joint ventures with foreign banks, and improvements in transportation, hotels, and resorts.

SAUDI ARABIA

SAUDI ARABIA—PROFILE

Population	20.7 million
Land..............................	850,000 mi²
Ethnic Groups	Arabs 90%
	African-Asians 10%
Religions	Islam 97.6%
	Muslim-Christian 3%
Education......................	Literacy rate 63%
Government	Monarchy with Council of Ministers

The Arabian Peninsula is the heartland of Islamic culture that is thir-teen centuries old, originating in Mecca. Arabia's inhabitants were the primary source of Arab expansion throughout the Middle East and Europe from 570–1258 A.D., the Golden Age of the Arab Empire. But Saudi Arabia as a nation is a product of the 20th Century, particularly because of oil discoveries and development.[12] In decades, its citizens have developed from a Bedouin tribal culture to a modern urban cul-ture. After hundreds of years of subsistence living, a nomadic, patriar-chal and impoverished society has been transformed suddenly into a more prosperous, educated, and internationally oriented one. Within this whirlwind clash between tradition and modernization, the affluent kingdom founded on Islamic principles experiences cataclysmic change. Popular magazines have described the nation as a desert superstate—a rich, vulnerable feudal monarchy being hurdled into the space age.

The People and Their Homeland

The kingdom's population has risen rapidly to 20 million and grow-ing. The country occupies 4/5 of the Arabian Peninsula, a landmass of 850,000 square miles, making it geographically one of the largest coun-tries in the region. Basically, it is a harsh rugged plateau reaching from the Red Sea on the west toward the Gulf on the east (called Arabian by the Saudis and Persian by the Iranians on the opposite side). Other Gulf states sharing that peninsula from north to south are Kuwait, Bahrain, Qatar, and the United Arab Emirates. The Saudi's northern frontier abuts Jordan, Iraq, and Kuwait, while in the south, it borders Yemen and Oman. There is wide variation in the Saudi citizens from desert to increasingly city dwellers—as Bedouin tribesmen in origin, they are a keen, alert, and astute people, never to be underestimated. The Saudis

Within this whirlwind clash between tradition and modernization, the affluent kingdom founded on Islamic principles experiences cataclysmic change.

live in an entirely Muslim country with an oil reserve of 257.6 billion barrels—compare that with other Middle Easterners. Approximately 1 million foreign workers and technicians are in Saudi Arabia to help build infrastructure and defense, to provide new technologies and services including Americans, Europeans, Japanese, Koreans, Filipinos, and other Middle Easterners.

With a literacy rate over 62%, rapid Saudi modernization and affluence has brought increased educational opportunities both at home and abroad for males and females. Throughout history, Arabic has been source of a great literary communication. While this language of three forms (classic, standard, and dialects) is principally used by Saudis, English is widely spoken or understood among the educated, commercial class. The citizens' three most common symbols are the date palm emblematic of growth and vitality, the unsheathed sword of strength rooted in faith, and the Muslim Creed described in Exhibit 14-1. Although the unique, flowing robes and headdress of the Arabs is preferred, cosmopolitan Saudis are equally at home in Western dress when appropriate.

Geographic Features and Cities

This country has four major topographical regions:

- ❑ Asir, a relatively fertile strip of coastal mountains in the southwest with peaks up to 10,000 feet and terraced farming.
- ❑ Hijaz, a mountain chain encompassing the rest of the west coast along the Red Sea.
- ❑ NAJD, the arid peninsula plateau with its Rub-al Khali or Empty Quarter, the largest continuous sand desert in the world, a place of oases in the north, as well as shifting sand dunes and untapped oil fields—the capital city of Al-Riyadh at its center is a "garden" because of springs and well water.
- ❑ Al Hasa, the eastern province where the principal oil and gas production occurs, along with agriculture in numerous oases, such as Haradh and Hofuf.

Saudi Arabia has fourteen principal population centers and four major cities. Riyadh, the royal capital, is a modern desert city with new freeways, hospitals, schools, shopping malls, and the largest airport in the world. The Red Sea port city of Jeddah is the nation's leading commercial center and hub of the country's 8,000-mile highway system. Jeddah's huge, $10 billion dollar airport handles the 800 million Muslim guests in route to the holy places. Assembling on the Plains of Arafat, the *haj*, or pilgrims, caravan to Mecca some fifty miles away. Then the pilgrim traffic heads for Medina, also a growing commercial center with a nearby new port of Yanbu. On the east coast, two more important

There is wide variation in the Saudi citizens from desert to increasingly city dwellers—as Bedouin tribesmen in origin, they are a keen, alert, and astute people, never to be underestimated.

commercial hubs are Al-Khubar and its nearby port city of Dammam, the Arabian rail terminus to Riyadh. Nearby are the two oil cities of Dhahran with its Aramco compound of American-style homes, and Ras Tannurah, the world's largest petroleum port. Fifty miles north up the coast is the new industrial city of Jubail with its giant new port and naval base.

Both Jubail and Yanbu are the two largest public works projects in history. They were built virtually *ex nihilo* since the 1970s and account for 10% of the world's petrochemical production today.[13]

Political and Social Conditions

The nation's history parallels the House of Saud, founded in the 18th century, which recaptured the traditional family seat of Riyadh in 1902 and then extended their control over what is now Saudi Arabia. This was accomplished under the leadership of Abdul Aziz ibn-Abd ar-Rahman. Called ibn-Saud, he was proclaimed king of the entire region in 1927; the new nation was named The Kingdom of Saudi Arabia in 1932. With the help of American petroleum engineers from Aramco, he launched the country and the company's future in 1939 by opening the valves for oil production at 4 million barrels a day; eventually hundreds of billions of barrels have been extracted and it is still flowing.

King Fahd now rules with assistance from a royal family of 5,000 princes. In 1995, King Fahd suffered a stroke and has since delegated more authority to Crown Prince Fahd's half brother Abdullah. Like his kingly predecessors, Fahd encourages economic, medical, educational and technological progress, friendly Western relationships, while maintaining orthodox Islamic teachings and supporting Arab world ambitions. Here also the Shariah governs national life and behavior. A judiciary interprets and advises the king on this law and in other matters not stated. The ruler is also assisted by a council of ministers chaired by the crown prince acting as deputy prime minister. Although there are no elections or legislature, the King and his governors of provinces, as well as the royal princes, govern by consensus but with absolute authority. In a system based on trust, they hold regular *majlis* or audiences where citizen petitioners may approach in open court to make requests, lodge complaints, or adjudicate grievances. Fahd opposes Western democracy and its institutions, while gently nudging his country forward on social matters without unduly offending right-wing conservatives. The country spends approximately $15 billion annually for a defense force to protect the kingdom from external enemies, but the real problems for the ruling family may be internal.

Islam permeates Saudi life—Allah is always present, controls everything, and is frequently referred to in conversation. Yet for all the fervor, the kingdom was jarred on November 20, 1979 when 350 armed religious zealots invaded Mecca's Sacred Mosque. The siege and intense

Although there are no elections or legislature, the King and his governors of provinces, as well as the royal princes, govern by consensus but with absolute authority.

fighting lasted two weeks before Saudi troops killed or captured these "renegades of Islam," as the ulama or theologians called them. At the same time in the city of Qatif, minority Shia Muslims rioted—the whole affair was thought to have been orchestrated by Iranian Shia pilgrims, followers of Ayatollah Khomeini who had overthrown the monarchy in Iran. Since then, Saudi rulers have sought to limit both non-Islamic influences and reestablish policies closer to the fundamentalist form of the majority Sunni Muslims.

Islamic tenets observed in Saudi Arabia enhance the status of women by limiting the number of wives a man may have, imposing restrictions on divorce, and ensuring a woman's rights to property and inheritance from husband or father. Following the impact of the Gulf War with Iraq, a silent revolution is in the making by females. For centuries, women in Arabia lived in extreme privacy, wore the long veil or *abayah*, and were protected by the males. Today, Saudi women are still socially segregated and very constrained in their movements and dress, and very much dominated by the husband or male family head. Yet with advanced education Saudi women have begun to enter the business world and the professions, especially teaching and social and public services. The so-called invisible women are said now to control as much as 40% of private wealth, much of it inherited under the law.[14] Despite social constraints on women, as well as bans on their driving, travel, and engaging in political activity—all enforced by the *mutawa* or religious police—cosmopolitan Saudi females slowly forge ahead. Their growing economic assets are increasingly used to invest in property and engage in business ownership—2,000 of the latter are registered with the Riyadh Chamber of Commerce.

The Economy

During the 20th century, Saudi Arabia's financial situation skyrocketed from the subsistence level based on herding and farming to wealth from oil and gas development. Over the past 70 years this developing economy has been transformed from a desert backwater with nomadic trade and barter to a rich, complex, global system. By mid '70s, the energy production accounted for 74.5% of the domestic gross product ($44 billion, 8 million barrels of oil per day), thus enabling the country to become the world's largest exporter of petroleum. Large-scale diversification into hydrocarbon-based industries is vigorously pursued. Provision of new infrastructure also spurred the growth of the non-oil economic sector, expanding private enterprise as well. A series of five-year development plans and over $91 billion in government expenditures on ports and roads have spurred commerce. Sheep, goats, and camels have given way to automobiles, jets, and supertankers making for a new mobility for both the populace and their products. By the '80s, with a proven oil reserve for the next 60 years, the country was producing 9.5

Over the past 70 years this developing economy has been transformed from a desert backwater with nomadic trade and barter to a rich, complex, global system.

million barrels of oil per day, contributing significantly to the economic well being of both the West and Japan. Yet by the '90s the GNP was down to $7,940 per person, almost half of what it had risen to in the previous decade. There has been a cutback on dependence on foreign workers, and more emphasis on young Saudis learning the skills necessary to operate the new economy.

Saudi Arabia wishes to become a member of WTO in 2000. To gain acceptance into the international trade organization though, Saudi Arabia will have to remove some if its protectionist policies. Two sectors of the economy that may be privatized are telecommunications and electricity.

As the world's largest producer and exporter of oil, Saudi Arabia's economy benefits from high oil prices. Only one company is responsible for producing 95% of the Saudi Arabia's oil, the state-owned Aramco Corporation. Saudi Arabia currently possess 25% of the world's known oil reserves. Currently, crude oil prices have been very low and the economy is experiencing problems with international cash flows.[15]

MIDDLE EAST BUSINESS CUSTOMS AND PROTOCOL

Consider this mini case in point:

A midwestern banker is invited by an Arab sheik to meet him at the Dorchester Hotel in London. A friend of both arranges the get-together, and facilitates the introduction. Dark sweet coffee is served. No business of consequence is discussed, but there is a sociable exchange. . . . Subsequently, the American is invited to a series of meetings in Riyadh. The Saudi greets the banker with, "There is no god but Allah, and Mohammed is his messenger." More strong coffee is served and sometimes others are present in the meeting room. . . . In time, a mutually beneficial business relationship is established.

This short episode encapsulates several important points for succeeding in Middle Eastern business ventures. First, nothing happens quickly and patience is a virtue. Second, trust is paramount, and it is cultivated over a period of time, often with the assistance of a third party acquainted with each. Although business customs will vary somewhat in the Middle East, by understanding Islam and Arab culture, an individual is in a better position to be effective. In this section insights on Saudi Arabia will be focused on so that one can be adapt and apply them elsewhere in the region, but remember all these tips are subject to change.

Among the modern institutions of higher education recently established within Saudi Arabia, King Fahd University of Petroleum and Minerals is among the best. There Dr. Mohammed I. At-Twaijri has conducted and published studies comparing Saudi and American man-

Only one company is responsible for producing 95% of the Saudi Arabia's oil, the state-owned Aramco Corporation.

agers, purchasing agents, and negotiators.[16] Some of his research findings and comments are offered for consideration:

- There is a trend toward "westernization" of Middle East managers, and Saudi managers are becoming less paternalistic.
- There are significant differences in the way Arab managers respond to questionnaire items in their native Arabic language as opposed to the English version of the same instrument.
- In negotiations, the Saudis have two dominant styles—competitive and collaborative, both of which are expressed within the Arab cultural context.
- For the hundreds of joint ventures underway between the U.S. and Saudi Arabia, foreigners are required to build extensive training programs for the locals into the project management. This is increasingly the trend in most Middle Eastern countries.

Apart from what has already been described about Middle Easterners and the Arab culture, remember these are a people of great emotion and sentimentality—sometimes of excess and extremes. They hold in high regard friendship, loyalty, and justice, and when events and behavior go against that sense of justice, Arabs are morally outraged and indignant. Arabs tend to be warm, hospitable, generous, and courteous. Like many Middle Eastern persons in commerce, the stereotype is that they are either very sincere and trustworthy, or the opposite, insincere and sly. It is dangerous to make generalizations about any culture, so one is advised to deal with each Middle Easterner as a person, and to treat him or her with respect and dignity. Semites, whether Arab or Jew, also have reputations as effective traders and sales people. Furthermore, Arab society places great emphasis on honor. Its concept of shame is somewhat alien to Western mindsets. Shame must be feared, avoided, or hidden, so one prays to Allah for protection from others (public exposure). Thus, foreigners should avoid shaming an Arab because of their powerful identification between the individual and the group—shame means a loss of power and influence, impacting the family, et al. In addition, the tribal heritage influences and values a high degree of deference and conformity, often expressed in a somewhat authoritarian tone. In return, the individual has a strong sense of place, and shares in the group's social prestige. That is why one typically worries about how decisions, acts, and behavior reflect on the family, the clan, the tribe, and then the country.

For a Saudi, as a case in point, the "self" is buried deep within an individual, in contrast to an American's which may be more open and close to the surface. This relates then to their sense of distance previously explained—because the "self" is personal and private, touching and jostling in public among males is quite evident. The latter, for instance, may hold hands and kiss each other on both cheeks, while this is not done with females.

Avoid shaming an Arab because of their powerful identification between the individual and the group–shame means a loss of power and influence, impacting the family, et al.

Business Tips

To an Arab, commerce is a most blessed career—the prophet Mohammed, after all was a man of commerce and married a lady of commerce. Thus business and trade are highly respected, so one is expected to be sound, shrewd, and knowledgeable. Some practices to observe among Middle Eastern business are:

❑ *Business relationships* are facilitated by establishing personal rapport, mutual respect, and trust—business is done with a "person" not merely with a company or contract.

❑ *Connections* and *networking* are most important, vital to gain access to both private and public decision makers, so maintain good relations with people of influence.

❑ *Negotiating* and *bargaining* are commonplace processes, and are an "art" in these ancient lands, so expect some old-fashioned "haggling."[17]

❑ *Decision making* is traditionally done in person, thus requiring an organization's representative of suitable rank; decisions are usually made by the top person in the government agency or corporation, and normally are not accomplished by correspondence, fax, or telephone.

❑ *Time is flexible,* according to the concept of "Bukra inshae Allah," meaning "tomorrow if God wills"; it is an expression of the cultural pattern of "fatalism." Avoid imposing Western time frames and schedules, though as they become accustomed to modern business practice, appointments may be set and kept.

❑ *Marketing* should be focused on specific customer-client segments; because centralized governments in many Arab countries hold the economic power and are the principal buyers, one must learn the public sector development plans for obtaining goods and services, then develop contacts and relationships with senior officials in appropriate ministries.

❑ *Socialization* in business is traditional, but deals are not usually concluded under such circumstances—social gestures, courtesies, and invitations are commonplace. Traditionally Arab women are not part of the scene, but mixed social gatherings in private are becoming more common; foreign woman in Saudi Arabia as spouses or on business will not only have to call upon inner resources, but take advantage of local support networks and female clubs (particularly in the expatriate communities).

❑ *Communication* is especially complex in the Middle East and outsiders should show harmony and agreement, following the host's lead—Arabic as a language is high context, manifested with raised voices and much nonverbal body language (wide gestures, animated facial expressions, eyebrow raising, tongue clicking, standing close,

To an Arab, commerce is a most blessed career. . . .

and eye contact, except with strangers on first meeting, a side nod of the head is often given as affirmation).

❑ *Taboos* are many, so caution is advised in unfamiliar circumstances.

IN THE MIDDLE EAST AVOID—

❑ Bringing up business subjects until you get to know your host, or you will be considered rude.
❑ Commenting on a man's wife or female children over 12 years of age.
❑ Raising colloquial questions that may be common in your country, but possibly misunderstood here as an invasion of privacy.
❑ Using disparaging/swear words and off-color or obscene attempts at humor.
❑ Engaging in conversations about religion, politics, or Israel.
❑ Bringing gifts of alcohol or using alcohol, which is prohibited in some countries, such as Saudi Arabia.
❑ Requesting favors from those in authority or esteem, for it is considered impolite for Arabs to say "no."
❑ Shaking hands too firmly or pumping—gentle or limp handshakes are preferred.
❑ Pointing your finger at someone or showing the soles of your feet when seated.

Business ethos in one country may frown upon baksheesh *or payments for "favors received," while elsewhere it may be tolerated, even encouraged.*

Global Managers Should Be Aware That:

❑ Nineteen states in the Middle East share the common Arab culture and practice Islam, but there are differences in interpretations and practices. Saudi Arabia is stricter in this regard as the Gulf's elder statesmen and protector of Muslim traditions, especially as perceived by the Wahhabi sect. Elsewhere social and business life may be more relaxed as in Bahrain, or between a country like Iran now under a fundamentalist religious regime, and Jordan under a progressive monarchy greatly influenced by British presence and customs. Business ethos in one country may frown upon *baksheesh* or payments for "favors received," while elsewhere it may be tolerated, even encouraged. In some Arab countries, a local sponsor or partner is essential for a successful joint venture, while in others it is not.
❑ It is helpful to develop a small vocabulary of Arabic words or phrases to be used properly for greetings and introductions, as well as to observe the protocol of names (e.g. "Ibn" meaning "son of") and titles (e.g. "Your Excellency").
❑ Middle Eastern food, while tasty and carefully prepared, may affect Westerners not familiar with the diet. Be cautious to drink bottled

water, not tap water, and if cooking with non-bottled water, one must purify it; peeling fruits and vegetables is advised.

❑ The future of the region may be shaped by the oil rich nations there, and those other Arab states without such wealth who generally are more populous and economically dependent upon the former.

❑ Middle Eastern country specific information is available in public libraries or the publications of the U. S. Government Printing Office and the U.S. Departments of State and Commerce, and also from the embassies, airlines, associations, and publications of Middle Eastern countries in your homeland.[18] Onsite, locally contact Chambers of Commerce and business-oriented clubs, such as Kiwanis International, or government-sponsored convention and trade organizations.

Middle Eastern Reactions to Americans

Peoples from ancient civilizations, like Egypt, Persia, Turkey, and Arabia, are proud of their past—its history, art, poetry, literature, and cultural accomplishments. Unfortunately, many Westerners and Asians carry distorted cultural images or stereotypes about the Middle Easterners and their contributions to human development. American media has been particularly inept, slanted, and at times false in their presentations about the Middle East and the Arabs. The image of the latter is further tarnished by a very small number of Islamic militants who engage in terrorist acts against innocent people, sometimes under the sponsorship of states like Libya, Iraq, Iran, and possibly Syria. Ugly American behavior and racism toward these peoples and their religion explains in part reactive "Anti-American" campaigns abroad that undermine both political and business relationships. That happened in Iran, a non-Arab country, in 1979 when American influence and actions threatened "Persian" identity and culture to the point of violent take-over and hostage taking in the U. S. Embassy.

Since 1936, Westerners have located 70% of the world's oil reserves in the Middle East. The resulting influx of Europeans, Americans, and even Asians into the region have brought repercussion from the indigenous peoples about these "guests" who come to engage in business and development. Here is a summary of the feedback from the Arab perspective:

❑ A feeling of superiority; they know the answers to everything.
❑ Many do not want to share the credit for what is accomplished by joint efforts.
❑ Many are frequently unable or unwilling to respect and adjust to local customs and culture.
❑ Some fail to innovate in terms of the need of local culture, preferring to seek creative solutions based on the situation in their homeland.

Westerners and Asians carry distorted cultural images or stereotypes about the Middle Easterners and their contributions to human development.

- ❑ Some individuals refuse to work through the normal administrative channels of the country, and do not respect local legal and contractual procedures.
- ❑ Americans tend to lose their democratic ways when on foreign assignments, becoming instead more autocratic and managing by instilling fear in subordinates.
- ❑ Americans and Northern Europeans are too imposing, aggressive, pushy, and rude.

Apparently, there is much misperception and suspicion of one another on the part of Middle Easterners, Americans, Europeans and Asians, particularly when it comes to each one's sense of space and eye contact.

Synergy: The Hope of the Middle East

> A few hours before boarding the plane that would take him to Washington for further peace talks, Prime Minister Benjamin Netanyahu stood on a stage here and handed out etched glass trophies to 53 foreign businessmen whose companies had each sunk $50 million or more into the Israeli economy. . . . In Israel, it is striking how the business community has not only accepted what it sees as the inevitability of an independent Palestinian state, but it already is preparing to profit from it. . . . Israel's economy is now far larger than all of its contiguous neighbors. . . . The peace process has already been good for business, Israeli executives say.[19]

Peaceful negotiations, mediation, and problem-solving skills are being used to resolve long-standing conflicts, instead of using weapons and violence.

Slowly and painfully a new cooperative relationship is emerging among the states and inhabitants of the Middle East. In addition to Arab unity efforts among themselves, unity and peace accords have included neighbors in the area like the accord between Egypt and Israel. Peaceful negotiations, mediation, and problem-solving skills are being used to resolve long-standing conflicts, instead of using weapons and violence. Gradually this approach extended to the Israelis who reached agreements with the Palestinians and Jordanians, and continues in terms of seeking comparable accords with Syrians and Lebanese. Even during the Gulf War, both Westerners and Middle Easterners realized the value of a coalition to oppose the tyranny of Iraq's invasion of Kuwait.

Middle Easterners of all types are beginning to prefer collaboration with one another, even former enemies, so as to realize the economic potential of the region. Since they are only a short jet hop away from Europe, the interchange with peoples on both continents has increased. Arabs fly regularly there to study, invest, engage in commerce, seek medical assistance, vacation, or even to reside. Europeans in greater numbers go to the Middle East seeking new markets and as tourists. In place of former colonial dominance, the present and future offer opportunity for a more *synergistic* relationships if both Europeans and Arabs learn to appreciate each other's cultural heritages and differences while seeking mutual benefit. Hopefully, the same strategy will be implemented between Middle Easterners and Africans, Americans and Asians. Practicing synergy is the key to peace and prosperity in the 21st century both for that region and the world.

SUMMARY

Although the business boom is currently over in the Middle East, global organizations will continue to seek commercial opportunities and relationships there. Thus, the authors have offered an introduction to the area in terms of its ancient glories, present diversity, and current difficulties. Particular attention was devoted to increasing understanding of both Islam and Arab culture, the dominant factors in the vast majority of populace in the area. Because it was not feasible for us to cover all the national conditions within the Middle East, we chose two target cultures that are more representative of the majority, acknowledging the presence of Jewish and Christian minorities in the area. Thus, in the context of doing business in these countries, we reviewed for each the people and their homeland, its geographic features and cities, political and social conditions, and the economy. Although each country is unique and different, we provided an overview of business and customs and protocols. We concluded with a call for cultural synergy not only within the Middle East, but because so many of its inhabitants now live and work in Europe, as well as Africa, America, and Asia.

Practicing synergy is the key to peace and prosperity in the 21st century both for that region and the world.

REFERENCES

1. Roaf, M. *Cultural Atlas of Mesopotamia and the Ancient Near East,* New York, NY: Facts on File, 1990; Nawwab, I. I., Speers, P. C. and Hoye, P. F. (eds.). *Aramco and Its World—Arabia and the Middle East,* Houston, TX: Aramco Services Company, 1981.
2. Lippman, T. W. *Understanding Islam: An Introduction to the Muslim World,* New York, NY: Mentor, 1990; Adas, M. (ed.). *Islamic and European Expansion,* Philadelphia, PA: Temple University Press, 1993.
3. Hourani, A., Khoury, P. S., and Wilson, M. C. (eds.). *The Modern Middle East: A Reader,* Berkeley, CA: University of California Press, 1994; Held, C. C. *Middle East Patterns: Places, Peoples, and Politics,* Boulder, CO: Westview Press, 1989; Spiegel, S. L. *The Arab-Israeli Search for Peace,* Boulder, CO: Lynne Rienner Publishers, 1992; Haddad, Y. Y. and Smith, J. I. *Muslim Communities in North America,* Albany, NY: State University of New York Press, 1994.
4. Bowen, D. L. and Early, E. A. *Everyday Life in the Muslim Middle East,* Bloomington, IN: Indiana University Press, 1993; Elashmawi, F. and Harris, P. R. *Multicultural Management—New Skills for Global Success,* Houston, TX: Gulf Publishing, 1993; Shusta, R. M., Levine, D. R., Har-

ris, P. R., and Wong, H. Z. *Multicultural Law Enforcement—Strategies for Peacekeeping in a Diverse Society,* Englewood Cliffs, NJ: Prentice Hall, 1994 (see Ch. 9, "Law Enforcement with Arab Americans and Other Middle Eastern Groups").

5. Feghali, E. "Arab Cultural Communication Patterns," *International Journal of Intercultural Relations,* 1997, Vol. 21, No. 3, pp. 344–378.

6. Lanier, A. and Gay, C. W. *Living in the U.S.A.,* 5th edition, Yarmouth, ME: Intercultural Press, 1996.

7. Hourani, A. *A History of the Arab Peoples,* Cambridge, MA: Harvard University Press, 1991; Nydell, M. K. *Understanding Arabs—A Guide for Westerners,* Yarmouth, ME: Intercultural Press, 1987, InterAct 5.

8. Mernissi, F. *Los Angeles Times,* June 8, 1990, p. VII/25.

9. Vincent-Barwood, A. "Georgetown's Bridge of Faith," *Aramco World,* May/June 1998, pp. 12–17.

10. Business and culture specific information for each chapter in Unit 3, as well as each country in the Middle East, is available from the International Trade Administration, Washington, D.C. 20230, USA. With reference to Chapter 14, their Office of the Near East (Rm. 2029B), has a fax number (202/482-1064) that can be contacted for relevant documents and reports. The code numbers for general regional data are 0101 thru 0118; then each nation has code numbers as follows: Algeria #0200-0211; Bahrain #0300-0306; Egypt #0400-0416; Iran # 0500-0503; Iraq #0600-0603; Israel #0700-0713; Jordan #0800-0809; Kuwait #0900-0917; Lebanon #1000-10005; Libya #1100-1102; Morocco #1200-1215; Oman #1300-1309; Qatar #1400-1407; Saudi Arabia #1500-1534; Syria #1600-1608; Tunisia #1700-1708; United Arab Emirates #1800-1811; West Bank/Gaza #1850-1856; Yemen #1900-1905.

11. *San Diego Union Tribune,* February 3, 1995, A 1 & 12.

12. Al-Hariri-Rifai, W. and Al-Hariri-Rifai, M. *The Heritage of the Kingdom of Saudi Arabia,* Washington, DC: GDC Publications, 1990; Altorki, A. *Women in Saudi Arabia,* New York, NY: Columbia University Press, 1988; Al-Farsy, F. *Saudi Arabia Revised,* New York, NY: Columbia University Press, 1986. Rihani, A. *Makers of Modern Arabia.* Westport, CT: Greenwood Press, 1983; Lee, E. *The American in Saudi Arabia,* Yarmouth, ME: Intercultural Press, 1980.

13. Pampanini, A. H. *Cities from the Arabian Desert: The Building of Jubail and Yanbu,* New York: Praeger, 1997.

14. *The Economist,* February 4, 1995, pp. 39–40.

15. Lexis-Nexis Academic Universe, Saudi Arabia, ABC-CLIO Inc. A division of Reed Elsevier Inc., 1999.

16. At-Twaijri, M. I., "The Negotiating Style of Saudi Industrial Buyers," *International Journal of Value-Based Management,* Vol. 5:1, 1992; "Language Effects in Cross-cultural Management Research, *International Journal of Value-Based Management,* Vol. 3:1, 1990; "A Cross-cultural Comparison of American-Saudi Managerial Values," *International Studies of Management & Organization,* Vol. 19:2, 1989; "Empirical Analysis of the Effects of Environmental Interdependence and Uncertainty on Purchasing: A Cross-Cultural Study," Industrial Marketing Purchasing, Vol. 3:1, 1988; "The Impact of Context and Choice on Boundary-Spanning Process," *Human Relations,* Vol. 40:12, 1987. For reprints, write to

Dr. Mohhammad I. At-Twarijri, Dean, College of Industrial Management, King Fahd University of Petroleum & Minerals, Dhahran 31261, Saudi Arabia (Fax: # 03 860-2772).

17. Moran, R. T. and Stripp, W. G. *Dynamics of Successful International Business Negotiations,* 1991; Elashmawi, F. and Harris, P. R. *Multicultural Management* (see Ch. 7, "Managing Intercultural Business Negotiations"), Houston, TX: Gulf Publishing, 1993.
18. Moran, R. T. and Braaten, D. O. (eds.). *International Directory of Multicultural Resources,* Houston, TX: Gulf Publishing, 1996; Middle Eastern Cultural Specifics: Each country usually has a Chamber of Commerce in its capital city which can provide information on doing business there. Inquire if business directories are available, such as *Saudi Commercial Directory* (PO Box 1257, Jeddah, Saudi Arabia).
19. Orme, W. E. "Israeli Business Flies Like a Dove, *New York Times,* 1998, p. 3WK.
20. Almunajjed, A. *Women in Saudi Arabia Today,* New York: Macmillan, 1997.
21. Chebel, M. *Symbols of Islam,* New York: St Martin's Press, 1997.
22. Cleary, T. (ed.). *The Essential Koran: The Heart of Islam,* San Francisco, CA: Harper, 1993.
23. Gouverneur, G. H. *Islam: A Pictorial Essay in Four Parts,* A 90-minute video produced for the Islamic Texts Society, 1986.
24. Norwich, J. J. *Bysantium: Decline and Fall,* New York: Alfred Knopf, 1996.
25. Nydell, M. K. *Understanding Arabs: A Guide for Westerners,* Yarmouth, ME: Intercultural Press, 1997.

Note: We recommend the colorful monthly magazine *Aramco World* that is complimentary if requested on business stationery. The Aramco Services Company of Houston, TX also publishes an informative book by the same title on the Middle East that may be purchased for $50. Contact *Aramco World,* Box 469008, Escondido, CA 92046.

15

DOING BUSINESS WITH AFRICANS

Africa is 20% of this planet's land mass. . . .

Africa has largely remained a mystery to the outside world, marked perhaps more by its isolation than any other feature. This stubborn reality can be traced to the earliest times and is reflected in the hopelessly misrepresented images of ancient cartographers, whose graphic distortions were as errant as the half myths and false science that passed for knowledge about a place long known among Westerners as the Dark Continent.[1]

Ancient civilizations flourished in Africa from Carthage in the north to black "empires" in the south.[2] Africa is 20% of this planet's land mass—11,700,000 square miles, lying south of Europe and the Mediterranean Sea, extending downward, bounded on the east by the Red Sea and Indian Oceans, and on the west by the Atlantic Ocean. Surrounding it are ten island groups: in the northwest, the Madeira, Canary, and Cape Verde Islands; in the west central area, there are the islands of Bioko and San Tome/Principe; in the southeast, the Seychelles, Comoros, Mauritius, Rodgriques, Reunion, and in their midst the largest island of all—Madagascar, just off the Mozambique Channel.

Geographically, the continent is split by the Equator and is contained between 38 degrees north and south latitudes. Lacking long mountain ranges to wring moisture from passing air masses, its rain patterns are extreme contrasts—the equatorial rain forest is deluged during two rainy seasons, while a single wet season north, south, and east prove quite insufficient. Relief from tropical heat may be obtained in higher altitudes of eastern and southern plateaus, while parts of the west coast have currents which transport seawater from cooler regions. For convenient analysis, this huge continent is usually divided into four parts—North and South Africa, East and West Africa. Although rich in its diversity of animals and fauna, many of these species are threatened by habitat

TUNISIA

AFRICA

MEDITERRANEAN SEA

MOROCCO

ALGERIA

LIBYA

EGYPT

WESTERN
SAHARA

MAURITANIA

NIGER

CHAD

SUDAN

MALI

ETHIOPIA

SENEGAL

BURKINA
FASO

SOMALIA

ARABIAN
SEA

GAMBIA

GUINEA

BENIN

NIGERIA

CENTRAL
AFRICAN
REPUBLIC

GUINEA
BISSAU

IVORY
COAST

TOGO

GHANA

CAMEROON

UGANDA

KENYA

SIERRA
LEONE

LIBERIA

EQUATORIAL GUINEA

GABON

CONGO

ZAIRE

TANZANIA

GULF OF
GUINEA

MALAWI

ANGOLA

ZAMBIA

MOZAMBIQUE

MADAGASCAR

ATLANTIC
OCEAN

ZIMBABWE

NAMIBIA

BOTSWANA

SWAZILAND

SOUTH
AFRICA

LESOTHO

INDIAN
OCEAN

411

destruction and extinction, so wildlife preservation in Africa is of global concern. By the turn of the century, a large majority of the population will live near Lake Victoria and the south coast of West Africa.

Approximately 52 countries share the African territory, from Algeria in the Islamic north to Zimbabwe in the southeast. National identities are difficult for diverse peoples assembled within borders imposed by departed European imperialists. Their partitioning of Africa in the past two centuries made no attempt to make national borders coincide with onsite ethnic groups and tribes. So one says "approximately" for boundaries on this continent as new states are continuously being reconfigured. Recently Eritrea broke away from ancient Ethiopia, and the so-called independent homelands of Swaziland and Lesotho someday soon may be absorbed back into South Africa. National names also change rapidly as when Rhodesia became Zimbawe, and Tanganyika became Tanzania.

With only one tenth of the global human population, Africa is home to almost one-third of the world's sovereign states. Most of the countries came into existence in the 20th century, and currently about half were formed as the result of coups, principally by the military. The redrawing of colonial boundaries need not mean smaller African states; it could simply mean more rational and viable political communities. The long-term scenario emerging from the crises may be the gradual redrawing of boundaries between Zaire, Rwanda, and Burundi. Unless the Hutu and Tutsi are partitioned into separate countries or federated into a larger, stable, and democratic political community, they are likely to turn against each other in a genocidal frenzy every few years. The international community should put together a large package of inducements and incentives to persuade Rwanda, Burundi, and Tanzania to create the United States of Central Africa. Parts of Zaire could one day seek admission into the new federation.[3]

Sovereign states with their bureaucratic controls are the hallmark of mass civilization; such historical experience was largely absent in sub-Saharan African kingdoms before the arrival of European colonialism during the past three centuries. Given this lack of strong statehood tradition on the continent, it is understandable why contemporary Africans struggle with the refinement and administration of government. Although by the year 1500, their ancestors had learned to smelt iron, the industrial stage of development was missed by most Africans who were mainly hunter-gathers, farmers, and herders; only a small minority lived in organized states and urban areas. Given this history with three centuries of predatory slave-raiding and direct European influence or rule, most Africans regained their independence and freedom only in the past several decades.[4] Thus, a dynamic process is underway throughout Africa to develop modern mass societies with the accompanying political, economic, and technological systems. One needs an *afrocentric* approach to appreciate fully this heritage and experience.[5]

MANAGING CULTURAL DIFFERENCES

INSIGHTS INTO AFRICA

This is a continent of immense natural beauty and resources, most of which is still undeveloped. It is a region of contrasts between the primitive and the ultramodern, a place where new industries, technologies, and cities emerge gradually. Yet for global leaders to be effective in their trade and development efforts within Africa, they must be realistic in their analysis of its peoples and their promise. First, there is great diversity to be found among the inhabitants in terms of stages of human and institutional development, manifested in the multitude of tribes, languages, customs, religions, education, and governments. Second, most of the people here are generous and traditional, eager to learn and hardworking. But in the past thirty years, their natural buoyancy and flexibility have been dampened by widespread famine, epidemics, exploitation, and social unrest. The world media often distorts our image of Africa by its emphasis on African tragedies—the horror of the mass poverty, the extensive droughts, the many civil wars, and the millions of refugees. Often overlooked in this reporting are the success stories— World Bank and UNESCO projects that work at the local levels, the green revolution that expands agricultural production, the many business enterprises that flourish, the African foreign students who return to apply their Western education, the shift from failed socialism to democratic and market-oriented policies.

Africa is in a state of profound transition as it enters the 21st century. The changes underway can also be summed up in three words—*tribalism, chaos,* and *developing.* To illustrate our choice of this terminology, consider this rationale:

Tribalism

The tribe is the basic sociological unit of Africa that provides one's sense of identity, belonging, and responsibility. When tribal members leave rural areas to go to the city for a job or to study, traditionally their enhanced stature brings with it responsibility for assisting their tribal brothers and sisters. Such social pressure on successful Africans may impose a burden to augment income by any means, legal or otherwise. Tribal bonds also lead to intergroup conflict, destruction, and corruption. As the force of tribalism deteriorates in modern, urban environments, Africans search for other substitutes, new institutional loyalties like membership in a religion, cooperatives, and political parties, often formed along ethnic lines.

For many, tribalism is the bane of independent Africa with its countless tribes and clans involving 2,000 language groups—Swahili, Zulu and Hausa being the most prominent. Leftover from the colonialists are areas where French, English, Portuguese, and a corruption of Dutch are widely spoken. National leaders seek to transform inter-tribal hostility

This is a continent of immense natural beauty and resources, most of which is still undeveloped. It is a region of contrasts between the primitive and the ultramodern.

into collaborative community endeavors. Tribalism is evident in elections when the voting favors the largest tribes, while the winners are only slowly learning that power should be shared with the minority losers. The challenge for many Africans is to build upon tribal heritage but move beyond tribal loyalties and constraints for the greater common good of the nation and its economic development.

Chaos

As Africans seek to move beyond their colonial past and dependency, while rapidly creating appropriate cultural institutions and opportunities, tumult abounds. The destablization process is compounded by a combination of factors. Sometimes it is caused by nature, when lack of rain triggers mass famine, or monkeys infect entire East African populations through the new plague of Acquired Immune Deficiency—the AIDS virus. Sometimes the disarray comes from:

❏ The rise of Muslim militants and terrorists as in North Africa and Sudan.
❏ The tribal conflicts in this past decade that escalated into civil wars, like Rwanda when the Hutu army oversaw the murder of a million Tutsis, while in Somalia the tribal warfare lead to the collapse of the government and anarchy.
❏ The ambitions and ideologies of local dictators and guerrillas to crush their opposition has lead to new tyrannies, which occurred recently in Nigeria, Liberia, Angola, and elsewhere.

Often the internal troubles get exacerbated by external intervention, as when:

❏ In past centuries Europeans imposed their controls upon the locals, so that today the influence of European cultures and dependency still may be found in former African colonies of Britain, France, Germany, and Portugal.
❏ In the 20th century, Western powers have twice involved Africans in their World Wars, as well as the Cold War between the U.S. and the former U.S.S.R.
❏ With the United Nations sent relief efforts and troops to such places as the Sudan, Rwanda, and Somalia.

The combination of such forces, overpopulation and the need for food and employment contribute to displacement of millions of Africans from their homelands. Many end up as refugees amid poverty on a gigantic scale. One effect of this chaos is threatening of the ecological environment of the continent. Deserts are widening, broad savannas and

For many, tribalism is the bane of independent Africa with its countless tribes and clans involving 2,000 language groups....

their communities struggle for existence, both wildlife and human life struggle for survival. Sometimes the confusion is simply *future shock* as tribal cultures and rural peoples try to cope with the demands of an urban, post-industrial way of life.[6] Finally, too many post-colonial nation-states and their political "leaders" are failing to liberate and protect their own citizens.

Developing

Africa has been classified as the Third World in economic terms. The continent often is viewed as either a "basket case" or a land of promise, rich in both natural and human resources to be developed. The full potential of Africa may be realized in the 21st century if Africans are empowered to build an infrastructure based on their own uniqueness and cultures. But to actualize this potential, Africans will have to learn how to (a) practice synergy among themselves; (b) control their populations; (c) advance their literacy, education, and productivity; and (d) connect with the Information Age and its technologies.

There have been promising developments. In the 1980s, 16 countries joined together to form the Economic Community of West African States, while in the 1990s, 9 more countries launched the Southern African Coordination Conference. In a sense the Organization of African States is a mini case study illustrating in its short history the significance of the above three terms and the promise of the future. Founded in 1963 to create greater unity among African states, the OAU has been both a disappointment and modest success. Too often it was used for demaguery, posturing, and junkets. Yet the organization also has achieved through its economic and technical projects, the improvement of the continent's communication and banking systems, and the maintenance of inter-state peace.[7] The hope is that the OAU will become the forum and mechanism for African recovery and self-restitution.

For individuals to be more effective in their business and professional relationships with Africans, it is helpful to have some insights into the diverse cultures of this continent. In the previous chapter we described the Islamic culture, which also dominates North Africa and the Muslim states elsewhere in this area. Within black Africa, there are some common cultural characteristics. The next section will review six dimensions of African cultures—family, trust/friendship, time, corruption, task orientation, and authority. This analysis may increase your awareness and improve interaction not only with Africans, but with the millions of descendants from this heritage who are found throughout North, Central, and South America, as well as in the Caribbeans and the United Kingdom. However, be cautious with such generalizations because African cultures are dynamic and changing to fit new times and circumstances.

The full potential of Africa may be realized in the 21st century if Africans are empowered to build an infrastructure based on their own uniqueness and cultures.

SELECTED CULTURAL
CHARACTERISTICS OF AFRICANS

The Family and Kinship

In traditional African society, the tribe is the ultimate community. No unit has more importance in society. The tribe is broken down into different kinship lines. It constitutes the primary basis for an individual's rights, duties, rules of residence, marriage, inheritance, and succession.

The basic unit of African society is the family, which includes the nuclear family and the extended family or tribe. In traditional African society, the tribe is the ultimate community. No unit has more importance in society. There may be some loose confederations, but they are temporary and limited in scope. In political terms, the tribe is the equivalent of a nation. It does not have fixed boundaries, but on its sanction rests the law (customary law like the English Common Law). All wars were fought on the tribe's behalf, and the division between "them" and "us" lay in tribal boundaries.

In some ways, the tribe is more than a nation. In Europe and America, ethical and moral standards are not given by national sanctions, but rest on religious and cultural traditions common to the whole continent. But in traditional Africa, except for areas under Islamic control, the tribe provides the guidelines for accepted behavior. The tribe bears a moral connotation and provides an emotional security. It is also a source of social and moral sanctions as well as political and physical security. The tribe provides its members with rules governing responsibilities, explanations of the responsibilities, and guidelines for organizing the society, and hence, the culture.

The tribe is broken down into different kinship lines. The concept of kinship is important to understanding African societies. It constitutes the primary basis for an individual's rights, duties, rules of residence, marriage, inheritance, and succession.

Kinship refers to blood relationships between individuals and is used to describe relationships in a narrow as well as a broad sense. Parents and their children are a special kind of kin group. The social significance of kinship covers a wide social field in most African societies. In Western culture, its significance usually does not extend beyond the nuclear family, but in the African culture, it embraces a network of people including those that left the village for urban areas.

The family—father, mother, children—is the ultimate basis of the tribe. But the tribal and family unit organization is being disrupted by changes in the economic organizational structure. The economic organization has tied reward to individual effort, and developed road, rail, water, and air communication networks that have increased the range and speed of contact and, therefore, the rate of intercultural contact and change. The reorganization has also brought tribes together as territorial units, thereby increasing opportunities for migration from one area to another and weakening family bonds.

As this new-found mobilization moves more people to the large urban areas, they try to maintain some family ties. This involves a responsibility to support family members still in the villages. It also affects Africans' business relationships with managers from abroad in terms of hiring practices and the need for extra income to support those at home. Earnings from business transactions are often used for this purpose.

Trust and Friendship

Trust and confidence are essential elements needed for successful enterprise in Africa. It is very important to get to know co-workers as individuals before getting down to actual business activities. Friendship comes first. Often, a friendship continues after specific business activities end. Socializing outside of the office is common. It is under those relaxed conditions that managers talk politics, sports, and sometimes business.

Contrast this with American business people who are interested primarily in getting the job done. There is some socialization outside the office, but only for business purposes. As soon as the job is done or the contract fulfilled, the U.S. manager moves on to other things. A friendship that develops outside of the office and continues for an extended period of time is unique.

In Africa, interpersonal relationships are also based upon sincerity. African societies are warm and friendly. People generally assume that everyone is a friend until proven otherwise. When Africans smile, it means they like you. When smiles are not seen, it is a clear sign of distrust.

Once a person is accepted as a friend, that person is automatically a member of the family. A friend can pop into a friend's place anytime. In African societies, formal invitations and appointment making are not common.

One of the most important factors to remember when doing business in Africa is the concept of friendship before business. Normally before a meeting begins, there is general talk about events that have little or nothing to do with the business at hand. This can go on for some time. If the meeting involves the coming together of people who have never met, but who are trying to strike a deal (an African and a foreigner), the African will try to reach out for friendship first. If an African tries to reach out but receives a cold response, he may become alert and suspicious and lose interest in the deal.

Time

The way an individual views the concept of time has a major impact on any business relationship. If two business people enter a situation with complementary goals, abilities, and needs, a successful arrangement can be thwarted if each has different ideas about time. Generally,

One of the most important factors to remember when doing business in Africa is the concept of friendship before business.

U.S. managers tend to be inflexible when it comes to time. Everything is done according to a schedule. Meetings must begin on time and end on time. The entire day is segmented into time slots, and Americans can become uneasy or nervous if the schedule is interrupted or if little is accomplished.

In Africa, time is viewed as flexible, not rigid or segmented. People come first, then time. Anyone in a hurry is viewed with suspicion and distrust. Because trust is very important, individuals who follow inflexible time schedules will have little success. The African wants to sit and talk—get to know the person before discussing business.

In the larger cities of Africa, the concept of time is changing. Punctuality is becoming more important. Contact with Western business persons have brought an increasing awareness and acceptance of the segmentation of time and its consequent inflexibility. But away from the capital city, time is still viewed in a relaxed and easy-going manner.

Time is not seen as a limited commodity. What cannot be done today can always be accomplished tomorrow. Meetings are not held promptly and people may arrive several hours late. Many times foreigners misinterpret this as laziness, untrustworthiness, lack of seriousness in doing business, or even lack of interest in the venture. However, lateness in meetings should be perceived as part of African life. It is understood among friends that even though everybody agrees to meet at a given time, they will not actually gather until much later. However, when Africans are dealing with foreigners, they normally try to be on time out of respect for the non-Africans' concept of time.

Corruption

Corruption in Africa is often a result of tribal responsibilities that individuals carry with them when leaving the village for a job or schooling in the city. The enhanced stature of city life brings a responsibility of assisting one's tribal family. This obligation often imposes a financial burden on the successful member far in excess of income. The worker is unlikely to resist the pressures of society, and is thus forced to augment income, often by means regarded by foreigners as corrupt. However, to the African, it is not. As long as great disparities in income and standards of living continue, the bribe system is also likely to continue as it has in many countries. In Africa, extra income is swiftly distributed through the extended family system to remote relations living in remote places. The tradition of sharing continues even as individuals move away from their tribal origins.

One of the greatest problems in Nigeria, for example, is the corruption in government on all levels. The following mini case is an example:

In Africa, time is viewed as flexible, not rigid or segmented. People come first, then time. Lateness in meetings should be perceived as part of African life.

Corruption in Africa is often a result of tribal responsibilities that individuals carry with them when leaving the village for a job or schooling in the city.

The company, Jones & Smith Food Company, is located in the capital of a large African country. However, they want to expand their headquarters to another state capital. To do this, they need approval from the federal government and the state government. The company sent in a written application a few months ago, but did not get any response.

The manager of the project went several times to the Federal Ministry of Trade and Economic Development but was always told to come back the next day. Mr. Jones became frustrated and mad at the clerks and officials involved. However, in the process of the argument, one of them said, "This is not America. It's Africa. If you want anything done on time, you've got to give a bribe. Kind of like a gratuity tendered before, rather than after a service is performed."

Mr. Jones, who is not accustomed to such practices, angrily stormed out of the office. In the car, he narrated the incident to the driver who advised him to give the "gratuity" or have the proposal denied.

In emergency meeting, the company's board of directors decided to offer the gratuity. To the company's surprise, the proposal was approved the next day.

But back in Jones' home culture a board of directors may frown upon such payments, and home country laws may consider such bribes illegal.

Respect for Elders

Age is another important factor to consider in Africa. It is believed that the older one gets, the wiser one becomes—life has seasoned the individual with varied experiences. Hence, in Africa, age is an asset. The older the person, the more respect the person receives from the community, and especially from the young. Thus, if an American is considerably younger than the African, the latter will have little confidence in the American. However, if sincerity, respect, and empathy are shown, the American will receive a positive response. Respect for elders tends to be the key for harmony in African cultures.

Young people may not oppose the opinion of elderly people. They may not agree, but they must respect the opinion. In some cases, especially in rural areas, young people are not expected to offer opinions in meetings. The informal and formal interpersonal relationships in Africa are based on cultural norms of various African societies.

In Africa, age is an asset. The older the person, the more respect the person receives from the community. . . .

CULTURAL SPECIFICS—NIGERIA AND SOUTH AFRICA

It is impossible here to cover the cultural aspects of doing business in all forty-plus African states. Such details are available without charge from the National Trade Data Bank of the U.S. Department of Commerce.[8] In this section we have chosen two key nations for in-depth analysis because (1) they have major economic implications for all of Africa; and (2) they present insights into what is happening with their neighbors.

NIGERIA

NIGERIA—PROFILE	
Population	110 million
Land..............................	357,700 mi^2
Ethnic Groups	250 tribal groups (three largest are Hausa-Fulani, Ibo and Yoruba = 65%),
Religions	Muslim 45%, Christian 48%, Indigenous African beliefs 7%
Education.......................	Literacy rate 51%, Six Years Compulsory

Nigeria's land mass is approximately 356, 667 square miles—about twice the size of the state of California.

The cultural history of this country and its peoples dates back to the 7th century B.C., and more advanced cultures have resided in Nigeria since the 12th century A.D. In 1861, the British seized the principal city of Lagos, supposedly to end the slave trade then flourishing there. The English social, financial, and political cultural impact has been considerable ever since. Even though the locals gained their political independence in 1960, they are still members of the British Commonwealth of Nations, often traveling to the United Kingdom for business, pleasure, or resettlement. English is often the language for business and national affairs.

Nigeria's land mass is approximately 356, 667 square miles—about twice the size of the state of California. Despite some border disputes with its neighbors over Lake Chad, this West African nation is bounded by Benin, Niger, Chad, and Cameroon, as well as the Atlantic Ocean on its southern edge. Its population of some 110 million is composed of 250 tribal groups of which 65% are the Hausa-Fulani, Ibo, and Yoruba, which also represent the three major language groups (Hausa, Zula, and

Swahili). There are five major religious influences present: Muslim—45%; Protestant—25%; Roman Catholic—12%; African Christian—11%; and Traditional African Beliefs—6% (percentages of the population are approximate). As with many African countries, foreign missionaries accompanied European colonists in previous centuries. Today Christian churches, schools, hospitals, and social institutions have significant influence on the culture, especially in the south, as do comparable Koranic schooling and enterprises in the north. A quota system guarantees students from the latter a share of university places; an undue share contend the southerners who view their school system as superior.

The People and Their Homeland

Nigeria's human resources have great potential. The literacy rate is 51% as a result of 6 years of compulsory education. Over 14 million students are enrolled in elementary (34,240) and secondary (5,970) schools and 48 colleges/universities. The Nigerian educational system is generally based upon the British system. What was generally believed about African culture comes into sharper focus in the context of Nigeria, once considered Africa's most advanced nation.

Social Structure

In Nigeria the family dominates the social structure. Nigerian tradition places emphasis on one's lineage through the male head of the household. In non-Moslem sections, these familial connections form vast networks that serve as a foundation for one's social identity. Marriage is seen as a way of producing more children to contribute to this lineage or network. Sterility is grounds for divorce.

Three forms of marriage exist in Nigeria. Among some Christians and non-Moslems, unlimited polygamy is customary. Wives are acquired through the payment of a "bride price" to the bride's parents. Moslem custom differs in that the number of wives is usually limited to four. The Western Christian marriage is relatively uncommon in rural areas, although increasing in the cities.

Women play a vigorous role in this society, although domestic authority always rests seemingly with the husband. There is a network of marketing and trading in commodities that occurs throughout the country. This is the exclusive province of women, who run their own businesses the way they see fit.

The stratification of Nigerian society varies with region. In northern Nigeria, rank is more important than it is in the south. In the east, some egalitarian tradition exists, while in the west there is a distinct aristocracy.

Women play a vigorous role in this society, although domestic authority always rests seemingly with the husband.

Groups and Relationships

Among the many tribes, the major ones are:

1. The Hausa are very religious and are Muslim.
2. The Yoruba are a festive people, outgoing and not secretive about their business activities.
3. The Ibo are excellent merchants, extremely resourceful, hard working and conscientious. They understand the value of money.

At state and federal meetings, protocol must be observed. Extreme politeness, respect for authority and a slower pace are normal. If an authority does not answer your question, it may mean they do not know the answer and do not want to be embarrassed.

It is helpful if a business person establishes a Nigerian counterpart. One needs expertise in dealing with the Nigerian business community. Because choosing a Nigerian counterpart or representative is crucial to the business success, the U.S. embassy's commercial officer can be of help. References should be carefully checked, and choosing someone with influential contacts is important. This local resource will prove invaluable in translating later what was said during a meeting. Even though the official language is English, the Nigerian accent can be difficult to understand. A Nigerian may be insulted when an individual does not comprehend his or her local version of English, often British in origin.

It takes a long time to become established in the Nigerian business community and it's who one knows that will make a difference. Connections are important and should be cultivated.

When investing in Nigeria, start at the state government level instead of the federal. Each state operates differently, but all want and need business, and consequently are very receptive. The state officials can greatly facilitate business formalities.

These important business attitudes exist in Nigeria:

❑ *Old family business tradition.* One does not share information because everyone else is a competitor. (This traditional attitude has often been reinforced by subsequent European influences.)
❑ *New U.S. training.* Free flow of information; share; communicate; trade knowledge. (Many young Nigerian business people are U.S. trained).
❑ *Moslem attitudes.* Predestination rather than free will; reliance on precedent; mistrust of innovation; unwillingness to take risks; learning by rote rather than by experiments or problem solving.

Because choosing a Nigerian counterpart or representative is crucial to the business success, the U.S. embassy's commercial officer can be of help.

BUSINESS TIPS

❑ Be formal and respectful.
❑ Be trustworthy—deliver when and what is promised.
❑ Relax, slow down—Nigeria is not on the same time schedule as Western cultures.
❑ Don't be overly sensitive to criticism or advice.
❑ American skills are technical not cultural. Learn about the people—take an interest in and try to experience the culture.
❑ Don't try too hard to "go African." Remain professional.
❑ Patience is the key to successful business in Nigeria.

It will almost always be necessary to deal, in some capacity, with Nigerian government officials. When a meeting is granted, whether with the desired official or someone else, there are important practices to be aware of. First, any significant business transaction is always conducted in person. Any attempt to conduct business either over the telephone or by mail is seen as considering the matter as trivial and unimportant. When visiting a colleague's office, tea, coffee, or other refreshments are always available and offered. These refreshments should not be refused, as this may be taken as offensive. Also, refreshments must always be available when the colleague comes to visit the foreign businessperson's office. A visiting businessperson will often be invited to a colleague's home for a meal. Once again, if at all possible, the invitation should not be refused.

When conducting negotiations with a Nigerian the tone of such meetings is generally friendly and respectful. Notice should be taken of titles to be sure the appropriate ones are used correctly. Age is highly respected in Nigeria and often associated with wisdom. Therefore, to maximize chances of success, an older person should be sent to meet with prospective businesspersons. Nigerians assume promises will be kept, so be realistic about delivery dates or price specifications.

It is not unusual for a Nigerian worker to try to involve his foreign manager or supervisor in politics. It is much better to not get involved in these politics, as sides will undoubtedly be chosen and one's authority will be minimized, and an air of hostility and tension will be apparent.

Any significant business transaction is always conducted in person. Any attempt to conduct business either over the telephone or by mail is seen as considering the matter as trivial and unimportant.

Decision Making

Decision making in middle level management is based on a centralized system and delegation of authority is almost nonexistent. Nigerians cling to authority and are dependent on supervision.

A Nigerian manager at a high level position may feel obligated to find jobs for his or her family and will not hesitate to "pull strings" to employ them. If the Nigerian is very powerful, there is nothing a foreign business person can do to stop this practice. This decision-making process based on family responsibilities can be very frustrating to an American business representative who is conditioned to merit selections and promotions.

Communication Tips

There are certain words that should not be used by a Westerner in Nigeria, such as "native," "hut," "jungle," "witchcraft," and "costume." The connotation behind these expressions tends to be that Africa is still a dark backward continent. Nigeria, as is true with many other parts of Africa, has made great strides in development and is proud of their advancement. Therefore, it is best to remember that a hut is a home and a costume is really clothing. Nigerians want to be friends with foreign visitors and they are proud to have them in their homes. They will go to great lengths to be a friend, but they do not want to be patronized.

Concept of Time

Time is viewed as being unlimited. As such, punctuality is not prevalent.

The concept of time in Nigeria can be summed up as unlimited. Lagos, the center of business is congested. Traffic jams can hold one up for several hours. Consequently, late appointments are common and usually anticipated, and telephone service is poor and unreliable.

Time is, therefore, not of the utmost importance to most Nigerians. As a matter of fact, time is viewed as being unlimited. As such, punctuality is not prevalent. Work is important to the Nigerians, but so is their leisure. Sports are a favorite way to spend time. Those that are most popular with the Nigerians are football, boxing, and horse racing. Hockey, tennis, cricket, polo, golf, rugby, table tennis, and softball are also played.

Greetings

Upon meeting a Nigerian business associate, the greeting is Westernized but formal. A simple, "Good morning Mister Opala, how are you?" is accepted as proper. Asking personal questions about one's family is a common practice. Once you have established some degree of familiarity, you can use a first name basis if the Nigerian initiates it.

Always shake hands when greeting someone. It is extremely rude not to acknowledge a person when entering a room or shake his hand. A typical situation for an American businessman unfolds as follows: He enters a room, shakes hands, is then formally introduced, shakes hands again, is announced as the new senior accountant, shakes hands again, prepares to leave the room, and shakes hands good-bye.

Forms of Address

Nigerians distinguish the levels of familiarity between one another by their forms of address. Friends will call one another by their first names. Older brothers and sisters are very rarely addressed by their first names. An older brother is addressed as N'da Sam and an older sister as N'se Sarah, which means "my senior Sam" or "my senior Sarah." This is simply a sign of respect towards seniority and age. The expressions "sir" and "ma'am" are always used when speaking to a businessperson, government official, someone older, or someone in a position of authority.

Social Customs

Nigerians are a proud and self-confident people. Much of this confidence comes from a knowledge that their country is a leader in Africa in many ways. They are extroverted, friendly, and talkative. Nigerians are known also for their hospitality. Strangers are taken in, fed, lodged for as long as the guest desires. Consequently, it is possible to make many more long-lasting relationships that are less superficial than in some other cultures.

When a friend, acquaintance, or relative becomes ill, it is customary for that person to receive many, many visitors. Anyone who even remotely knows the sick person will come to visit. It is the Nigerian way of saying, "I want to know for myself how you're feeling."

When two people are considering marriage, a proper procedure must be followed. The first step is for the prospective groom to send an intermediary to the woman's home to present the idea of marriage to her parents. Gifts are sent to the woman and then the man himself comes to the woman's parents to discuss the marriage. So far, nothing has been said to the woman about the pending marriage. If everything is in order with the prospective bride's family, the woman then goes to live with the man's family to make sure this is where she wants to live. If so, the marriage can occur. The dowry involved in the marriage is not a fixed amount. It is an insurance against maltreatment for the woman. It is not until the wife dies and is buried in her natal land that the dowry is paid to her husband, if she has been treated well.

Most Nigerian cultures are patriarchal. In some areas, particularly the rural ones, polygamy is still prevalent. However, in urban areas, it is much more common to find one-man, one-woman marriages. Marriage

Nigerians are known also for their hospitality. Strangers are taken in, fed, lodged for as long as the guest desires.

age is becoming more of an economic decision. Couples wait until they have an education and can afford a marriage.

Nigeria is a "right-handed" society. As in many cultures, the left hand is unclean, as it is the "toilet hand." It is extremely impolite to extend the left hand to others or to eat with it, even if the person is left-handed.

Although mentioned before, it is important to reemphasize the importance of age in Nigeria. There is a profound respect for one's elders. Older people are not placed in nursing homes when they become ill. They are taken in by their families, looked after, and revered. The importance of the elderly seems to lie in their capability to pass on family history and tradition. Although Nigeria is growing quickly and becoming more modernized, traditions are still very important to the people, as can be evidenced by the fact that local customs still play a very significant role in Nigerian life. One such ritual, which is quickly disappearing, is found strictly in the western portion of the country and has to do with tribal marks. When a child reaches the age of two or three years, he or she has the appropriate tribal marks burned into his face, very similar to the branding process. These marks reflect tribes or family. When one sees the marks, it is not necessary to ask what the person's last name is or from what tribe he comes. It is said that if the child cannot withstand the pain during the ceremony, as there is no anesthesia, he or she is not worthy of that family or tribe. The whole process is very unhygienic and dangerous, and seems to be dying out gradually.

Intermarriage between tribes currently is very rare in Nigeria. It is more common for a Nigerian to marry a foreigner than out of his tribe to another tribe member. There is still a great deal of rivalry between the tribes and the intent seems to be to try and keep them pure. However, if such an intertribal marriage should occur, oddly enough, the stranger will be treated almost royally by the other members of the other tribe. The reason for this is that the non-tribe's member is viewed as having made a supreme sacrifice by giving up his/her tribe and their traditions and adopting those of the spouse, as they almost always do in this situation.

The custom of eating with one's hands is practiced in Nigeria. If there is a big festival, or even in a private home, where there are foreign visitors not used to this custom, allowances are made and silverware is often provided them. However, an honest effort will be greatly appreciated. Before eating, a communal bucket is passed around for everyone to wash their hands, prior to the beginning of the meal. Once again, it is important to use only the right hand.

As in all of Africa, the role of women in Nigeria is changing with modernization. Females have always performed the major laboring tasks from farming to road building. Now with increased education and opportunity, they are moving up in commerce and industry, as well as in government and the professions. Perhaps the Nigerian women achieving positions of leadership and influence in the political and economic arena, will also set the example for the liberation of women elsewhere on the continent.

Intermarriage between tribes currently is very rare in Nigeria. It is more common for a Nigerian to marry a foreigner than out of his tribe to another tribe member.

Geographic Features and Cities

Ordinarily, Nigeria is hot and dry in the north and hot and wet in the south where the climate is more tropical because of its equatorial location. There are 22 principal cities in the country, of which Lagos, in its southwestern tip on the Bay of Benin, is the largest. This is the nation's main port and commercial center. Like the next largest urban area, Ibadin (historic center of Yoruba people), both have populations well over a million. About a half million, more or less, inhabitants are found in four other cities—Ogbomosho, Kano (an ancient Moslem center), Oshogbo, Ilorin. Sixteen other leading cities have populations ranging from 200,000 to over 300,000. Smaller places like Benin City are fascinating for their age, galleries, museums, and palaces, or Jos in the country's geographical center with its archeological excavations and museums with artifacts thousands of years old.

Political and Social Conditions

Despite the long tribal history within this region, the Federal Republic of Nigeria was not established until 1963. The boundaries provided by the British brought together four peoples who have had a continuous rivalry going since then. In 1967 the Eastern region seceded to found the "Republic of Biafara"; the subsequent civil war lasted three years and caused over a million deaths, mainly from starvation. Since its formation, Nigeria has experienced struggles whether the government should be ruled by civilians or the military. In 1985, Maj. Gen. Ibrahim Babangida seized power, and in 1992 when Moshood Abiola, a Yoruba, was elected president, in an election organized by the military, the northern generals annulled the results. Instead, the president was put on trial for treason and one of the military cabal, Gen. Sani Abacha, became the self-appointed ruler.

With General Abacha's death from a heart attack in 1998, General Abdulsalam Abuubakar was sworn in as Nigeria's tenth head of state. The Provisional Ruling Council of military men made this appointment. There is growing consensus that military rule by soldiers who get rich has had its day—28 years out of the nation's 38 years of independence. Politics has been reduced to matters of stealing, or chopping as it is called here. The new president has released political prisoners, opened a dialogue with civilian leaders, and announced a reasonable date to hand over power to a civilian government. He has also promised to disband the five political parties set up by the previous dictator, and let the electorate establish parties of their choice. Reality is that multi party politics, a product of industrialized societies and often based on social class, has yet to succeed here or in the rest of Africa, where loyalties are tribal. Also, Abubakar said he would break up state monopolies in several industries, partially privatize big corporations, introduce competition, and end the country's crippling domestic fuel shortage. Yet Nigerian

Nigeria is hot and dry in the north and hot and wet in the south where the climate is more tropical because of its equatorial location. Multi party politics, a product of industrialized societies and often based on social class, has yet to succeed here or in the rest of Africa, where loyalties are tribal.

institutions are discredited and restoring them is as important as elections since the long-suffering citizenry is disillusioned. Like elsewhere on this continent, people have no trust in their unscrupulous "leaders" who stir up ethnic chauvinism, undermining national integration.

The only time there was expressions of real unity between the tribes and religions was during the World Cup games when traditional rivalries were put aside to cheer the national soccer team! When oil was discovered in coastal swamps, the revenues strengthened the federal government and its powers over the states and increased tribal hostilities about sharing the wealth. The ultimate solution for Nigeria may be a genuine federal constitution, with power devolved from the center to the six main regions. This would necessitate a commitment to share political power among the Hausas in the north, the Yorubas in the south, and Ibos in the East who already fought and lost their civil war. Still other Nigerians question whether a federation can survive, proposing instead a confederation or "coassociation" of states. Nigeria's motto is *Unity and Faith,* but there is so little of the former and so much of the latter.

The Economy[9]

As Africa's most populous country, Nigeria represents an enormous market for goods and services. Over a hundred companies are doing business there with an investment of some $2 billion, two-thirds of which is in the petroleum industry. Its most important international trading partner is the U.S., which imports 58% of its oil production. Expatriates from many countries abounded when Nigeria was awash with oil money, especially in the capitol of Lagos. Today, though less in numbers, expatriates comprise business persons, construction engineers, agricultural experts, educators, and technocrats.

Nigeria's natural resources besides petroleum are tin, columbite, iron ore, coal, limestone, lead, zinc, natural gas, marble and fish. Agriculture and foodstuffs are big business, along with major industries in beverages, tobacco, vehicles, chemicals, pharmaceuticals, iron/steel, rubber, printing, building materials, lumber, and footwear.

SOUTH AFRICA

SOUTH AFRICA—PROFILE

Population	43 million
Land................................	471,433 mi^2
Ethnic Groups	Black 75%, White 14%, Coloured 7%, Indian 3%
Education.......................	Literacy rate 76%

There are multiple visions of what South Africa has been and should be.[10] One vision is that this is a land of promise—the most advanced economy on the continent; a country with enormous natural beauty and resources. However, South African society is in the midst of transformation that could lead to prosperity, if white citizens who have been in control truly share their political and social institutions and power with the black majority who have been oppressed. If a multicultural society of equal opportunity can be created, then civil war between the races may be avoided.

South Africa has a heritage of pioneering, colonization, wars, building a modern infrastructure, and *apartheid*—a failed policy of separation of white and blacks that was internationally condemned and finally abandoned in the '90s.[11] Three centuries ago the land became home to Bushmen and Hottentots, Bantu-speaking black tribes. In the mid-17th century, the European whites arrived; first were the Dutch who built a trading settlement at the Cape of Good Hope. They were joined by Germans and French Huguenot refugees in 1688. Together these colonists were to become known as Boers (farmers). The British invaded and captured the Cape in 1806, gaining formal possession of the colony in 1814 as the result of the Napoleonic wars. To avoid English rule, the Boers migrated to the undeveloped interior of the country from 1835–48, defeating the indigenous Zulus and other black tribes in the process. With the discovery of gold and diamonds in that territory, Britain annexed parts of the area, which led to the Boer War that they won in 1902. The British then combined their colonies of Cape and Natal with the Boer Republics of Orange Free State and Transvaal, creating in 1910 the Union of South Africa as it is today.

Thus, this is a nation of four cultural influences or ethnic groups: the native African majority; the minority populations consisting of the Dutch who were to become known as Boers and *Afrikaners;* the British and Asian immigrants, mostly from India, designated later as the *Coloureds.*

As British power waned, the Afrikaners increased in power, taking control of the government with the election of their National Party in 1948. During the 1960s, Afrikaners introduced the oppressive apartheid system separating blacks from whites, creating two unequal communities. Another flawed policy was launched that forced settlement for the majority black Africans in separate and supposedly independent homelands. Since the 1960s, the domestic turmoil and violence caused by these inhumane political actions have brought international protests and boycotts, including trade sanctions by the United States and condemnation by the United Nations.

To fight for black human rights, the African National Congress was formed in 1955 and eventually coalesced with other black groups' campaigns against the white power government. Finally, the economic and social impact of multinational sanctions lead to the resignation in 1989

South Africa has a heritage of pioneering, colonization, wars, building a modern infrastructure, and apartheid.... *To fight for black human rights, the African National Congress was formed in 1955 and eventually coalesced with other black groups' campaigns against the white power government.*

of the president of the Republic of South Africa (RSA), P. W. Botha. His replacement, F. W. de Klerk, implemented a series of democratic reforms, beginning with the freeing of political prisoners, the desegregating of institutions, and the legal recognition of the ANC as a political party. The outcome was the signing of a peace agreement between the latter and the ruling elite providing for power sharing, the dismantling of apartheid, and the holding of open elections. In that 1994 election, all RSA citizens voted for the first time, electing ANC leader Nelson Mandela as President and de Klerk as Vice President of a multiethnic government. For their peacekeeping success, both men were award the Nobel Peace Prize.

The People and Their Homeland

Today there are approximately 43 million South Africans, almost equally divided between males and females who together have a life expectancy between 61–67 years. This is a relatively young population, about 70% or more are under 50 years of age, with 26% under the age of 10. The Black Africans (74%) consist of nine tribal groups—Zulus (the largest), Xhosas, North and South Sothos, Tswanas, Shangaan-Tsongas, Swazis, South Ndebeles, and Vendas. Each has its own special cultural heritage, language, and sense of identity. During the apartheid period, the tribal groups had been assigned by the racist government to ten ethnic "homelands" that were to have self-rule, but actually were dependent on the white statecraft—these are being dismantled under the new regime. Although English and Afrikaans (a Dutch derivation) are the official languages, the Blacks among the four major tribes speak varying forms of Bantu. The whites (14%) have zero population growth, but were reserved 85% of the land under the old system. The whites are divided into two groups—the English-speaking descendants of English, Scottish, and Irish settlers and the Afrikaan-speaking offspring of the Dutch, German, and French colonials. The English-speaking Coloureds constitute 9% of the inhabitants—mixed descendants of early white setters, native Hottentots, imported Dutch East Indian slaves, and indentured laborers from India (now 3% of the population and Hindi speakers).

In terms of religious affiliations, most South Africans are Christians, divided among the Dutch Reformed Church of the Afrikaners, part of the apartheid problem, and other denominations, such as Anglican, Methodist, Presbyterian, Roman Catholic, as well as African Charismatic, a combination of Christian and traditional African rituals. The Indian community consists of both Hindus and Muslims. There is also a small number of Jews.

Compared to other African nations the overall literacy rate of 76% is high among the citizenry, with variations of 99% for whites as compared to 50% for blacks; 3.8% of the GNP is devoted to education with

The whites are divided into two groups—the English-speaking descendants of English, Scottish, and Irish settlers and the Afrikaan-speaking offspring of the Dutch, German, and French colonials.

over 8 million students enrolled in elementary schools, 1 million-plus in secondary, and 282,000 or so in third or high levels of education. The school system is an adaptation of the British educational model, but in transition to integrate blacks.

Cultural Clues in South Africa

❑ *Family structure* in the black community has been destabilized by past apartheid policies and its constraints; dislocation caused by job searches contributes to 7 million living in poverty. In the black extended family there is great respect manifested toward the elderly, and obedience to parents. The white community's family is nuclear, close-knit and privileged.

❑ *Life style* among the white community is comparable to that of the average European or American experience, relative to socialization, work, and recreation. Afrikaners are very independent and nationalistic with a sense of superiority and pride. Among the blacks there is more vibrancy, naturalness, and brotherhood, sometimes marred by inter-tribal conflict and power struggles.

Geographical Features and Cities

Located at Africa's southern tip, this land mass of 471,433 square miles lies between the Atlantic and Indian Oceans, about twice the size of Texas. It is bounded by Namibia in the northwest (once a South African protectorate); Botswana and Zimbabwe in the north; Swaziland in the northeast. The terrain is a vast interior plateau (average 5,000 feet above sea level) of savannah and desert, rimmed by rugged hills and narrow coastal plain. Climate is generally semiarid except for the narrow coastal belt, which is subtropical on the east, and like the Mediterranean along the southwestern cape. Seasons are for the most part the opposite of the northern hemisphere, and snow may be found in the eastern mountain ranges.

There are 22 urban areas with three cities having populations between 1–2 million people—Cape Town (one of the world's most beautiful cities, set on the harbor at the foot of Table Mountains); Johannesburg (the largest and most cosmopolitan city); and East Rand. Pretoria lies in the northeast and is the administrative capital (823,000 people), as well as a center of the Afrikaner constituency. Many of the segregated black townships, such as Soweto where the great black student protest of 1967 occurred, have large populations and are on the way to becoming cities in themselves. Among the artificially constituted black "homelands," Lesotho is presently politically independent and located on an eastern plateau, totally surrounded by the Republic of South Africa; its status is subject to change and may eventually be incorporated into the larger nation.

In the black extended family there is great respect manifested toward the elderly, and obedience to parents. The white community's family is nuclear, close-knit and privileged.

Political and Social Conditions

The Republic of South Africa (RSA) was founded in 1961 when it gained independence from Great Britain. Presently it is a laboratory of social experimentation that has implications for the whole continent. With the ascendancy of the ANC leadership to the national government in 1994, and the new approach to white/black power sharing, the inequitable, segregated apartheid political and social system is being transformed. Here are examples of the change process in a corrosive legacy.

❑ A *suffrage policy* that at first limited voting rights to whites only, then extended it to the Coloureds, and now finally includes the blacks who formerly could only vote in local "homeland" or township elections. The shift in political parties and power has been from the National Party and Conservative Party to the African National Congress, the Inkatha Freedom Party (Zulus), and the Democratic Party.

❑ A *parliament* that once consisted of three houses for Whites, Coloureds, and Indians, but now is being redesigned into a national legislatures representing all citizens regardless of color or race.

❑ Restrictive and racist *national policies* that left a legacy of social institutions that deprived blacks or provided underfunded, inadequate and inferior schools, hospitals, and public facilities.

In the social and democratic revolution underway to provide more equity for black and Coloured communities, there is resistance from small but powerful hardcore racists who seek to preserve the past status quo of white supremacy. Some racists attempt to continue the violent actions of the former government-sanctioned *Vlakplaas,* an elite police unit that engaged in mayhem and terrorism including bombings, killings, and false imprisonments. Fortunately, its military commanders are presently being prosecuted, while most well-meaning South Africans seek to re-invent their nation as a place where human and democratic rights are protected. The ongoing struggle for equity extends from housing to employment, but is most evident in the attempts to integrate education. In January 1995 the black-led government inaugurated desegregation of schools, so that all-white schools are now open to children from all races, 11 million of whom are non-white. Multiracial education also involves redesigning the curricula, the textbooks, and even the language of teaching (previously it was just Afrikaans). The National Education Training Forum is leading the changes in syllabus, courses, and policies that previously supported apartheid.

Today's challenge for the more democratic government is to bring equity to blacks, while leaving their former oppressors comfortable enough to stay in the country. The fringe separatist group, *Afrikaner Volksfront,* have a resistance movement underway and would create a separate all-white state for themselves with a confederation. The issue is whether the black and white communities can create not a common culture, but a dynamic and truly civilized society in which both live in peaceful and human co-existence.[12]

The Economy

The strongest and most diversified economy on the African continent, the situation should improve further with the lifting of global economic sanctions and diminishing civil protests. The challenge is whether the high standard of living enjoyed by the whites can be shared somewhat by the masses of black citizens, developing in the process a broader middle class. The gross national or domestic product average is obviously much higher for whites than blacks; reducing unemployment among the latter by creating new enterprises and jobs is critical to the growth of the new multiracial society. In the past, the economy was largely based on varied agriculture and the mining of diamonds and gold until the manufacturing industries took hold. South Africa has vast natural resources including chromite, coal, uranium, platinum, natural gas, and fish. Today this diversified economy has a large industrial base from metal products, chemicals, and foodstuffs to machinery, vehicles, and textiles—all part of a strong exporting program. With a good infrastructure in transportation and communication already in place, as well as an educated population, this nation has great potential for developing high technology, information, and tourism industries.

AFRICAN BUSINESS CUSTOMS, PROTOCOLS, AND PROSPECTS

With a continent as vast and diverse as this, it is impossible to generalize on preferred business and trade practices. The customs and protocols in North African countries with their Islamic cultures are more akin to those described in Chapter 14; the same might be said for other Muslim-oriented states elsewhere, such as northern Sudan and Somalia. However, in what is typically referred to as "Black Africa," whether in the west, east, or south, the following observations may prove useful and supplement what has already been described in the two country-specific sections.

Business and Common Courtesies

Business is normally discussed in the office or in a bar or restaurant—always outside the home. When an African is the host of such meetings, he or she will pay for everyone. If a foreigner is the host, he or she should pay.

This diversified economy has a large industrial base from metal products, chemicals, and foodstuffs to machinery, vehicles, and textiles—all part of a strong exporting program.

Home matters are not discussed in business meetings. What happens in the home is considered private. When invited to someone's home for a meal, do not discuss business.

As indicated earlier, age commands respect. Age and wisdom are seen as the same, and the norms of the elders must be followed to ensure smooth business dealings.

In general, Africans are in transition from their traditional cultures based on a rural, agricultural, and tribal way of life. Rapidly, they are moving toward an urban lifestyle that is based upon industrial and technological development.

Prospects for African Business Synergy

Africans are in transition from their traditional cultures based on a rural, agricultural, and tribal way of life. Rapidly, they are moving toward an urban lifestyle....

Foreign business, professional, and development workers have done much to promote greater African prosperity, whether through the United Nation's agencies, their own governments, multinational corporations, or financial investment. However, much more can be done if non-Africans would encourage and participate in the following endeavors:

❑ *Effective leadership* (replacement by second generation leaders who are better educated, more competent, more foresighted, and more aware of international interdependence). This will require cultural change so that Africans become more goal oriented and less fatalistic.
❑ *Rural development* (less emphasis on urban development and more on rural opportunity and agricultural production).
❑ *Population control* (traditional large families that enlarge tribal power bases have to be regulated, while social security provisions are made for the aged). Only then can tough problems be solved in black Africa related to infant mortality, illiteracy, health care, and political instability.

Africa covers 20% of the world's land mass and has 10% of its people. Yes, it has problems, but nothing north-south dialogue and collaboration cannot resolve, for Africa is a potentially rich continent.

AVENUES FOR IMPROVED TRADE RELATIONS
IN AFRICA ARE:

....

❑ Seek information about African business conditions and cultures from voluntary agencies with sound experience in Asia—such as the Peace Corps, Canadian International Development Agency, British Voluntary Service Overseas.
❑ Send trade missions of related business groups to Africa and arrange for them to meet with high-level contacts. Trade shows are

not the way to enter the African market since there is no middle class in most of the countries.

❑ Use the services of the African-American Chamber of Commerce headquartered in Los Angeles, and recruit American business representatives from the land grant universities in the U.S. that are predominantly black with students of African heritage.

❑ Obtain explicit clarification from African host governments concerning guarantees to be received, expropriation risks, tax or duty breaks, taxes on corporations and properties, labor regulations and currency practices.

EMERGING AFRICAN MARKETS

There are many forecasters who believe that Africa will come into its own economically in the 21st century. Perhaps the following media summaries convey how this would become a land of plenty through more cooperative actions applying the previous insight.

Dr. Chaman Kashkari, a professor of engineering at the University of Akron, received the Presidential End Hunger Award in White House ceremonies on October 16th, World Hunger Day. The honor was in recognition of his work as director general of the Global Energy Society for the Eradication of Poverty & Hunger and the AFRICA-1000 program. The organization provided water to 1,000 African villages by the year 1995 and another 5,000 by year 2000 through the use of manual and energy pumps. The pilot project in Senegal demonstrated that wind mills and deep aquifers 200 feet below the parched African surface can produce water and vegetation, including potatoes. Using this technology, Kashkari predicted that hunger could be eradicated on this continent in 20 years.[13]

Investment managers and banks that peddle emerging-market funds are turning their attention to the world's last great investment wilderness—Africa. Few investors may be able to name many African stock markets north of Johannesburg. Yet the continent now has 12 others up and running, including one in Zambia; Malawi, Uganda, and Tanzania have plans to launch their own bourses too. . . . Andrew Sardanis (chairman of the Meridien Corporation, the parent company of Meridien BIA, which operates commercial banks in 20 African countries), is equally bullish. "Anybody who puts cash into these new stockmarkets is going to make a great deal of money," he says. . . . The World Bank forecasts that sub-Saharan Africa's economy, boosted by trade with the post-sanctions South Africa, will grow by 3.9% a year in 1994–2003—an impressive rate by African standards.[14]

About 6 million Africans are refugees. Eighteen of the world's 41 countries with food shortages are in Africa, as well as 18 of the 20 poorest countries. Africa's debt burden stands at $300 billion. Wars are being or

There are many forecasters who believe that Africa will come into its own economically in the 21st century.

have just been fought in Rwanda, Sudan, Niger, Angola, Mali, Liberia, and Sierra Leone. Post-war Mozambique has 1 million dead and wounded, while Somalia has been without a government since 1991 and its warlords engage in violent tribal conflict. . . . "The leadership of Africa is in a state of deep-seated bewilderment," said Jonathan Moyo, a Zimbabwean political scientist at the Ford Foundation in Nairobi. . . . The sheer size of Africa (four times larger than the United States, spanning seven time zones) and its diversity . . . were sufficient to undermine the dreams of a united Africa. However bleak the immediate future may seem, Moyo and other African commentators believe one tragic era is ending and a more hopeful one is beginning. These are the signs:

❑ Most of the 52 states are young and struggling to put in place institutions that will work.
❑ In the 1990s, dozens of countries here are drafting new constitutions, holding multiparty elections, loosening restraints on freedom of expression, and moving toward free-market economies.
❑ Initiatives for political reform and increased respect for human rights have generally been undertaken by Western donors who demand rehabilitation as a condition for continued aid.[15]

But new attention to improved governance comes not just from the World Bank and the United Nations, but also from the African masses who have taken to the streets by the thousands to demand change. As Uganda's vice-president Samson Kisekka wisely observed, "We Africans have a duty to reexamine the type of leadership we offer to our people."

War, Terrorism, and Prosperity in the Heart of Africa

At the beginning of the 21st century, Central Africa is again in internal turmoil and conflict. Rebellion in the Congo involves its neighbors, Zimbabwe, Rwanda and possibly Angola. Some fear the breakup of the Congo, with Rwanda and Uganda carving up the eastern regions for themselves. In the south, the 14-member Southern Africa Development Community (SDAC) is split by conflict between the leaders of Zimbawe and South Africa.

To make matters worse, outside forces have come into the continent and made the American embassies in Africa a target of terrorists. The bombings in both Kenya and Tanzania caused many local casualties and much destruction, but seemingly were the work of agitators from the Middle East angry at U.S. policies.

In counterpoint to such conflict and violence are positive developments. In 1997 a summit meeting was held for 30 heads of African states and 7,000 delegates from the African diaspora abroad. The intention of this seminal gathering of African and African-American political and business leaders was to foster closer relations and increase trade between the two continents. As Jesse Jackson wrote, "In the new global economy, Africa is a backwater." Per capita income in sub-Saharan

As Uganda's vice-president Samson Kisekka wisely observed, "We Africans have a duty to reexamine the type of leadership we offer to our people."

African nations fell during the 1980s. Foreign aid is hard to get. And debt burdens continue at crushing levels; more capital is shipped out to pay off debts than is received in aid or investment.[16] By practicing synergy, this conference intended to find solutions to these problems.

Similarly, several non-profit, non-governmental organizations and foundations from around the world are seeking to assist Africans cope with their on-going problems through self-help solutions. Among such private enterprises, one success story is the Carter Center (One Copenhill Ave., Atlanta, Georgia 30348, USA). Their Global 2000 program includes a partnership with the Sasakawa Africa Association (SG2000). It has enabled Ethiopia to produce a food surplus for the first time. As their newsletter reports: "By instituting sweeping governmental policy changes, joining together with thousands of farmers, and collaborating with SG2000, the people of Ethiopia have begun to lead their country to a newfound prosperity." Under the leadership of former U.S. President Jimmy Carter and his wife, Rosalynn, the Center has promoted this program that empowers small-scale farmers to increase food production by improving the yield and quality of their crops with high yielding seeds, new fertilizer methods, plus more productive timetables for planting, weeding, and harvesting. As a result of this private initiative, the government began an Intensified Extension Campaign (EMTP) to replicate the SG2000 methodology that also aims to improve the country's infrastructure in processing, storing, and transporting maize to other countries. The Ethiopian government now sponsors 350,000 EMTPs, and pledges to redouble efforts in these innovations that have lead to a million ton surplus of maize. Maybe the 21st century will find Africa moving beyond its colonial past and contemporary problems to self-sufficiency in a more peaceful environment by more concern for protecting the continent's vast natural resources, including its peoples, while at the same time encouraging tourism.

SUMMARY

Global managers appreciate both the potential of Africa's human and natural resources. Synergistic partnerships, such as joint ventures, can do much to contribute to the development of the area and its peoples. The chapter underscored this significance and contemporary realities.

When comparing the American and African cultures and how they affect the business environment, it is necessary to understand that the U.S. is a low-context culture. It is technologically oriented with emphasis on individual achievement rather than group participation. In the communication process, a low-context culture places meaning in the exact verbal description of an event. Individuals in such a culture rely on the spoken word. This is typified by the common statement, "say what you mean."

Several non-profit, non-governmental organizations and foundations from around the world are seeking to assist Africans cope with their on-going problems through self-help solutions.

Africa's culture is high-context. In the communication process, much of the meaning is not from the words, but is internalized in the person. Meaning comes from the environment and is looked for in the relationship between the ideas expressed in the communication process. High-context cultures tend to be more human oriented than low-context cultures. The extended family fits into the high-context culture.

Business persons from Africa and elsewhere can profitably work together if they accept the differences between them and work to create an atmosphere of nonjudgmental acceptance. On the part of the American, it means slowing down; not being tied to a time schedule.

REFERENCES

1. French, H. W. *The New York Times,* "Clinton's Spotlight Now Turns to Africa," March 21, 1998, p.3 WK.
2. Oliver, R. *The African Experience—Major Themes in African History from Early Times to the Present,* New York, NY: Icon Editions, 1992.
3. Mazrui, A. A. *Los Angeles Times,* "Redraw Colonial Borders to Quell Frenzy," November 13, 1996.
4. Pakenham, T. *The Scramble for Africa—The White Man's Conquest of the Dark Continent from 1876-l912,* New York, NY: Avon Books, 1992.
5. Asante, M. K. *The Afrocentric Idea,* Philadelphia, PA: Temple University Press, 1987.
6. Davidson, B. *The Black Man's Burden: Africa and the Curse of the Nation-State,* New York, NY: Times Books, 1992.
7. Davidson, B. *The Search for Africa,* New York, NY: Times Books, 1994.
8. National Trade Data Bank, International Trade Administration, U.S. Department of Commerce, Washington, D.C. 20230 (Tel: 1/800-USA TRADE). There is a country code for information on all nations of Unit 3 and this chapter on Africa. You can obtain the code number (for example, South Africa is #3000), and call the "hotline" directly for data to be sent to your fax number (Tel: 1/202 482-1064 or 1860). Major U.S. cities also have local offices of USDC with commercial advisors to provide counseling and resources to business persons seeking data or connections abroad in a specific country or area within that target culture. Consult the local telephone directory under "Government Pages" for the United States Government Offices, and the Federal Commerce Department listing.
9. For further information on Nigerian culture, business, and travel, contact the Embassy of Nigeria, 2201 M St., NW, Washington, DC 20037, USA (Tel:202/822-1500). The Office of the Commercial Attache publishes *Investment Policy of Nigeria.* The U.S. Department of Commerce also publishes *Export Programs—A Business Directory of U. S. Government Printing Services,"* which describes how to access their Country and Regional Market Information (for Nigeria and South Africa, the code # is 3000 @ telephones 1-800-872-8723 or 202/482-1064).

Africa's culture

is high-context.

10. Brown, J. et al. (eds.). *History from South Africa: Alternative Visions and Practices,* Philadelphia, PA: Temple University Press, 1991.
11. The authors acknowledge that the insights for this profile were partially obtained from a *Culturgram for the '90s—Republic of South Africa.* The Culturgrams are published on various cultures discussed in Unit 3 and are available from the David M. Kennedy Center for International Studies, Brigham Young University, 280 HRCB, Provo, Utah 84602, USA (Tel: 801/378-6528).
12. For further information about this nation and its culture, contact the Embassy of South Africa (3051 Massachusetts Ave., NW, Washington, DC 20008, USA) and the South African Tourism Board (747 Third Ave., 20th Floor, New York, NY 10017 or 9841 Airport Blvd., Ste. 1524, Los Angeles, CA 90045, USA).
13. *The Beacon Journal,* October 21, 1900.
14. *The Economist,* June 11, 1994.
15. *Los Angeles Times,* June 27, 1994.
16. *Los Angeles Times,* July 27, 1997.

INDEX

Philip R. Harris, Ph.D., a management and space psychologist, is president of Harris International Ltd. in La Jolla, California. A former Fulbright professor to India who has lectured at numerous universities worldwide, he also served as vice-president of St. Francis College in New York, and Copley International Corporation in San Diego. As an international management consultant, Dr. Harris has helped more than 200 clients around the world to better understand and manage the impact of cultural and organizational dynamics. He is the author/editor of some forty books and is on the advisory board of the *European Business Review.*

Robert T. Moran, Ph.D., is a professor of International Studies at Thunderbird/ American Graduate School of International Management in Glendale, Arizona. As a global consultant, he has worked with some of the world's largest corporations including Aramco, AT&T, Bayer, Ericsson, General Motors, Intel, Exxon, Volvo, Singapore Airlines, and many others. A Canadian by birth, Moran's international experiences range from hockey coach in Japan to visiting professor in a French and a Chinese University. A former columnist for the magazine *International Management,* he has edited or authored several books on global management and culture.

- shock
- map
- video

- call Jackie for Do's & Don'ts on this
- group process write paragraph.